FEAST

Why Humans Share Food

MARTIN JONES

OXFORD
UNIVERSITY PRESS

OXFORD

UNIVERSITY PRESS

Great Clarendon Street, Oxford OX2 6DP

Oxford University Press is a department of the University of Oxford.
It furthers the University's objective of excellence in research, scholarship,
and education by publishing worldwide in

Oxford New York

Auckland Cape Town Dar es Salaam Hong Kong Karachi
Kuala Lumpur Madrid Melbourne Mexico City Nairobi
New Delhi Shanghai Taipei Toronto

With offices in

Argentina Austria Brazil Chile Czech Republic France Greece
Guatemala Hungary Italy Japan Poland Portugal Singapore
South Korea Switzerland Thailand Turkey Ukraine Vietnam

Oxford is a registered trade mark of Oxford University Press
in the UK and in certain other countries

Published in the United States
by Oxford University Press Inc., New York

© Martin Jones 2007

The moral rights of the author have been asserted
Database right Oxford University Press (maker)

First published 2007

British Library Cataloguing in Publication Data

Data available

Library of Congress Cataloging in Publication Data

Data available

Typeset by SPI Publisher Services, Pondicherry, India
Printed in Great Britain
on acid-free paper by
Clays Ltd, St Ives plc

ISBN 978-0-19-920901-9

1

To my father, John Jones, who always enjoys a sociable meal

Contents

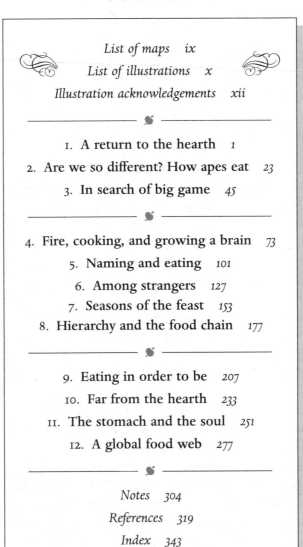

Acknowledgements

This volume first took shape within the uniquely stimulating context of the Bellagio Study Centre funded by the Rockefeller Foundation, where I had the privilege of holding a month's residency in 2002. I would like to extend my warm thanks to Gianna Celli and her staff, Alice and Warren Illchman, and my co-residents who each contributed greatly to nurturing and encouraging partially formed ideas.

My exploration of the individual case studies depended just on published sources, but also upon direct communication with the researchers and in several cases accessing primary and sometimes unpublished data, thanks to the openness and great generosity of many colleagues, among which I would make especial mention of Martin Bell, Philip Crummy, Richard Evershed, Paul Halstead, Frances Healey, Glynis Jones, Tony Legge, Jacqueline McKinley, Roger Mercer, Matthew Pope, Mike Richards, Jiri Svoboda, Ehud Weiss and George Willcox.

For reading through passages of text and offering related supportive input and advice I would like to thank: Leslie Aiello, Martin Bell, Lisa Bendall, Adrian Chadwick, Philip Crummy, Richard Evershed, Felipe Fernandez Armesto, Robert Foley, Peter Garnsey, Paul Halstead, Richard Hingley, Frances Healey, Camilla Hinde, Glynis Jones, Leslie Knapp, Elizabeth Leedham Green, Tony Legge, Martin Millett, Nicky Milner, Iain Morley, Tamsin O'Connell, Matt Pope, Sandy Pullen, Tjeerd Van Andel, Marijke Van der Veen, Lucy Walker, Ehud Weiss, George Willcox, Kathy Willis and Richard Wrangham. The responsibility for errors and inconsistencies in the text nevertheless remain entirely my own.

I have been supported by a very able and effective production team, and would wish to express my especial gratitude to Sandra Assersohn for her imaginative picture research, Mary Worthington and Andrew Hawkey for their scrupulous copy editing, and the staff at Oxford University Press, in particular Luciana O'Flaherty, Deborah Protheroe, Matthew Cotton, Catherine Berry, and Kate Farquhar-Thomson. Throughout the project I have been ably encouraged, supported and stimulated by my agent, Clare Alexander, to whom I extend my sincere thanks.

List of maps

List of illustrations

Illustration acknowledgements

Author, adapted from data within Daniel Nadel (ed.): *Ohalo II, A 23,000-Year-Old Fisher-Hunter-Gatherers' Camp on the Shore of the Sea of Galilee* (2002): 11; Bibliothèque Nationale, Paris, France/Archives Charmet/The Bridgeman Art Library: 32; The Trustees of the British Museum: 20; from Josef Wilpert: *Fractio panis: Die alteste darstellung des eucharistischen opfers in der 'Cappella greca,' entdeckt und erla utert.* Herder, 1895: Morrison.a.40.51. Syndics of Cambridge University Library: 27; © Gerard Campeny/Institut Català de Paleoecologia Humana i Evolució Social: 10; Munawar Chaudhry, Darwin College, Cambridge: 2; watercolour by Piet de Jong, digitally restored by Craig Mauzy. Courtesy of the Department of Classics, University of Cincinnati: 17; courtesy of the Department of Classics, University of Cincinnati: 18, 19; oxygen isotopes curves adapted and redrawn from data within M. Cross: *Greenland summit ice cores* (1997), and S. C. Porter, *Quaternary Research*, 32 (1989): 8; Philip Crummy: 22; English Heritage Photo Library, drawing by Peter Dunn: 6; www.janegoodall.org: 4; INDEX/Pedicini: 21; Archives of the Institute of Archaeology, Academy of Science, Czech Republic (excavations of Bohuslav Klima): 1; from Ghislain Lancel: *L'Etoile et son histoire*, Picardie: http://g.lancel.free.fr: 28; Simon Mays: 26; used with permission from McDonald's Corporations: 33; William C. McGrew, Leverhulme Centre for Human Evolutionary Studies: 3; from Roger Mercer and Frances Healey (in press): *Hambledon Hill, Dorset, England. Excavation and survey of a Neolithic monument complex and its surrounding landscape.* London: English Heritage Monograph Series: 15; Musée national d'histoire et d'art, Luxemburg: 23; Daniel Nadel, University of Haifa: 12; National Museum of Denmark: 24; Matthew Pope and the Boxgrove Project, University College London: 7; from *Revue archéologique de Picardie*, special 19-2001: 29; © Francesc Riart: 9; Louie Psihoyos/Science Faction Images: 31; adapted and redrawn from Geza Teleki: *The Omnivorous Chimpanzee*, January 1973 Copyright © 2006 by Scientific American, Inc. All rights reserved: 5; Danielle Stordeur, Centre National de la Recherche Scientifique : 13, 14; Swanson® is a registered trademark of CSC Brands, Inc. Used with the permission of Pinnacle Foods Corporation: 30; Gonzalo Trancho, Universidad Complutense de Madrid: 25; from Yoshinori Yasuda: *The Origins of Pottery and Agriculture*, Roli Books, New Delhi, 2002: 16.

Map acknowledgements

From *Cambridge Encyclopedia of Human Evolution*, 1992; map by Swanston Graphics; hand-axes from François Bordes: *Typologie due paléolithique ancient et moyen*, CNRS Editions, 1981, plates 65(2), 78(2), and K. Paddaya, *The Acheulian Culture of the Hunsgi Valley*, Deccan College Postgraduate & Research Institute, 1982, fig. 17(1): **Map 2**; from Richard G. Klein: *The Dawn of Human Culture*, Wiley, 2002, fig. 6.3: **Map 3**.

1. Excavations at Dolní Věstonice in the Czech Republic. A Palaeolithic hut has been exposed by digging through accumulations of wind-blown sediment.

1

A RETURN TO THE HEARTH

BENEATH a tangle of overgrown vegetation, the earthen face of an abandoned quarry is interrupted by a dark horizontal band, a meagre stripe of charcoal. The quarry in question survives as a series of overgrown steps and bluffs, cut into the gently rolling topography of the vineyards of Southern Moravia. Making up that earthen topography are fine sediments that glacial winds once carried across the valleys and plains of Central Europe, reaching tens of metres in depth over many thousands of years. Those deep accumulations trap the occasional trace of a human visitor, a few flints, the bone of a captured animal, or the charcoal from a hearth that has left that dark horizontal band. They provide us with some very early evidence for an activity that the anthropologist Claude Lévi-Strauss argued separated humans from the rest of the living world—cooking.[1]

Close to 30,000 years has passed since the cooks in question prepared their meal. They were not the first to use fire as a taste-enhancing form of pre-digestion: our more distant ancestors may have harvested fire after lightening strikes, even initiated it within their rock shelters. However what survives as traces in abandoned quarries of Moravia is something more substantial than mere opportunistic use. The charcoal came from hearths that were constructed and sustained at the very heart of human life, foci of activity housed within the oldest known built architecture, structures fashioned from skin, branches, and mammoth bone.[2] Within these spaces we can envisage small communities sitting round the fire, face to face, talking, smiling, and laughing, and sharing food. And Lévi-Strauss was right to point out how unusual a behaviour this was.

In other species, fire is not the only element of this scene that would spell threat and danger. Direct eye-contact is more typically hostile, as is the opening of mouths and the exposure of teeth. Combine these with the placing of food, midway between a group of a individuals other than parent and child, and we have a clear recipe for conflict and violence. At some point, our own ancestors turned those danger signals around and transformed them into the very essence of conviviality that defines humanity.[3] We now use the shared meal to punctuate the day, celebrate the great occasions of life, make transactions, and define who is inside and outside any particular cultural group. How did this inversion of the signals of danger come about, and how did it unfold into the enormously diverse fusion of ecological complexity and social drama it is today?

The unusual behaviour displayed at a meal has attracted the attentions of several anthropologists and historians. They have drawn on direct observation, and reached back into the past through written sources. Those sources are widely available for the last 2,000 years, and can be traced in more fragmentary form back another 3,000 years, as far as a series of clay tablets inscribed with inventories for the provisioning of Ancient Sumerian feasts. It is clear from those earliest texts and some accompanying images that feasts were already complex affairs, bringing luxurious and exotic ingredients together with an elaborate protocol of manners, gestures, and dress.[4] The hearth-centred meals whose remnants are trapped within the Moravian hills may be less lavish, but also bear many of the structural hallmarks of the modern human meal, and they are six times as old as the earliest texts. To explore the various elements of the meal, the use of fire, the roots of cooking, and sharing food with strangers, our timescale of enquiry needs to be 100 times greater still. The route to those deeper timescales is archaeology, a field which has in recent years undergone a methodological revolution. As a result of that revolution, we are coming much closer to the ancient traces of people engaged in sharing food. Before considering what archaeo-logical methods can reveal, let us pause within those vineyards to reflect on the remains beneath their soils.

The episodes preserved around the small village of Dolní Věstonice have been scientifically dated to around 25,000–30,000 years of age. As we face to the north-east from the hills above the village today, the view before us takes us across one of the most important natural corridors of human movement across Europe. On a clear day, the Carpathian Moun-tains can be seen stretching out to the east. They reach almost as far as the Black Sea. The ridge of the uplands that encircle Bohemia can be made out to the west. Some way behind us lies the valley of the Danube, stretching out along the southern edge of these ranges. This long river has been one of the principal avenues across Europe throughout human history. Straight ahead of us, the gap between the uplands, known as the Moravian Gate, opens into the vast plains of northern Europe. This gap has served as a corridor for the movement of humans, along with the species upon which they preyed, from the first appearance of hunter-gatherers to the Napoleonic campaigns. It has also served as a wind tunnel, particularly during the colder epochs when glaciers spread across northern Europe and down from the Alps, and searing periglacial storms filled the Moravian Gate with the dust that built the hills beneath today's gently rolling vineyards. Those same dust-storms trapped moments in ancient human journeys within the region, burying their campfires and food debris beneath fine wind-blown sediment.[5]

Two years ago, a group of us met up to plan a new investigation into these excellently preserved traces of early meals. We were not the first to probe into the deposits. These sites have been meticulously excavated over the past eighty years by a series of Czech and Slovak archaeologists.[6] The hills around the village preserve a number of these relict hearths, marking out the vantage points from which hunters could survey the valley below. From the stone tools and bones, a picture had been built up of hunting communities, camped out on higher ground with a view over the moving herds of deer and mammoth. These were communities of anatomically modern humans, biologically indistinguishable from ourselves. Whereas we have now long since thought of humans as masters of the world, we are originally an African species, adapted to sub-Saharan climes. Our Moravian ancestors were doing something quite unusual and novel in pressing northwards into some of the coldest of regions. Recent climatic modelling suggests that some of these early hunters pressed northwards to where the winter night-time temperatures fell to $-20°C$ degrees below. We wanted to find out more about the lives of these pioneers. How did they get fuel to stay warm on the outside, and calories to fuel them on the inside? How did they move around the landscape from season to season, what foods did they find, and what was the significance of the hearths to which they repeatedly returned?[7]

From the earlier excavations, a number of plans had been carefully constructed of those centrally placed hearths, the clear spaces where diners gathered in a circle, the flints they used to catch and butcher their prey, bones discarded from their meals, and the mammoth bones and tusks used in the construction of shelters or 'houses' around the hearth. When we followed the charcoal smears to embark on our own excavation of these early hearths, we followed in this tradition of careful three-dimensional plotting to reveal the use of space. We recorded the elegant thin blades of blood-red stone brought from the Carpathian Mountains, visible in the distance. They were found alongside marbled grey blades gathered from the glacial moraine out of sight to the north in modern-day Poland. We plotted in butchered bones of reindeer, mammoth, wild cow, and even cave lion, all around concentrations of charcoal and reddened earth. In addition to these more conventional finds, we bagged up and labelled over a thousand samples of sediment, to be put through a range of processes to recapture fragments of food, large and small, even molecular traces, and plot them carefully in space—sources of data we hope to assemble into a picture of the lives of these early diners. One of the things we could immediately see from the stratigraphy was how close these diners were to the searing periglacial winds. Sediments from the dust-storms were found above and below the hearths, and even within distinct firings of the same hearth.

Sharing our own meals and a glass of Czech beer at the end of a day's digging, the team would discuss the analyses we had in mind, and what we would make of all that new data. A name that cropped up from time to time in those conversations was that of a twentieth-century anthropologist who had thought and written a great deal about the food quest. Marvin Harris grew up in a relatively poor family in 1930s Brooklyn to become one of America's best-known anthropologists. I would presume that both his childhood and his early research fieldwork in Portuguese Mozambique gave him several opportunities to witness first hand how tough the food quest could be. Throughout his life, he was interested in how ecological needs, the struggle to acquire sufficient food, shaped the richness and diversity of human culture. After his research in Mozambique in the 1950s, he was able to observe other cultural ecological patterns, particularly in South and Central America. On the basis of such observations he argued that the various aspects of human life could be represented as a pyramid. At the base were the physical environment, the biological features of our species, and the means we had of acquiring food and sustenance. Further up the pyramid were the variable structures of society by which family, tribe, nation, and so on were arranged and organized. At the apex of the pyramid were the 'superstructural' elements, including religion, art, music, and dance.

Family life, political structures, food taboos, cannibalistic practices, and every feature and practice displayed in the consumption of food could, in his view, be ultimately connected to the struggle for survival, and to a balance sheet of calories, proteins, and reproductive success established at the infrastructural base of this pyramid. The anthropologist's job was to chart the mechanisms and connections, to look beneath the pattern and mythology of different cultures to the universal logic of nature beneath.[8]

Rather like the cultural groups that Harris was comparing, we archaeologists also tend to cluster into sub-cultures, each one adapted to its own style of data. A passion for Egyptian hieroglyphs, crumbling classical ruins, and buried bones each leads to its own distinctive style of archaeology. The differences are not just in the form the evidence takes but also in modes of reasoning, thought, and narrative—even the personal styles of the archaeologists can display sub-cultural traits, features that Marvin Harris would have no doubt related to the evolutionary fitness of the different branches of the disciplines. My own academic sub-culture no doubt displays its own suite of cultural traits, but is defined by methodology rather than epoch of study. We 'bio-archaeologists' employ a range of scientific methods to study the archaeology of food, in projects whose focus spans from the historical period back to the age of the Neanderthals and beyond. To do this we work closely with a range of period specialists, and in the process experience a wide diversity of thinking about culture, food, and the shared meal.

Without going too far down the path of caricaturing my colleagues, it seems generally that archaeologists of the earliest human epoch, the Palaeolithic, are most at home with the theme of small communities engaging with the massive forces of nature. Harris's emphasis upon evolutionary forces fits well with such a theme. However, when discussing anthropological themes with archaeologists of the much later classical and historical epochs, periods of nation-building, empire, and conquest, I might hear less about Marvin Harris and more about Jack Goody, for whom the analysis of a shared meal leads not so much to an exploration of nature than of the internal shape of society itself. Goody's insights have largely been influenced by time spent in Africa and around the Mediterranean, areas of the world he experienced at various stages of his life as soldier, prisoner of war, and anthropologist. They were experiences that highlighted to him the importance of difference— difference, for example, between rich and poor, East and West, literate and illiterate, oppressor and oppressed. His work has provided key insights into culinary differentiation, between for example *haute cuisine* and *basse cuisine,* and how the sharing of food marks out the internal workings of social class and power.[9]

In the intervening epochs of prehistory, we encounter the enigmatic landscapes, monuments, and elaborate burials of our Bronze Age and Neolithic forebears. These are epochs in which many recurrent features of 'civilization', such as towns, texts, markets, and religion, make an appearance. In making sense of these, archaeologists have sought inspiration from a range of anthropological thinkers of the twentieth century.

While Marvin Harris was growing up amidst the bustle of 1930s Brooklyn, a very different mind was maturing in the quieter English setting of Roehampton, at the Convent of the Sacred Heart. It was in this contained world of order, regulation, and religion that one of its pupils would develop her ideas about the way her own society and others structured and made sense of the world around them, through classification and ritual. While Harris was to become concerned with 'culture' as a mechanism with which society tackles the struggle for survival within 'nature', Mary Tew (later Mary Douglas) would become interested in how such categories as 'culture' and 'nature' might form in people's minds in the first place, and indeed how other classifications of the world formed in the minds of other cultures.[10]

She was looking at the world in a way that could be compared with another key figure of twentieth-century anthropology. In the mid-1930s, a young Belgian scholar, who had dabbled widely in law, politics, and other topics, set sail from the port of Marseilles for South America. Claude Lévi-Strauss was travelling to join the French Cultural Mission to Brazil. A visiting professorship at the University of São Paolo would allow him to embark on a series of journeys into the Amazon rainforest, journeys to which he returned at various points in his life, and which equipped him with profound insights into a world that was about as far from the worlds of Europe and America as it was possible to get.[11] Like Douglas after him, he was keen to look 'beneath the surface' of human experience to the underlying structures that shaped the things people did. In different ways, their pursuit of that interest led both Lévi-Strauss and Douglas to reflect on how the underlying structures of society both became manifest, and were reaffirmed, in conversational circles around the hearth, sharing food.[12]

I wonder what these three social anthropologists would make of our ancient Moravian campfires. In each case, periods of immersion in distinctly non-European regions of the tropics, Goody in Ghana, Douglas in modern-day Zaire, and Lévi-Strauss in Brazil, had sharpened their eyes to the tacit assumptions of the Western world in which they had been raised.[13] They each strove to uncover the logic of human societies, drawing a distinction between the inside, the home and hearth, fixed and secure and the outside, the dangerous, the changeable, and the uncertain. It was around the hearth that the world was put to order, people, processes, and things classified and allotted their place.

If they had been able to visit our excavation, I would have also liked to have taken them down the hill to another of the hearths on its slopes. It is in the section through this hearth that we can really sense the harsh periglacial winds from which they were sheltering. The dust from those winds has smothered one reddened hearth, but the fires were relit. Later on, the hearth was once again covered by the wind, and then relit. The alternation of wind-blown sediment and reddened earth repeats itself six or seven times within a few centimetres of the profile. Within a landscape that was being constantly remoulded by global forces, and across which these early hunters roamed for hundreds of kilometres to find the best stone and to gather food, they returned again and again to precise points to gather, adorn themselves, and share food. On a neighbouring hillside, the first excavations of the Dolní Věstonice hearths yielded other objects besides, which can still be seen in the Moravian National Museum at Brno. There were beads of drilled shell and teeth that had slipped from bodily adornments worn around the fire. Around these ancient hearths the world's oldest known human forms were being sculpted, with the first attested use of fired clay. Some other fragments of clay retain the imprints of the world's oldest known weaving, and woven cords are also portrayed on some of the clay figurines. A few carefully drilled animal bones have been interpreted as flutes. It seems that music was also playing. There was model-making, crafts, and weaving, arenas rich in imagery and colour, no doubt also storytelling and conversation. Was Harris right that all this was about calories and biological survival, simply obscured in complex social code?[14]

Mary Douglas's analyses of the shared meal shifted the focus from biological function to social drama. Scrutinizing the modern American family meal, she noted seating arrangements and dress codes differentiating mother, father, and children, and tacit rules about the preparation, order, and consumption of food and drink, and the presence or absence of background music, radio, television, and other entertainments. These modern meals observed by Douglas followed a seasonal cycle, marking out, for example, religious festivals, Thanksgiving, Sunday lunch, all superimposed with another set of meals marking birth, coming of age, marriage, and death. All this was interwoven with the daily cycle of three meals, with their allotted time and format, and their own distinctive character, and in many cases initiated with a brief word of thanks to God for making the whole thing possible.[15]

Lévi-Strauss had suggested that food was 'good to think'. Much of what Douglas observed might be expressed by the notion that food is good to communicate. The whole sequence of meals through a lifetime was like a long conversation, or an extended narrative, broken down into episodes, chapters, paragraphs, and sentences. That narrative expressed and reaffirmed relationships within the family and between families, followed life stories from the cradle to the grave, and charted and celebrated major turning points in the community's history. Looking more closely at each particular meal, just as sentences broke down to words and syllables, meals broke down to courses and mouthfuls, each articulated with a certain amount of individual expression, but essentially following a shared corpus of grammatical rules.

Those conversations, culinary and actual, continuously put the world into order. The shared meal remains a very central feature in our social lives, a marker of who our friends and relations are, and what it is to be human. In many languages the actual vocabulary of the meal separates it as quite distinct from the more individualistic feeding of animals. In English for example, we talk of a human 'meal' but animal 'fodder'. We 'dine' and they 'graze', and so on. To Claude Lévi-Strauss and Mary Douglas, this separation was profound. In the sharing of food and the accompanying courtesies and conservations, humans exhibited their fundamental distinction and separation from nature. The story of the meal was a story of social relations and the notion of 'culture', that key attribute that we humans have, and other species lack.

Marvin Harris was not persuaded. He was of the impression that Lévi-Strauss and Douglas were absorbed in the intricacy of a surface pattern that obscured an underlying process of a more fundamental and scientific kind; moreover a process that applied equally to humans and all other species. In the final analysis, meals were in his view about the necessary function of feeding the body, and are bound to be shaped by the requirements of nutrition. If the elaborate drama of a meal failed to provide enough individuals with sufficient energy, protein, vitamins, and minerals to reproduce and raise offspring, the dramatis personae would simply leave the stage, making way for those displaying greater evolutionary fitness. In order to explain and understand the drama, Harris argued that we need simply to crack the functional code, to reveal the linkage between rules, manners, social relations, and productive efficiency. Then the veneer of mystery surrounding the elaborate human meal would fall away. We would be revealed as yet another naked species caught up in a similar struggle for survival. However distinctive and unusual humans may seem, Harris argued that they surely cannot lie outside the evolutionary logic of natural selection and optimal fitness.[16]

If Marvin Harris had joined our other eminent twentieth-century anthropologists in this fantasy field visit among the Moravian vineyards, he would have surely pointed his finger at those accumulations of storm-laid dust, interleaved with successive episodes of hearth repair. Who could doubt that these pioneer modern humans were struggling to survive in the toughest of worlds, which must have framed their every action? Douglas may have responded with the observation that humans were not the only large mammal to colonize this challenging landscape, and no other species followed anything like this path. Can we really draw upon a logic of nature to explain a trajectory so foreign to most of the natural world that led to music, conservation, bodily adornment and craft, architecture, and order? Their differences, however, are not really about deciding who has the better argument to explain the same set of evidence; they reach deeper into the argument, to fundamental differences of view about humanity and the world.

The person and the organism: who is dreaming who?

Those differences relate how we understand the relationship between two aspects of human life, the social person and the biological organism. This has proved an area of great contention, not just in the study of food, but in all studies of the human condition. There is a strong sense that one of these aspects is 'contained' within the other; the latter is the more powerful, the driving force that shapes history. However, there is no consensus on which is driving which. Some would argue that the biological organism and nature constitute the larger arena; culture is something in which certain organisms engage as part of their survival package. Others would turn this argument around, proposing instead that the social person engaged in discourse forms the larger arena; 'nature' is simply one of many possible cultural constructs used in one of many possible discourses. One of the major traditions of modern science grew out of this very debate.

Towards the end of the eighteenth century, two essayists each pondered on the causes of shortages of food, and consequent human misery in the world. One was a friend of the American radical Tom Payne, and husband of Mary Wollstonecraft, one of the inspirational figures of early feminism. William Godwin was convinced of the power of the social person to drive the course of history, and was convinced that social inequality was the source of contemporary ills. Within the peaceful courtyards of Jesus College Cambridge, Godwin's writing was prompting a contrary view. Here, Thomas Malthus argued that the forces of nature faced people with some hard truths; they had to accept that as biological organisms they had to mould their lives to nature's laws. History was shaped by how effectively they did that. Malthus's ideas were subsequently critical in shaping the ideas of Charles Darwin, whose thesis of evolution continues to shape our studies and understanding of both nature and human society.[17]

The essential difference of view has persisted. There has been a long tradition of social scientists and anthropologists who give primacy to social persons and the power of discourse and engagement between them. Claude Lévi-Strauss and Mary Douglas fall within this tradition, and some who have drawn on their work have granted the dynamics of the biological organism a very local status indeed. Just as some groups of social persons converse about ancestry and shamans, other groups of social persons converse about 'biology' and 'organisms'. These are simply their local narratives employed to organize and make sense of the cosmos. On the other side of the debate, Darwinian evolution has generated many arguments that, like Malthus, give primacy to the biological organism, regarding discourse between social persons as just one means by which the organism engages with the overarching forces of nature. Marvin Harris is an exponent of the latter position. He has taken both Lévi-Strauss and Douglas to task for elevating the discursive aspect of a meal to too significant a place in their explanations of the way we eat. Just as others reduce the biological organism to a piece of local narrative about how the world works, Harris tended to reduce the social person to the visible tip of a larger evolutionary strategy for coping with nature.

The person and the organism are battling it out in the wider world of research into the human condition, and the easier route is to opt for one or the other. The different sub-cultures within archaeology have tended to differentiate themselves into biological and social camps. The trend has been for archaeologists working in recent periods, especially those in which there are documents and texts, to emphasize the social dimensions, and for those studying the distant past, in which bones and stone tools are prominent among the data, to explore the biological dimension. As a consequence, archaeological narratives tend to segregate around thresholds in time, points of origin at which one manner of being human is left behind, and another takes its place. For many who focus upon the food quest, a critical threshold has been the origin of agriculture, an event placed at around 10,000 years ago, before which humans were part of nature, reacting to its fluctuations as biological organisms, and after which they gained control of nature as social persons, and set about shaping a turbulent history. The birth of agriculture is one among a number of such origins, around which the complexities of being human are conveniently disaggregated into disconnected episodes.

My limited experience of the human species leaves me uncomfortable with the idea that human communities can be subdivided into 'types' in this way, some more 'social', others more 'biological'. Across some very marked cultural boundaries, admittedly within a single lifetime, I have never been other than conscious of the continuous movement between social discourse and biological necessity that seems to characterize all human life. It may be the case, especially in societies like my own, used to specialized roles, that certain activities can be meaningfully segregated into social and biological; appreciation of art clearly has a strong social dimension, just as keeping warm is essentially a biological prerogative. Other activities nonetheless resist attempts to distance the person and the organism, and these offer some insight to their interconnectedness. Such activities include birth and early motherhood, sexual union and death, and most frequently of all, the meal.

Each day, or for the more fortunate several times a day, the sharing of food brings people once again to the intimate interconnection between social person and biological organism. At such a point, attempts to dissolve one and subsume it within the other are confounded; these points reveal their interdependency. As well as being the most frequent union between the person and the organism, for an archaeologist, the meal is also the most accessible. It leaves a lot of material traces, from the arrangement of space around the hearth or table, to the equipment used to prepare and consume the food, and the remnants of the meal itself. It was this resistance to separation of the person and the organism that drew me to explore the archaeology of the shared meal, though it is only recently that the methods of archaeology have diversified to a degree that such an exploration might have some substance.

The changing tool kit of archaeology

Some durable traces of the meal are well known to archaeologists. It was a few meat bones that alerted a local monk to the remarkable archaeology of Dolní Věstonice over eighty years ago. When excavations began, although it was the small models or humans and their animal prey that captured the public's attention, the most plentiful finds were the stone toolkits of the hunt. During the following decades, bones and stone tools formed the core data of hunter-gatherer archaeology, their study ever growing in refinement. The surface of the tools could be scrutinized, and their manufacture and use explored. The animal bones could be identified, sexed, and their age at death established. Herd structure and culling practice could be inferred. The study of plant foods took longer to get under way. Although the ancient hearths are rich in charcoal, up until our own project, only a single small bag had been scanned for charred food, revealing traces of the gathering of wild roots. During our excavation, we took hundreds of large bags of sediments to sieve and float over water, in order to scan much larger quantities of charred plant remains. Within those remains, we shall look for seeds, nuts, roots, and tubers, and from the species of charred woods infer the wider range of available foods.[18]

The core data in the archaeology of food are fragments of bone, antler, and shell, and the charred fragments of plant tissue. What they have in common is that they are solid, durable, and identifiable through visual observation and the microscope. As such, the evidence they retain of the food quest tends to relate to those earlier stages of that quest when the plant and animal tissue was still reasonably intact. From bone studies we may learn about the movement of the herds and the nature of the hunt and the kill, from plant remains such things as harvest times and soil fertility. The closer these food species get to the meal itself, the more they are chopped up, pulverized, mixed, and transformed, and the more we need to look at evidence that survives in different ways, often involving observation at a finer scale. The surfaces of even tiny fragments of bone retain cut-marks which provide testimony of a sequence of stages, from butchery of the carcass to subdivision at the meal, and individual consumption of meat. A wealth of information remains at a smaller scale still, within the microscopic particles and molecular traces that service the vigorous transformations of meal preparation.

Food plants in pulverized form may leave identifiable sub-cellular granules in their wake. There are two principal kinds: fragments of silica and granules of intact starch. In the right condition, these dust-sized fragments can endure for thousands of years. The most minute traces of all are the molecules of which the food is made, most of which are quickly digested, but a small proportion of which endure for a considerable time. These include proteins, lipids (a collective term that includes fats, oils, and waxes), and DNA, which can persist for tens or hundreds of thousands of years, and in the case of some lipids, a hundred million years or more. These may be found within the food itself, or as traces in food-preparation equipment, such as grinding stones, and vessels in which the food was prepared and brought to the meal.[19]

In the more recent archaeological sites, particularly those of farming societies, the finest molecular traces are bringing new life to the study of the most familiar archaeological marker of the meal, the food vessels themselves. For historical reasons, the study of pottery has been dominated by stylistics, which has much to do with the long-standing use of pottery as a means of dating sites, and ascribing cultural affinities. Even after half a century of the radiocarbon method, scientific dating remains something of a selectively conducted calibration back in the laboratory, after the fieldwork is over. Out in the field, it is the fragments of stone and pottery, and the style in which they have been fashioned and shaped, which immediately indicate that a site has been found, and the nature of its affinities and date. In comparison to this stylistic enterprise, there has been surprisingly little enquiry into how pots were used, what was in them, and how many people shared their contents. Scanning the shelves of an archaeology museum, it is not at all difficult to find pots whose users would have been numerous. Indeed, a selection of cups, saucers, and plates from a modern Western family would look markedly individualistic alongside. An awareness of the potential of exploring pots as containers of food is now growing, encouraged by the fact that the new molecular archaeology is revealing that many pot fragments retain traces of their contents, particularly as proteins or lipids. In some cases, it is possible not simply to ascertain the ingredients in a pot, but whether they were boiled, roasted, or fermented.[20]

There are now various avenues open for following food from its production and preparation through to its presentation at the meal. In a few cases, we can follow it further through the human gut. Perhaps the most familiar sources of evidence for ancient meals are the stomach contents of the so-called 'bog bodies'. These are the unfortunate victims of an untimely death and submersion into the highly preservative medium of a peat bog. While a rather particular group, largely belonging to the last 3,000 years, their stomach contents have contributed something to the much wider set of data from conventional archaeological sites. However, if it is unusual to find a meal still within the human gut, it is more commonplace to encounter it at the close of its alimentary journey. Fossil faeces, or coprolites, are among bio-archaeology's great treasures, encountered where human settlement is physically constrained, as in rock shelters, and where functional latrines are built, as in urban societies. As well as their visually obvious contents of undigested plant tissue and small bone fragments, they preserve a range of molecular data, and are currently proving a good source for ancient DNA.[21]

The diners themselves preserve a record of their meals, not just through the material passing through their guts, but also in many aspects of their skeleton. All food passes their gums and teeth, which are progressively polished, ground, infected, and decayed as a result of feeding, and in a manner that a dental archaeologist can decipher. As different kinds of protein, fat, and carbohydrate enter the bloodstream, new tissue is built retaining a chemical signature of those ingredients. Those signatures may include specific compounds, for example of a drug plant, or, more commonly, particular elements, or forms (isotopes) of those elements. By looking at hair, teeth, and bones, and indeed different fractions of those separate tissues, bio-archaeologists are gaining an increasing understanding of precisely how those signatures reflect diet. That does not just apply to human feeders. Within our Moravian project we are working towards an 'isotopic ecology' of the whole food chain linked to the site, exploring the diet and movement of the animals upon which those early humans preyed. To extract a suitable sample, a miniature power saw is taken to a 28,000-year-old mammoth bone, and the disturbing smell of a dentist's surgery fills the air. That is the smell of burning collagen, a sure sign that these ancient bones are still rich in the molecular traces from which so much information can be gleaned.[22]

All these new developments within archaeology, which are enabling us to look more closely at past meals, relate to some novel ideas about what might serve as an organic or molecular marker. There are, however, other developments in archaeology that are equally important in this endeavour, and they involve an enhanced awareness of time and space in the archaeological record.

One notable legacy of eight decades of Moravian archaeology is some superb three-dimensional plotting, from which we can see how structured their living and food-sharing spaces were. It is not difficult to find twentieth-century excavations where the spatial plotting was far coarser; fine plotting was hard and time-consuming work when everything depended on cloth tapes, plumb-bobs, and fragile and cumbersome optical equipment. On today's excavations, plotting is achieved through laser technology, with immediate computer input and connection with geographical information systems. Against the background of an important legacy of finely plotted distributions from twentieth-century projects, the sheer availability of information about spatial pattern is now proliferating. It is that fine spatial pattern in microscopic debris that will reveal more and more about how humans gathered and interacted in the sharing of food.

A constraint on these spatial plots is adding the third dimension of time. We may, for example, find within an accumulation of sediments something we call an 'occupation deposit'. We call it that because, in contrast to the layers above and below, it contains small fragments of charcoal, bone, and artefact throughout. We can chart its profile in the section, measure its depth, and count and identify the fragments within it. However, none of these alone will indicate the actual rate of deposition. On even a single excavation, we can glance at two finds trays sitting adjacent to one another, each containing fragments of pot, bone, and stone. For all their superficial similarity, it may be that one corresponds to an accumulation of several centuries, the other to a single afternoon. Without this knowledge, we are in no position to relate those contents to any particular meal or meals. A promising route to understanding how fast or slowly those deposits built up is through sedimentary analysis and 'geo-archaeology', a field that is growing as fast as 'bio-archaeology'. While it is often difficult from old excavations, however well recorded for their time, to answer the question of duration, it is increasingly possible with modern scientific excavations so to do.

While others on our excavation were lifting stone tools and bones, and labelling up samples of loose sediment, others could be seen meticulously and patiently working a thin knife into one of the exposed sections. They were in the process of removing blocks, a few centimetres across, of the sedimentary accumulation intact and undisturbed. Carefully removed, packed up and labelled, the fragment would then travel to a Cambridge lab to be impregnated with resin, sectioned again, and scrutinized under a microscope for the minute traces of sedimentary process. It is these methods that we hope will eventually tell us whether those oscillations between hearth reconstruction and dust-storm burial were weekly, seasonal, or span much longer periods.[23]

From such fine observations of stratigraphy, it is clear that on some archaeological sites deposits built up very quickly indeed, trapping the kinds of moments in time that would correspond to a relatively small number, perhaps even a single meal. This may be a destruction deposit, burying the debris of a particular moment under ashes, a coastal deposit, in which successive tides leave their coating of sediment, or even a pit containing the residue of a meal, speedily backfilled. If we can recognize such captures of a brief moment in time, much information can be gleaned from arrangements in space, and the recording of such arrangements has greatly improved in recent years. The traditional emphasis within archaeology has been on chronological sequence, such that many older excavations record what things are on top of each other with greater rigour and care than their records of what things are next to each other, but such spatial arrangement can be highly informative in understanding something like the sharing of food.

A culinary journey

Our Moravian excavations have just begun. There is much work ahead for many specialists in different fields. The following pages chart a personal journey of enquiry that has led me to the project. That enquiry was rooted in a sense of how my own field of bio-archaeology was changing fast, and had the potential to address a wider range of issues than we had traditionally addressed in our laboratory. The issue that particularly intrigued me was that elusive interplay between social person and biological organism that might come into view through examining the sharing of food at a meal. The steps of my enquiry have entailed a close scrutiny of, and reflection upon, a series of projects that in some way or other resonate with what we hope to achieve in Moravia; they each combine imaginative and careful archaeology with the fortune of discovery to open our eyes to a variety of particular meals. Several of those meals are a mere fraction of the age of the Moravian hearths, some

MAP 1. Map of Europe and the Mediterranean, showing archaeological sites mentioned in the text. The principal case studies are indicated by their chapter number.

are older, one almost twenty times as old. There is nothing comprehensive about the coverage; they are more like a series of stepping stones across a sizeable stretch of the human past, selected both according to expediency and with the aim of casting light on the unfolding nature of the meal as a social and biological phenomenon.

At an earlier stage of this culinary journey, I considered choosing examples from across the world. There are several case studies from the archaeologies of America, Australia, and Asia that are at least as detailed and innovative as those in Europe. The choice of a broadly European focus (with a few key exceptions) allows the exploration of some interconnecting themes. This harks back to Mary Douglas's idea that meals constitute a kind of narrative. Like all narratives, they allude to earlier narratives, retelling and reshaping earlier stories. In a single festive meal in northern Europe today, the ingredients may celebrate the modern 'global village' of world trade at the same time as the shape of the courses alludes to the *haute cuisine* of the Renaissance aristocracy. The meal may open with a grace that harks back to the days of an opening sacrifice to the gods, and the roast joint may be conspicuously carved and served by a leading male, an allusion to a distant heritage of Palaeolithic hunting.

Moving back in time, such culinary narratives are decreasingly accessible, and increasingly speculative. In each chapter, nonetheless, my observations on hard evidence are preceded with a narrative, built from a varying combination of analysis, memory, and fiction. I have employed a fictional mode to connect the analytical fragments currently available to us. These narratives serve first of all as a means of exploring what novel archaeological approaches can reveal about ancient meals, and then to address a series of central questions. Why should one of the most basic biological functions, eating, develop into an elaborate costume drama of manners and gestures? What is all this about? When and how did biological function turn into a complex social performance? What do such social dramas contribute to the food quest, and indeed, how has the food quest found itself at the heart of social life?

These 'real-time' narratives at the start of each chapter impose an important discipline on myself as author and observer. It constrains my analysis of each meal and its context to a common scale, a distinctly human scale of space and time. Much of the interplay between the social person and the biological organism may come down to shifting scales in space and time, an argument developed by the historian Fernand Braudel.[24] Our common tendency to view early prehistory over large stretches of space and time, while we view more recent epochs within successively shorter intervals, can itself create an impression of transition from a predominantly biological state to a predominantly social state of being. By initiating each chapter from a common scale of observation, and moving in reasonably ordered fashion through larger scales, my aim is for a reasonably equitable treatment of suburban TV watchers, medieval monks, chimpanzees, Roman soldiers, and Neanderthals.

The different anthropologists mentioned in this chapter might have different expectations of where such an exploration might lead. Marvin Harris would expect that unfolding of scales to reveal the linkage between each social ritual and performance and the unswerving logic of natural selection and survival of the fittest, favouring the reproductive success of one mode of sharing food over another. Mary Douglas might have expected instead an assembly of social commentaries, in which manners, gesture, and cuisine mirror and document the structures of contemporary societies and contemporary worlds. Jack Goody might take that line of reasoning further still. He has argued that the language of the meal is more than a local commentary; it can also unfold into large patterns of social and political history and geography. A global map of *haute cuisine* can separate whole continents in relation to their histories of social hierarchy, to explore those commentaries as active agents of historical change. In the state of Ghana, within a continent where *haute cuisine* has not been a traditional agent for separating the elite from the masses, he observed how modernization was now proceeding in part through the manner of metropolitan eating in hotels, universities, businesses, and government offices, a sort of culinary Esperanto.[25]

Culinary conversations between humans now form a global force indeed. Aside from the vast range of political, social, and economic manoeuvres enacted in billions of such conversations around the world each day, the ecological impact of humans sharing food is immense. A recent projection estimates that 31 per cent of the net primary productivity of our planet's biosphere is appropriated for human needs. Major components of this percentage comprise the plants and animals we eat and the fuel with which they are cooked. We have conscripted vast stretches of the earth's surface into a production line for cereals, grass, fuel, poultry, and livestock, all stocking a multitude of meal tables. If we reflect on that livestock, mammals like ourselves shaped by the same logic of natural selection, we are reminded how distinctive is the particular course that humans have taken.

A field of cattle will spend much of their waking hours grazing. In doing so, they naturally create a sense of individual space, avoiding eye-contact as they proceed in quiet, unending, solitary, consumption. That is a commonplace pattern among animal species, and quite distinct from the routinized, ritualized, social meals of our own species. At some stage our ancestors departed from that more commonplace animal behaviour to our unusual pattern of eating together, face to face. That pattern subsequently evolved to generate one of the most central and character-istic, yet also one of the most diverse aspects of what it is to be human. It is a pattern whose beginnings and unfolding history have long remained obscure, but which new methods and approaches in archaeology are now gradually bringing to light.

2. The author, gathering together with dining
companions at the start of a Cambridge college feast. (*top*)

3. An adult male chimpanzee in the Gombe reserve,
consuming the head of a red colobus monkey. (*bottom*)

2

ARE WE SO DIFFERENT? HOW APES EAT

Location: Gombe National Park, Tanzania, September 1980

As Passion and her family approach the strychnos tree, Pom, who is leading, turns, pant-grunts softly, and touches her mother's brow. She runs on ahead; Passion, with a small sound of threat, rushes after. They reach the tree together. Passion climbs at once and three year old Pax follows, but Pom, after gazing at the sparse crop, moves on. Passion feeds for ten minutes, banging the hard fruits against the trunk to crack them open, then picking out the flesh with her lips. The fruits are unripe and bitter and as she feeds, she salivates copiously. Pax picks out a few but is too young to be able to open them. Presently Passion climbs down, carrying four unopened strychnos, and sits to eat them in comfort. Pax begs and eventually gets a tiny piece. As he chews, a dribble of saliva trickles down his chin; instantly he picks a blade of grass and dabs at the sticky juice. As he continues to feed, he repeatedly wipes his mouth with tiny pieces of grass. He uses nine of these napkins in the five minutes it takes him to consume the morsel. Passion does not clean herself at all and at the end of her meal has a mess of saliva and fruit juice all over her chin, chest and hands.[1]

A T a discrete distance from this family of chimpanzees, a human being looks on, a member of the *Gombe Stream Research Centre*, observing carefully and taking these notes. It may be some time before she returns to the Centre to share food with members of her own species; these chimpanzee 'follows' start early in the morning and finish late. Observational sessions can continue for days, even weeks. Back at the Centre, the meal she shares with other researchers is less intimately connected with the surrounding forest than Passion's strychnos feast. While Passion sat at the base of the very tree that produced her fruits, ingredients of the humans' meal will have travelled at least from the far side of Lake Tanganyika. Others ingredients will have been carried in tin cans yet further distances, even from different continents. Such human meals are separated from the environments that produced them, not just by distances, but also by architecture and chemistry. The walls and roofs of the Research Centre enclose them, and in the kitchen, a range of chemical and pyrotechnic wizardry transforms leaves, seeds, and flesh into culinary creations. Yet for all this physical and chemical separation that lend to it a particular ecological remoteness, the human meal is also characterized by a surprising intimacy for which it is hard to find parallel in the natural world.[2]

Passion and Pom are mother and daughter. They certainly cooperate in their quest for food, but we can sense a certain tension, an ambiguity about who will get the strychnos fruits. Passion and Pax are mother and young dependant son, but he still has to beg and wait for his morsels of food. Back at the Research Centre, their human observer will freely pass and receive plates of food. She will not be surprised to sit alongside a fellow diner she had met only a month, a week, or a day earlier, and to share food from a common dish. There may be any number of unrelated diners sitting around the meal table, face to face, an attitude that many species would find very threatening. The thing that allows this unusual intimacy of a human meal is a quintessentially human attribute, an ingredient of the meal at least as important as the food itself—endless lively conversation.

There are nonetheless several features of Passion's meal that resonate with that of her human observer. While Passion's diet did not draw from the same global ecosystem as her observers, it did draw extensively from the fauna and flora of the Gombe forest in Tanzania where she lived. Of over 600 plants recognized by humans in the Gombe forest, round about a quarter are recognized by its chimpanzee population as sources of food. Some of those foods, soft leaves and flower heads for example, are fairly straightforward to eat. Others, such as pods, hard fruits, and stems, require a certain amount of dextrous unpacking, for which the jaws are assisted by that characteristic feature of primates, their nimble hands. As the soft interior of many of these unpacked food plants does not remain edible for long, they also require a certain sense of timing and of natural life cycles.[3]

In addition to these features of manual dexterity and awareness of 'natural history', Passion's meal also displayed a social dimension. It is true that a competitive tension can be sensed between mother and daughter, between Passion and Pom, in relation to the strychnos tree. Viewed, however, in the context of how many species feed, they had engaged in quite a complex social negotiation. It might be misleading to describe either Pom's pant-grunt or Passion's threat call as 'language'; at least it seems clear that such sounds are never woven together into 'sentences'. The Gombe researchers have learnt over the years to recognize a range of vocal calls and bodily signals, a number of which relate specifically to the enjoyment of food. In more masculine chimp meals, an alpha male at the centre of the action might let forth a loud 'food aaa call' which will draw other diners to the scene, who in turn will issue a repertoire of softer 'food grunts' as they tuck in. In the strychnos meal of Passion's family, Pom's soft 'pant-grunting' is a more general and personal token of respect; it acknowledges her mother's higher social rank as they both catch sight of the strychnos tree. The slight sound of threat from Passion conversely emphasizes her daughter's inferior rank, and the implicit message is: 'Don't start on that meal before your mother reaches the tree!' As we see, the net result is that Pom deferentially leaves the meal to her mother and younger brother. Passion's relationship with her 3-year old son is quite different from that with her daughter. If Pax were a little older, the age of his absent 9-year-old brother Prof, then he might well be competing with his mother for food, exchanging the occasional threatening sound and posture. Prof is still spending a lot of time with his blood relatives, but is significantly out of the frame during this meal. He may well have temporarily joined up with a few other males, jostling for rank and generally 'out on the razzle'. His younger brother still looks to his mother for food and protection. These various communications established a clear social relationship between dominant and submissive parties within the family that set the stage

4. Passion, a chimpanzee in the Gombe reserve, together with two of her offspring, Pax and Pom, observed in November 1978.

for the meal quite as definitively as a paterfamilias taking his place at the head of the table to carve the Sunday roast. Passion was, however, very far from being the most sociable of chimps. The more closely the whole community of Gombe forest chimps is observed, the more clear the social dimension of food-sharing becomes.

Going back to the year before the birth of the infant Pax, it was Passion's turn to be closely observed through a 'long follow', as she roamed with her two older offspring across ridge and ravine through the rich variety of trees that clothe the rugged slopes that descend to Lake Tanganyika. Even though this long follow took place towards the end of the dry season, the air remained moist and hot. Each evening, as the air cooled, Passion and Pom prepared for the night by stripping oil palm trees of their fronds. They would use these high up in the trees, to build their night nest. Each following day, the small family roamed for several kilometres, and around half their waking hours would be spent feeding. A great deal of that time, the chimps would move from tree to tree plucking leaves, and in the appropriate seasons, blossoms, fruits, insect galls. Bark, pith, and resin were also occasionally consumed. In this way chimps acquire food from around 150 plant species, around a quarter of the entire recorded flora of the Gombe forest.[4]

For all this diversity of plant foods, Passion was certainly not a vegetarian. Back in the 1960s, she was one of the first chimps that Jane Goodall had watched 'termite-fishing'. In this delicate and skilful procedure, the chimps would insert some suitable tool, such as a grass stem, into a carefully opened termite mound, and slowly withdraw the stem together with its clinging prey. During the long follow she was also seen killing and consuming two newly born fawns of a deer-like creature called the 'bushbuck', and sharing the tasty meal of meat, blood, and brains with her children, Prof and Pom. All the time, a member of the Gombe Stream Research Centre would be taking notes, recording distances travelled, nesting sites, food species consumed, and so on. They looked at the remains of nests, of tracks on the ground, the broken and discarded shells of the strychnos and other fruits, and the 'scats' or faeces. With the aid of a makeshift tin, holes punched in the bottom, these scats could be 'dung-swirled' down by the stream. After the water dispersed the more digested food, some quite large fragments remained, of meat, fruit-stones, and the like which contributed greatly to our understanding of chimpanzee diet. Jane Goodall had come to know the individual chimpanzees sufficiently well to give them names and to record their biographies. In this way, they were able to check who was travelling with whom, which chimps were coming together to share food, to threaten each other, and who was engaged in sexual relations with whom. The different chimpanzee groups dispersed and reassembled in various ways, bringing together feeding, tenderness, violence, and bloodshed in a variety of permutations. By the time of Passion's long follow, she had become fairly antisocial, sticking with her own immediate family, avoiding, and being avoided by, many of the other female chimps in the nearby woods. They had good reason to steer well clear. While many enjoyed eating bushbuck, bushpig, baboon, or colobus monkey, Passion and her teenage daughter Pom had acquired a taste for the flesh of their own species, and had spent the last few years intermittently terrorizing local chimp mothers, brutally wresting their newborns from their breast, and consuming them in full view of the bereaved, wounded, and traumatized parent.[5]

Turning back, just over a decade before Passion, Pom, and Pax reached the strychnos tree, to a time before Pax was born and Pom was no older than he, we can get a glimpse of some rather less antisocial meals among the Gombe chimps. As well as being a bit of a rough diamond in later years, Passion did not strike Jane Goodall as the ideal textbook mother when Pom was growing up, and her infant daughter was known to roam fairly free. On one such occasion, she happened upon an elaborate feast that lasted from 8.00 a.m. in the morning til 5.30 p.m. in the afternoon.[6]

All the great and the good from the Kasakela community were there. This name was given by the researchers to the community of chimps which ranges across the Kasakela and Kakombe river valleys, in the middle stretch of the Gombe reserve, in the middle of which the Research Centre is located. At the heart of the feast was the community's alpha male, the temperamental and rather unlikely figure of Mike. He seems to have risen through the ranks from a quite lowly position by a combination of guts, intelligence, and threatening use of the empty kerosene cans that he found around the Research Centre. Mike had captured a young colobus monkey, and this tasty treat was to become the focus of the ensuing feast. The kill had attracted other males that would experience high rank at some stage in their lives. There was a previous alpha male, Goliath, who Mike had displaced from the top, yet with whom he would become friends. Also there was a future alpha male who would displace Mike's own successor and rule for several years. His name was Figan, who would before long be propelled to the top with the help of his brother and sidekick, the disabled Faban, and the help of his mother, to whom we shall return. Then came Charlie, who would never make it to alpha male in the Kasakela community itself, but in a couple of years would reach the top in a breakaway community centred on the Kahama valley further to the south.

Some powerful females had also gathered to the feast, such as the adolescents Melissa and Nope, along with Mandy and Athena, who

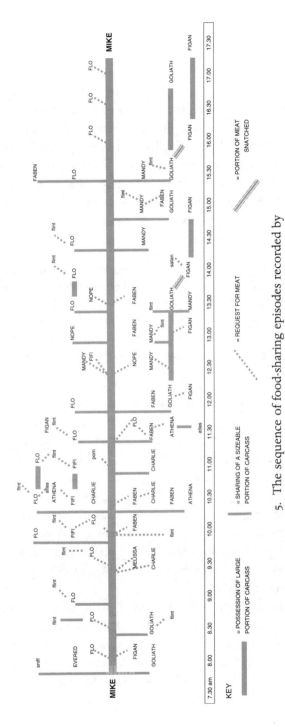

5. The sequence of food-sharing episodes recorded by
Giza Teleki in the Gombe reserve during a day-long consumption of a captured colobus monkey.

arrived with her one-year-old daughter, Atlas. The most notable female in their presence was twice the age of these adolescents, and had quite a hold on the assembled community, male and female alike. The matriarchal figure of Flo, now approaching her fortieth year, was mother to four of the other feasters, the future alpha male Figan and his brother Faben, their 10-year-old sister Fifi, and 4-year-old brother Flint. At many points in her life she had exerted a strong sexual hold on many of the community's males. At the time Flint was conceived, she could be seen with a retinue of as many as fourteen males, one of whom was the current alpha male, Mike. Eight years on, she became the first non-human to earn an obituary in the Sunday Times, from which the following is an extract:

> Even now a month later it is hard to believe that Flo is dead. For more than ten years this old chimpanzee had been an integral part of life at the Gombe stream, with her torn ears and bulbous nose, her occasional spells of wild sexual activity, her dauntless, forceful personality... She was lying at the edge of the Kakombe stream. When I turned her over, her face was peaceful and relaxed without sign of fear or pain. Her eyes were still bright and her body supple.[7]

At the centre of this far from anonymous group, the slightly uncertain Mike clung to his dying colobus monkey. Possibly because of his less than certain grip on his current alpha male position, Mike tended to be a generous food sharer. Over the following nine hours, around forty food-sharing negotiations were observed with Mike himself, and around the same number of negotiations on the periphery for subdivided portions. Those negotiations occasionally involved a snatch, but were mostly achieved through supplicant behaviour, peering or touching, or even throwing an infantile tantrum. In response to these, the higher-ranking individual would either diffidently refuse, or give freely to the lower-ranking individual.

The 3-year-old Pom, wandering away from her mother to find this feast, made just one, inconsequential request to Mike. In general, the four infants at the feast only got food by way of a female, or some more compliant male, such as the has-been, Goliath. The one infant to succeed in getting food direct from Mike was Flint, but he was well connected.

His mother was the most successful recipient of all. On twelve occasions during the day, sometimes sizeable portions of meat passed from Mike to Flo.

At the end of the day, thirteen out of the seventeen chimpanzees assembled had succeeded in sharing in the colobus monkey feast. A careful recording of each food-sharing event revealed a full spectrum of relationships in which a higher-ranking individual passes a share of the food to a lower-ranking individual, in response to some form of begging or supplicant behaviour that both signifies and reinforces each relationship. In this way, food is passed from the alpha male to males of a lower rank. It is passed from male to female, sometimes in the context of sexual engagement. It is passed from adult to child, and particularly from mother to child, the primary engagement which all the others, in some way, echo.

A stranger species still

Reading through these remarkable accounts of the shared meals of our closest living relatives, accounts that bring together tenderness and hostility, minute dexterity, and bloody violence, my thoughts turned occasionally to a Cambridge college feast I myself had recently attended. That too was characterized by an enormous diversity of leaves, seeds, fruits, roots, tubers, and flavourings from a very long list of plant species. Against this vegetative backcloth, a drama was also enacted with the flesh of a smaller number of animal species in starring role, a drama at least in the presentation, if not the actual kill. Like the Gombe chimps, I too gather with members of my own species in different permutations to share food on different occasions, in each case acknowledging rank and status in a variety of ways.

Many of the diners at that college feast I had not previously met—they were complete strangers to me. In the context of the natural world, that is a most unusual state of affairs. Close kin yes, but we know of no other species that will gather to share food with a complete stranger, and I am not always so intimate with strangers. If I take my packed lunch to a busy park, I create my own personal space along with many other lunchers, our virtual boundaries around individual patches of grass, rather like a field of grazing animals. My human meals are yet more socially bounded, and certainly more emphatically enshrined in architectural space. At the same time they are more ecologically open, reaching far and wide into a global ecosystem.

Those boundaries subdivide the totality of our human existence in a variety of ways. Sex and death may be more repeatedly alluded to, but have not been welcome in material form at any meal to which I have recently been invited. Bodily contact in general is rule-bound, as is contact between my body and my food, and the different foods with each other. At that recent college feast, scanning the cutlery, crockery, table linen, and so on, I counted thirty-three items of food-sharing technology around my own seat, provided to ensure that none of those boundaries was breached. Beyond that, the most elaborate architectural provisions for food preparation, consumption, and disposal opened up around me, all suitably partitioned and separated by walls and doors. In the language of anthropologist Mary Douglas, the rules of punctuation are strict indeed. I had furthermore enclosed my own body in ten items of attire to ensure that my personal visual signals and boundaries were in place, including such things as an academic gown, a dinner suit, and the associated, shirt cuff links, and tie. Seven of these ten items I reserve entirely for the purpose of feasting.

Adhering to those rules and manoeuvring through those social bound-aries, we find that in ecological terms the food we eventually reach at our feast is conspicuously open-ended. The chimp meals in Gombe forest display a similar diversity, but they are bounded by the perimeters of the forest itself. The Mahale mountains run alongside Lake Tanganyika only 140 km to the south of the Gombe forest. Here too, another long-term chimpanzee observation project has been carried out. The Mahale mountains also support a large number of plant species, in this case a third to a half of which are recognized by chimpanzees as sources of food. What is really interesting about the comparison between the Mahale and Gombe chimp diets is the range of mismatches. Bringing the two recorded food lists together, we can assemble a list of potential food plants for chimps. Of these, less than 60 per cent are consumed in both areas. As the Tanzanian chimps move through their home woodlands, they repeatedly encounter plants that chimps readily consume in remote communities, but pass them by. These 'cultural' differences between communities are revealed in other ways, for example in differences in the items used as wands for termite fishing. The more we learn about chimpanzee communities, the more we appreciate how bounded their practices are in ecological space.[8]

More or less bounded or immobilized at my predetermined college seat, the feast unfolding before me situated the diners within a food chain that spanned the world. At various stages during the meal we sampled several of the species that dominate the global human food chain in calorific terms: wheat, originally from south-west Asia, potatoes originally from South America, and rice, originally from China. We ranged omnivorously, up and down that food chain, consuming the flesh of herbivores and carnivores from sea and air, and the rivers and land-surfaces of several continents. Not much is known about the response of the different African forests to the grazing by chimps of so many of their component species. At the same time, the world's human community, by gathering around meal tables, hammers planet earth, day by day, with an environmental force comparable with the movement of glaciers, the eruption of major volcanoes, and the impact of comets.

I do not share food in that elaborate manner very often, but similar themes may be observed at meal tables that are more ordinary by far, such as the one to which our observer of Passion's family looked forward, back at the Research Centre. In her various books, Jane Goodall alludes to such simple fare on many occasions, from a hastily snatched breakfast of toast and coffee at 5.30 in the morning, through to restful evening meals on the veranda, or alternatively, like the chimps, alfresco under the night sky. Even those alfresco meals around the campfire share many of the hallmarks of this uniquely human institution. Just like the college feast, they sit around in a 'conversational circle' facing each other, accompanying the food with leisurely talk, gossip, and laughter. Goodall might be accompanied by familiar kin, her husband Hugo and mother Vanne, fellow researchers and other non-kin, some of whom may have been new to Tanzania and the Centre. There was a drama to these simple meals; they might start with drinks and taped music, and end with coffee and the playing of games. In between, the sequence and assembly of such ordinary ingredients as baked beans, tinned bully beef, tomatoes, onions, and bananas would be stage-managed accordingly to culturally familiar culinary practice, taking the diners through a preordained sequence of 'courses'. At Christmas, this culinary drama would intensify to connect this remote and unusual African community with a large part of the English-speaking world. A meal of stuffed roast chicken and plum pudding would connect Goodall simultaneously to her own roots and to Britain's heritage. The ingredients of the plum pudding alone, figs, raisins, and brandy from Europe, sugar from the Caribbean, cinnamon and cloves from Sri Lanka, nutmeg from the Spice Islands, read like a map of Britain's global colonial history.

As in these meals in the Gombe reserve, so our college feast simultaneously unfolded as a rich social drama. One of the more unusual items of my dining attire is an academic gown. Its style and length, as well as odd bits of appliqué fabric, signal to the initiated with whom I am about to share food what degrees I hold, and by which university they were awarded. The complex trajectory of initiation processes and rites of passages, within educational and academic institutions, that had brought me to that particular table wearing that gown, stretch over a large part of my life and have absorbed a significant portion of my energies. Around me I could see seats I might have occupied at an earlier stage in my life, a few rites of passage back. There are clearly some newcomers, staying close to their host and cautiously attentive for discreet guidance on any idiosyncratic elements of protocol. I could also look round to points around the table I remain too junior to occupy. Occupying a prominent position at the centre of this elite group was our alpha male. We waited until he was seated before we took our seats, and waited until he commenced each course before we did the same. Similarly, he rose from the table first, and we followed. We rose and sat following this slightly staggered sequence at certain points within the meal. On such occasions, and sometimes clasping a preparation of the narcotic my society uses, we cried out to higher beings whose presence around the table lacked material form. One was the constitutional head of our tribe. Another was the deity to whom our elders subscribe and pay homage. A third was the ancestor whose benefaction had allowed this feast to take place on an annual cycle stretching from here to eternity.

Intimacy among dinosaurs?

After four decades of observation in the Gombe reserve, in which individual chimps are recognized and named by their human observers, quite a lot is known about their blood relationships, and it seems quite clear from these observations that food-sharing goes well beyond maternal care and courtship. But what about the wider world of nature? How social are the meals of other species?

When dinosaurs roamed, we suspect that mother and child would have become quite independent feeders soon after the infant dinosaur had hatched. At least that is what we infer from living reptiles. In a rather more diminutive group of living lizards, the 'skinks', the mothers will allow their newborn to snatch food from under her in the first fortnight of their lives, but that is about as far as it goes. Among crocodiles and alligators, the care of nests of eggs will extend as far as helping the newly hatching offspring to break out of the egg, but from then on, they fend for themselves. In many turtles and iguanas, the independence is greater still. A moist place is found, under rocks, debris, or mud, in which to deposit the eggs and then the mother moves on; the next generation is on its own. Among these reptiles, as with most amphibians, fish, and much of the animal kingdom, feeding is a self-interested thing, an individual quest in the struggle for survival. Yet, as the great dinosaurs dwindled, other animals diversified, and went on to dominate the exposed surface of the planet, and the skies above. With the domination of the land and the skies came a break in an age-old pattern of self-interest.

For a period after a baby mammal has emerged from the womb, or a baby bird from its egg, its mother's behaviour will not be competitive, but instead may be described as 'pro-social'. She will actively devote time and energy, not to her own welfare, but to the well-being of her offspring, by protecting them, sheltering them, and passing food from her own mouth, or beak, to those of her children. Particularly in birds, the father may also play a key role in gathering food for mother and offspring, or even take over all parental care. All the evidence suggests that the sharing of food finds its origin in this pro-social relationship between parent and child, the only really widespread forms of pro-active food-sharing in nature. Such pro-social feed relationships are certainly seen among our immediate relatives, the primates, in this case, aided and elaborated by unusually dextrous forelimbs. Such limbs with their nimble digits allow mouth-to-mouth food-sharing to be supplemented by hand-to-mouth and hand-to-hand sharing. Mouth-to-mouth sharing remains the predominant mode among mammals and birds. Among the Kalahari !Kung, and the Highland peoples of Papua New Guinea, we can find the human version of this, sometimes known as 'kiss-feeding', in which a mother affectionately passes a morsel of food from her own mouth to her infants.[9]

Food and sex

Parental care quite often displays features in common with courtship. It is as if the parental behaviour in caring for a young child is 'borrowed' by courting couples. This is certainly true of the meeting of mouths or beaks during food-sharing. A very wide range of birds, from ravens to parrots, herring gulls to woodpeckers, pass food from beak to beak, not just from parent to offspring, but between courting couples. In courtship, the actual transfer of food may have disappeared, and affection be communicated by the meeting of mouths alone. A sea lion will rub snouts with its young offspring, and employ the same behaviour during courtship. A female shrew will allow saliva to be licked from its mouth, by its young offspring, or alternatively by a courting male. In some human societies, the kiss-feeding of infants is known, and the behaviour may also occur without the actual transfer of food. In other human societies, mouth to mouth kissing becomes the sole reserve of courtship.[10]

The intimate relationship between feeding and courtship may be understood in the evolutionary context of reproductive success, but sexual encounter is not invariably connected to courtship and mating. Food and sex may also come together in a more immediate way, through the sensual pleasure that each provides. Indeed, the one may be implicitly or explicitly traded for the other. We can observe this in our own species, and in another of our close relatives, a species in the same genus as the chimpanzee, and sometimes referred to as the 'pygmy chimpanzee'. It is better known as the bonobo.

This diminutive primate, first mistaken for an immature chimp, was only recognized as an independent species in 1933. Since then, its study has revealed a number of similarities to humans in terms of sexual behaviour. Females are sexually receptive throughout their cycle. A number of sexual positions are adopted, involving both same-sex and mixed-sex unions, and are used pleasurably to relieve tension and generally socialize. Not surprisingly, many bonobo activities, including the sharing of food, involve some aspect of sex. Field researchers in the Lomako forest of central Zaire carried their dictaphone, camcorder, portable balance, and tape measure to the feeding grounds of the Eyengo community of bonobos. They watched closely and recorded as these animals sought out and then shared breadfruits, the occasional catch of squirrel or some other small prey, and charted the associated behaviour, which was frequently sexual. The most common behaviour was the rubbing of genitals between two females as a prelude to sharing the breadfruit's tasty orange seeds. Copulation was also a recurrent element of negotiations over food, though not always on equal terms. One of their records describes the sustained sexual activity between a vigorously begging female, and a male in possession of food. After seven successive copulations, he still would not give her a bite of his breadfruit.[11]

This may all seem a long way from the Cambridge college feast, but that meal too displays an intimate association with sex, not by way of its engagement, but conversely of its prohibition. Acts of sex are commonly excluded from contemporary human meals, and for several centuries Cambridge college meals placed certain limits on such possibilities by excluding one sex altogether. When in the 1960s Jane Goodall arrived in Cambridge to undertake her doctoral research, she was not eligible to enrol at the college of her supervisor, and certainly not to join him at the feasts of his own college. Had she lived half a century earlier, she would not have been eligible to join the Cambridge academic community at all. Half a century earlier still, the fellows dining at college feasts would have been expected to abstain from sex and matrimony altogether.

Meals that are as strictly bounded by moral code are by no means confined to these rather rarefied circumstances, but are widespread among human societies around the world. Indeed, human meals of all kinds are framed within moral codes about sex, age, rank, and ethnicity, and the diners do not typically sense that these rules are negotiable. They are set at some other time, by some other authority, part human and part divine. The rules of conduct are passed down from each generation to the next.

This seems to mark us apart from our closest relatives. Chimps and bonobos clearly have a social structure and a mutual sense of rank. They evidently move and feed in groups that are broadly single sex from time to time. Our general sense, nonetheless, is of a series of strategies that are negotiable, that can be constantly reassembled in different ways in different places. It may normally be the case that 3-year-olds feed with their mother, but the 'lightly parented' Pom may nonetheless wander off to join a 'power feast'. It may generally be true that the males do the hunting, and share the kill widely, while the female chimps fish for termites and gather, eating in intimate groups of kin. However, such females as Passion also hunted occasionally, and some plant foods have been shared beyond the family. The lives of chimps and bonobos are framed by two interwoven strands of social norm and ecological reality. Within that fluid frame, they inhabit their bounded ecosystems amply and flexibly, and with far less instruction from the previous generation. Contemporary humans inhabit a much more open and global ecosystem, but through the bounds of a more rigid social 'architecture'. The use of the word 'architecture' emphasizes that these bounds have a permanency, and a source beyond those who move within them, and passed down in detail from one generation to the next. The architectural spaces of the modern human world separate our activities into different types. In some spaces, we are social persons, listening to each other's words and music, creating and consuming cultural artefacts. In other spaces, we are biological organisms, taking care of bodily needs, sleeping, defecating, washing, and recovering from illness. Elsewhere we are economic beings, turning the soil, working the machine, creating the wealth that underpins our existence as social persons or biological organisms. However, some of our activities refuse to be thus compartmented, to be removed to separate realms of existence. These are activities in which person and organism remain intimately connected within a common whole. For all their social shaping and ritualization, they remain as gateways that interconnect our compartmented selves, points at which social person and biological organism inextricably combine.

Origins

Close observation of chimps and bonobos provides us with something of an observation post, from which we reflect upon our own species and its peculiarities. But it is important to remember that, in evolutionary terms, these two species are our close cousins, not our ancestors. They are level tips of the same evolutionary bush rather than points beneath us on our own evolutionary tree. They too have an evolutionary history of changing circumstances and changing responses. That much is clear from comparing and contrasting what chimps eat in two distinct forests. Looking beyond chimps and bonobos on the living tips of our evolutionary bush, we encounter around 200 species of living primates, each of which also has its own evolutionary history. What we can do by viewing the living tips of the evolutionary bush is draw upon some commonalities which, in conjunction with the fossil record, allow us to project a certain amount back in time.

One clear commonality is that most primates are conspicuously social animals, recognizing and engaging with a significantly larger group than immediate parents and offspring. The branch of primates that includes monkeys and apes and ourselves displays a very diverse range of social patterns sometimes involving social networks measured in tens of individuals, occasionally running into three figures. We can reasonably assume that the degree of social complexity apes and monkeys share was also shared by their common ancestor. Fragments of that ancestor, or at least something quite close to it, have occasionally emerged from quarries within the Fayum depression of Egypt, and the genus name *Propliopithecus* has been ascribed to them. Their teeth and bones were laid down near to the tall trees that flourished in the hot humid lagoonal rainforest that occupied the depression 32–5 million years ago. Some of the fossilized tree trunks also survived. These skeletal fragments belonged to a small monkey-like primate, its limb bones indicating the manual dexterity which is typical of primates and with which it ascended into the tall trees, to unpeel soft fruits with delicate fingers and teeth. Its somewhat dog-like skull had space for a brain of around 30 cubic centimetres. That was an unremarkable size for primates, but substantial in comparison with most animal species. Brain size was to become a significant attribute when it came to managing a complex social life.[12]

It is not for another 10 million years that we can add much definition to those complex social lives. From this point our evolutionary line differentiates into monkeys and apes, allowing us to focus in upon these two related groups. The majority of species of forest-dwelling monkeys in Africa today build their social groups around female lineages. Mothers, sisters, and daughters cluster around sources of food, and a variable number of males cluster around them. There is an ecological logic to this pattern, concerning the different constraints of being a mother and a father. A mother has a tough time reproducing, from conception, through gestation, lactation, and upbringing to the eventual independence of their offspring. All this needs a lot of energy, and places heavy demands upon food supply. Food is a limiting factor for the mother, and one way of maximizing evolutionary success is for related females to club together around a food source and cooperate on feeding and defence. Reproduction is theoretically less of a challenge for the father, who can assure a future for his genes simply by impregnating as many females as possible. That assumes of course that sexual engagement itself presents no challenges, something that is not true for every male. In order to win a mate, he may need to compete with others and prove himself in food-sharing largesse such as has been observed in the Gombe forest. It seems that for many species, food is limiting for reproductive females, while access to females is limiting for reproductive males, and that may account for the kind of social structure seen in many species of forest-dwelling monkey today, in which related females cluster around food, and unrelated males around them. A similar pattern might be projected back to their common forest-dwelling ancestor 25 million years ago. What was happening in our particular sub-branch, the apes, is more complex.

Living apes do not fall into the kind of recurrent social pattern which would allow a simple projection back to their common ancestor. Orang-utans lead relatively solitary existences; gibbons form monogamous families, with the sexes sharing equal roles in the defence of territory; male gorillas connect with 'harems' of females, while chimps and bonobos can disaggregate and reaggregate in multiple social groupings. It may indeed be that flexibility rather than any one social norm is what characterizes the evolution of apes, a flexibility observed both between species and within some species of ape, including our own. Negotiating with large social groups of recognizable individuals places considerable demands on the capacity of the brain to manage that information. Flexibility in the relationships that are formed between those large groups places yet more demands on the managerial capacity of the brain. It is indeed within some of the apes that brain size grows to truly unusual levels, notably within a genus that differentiated around two million years ago, our own genus *Homo*.[13]

What are our distinguishing features?

There have been a number of ideas about distinguishing features of humans, separating us from the animal world, that have one by one fallen by the wayside as observations of our primate relatives intensified. The best known among these was the use of tools, which are certainly central to the manner in which we humans prepare and consume a meal. However, it is now clear that tool use is widespread among our close relatives, and also encountered in a number of other mammals and birds.[14] A deep and intricate knowledge of natural history is another feature that has in the past been linked specifically to humans. The remarkable diversity of the human diet, comprising thousands of species of reasonably familiar organisms, and many more obscure foods, has been connected with our ability to classify, recognize, and experiment. Feeding observations of primates have repeatedly demonstrated their vast awareness of natural history and the species around them, and the manner in which their food acquisition varies from place to place, presumably arising from a propensity to experiment. Much of these diets is made up of plant foods, but observations since the time of Jane

Goodall have repeatedly witnessed primates hunting other mammals, also robbing 'man the hunter' of his singular place in nature. Linked to the hunting of sizeable beasts is the sharing and negotiation of food beyond the parent–child union, and here too, evidence of such negotiations within other species can be found.

The emergence of none of the above features is entirely unique to the genus *Homo*. They were in the primate line long before early humans differentiated into a distinct line. The differences are no longer absolute; instead they differ in scale and diversity. However, those changes of scale and diversity are in many cases immense. Our tools are considerably more complex and our natural histories more intricate. The change in scale with greatest archaeological visibility is the size of the beasts we cull. Early in the history of our genus, these beasts may exceed the size of a chimp's prey by a factor of twenty or more. We can find later prehistoric deposits in which many such beasts have been slaughtered together for a feast. The social groups that gather on such occasions probably numbered thousands.

In addition to these quantitative differences, it does seem that there remain some distinctions of a qualitative kind. These bring us back to Mary Douglas's consideration of the meal as a kind of structured language. Our close relatives the chimps spend a great deal of time feeding, and it is broadly continuous and opportunistic. We humans have cycles of eating, which are diurnal, weekly/monthly, seasonal, annual, and biographical. Each meal has a beginning and end and a certain drama and sequence, not just the Cambridge feast but also the working meal at the Gombe Research Centre. In time, this intensive structuring and ordering of consumption unfolds into a rigid architecture around food, not just the physical spaces in which dining is permitted (or not), but also the food-producing landscape, partitioned off into plots and fields. Indeed, the practice of agriculture upon which most contemporary meals depend may be seen as the rigorous organization of plants, animals, and people into precise blocks of space and time.

That was not a particular issue of note when Passion, Pom, and Pax happened upon a strychnos tree one day in 1980. Neither did it really figure a decade earlier, when the whole day was spent negotiating meat from a colobus monkey. That monkey was around 20 kilo in weight. Nor was it likely to have been a significant issue for the early humans. It is, however, within the archaeology of early human species that we witness the consumption of beasts of several hundred kilos in weight by primates with unusually large brains. The following chapters explore those two significant changes in biological scale, and ask questions about parallel changes in the scale of social organization, questions about structure, order, and the focus of the greatest scalar change of all, communication.

6. Imagined scene of the butchery of a wild horse, half a million years ago
    along the coast of southern England at Boxgrove.

3

IN SEARCH OF BIG GAME

Boxgrove, near Chichester, southern England, circa 500,000 years ago

She crashed down at the edge of the water's edge, her body disappearing beneath the grass. All that could now be seen from the cliff was the flailing motion of the long, slender hardwood spear lodged in her shoulder, and tagging her staggered movements across the mudflats. They hurried down the scree onto the mudflats to join the spear-thrower, the stronger among them making good headway. Around half a dozen of the others lingered at the flint scree; even though others had already reached the injured horse, they knew their own turn to eat would come. High above, birds gathered and began to circle, it seemed with a similar wisdom. Down below, flint nodules were being checked, turned over, and a few of the better-shaped ones selected. Others had brought their own carefully fashioned stone tools with them.

Making their way carefully across the salt marsh, creeks, and mud slurries, they reached the point where their faster relatives had brought the wild horse down. They were already circling the carcass. Their anxious eyes were wide open, all the while scanning the horizon. An open watery place was a dangerous place to linger. Hurling sticks and stones at hyenas was one thing—big cats were something else. They might have to abandon the whole thing if one of those lions got too close. They would remain on guard for as long as it took—probably several hours. The chosen nodules were placed at various well-chosen points around the carcass.

Activity centred on the last arrivals at the scene. Each laid their spear beside them, pulled from their hide waistband an antler hammer, and settled in the position they had carefully chosen, with one foot extended, the other bent at the knee to serve as an anvil. They began to strike. The physical contact with the nodule was critical to getting the impact right. An impact at the wrong point, or in the wrong direction, would have no visible impact on the flint. A strike, which to an observer displayed the same natural fluency as breathing or walking, would cause the nodule to fall into two, the freshly exposed faces moistly gleaming with a deep blue-black hue.

Within minutes, those moist new surfaces would dry, their rich dark colour dull, and newly created edges lose some of their sharpness. For the next few hours, however, those edges would be among the sharpest edges ever fashioned. By turning and striking, turning and striking, each globular flint nodule was transformed into an elegant oval shape, its matt white surface removed to reveal the shimmering blue-black surface beneath. Others were sharpening the tools they had brought with them.

A lead hunter carried his butchery tool or 'hand-axe' across to the carcass, the guards letting them by. First slicing open a main neck artery, in order to ensure the animal was lifeless, and then plunging deep and low into the horse's belly, the newly prepared blade was dragged up the throat. Immediately working on the head, the tongue was cut out and the skull smashed open. A constant chattering from those who brought the horse down ensured they were included in the distribution of these tender tissues. By the time the liver, kidneys, stomach, and intestines were eased out and consumption had begun in earnest, yet more feeders arrived at the scene.

The original hunting party was now joined by many others, jostling noisily. Some were presenting themselves for sex in the hope of food shared in exchange, an offer that would be taken up on several occasions before the meal was over. Young mothers begged both for meat and for the soft and oily layers of horse fat. The jostling males occasionally allowed them access to the flesh without any further bargaining.

Things were settling down around the dead animal as empty stomachs had gradually filled. The guarding of the kill had found a more settled rhythm. There was certainly a band of hyenas lurking at the woodland edge on top of the cliff, but so far, the cats has chosen to stay back from the commotion. Two of the group each had sections of the rib-cage clamped firmly between their jaws. A skilful wrench of the neck muscles would peel the ribs back, freeing the heart and lungs for consumption. A few fragments of tissue were quickly consumed by the bolder gulls that had been circling for some time up above. More skilful blade work was in progress now, with neat incisions around each hoof, around the eye sockets and across the skull. The blades could then be used to ease the hide off the body.

One of the older flint-knappers bared her teeth and cried out. She was vigorous in defence of her prized hand-axe. She moved quickly to the skinned animal, and with a well targeted strike, plunged her axe into the prize—the socket of one of the rear legs. She allowed her immediate kin to get close and help with the limb's detachment. After much striking, bending, and slicing through meat and tendons, the leg came free and was dragged to one side. Another of the knappers was already at work on the second hind leg, and others were moving to the forelegs.

By now, the feeders had aggregated into separate clusters, each with their own fragment of the carcass, and the job of cutting off fillets of meat began. The more urgent competition now behind them, a member from each kin group set off towards the coast in search of large pebbles. On their return, the meat filleting was already drawing to a close. Slabs of meat were being parcelled up in strips of the horse hide and skewers by the spears for ease of transport. The work on the carcass had moved to the scraping of the bone surfaces, in preparation for fracture.

With a bone held firmly down upon one beach pebble, another pebble was hammered down from a full arm's length to shatter the bone and reveal the soft, tasty marrow. The entire skeleton was smashed up in this way, the scene opening up into a feast of happy sucking and chewing.

This meal had taken several hours, and they had hardly started on the actual meat, which was now all rolled up and ready for transport, back up the cliff and into the woods. The tools they had carefully manufactured at the site were also taken with them. Even without consuming the meat they felt bloated and somewhat heady after their vast intake of protein.

They set off with their food parcels, leaving precious little soft tissue behind them. The hyenas did eventually come over to the site, to chew away at a few pieces among the scatter of fractured bone and viciously sharp flint. However, the rewards were minimal and the walking surface decidedly unpleasant. It was left to the birds to dispose of most of the debris. A few days after the flesh had gone to the woods, most of the bones had gone to the sky.

MUCH of the carcass had disappeared, but not all. That some bone fragments remained was critical in building towards the storyline above. Around 180 of these fragments were carefully picked from a sand and gravel quarry close to the coast of southern Britain. The roughly cratered landscape of the quarry has in modern times been populated by scrub, weeds, and the heavy machinery of mineral extraction. In a few places its irregular surface had been interrupted by neat rectangular trenches, their sections straightened and cleaned, their exposed surface peppered with small black flags, marking where some tiny flint flake or bone fragment had been exposed by meticulous excavation, and its precise position plotted. One set of black flags in the sand mapped out a brief episode half a million years ago when flint blade and wild animal prey came together in the quest for food. Archaeologists have undertaken several seasons of excavation in the Boxgrove quarry, plotting the finds trapped within the accumulating sediments. In 1989, they unearthed the scatter of bones and flints from which the above narrative was assembled, a narrative that captures one striking feature of the human food quest, the consumption of very large animals. The 180 bone fragments were scattered across around 70 square metres of a buried sandy surface. Also scattered across that same surface were a multitude of chipped flints.[1]

The most striking items among these flints from the Boxgrove quarry are a series of elegantly fashioned 'hand-axes', large tools, skilfully shaped on both sides to create one of the most durable artefacts the world has ever seen. More numerous by far were the courser flint fragments of various sizes which the archaeologists could occasionally fit together along the lines of their original breakage, in the manner of a three-dimensional jigsaw puzzle. The task is laborious but rewarding; if enough pieces are recovered, a void can be reassembled, capturing the

7. Dense distribution of primary flint-knapping debris at the horse butchery site at Boxgrove.

shape of the hand-axe within. Because the final location on the sand surface of each fragment was recorded, and their relative position on the original flint nodule known, three dimensional cameos can be built up of human action in the fracturing or 'knapping' of the flint. Both the preservation of these spatial patterns and the freshness of the flint surfaces confirmed what the pattern of accumulating sediments also indicated. These scatters were buried fairly quickly in an active

49

coastal landscape; the moments in time were quickly covered up and conserved. The pattern of the scatter is in places so precise that the sitting position of the knapper can be established, and the 'spray' of shattered debris followed from the knapper's hand. The pattern preserves a precise echo in flint fragments of a series of instances of flint working around whatever it was that had generated the scatter of fractured bone.[2]

To the untrained eye, those fragments of bone looked unpromising, and certainly gave the impression that most of the skeleton from which they came had disappeared. The small portion that remained, when carefully cleaned and inspected under a scanning electron microscope, was quite enough to reveal the fine details of the series of events narrated above. Take, for example, the pieces of backbone. A trained eye can recognize not only that they were vertebrae, but also at which position on the backbone they belonged. Through comparison with modern reference material, it was confirmed that their particular shape and size matched the wild horse, *Equus feris*. That much was accomplished with the naked eye. A low-power microscope allowed analysis to proceed further, into how the animal was divided for consumption. Under magnification of seventy-five times, a pattern is discernible across each vertebral surface. These marks resemble tiny plough furrows, even including a miniature version of the 'feathering' effect that can be seen on dragged soil. It is possible to create very similar marks on a fresh modern bone by scoring it with a fresh flint blade. In the context of a surface scattered with freshly knapped flint, it could thus be inferred that what were visible under the microscope were cut-marks, traces of the passage of a sharp flint blade along the axis of the spine. This is precisely the motion needed to separate the rib-meat from the bone. An exciting result, but by no means unique. On close inspection, almost half the remaining fragments carried marks of this kind.[3]

It is precisely cut-marks such as these that have taken the study of ancient animal bones far closer to meals of the distant past. Routine analysis of animal bones from archaeological sites has aimed to establish species, sex, the age of animals at death, and whether different elements of the body are present in different proportions. These data alone can tell us a great deal about the living population, and a certain amount about how they were hunted, scavenged, or culled. From the moment a blade makes contact with the skeleton a whole new realm of forensic evidence begins to accumulate. Fresh bone is comparatively soft, inasmuch as even a dinner knife can leave a durable cut-mark. It is not only the strike of a hand-axe, but the careful filleting of meat from the bone, or the removal of hide from the body that leaves a characteristic mark behind, a mark that becomes fixed as the bone dries out.

There are many ways of taking an animal apart. It can be fairly randomly hacked into meal-sized chunks, or systematically dissected into component meats. The vertebral elements may all be sliced in two, an indication of the division of 'sides' of meat for transport and storage, or cut laterally to prepare rib steaks. In recent centuries, when butchery practices have actually been written about, it is clear that they reflect not just preferences for particular cuts and joints of meat on the table, but the actual context of those preferences in narratives of social hierarchy and religious belief. Certain cuts may be considered impure, and forbidden; other cuts may be reserved for sacrifice to the gods. In a contemporary cosmopolitan city, butchers from each of the major religions may have separate establishments, dividing the carcass with different equipment in different ways. In medieval Ireland, the carver of the meat at a feast was a significant figure; it was he who indicated the status of the diners by the cut they received. Half a million years earlier, we have no texts, but we can follow the sequence in which the wild horse carcass at Boxgrove was divided.

The direction of the actual cut-marks can be informative. On one particular vertebral fragment from high in the back, close to the neck, the flint incisions ran at right angles to the body. This is consistent with the separation and removal of the horse's head. Other marks differ, not in their direction, but in their form, indicating scraping or smashing, rather than skinning. As with the flint incision, experimentation with fresh bones provides a useful route to interpretation. Striking a bone with a large pebble can release a rounded chip, and replicate the patterns seen on some of the ancient bones. A fragment of the upper-left forelimb has the scar from such fractures on opposite sides of the bone, one corresponding to the striking pebble, the other to the anvil. Those large pebbles were presumably being used in the breakage for marrow. Yet another fracture is different again; it is a semicircular wound on the surviving fragment of one of the shoulder blades. It seems to be a projectile wound, and is broadly consistent with the impact that would be expected from a form of artefact that has been recovered from a slightly younger archaeological site in Germany. Close to the modern settlement at Schöningen, between 400,000 and 350,000 years ago, three sharpened lengths of wood, around two metres long, were laid down in the archaeological sediments. They were found together with a shorter implement sharpened at both ends, reminiscent of contemporary Australian aboriginal throwing sticks. These artefacts were interpreted as wooden spears, of the kind that could have certainly inflicted the Boxgrove shoulder wound and brought the wild horse down.[4]

Horses that are truly wild no longer roam the earth's surface, but they have left enough skeletal evidence for us to estimate their size. The bones at Boxgrove indicate a pretty large animal, producing somewhere in the order of 400 kilos of edible tissue. What is more, another feeder has left its marks on the bone, and in a most informative way. As well as the narrow grooves left by the flint, a few of the bones carry a broader, deeper groove, of a type that matches teeth rather than a blade. A comparison with modern bones chewed by known animals comes up with a good match, the spotted hyena, whose bones are also known from Boxgrove.

These gnawing marks tell us something else, about patterns through time. Occasionally, the toothmarks of a hyena and the cut-marks of a stone tool could be found on the same bone. Inspecting those coincident marks under a lens, it became clear that, each and every time this has happened at the Boxgrove horse kill site, it was the hyena tooth marks that cut through the flint tool marks, and never vice versa. This apparently was not the occasional return of two types of scavenger to the carcass, but instead, two distinct episodes. The humans consumed, departed, and only then did the hyenas feed. This gives us some sense of the timescale of the whole episode. All this was going on in an open landscape of salt marsh and mud slurries, close to patches of open water. This much we can infer from the morphology of the sediments above and below the Boxgrove finds, sediments that preserve direct traces of marine washing, and unstable stream formations. It is further elucidated by identifying the shells and bones of small animals that have been carried along and then trapped within these sediments. Over 100 such species provide a detailed reflection of the ecology of the site.[5]

Some of the other bones uncovered from the quarry levels remind us how different such ancient open watery places were from the ones we know today. Not far from the wild horse bones the archaeologists unearthed the complete skull of a wolf. A little further away, they uncovered the paw bone or 'metatarsal' of *Panthera leo*, the lion. Placed alongside the equivalent bone in a modern African habitat, it became clear that the beasts that also roamed that coastal marsh were substantially larger. As these fast-moving carnivores waited for their own prey, they knew that patches of water would attract mammals of all sizes; the open landscape made it easy for these top carnivores to sit and wait, and in this open wet grassland, the stench of the carcass would be drawing every predator for miles. However large the task, it seems reasonable to infer some sense of urgency among our human feeders. At the very most, this episode will have spanned from dawn until sunset in a single day.

Let us compare this with the chimpanzee 'feast' recorded a quarter of a century ago in the Gombe reserve, and discussed in Chapter 2. The distribution of meat from a colobus monkey brought together a significant number of the most powerful males and females within the Kaseleka chimpanzee community. One of the most socially complex episodes of food-sharing ever recorded in the animal world took nine and a half hours in the distribution of less than 20 kilos of meat. Over a similar period of time, quite possibly less, a group of hunters, half a million years ago near the Boxgrove coast, dispatched twenty times that quantity of edible tissue—400 kilos dispatched between dawn and dusk.

So far, the roots of the opening narrative have been hard material evidence, evidence that has gone much further than identifying the meat and the toolkit. The Boxgrove team have built up a picture of the ancient landscape, a chalk cliff, coastal mudflats, and a distant beach, and populated it with wildlife. From the source of the pebbles and flints they have plotted the hunters' movements through that landscape, and nowhere with more precision than when they paused to fashion their flint butchery tools. We can follow our flint-knapper from how she or he was sitting on the ground for one stage in the process, got up and walked one to two metres to finish off the core tool, and then identify the traces of those tools along the animal carcass itself, and how the jaws were used as a 'third hand'. A series of independent foci of hand-axe preparations can be carefully charted at different points around the carcass.

Their research has provided us with superb stage directions, but what about the plot and the lives of the players? The narrative I have woven through the results of their research goes far beyond those stage directions to allude to role-division, kinship loyalty, and competition, small and large group cooperation and trust, bargaining, double-crossing, hissing, tooth-baring anger, and repeated acts of sexual congress even as the tasty intestines were still being passed round. Where did all that come from?

The idea of the 'primitive'

The renowned fictional detective, Sherlock Holmes, famously proceeded by excluding all impossible scenarios until he ended up with the truth. He used reason and forensic evidence to narrow the corridor of plausibility to such an extent that only a single story could pass through. I doubt that is ever achievable in real life, let alone real lives from which we are separated by thousands of years. Instead, we have to guide ourselves along these corridors of plausibility by borrowing patterns observed amongst living peoples who were engaged in a similar kind of food quest. This would have been a rather easier task in the late nineteenth-century London with which Holmes is connected than it is now, for the simple reason that his contemporaries had a far more straightforward idea of the 'savage'. This was the time when Buffalo Bill's Wild West shows were travelling to London and other European cities, and in which his troupe portrayed the 'wild rivalries of savage, barbarous and civilized races'. Those three categories were not just the stuff of entertainment; they were how critical observers, even sympathetic ones, shaped their accounts of the progress and development of humanity. One of the most influential observers was the nineteenth-century American scholar Lewis Henry Morgan. His descriptions of the American Indian would shape the narratives woven around unearthed bones and ancient stone hand-axes for generations.

In 1859, when Charles Darwin's *Origin of Species* took the public by storm and opened minds to the possibility of a long prehistory of human big-game hunters, Morgan set out to explore the American west, in search of a deeper knowledge of native American life. On his frequently difficult journeys up river and across prairie, he encountered and recorded an enormous diversity of communities, who combined different patterns of farming, fishing, and hunting. His journeys across space seemed like journeys back in time, rather in the manner of an archaeologist peeling off layers of earth. Using his words, he was leaving *civilization* behind, to record the kinship patterns and ways of life of communities who remained in a state of *barbarism*, in other words rudimentary farmers. Upstream on the Missouri River and westward into the Kansas prairies, he encountered communities further still from civilization and yet closer to nature. They hunted big game, the North American buffalo, and he described their state as *savagery*. A century and a half later, a word like *savage* has a disconcerting and derogatory sense. For Morgan, who had a much greater respect and sympathy for native Americans than many of his contemporaries, the term was closer to the French *sauvage*, alluding to the 'wild', 'untamed' aspect of these communities. They had yet to adopt the trappings of high culture and existed within a more innocent world of nature. In the eye of east coasters and contemporary Europeans, they conveyed an image of timeless harmony with natural cycles, not yet diverted to the path of history and progress.[6]

The people he called 'savages' were mobile, tracking the seasonal movements of the buffalo, and dovetailing their intensive periods of hunting with the life cycle of their prey. As the buffalo gathered in large groups, so would their human predators. During midsummer, the peak of the buffalo rut, when hunting would have been dangerous and counter-productive, the human predators instead engaged in the ritual of the sun-dance. Here, they would celebrate the cyclical harmonies of nature, of death, rebirth, and regeneration. Through trance, and sometimes through extremes of self-inflicted pain, participants would lose their sense of individuality, and merge with the harmony of the universe. The buffalo was a central feature of the ritual, which would often be accompanied by buffalo dances, buffalo songs, and feasts of buffalo meat.

Morgan's savage from the High Plains could be transferred back through time with relative ease, and to the large animal bones and hand-axes then being unearthed by quarrymen and antiquaries across Europe. Without the fine constraints of detailed excavation, a broad corridor opened up, along which narratives could easily pass from hunters of the nineteenth-century world to hunters of the Palaeolithic. Well into the twentieth century, an account of the Boxgrove episode would have been heavily populated by Plains Indians and Inuit Eskimo in all but name. We would have talked of tribes and bands, perhaps of ceremonies and totemism. I would have recreated a nobler, less animalistic scene. We might have given them tepees, perhaps some interesting headgear, and a little warpaint. But by the time of the meticulous work of the Boxgrove project, however, the corridor of possibilities had greatly narrowed. A modern-day Sherlock Holmes would have drawn attention to two simple and basic features of the scene. The first is a seeming mismatch in the data, the second a few fragments of bone.

The mismatch is between two strands of evidence that lead to opposite impressions of Boxgrove hunters' versatility of action. Both of these strands connect to the site's most characteristic artefact, repeatedly created in the vicinity of the Boxgrove horse carcass—those elegantly made hand-axes. Tools of this kind have been found from deposits spanning a vast stretch of space and time. During the nineteenth century, large numbers were recovered from a gravel pit above the River Somme at St Acheul, attracting many of the pioneers of archaeology to visit. The village lent its name to the entire worldwide corpus of bifacial 'Acheulian' hand-axes. Rather similar tools have been found at sites like Olduvai and Olorgasailie close to the heartland of human evolution, and also in the southern and western ends of the African continent. They are found as far east as India and across Western Europe, for example at Torralba and Ambrona in Spain. Their latitudinal range spans from south of the Tropic of Capricorn in Southern Africa to northerly sites like Boxgrove itself. This geographical spread must have corresponded to an equally vast ecological range with substantial variations in climate, topography, and available species of plant and animal. The lives of those who fashioned these tools must have displayed a considerable ecological versatility. In that way they can indeed be compared to the American Indians observed by Morgan who, within a few thousand years of their appearance in the New World, had diversified to consume fish, whales, game, seeds, squashes, fruits, and tubers from the Arctic to the Amazon forest, from the waterholes of Florida and the chilly bays of Patagonia, to some of the most sun-parched arid regions on earth. Similarly, a muddy, windy saltmarsh in north-west Europe is not a lot like the East African heartlands

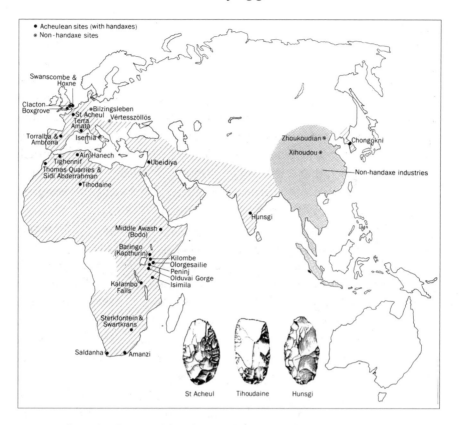

MAP 2. The Acheulean world with some key sites indicated, together with three representative tools: a hand-axe from St Acheul in France, a cleaver from Erg de Tihoudaine in Algeria, and a hand-axe from Hunsgi in India.

of human evolution, yet the Boxgrove hunters had managed to switch the skills and knowledge that their ancestors had acquired in quite different ecosystems to an alternative group of species and environments.

Yet as they squatted by their kill to prepare their cutting tools, they displayed a distinct difference from the American Indian, whose material culture is at least as diverse as their ecology. By contrast, the Boxgrove hunters' artefacts display a profound lack of diversity. The ease of transformation and changed practice evident from their ecological range could not be discerned in their manner of knapping flint. We see no evidence of the redesign of the blades to fit new species of prey, none

57

of the artefact diversity that the recent American Indian hunters have shown in abundance. Instead, they embarked on the monotonous production of a tool that broadly shared its design specifications with tools created a million years earlier in quite different environments, and continue to be created in diverse places for hundreds of thousands of years to come. What was going on in the mind of those ancient knappers, whose chilly northern surroundings bore witness to great versatility in engaging with nature, but whose expert hands struck away at the flint nodule without innovation or invention, their movements locked instead within an unchanging script? The answer may lie in the second key piece of evidence, a few fragments of bones.

The fragments in question number only six, and derive from a single leg bone, a tibia, from a member of the hunting community which lived around the general period when the horse met its fate. This fragmented tibia, carefully reconstructed and measured, was estimated to have come from an individual of six foot in height, and quite a sturdy individual at that, with an estimated body weight of around 80 kilos. Taken together, the measurements indicate a sturdiness that lies outside the range of modern humans. The Boxgrove hunters belonged to a species of early human that was physically quite distinct, with a more robust skeleton and a somewhat smaller brain. The differences are sufficient to place the fragments within a separate species, known from a scatter of sites around the Old World, and labelled *Homo heidelbergiensis*. The differences in their bodies, which could be recorded and measured on their skeletons, raises the question of whether there were also differences in what was going on in their minds.[7]

When Morgan was observing the big-game hunters that would come to serve as a modern analogue of ancient hunters, he knew little of other species of humans, beyond the news that had spread across the world three years earlier of the strange half-man half-skeleton that had been unearthed in Prussia from the Neanderthal ravine. Archaeologists today are much more familiar with the idea of different human species roaming the world at different times in the past. However, it is only quite recently that the full implications of their belonging to another species have been tackled head on, with profound implications for how we reconstruct the Boxgrove scene.

A different kind of humanity

The idea of fundamental differences between types of humanity is not new, and did not actually depend on finding new species of human. Indeed, many of Morgan's contemporaries believed the savage 'Red Man' to be intrinsically different from the civilized 'White Man'. The Red Man was close to nature and subject to her rules. The White Man was liberated from nature and able to embark on his cultural journey through history. Such a difference for a long time informed and shaped our views of ancient hunters. Also being close to nature, they could be treated as biological organisms, following nature's laws and as much subject to her constraining powers as birds, animals, and fish. At some point in the past, White Men had become liberated from nature, to become social persons, shaping history and the world about them. We are now far more aware both of the rich social and historical complexity of American tribes, and also of the profound importance of biology in shaping contemporary cosmopolitan societies. We also know that Red Man and White Man are virtually identical in genetic terms, that the skin colour implicit in 'red' and 'white' is a poor proxy for the tiny genetic variations that do exist, and that all are simultaneously biological organisms and social persons within a single, fully interfertile species.

By contrast, analysis of DNA fragments from our very closest extinct relatives, the Neanderthals, has revealed that the genetic distance between us and them is significant.[8] If we could access the DNA of more distant relatives in the genus *Homo*, such as those from Boxgrove, we presume the difference would be greater still. This issue of difference within the human genus has been considered in depth by Steven Mithen, an archaeologist who believes that paradoxes in the archaeological evidence such as the one explored above lead us directly to the workings of the early human mind. By drawing on modern advances in our understanding of the living brain, he argues that the kind of paradox we have observed above between ecology and tool-making may be resolved by imagining that early humans operated, not with a single fully interactive intelligence, but instead by a cluster of 'domain-specific' intelligences. Mithen compares the workings of the mind to a cathedral, in some cases accommodating a single service, in other cases fragmented into separate services in distinct chapels. Whilst in the modern human mind, movement within the entire cathedral is fairly fluid, he argues that in some early human minds, the chapel model fits better with such data as we possess. In one 'chapel', they had a rich understanding of the living world, its different species and aspects. That would be an 'ecological intelligence'. Lateral thinking in this compartment could clearly take them to countless different ecosystems on the planet. Another 'chapel' guided dextrous hands to work with, and to shape inanimate materials, a 'technical intelligence'. This compartment adhered to stricter norms, repeatedly fashioning the same sort of tool out of the same kind of material. A third chapel facilitated recognition of its own species, and guided it through social interactions with its own kind, a 'social intelligence'. Mithen's model, which cleverly addresses a number of initially unusual features of the archaeological record, is also supported by certain forms of mental illness that uncover the potential of the brain activity to be compartmented. It also has implications for a critical feature of modern food-sharing. There is one attribute among our own species that involves a great deal of cross-reference between different sections of our mental cathedral. It involves a constant interplay between social recognition, reference to both animate and inanimate objects, and movement of our body. That attribute is as much a part of the modern human meal as the food itself—conversation.[9]

There can be little doubt that early humans expressed themselves through sound, since many other primates communicate vocally in quite precise ways. A few examples were touched upon in the context of Passion's meal explored in the previous chapter. There are examples among several primate species of alarm, warning and greeting signals, as well as socially reassuring equivalents of 'grooming'. It seems reasonable to assume a fair lexicon of these, and I have therefore alluded to vocalization within my narrative. There is quite a distance, however, between a lexicon of vocal signals and a 'conversation' in the modern human sense.

Imagine a conversation between two modern humans standing over a fresh kill, planning the collection of pebbles for bone-smashing from a nearby beach. That conversation would necessarily involve such details as: directions to the beach, warnings about the lions on the way, and so on; a fairly basic conversation perhaps, but one that at minimum would involve sentences, syntax, connections between individuals, things, and landscapes and a range of tenses including the future and the conditional. Is that likely to have been within the abilities of early humans?

There are a number of ways that question can be addressed, from both the remains of early human skeletons, and from the archaeological traces they leave in the landscape. From fragments of their skulls and spines, anthropologists are generally agreed that all members of our genus were endowed with both the bodily equipment required to generate a wide range of vocal sounds, and the brain power to do something interesting with those sounds. Whether or not that 'something interesting' corresponded to what we might call language and conversation is a point that has been queried in relation to the objects and material traces left within the archaeological record. There are a number of such traces that have what might be called a 'narrative' quality about them; they imply a sequence of connected ideas, a storyline. They might be artefacts that require a number of different steps in their manufacture and a template in the mind of the maker. It is hard to imagine how the ability to fashion such objects could be learnt without a narrative form of language. More directly, they might be items that we would describe as 'art', that employ representations or symbols of an idea to tell a visual story. Musical instruments would imply something similar.

Uncontentious traces of this narrative kind come from sites associated with one single species of human, our own. There are a few, strongly contested claims for Neanderthal art, music, narrative thought, and projections to the future, but other species within our genus leave no artefacts that so obviously connect with a narrative way of thinking. Indeed, the monotonous uniformity of the Acheulian biface might suggest the opposite. Returning to Stephen Mithen's idea of a compartmentalized intelligence, it could be that the large brain and vocal capacity simply did not make strong connections with the creation of artefacts. Language may not have been directly connected with technological intelligence. Instead it might be closely attached to one particular chapel of the mind, the chapel concerned with social intelligence, for example. Mithen comes down on the side of a social language in early humans, with a rich vocabulary of reassurances, acknowledgements, warnings, and greetings, and enabling a large group to interact successfully around a sizeable kill like the wild horse, but not substantially connecting with other chapels of the mind.

Begging and bonding

Following Mithen's reasoning, the Boxgrove horse kill could have been the site of a great deal of 'chattering', whose principal impact was to enable a reasonably large group of early humans to coexist at the site for as long as it took to dismantle this rich source of food, and to focus on external dangers without the whole thing erupting into intra-group violence. We might speculate that the power of early human chattering to serve as a kind of low-cost grooming was repeatedly stretched to its limit, as larger groups dispatched larger animals with growing pace. That has drawn me to imagine that sexual bargaining played a part in this episode of food-sharing, much as has been observed in chimps and bonobos.

Alongside these exchanges, a parallel negotiation is portrayed in the narrative in which young mothers successfully begged for meat and fat. It may not have been that different from the chimp mothers who begged some monkey meat from Mike in the Gombe forest; that transaction too seemed to be underwritten by a memory of sexual engagement in the past. In general, however, chimp mothers raise their young independently. That may have been true with early humans, but two key changes would have greatly shifted the economic costs of feeding and sharing. First, early humans were evolving with much larger brains. Pregnant and lactating women were carrying a greatly increased nutritional burden of growing their offspring's massive brain. Second, those same early humans were moving through landscapes in which the diversity of plant foods was diminishing, and hunting of large animals played an increasingly central role. This was an activity in which younger, fitter males would always have the competitive edge. Older males and the bolder females may also have been at the heart of the hunt, but it would have been tough for pregnant and lactating females to compete. It is the context of such an imbalance that some form of kin cooperation might be favoured in evolutionary terms, between mother and grandmother, for example, or between mother and father.[10]

It is a long way from the reconstructions that drew heavily from Lewis Henry Morgan's observations of the American Indian; that simple equation between big-game hunters of the very recent and very distant pasts no longer stands up to close scrutiny. The Boxgrove hunters belong to a different species of human. In genetic and cognitive terms we and the American Indians are more or less identical. We cannot transfer their world of culture back half a million years. Neither can we transfer their world of nature back in time. It too has a complex dynamic of transformations, a feature that lies at the very heart of the history and evolution of human food-sharing.

The changing world of nature

When Morgan described the woodlands, river valleys, and prairies in which he observed Amerindian life, words like 'nature' and 'environment' had little scientific shape. They expressed concepts that were essentially poetical or aesthetic. While Morgan himself was keenly aware of the food quest and its role in shaping the lives of the communities he observed, placing them within a 'natural environment' would have conveyed more of a romantic idea than a scientific analysis. Part of that romance endowed nature with a sense of timelessness, a serene removal from history and change. It was an impression of nature that did not fit with observations that were currently being made of peat bogs on the far side of the Atlantic.

Across large stretches of the northern latitudes, a treeless horizon is softened by the gently domed surface of peat, carpeting moist cool expanses and throttling any over-adventurous seedling that takes root. As these peaty areas were dug for fuel and fertilizer, many cuttings exposed whole forests of tree stumps, sometimes metres below that treeless surface. It was from exposures such as these that Morgan's European contemporaries realized that the world of nature was not so timeless and serene. Even in these wilderness areas, far from the settler's axe, woodland was being replaced by open land, at a later stage to return once again to woodland. They did not have good dating methods, but they knew that peat grew fast. These successive bands of wooded and open peat were not separated by vast tracts of geological time.[11]

The Scandinavian peat studies had been read by an American naturalist who grew up a generation after Morgan's travels, not far from the end of his historic westward journey. Frederick Clements was more attuned to the idea of environmental change at the hands of farming settlers like his own family. As he looked eastward from his Nebraskan home, he saw that much of the valley woodlands that Morgan had described had been cleared for wheat. Looking westward towards what remained of the open prairie, he still saw an essentially timeless big-game hunter, the Plains Indian, hunting buffalo across the essentially timeless prairie grassland. From these various elements, however, he did extract a logic of environmental change. That logic comprised two fundamental models that would go on to form the foundations for the fledgling science of ecology.[12]

One of these models was 'succession'. He combined the Scandinavian observations of change between wooded and open ground through time, and his own observations of an equivalent change across space, to argue for a gentle ebbing and flowing of vegetation bands back and forth, propelled by either slow climatic change, or more rapid human action. As the vegetation bands ebbed and flowed, they did so in a predictable sequence, and that sequence was 'succession'. The second model was the 'food chain', to which other pioneer ecologists attached the terms 'food web' and 'ecological pyramid'. These connected animals to the vegetation bands through the pattern of their feeding links. Buffalo grass–buffalo–High Plains Indian is a simple example of such a food chain. As the vegetations bands ebbed and flowed back and forth, so did the chains that they supported. These two simple models provided the theoretical basis from which visual inspection of peat cuttings could blossom forth into a detailed study of changing environments over the last two million years, or 'quaternary science', as it is known. Peat sections were complemented by river gravel exposures, lake and seabed sediments, and tree stumps were complemented by pollen grains, insects, vertebrates, shells, and algae. In the century since Clements's work, they have charted and described the ebbing and flowing of the world's natural environments in fine detail.[13]

An important element of these quaternary reconstructions is the climatic driver of the ebbing and flowing, temperature change. One of the best records of temperature change is the balance between different types, or 'isotopes' of oxygen, tracked in microscopic plants within sediments cored from beneath the seabed. The marine cores go so deep that an oxygen isotope record of temperature can go back millions of years. The complex patterns of temperature changes are subdivided into distinct episodes or 'isotope stages'. At the top of the sequence is isotope stage 1, in which we live today, a relatively mild period. Going back 20,000 years, the climate was much colder, and the cool period is isotope stage 2. Following the marine core down through increasingly distant periods of sedimentation, towards half a million years ago we reach isotope stages 11–13, during which period the Boxgrove horse was consumed.[14]

Back on land, geological exposures and cores through peat and lakes allow us to populate those temperature fluctuations with the ebbing and flowing of plants and the animals they carry in their food chains. In a warm period, the tree stumps will appear in those Scandinavian peat bogs, and retreat again in the cooler periods to more sheltered spots and lower latitudes. The pollen enriches that picture with long lists of plant taxa, and insects, shells, and bones do the same for other parts of the food chain. The Boxgrove archaeologists could argue that they were in isotope stage 11 from a combination of different dating methods, and then populate it with animal species determined from the study of bones from the site. The bones actually go further than invoking a landscape populated by lions, hyenas, and rhinoceroses; they can serve as a dating methods in their own right. This is because a certain number of species only occur in particular isotope stages. After that they disappear, providing us with a convenient chronological marker. In doing so, they incidentally also challenge a fundamental feature of the whole ebb and flow model on which the reconstruction is based.[15]

Equilibrium and disequilibrium

Extinction was not really explained by Clements's successional model. The different species should simply move back and forth between warm and cold latitudes, altitudes, and refuges as the climate fluctuated; there was no reason for them to disappear. Yet extinction is sufficiently widespread and common to serve as a dating tool. Why is this, and what is it telling us about the natural environments in which big-game hunters lived? It turns out that the answer may also be sought from the metaphor of an ebbing and flowing tide, not in the repetitive movement back and forth of the tide itself, but in the ephemeral crashing of waves on its surface. Waves form and then break because the tide is moving fast, the vast release of energy creating turbulence. It is as if the water itself has difficulty 'keeping up' with the massive energy it is dissipating. It seems that the quaternary climate has also been moving so fast that certain species and parts of the ecosystem have also had difficulty keeping up. It is a difficulty that has left its marks in recent sediments, and can be observed directly in an exposed cliff face on the Welsh coast.

Back in the 1970s, some fragments of ancient insects were collected from dark bands of organic sediment exposed in this particular cliff. The ecological traits of these particular species of insect allowed a picture of climatic change to be assembled, over the period from 15,000 to 10,000 years ago when the sediments had accumulated. At the bottom of the cliff sequence were fragments of insects characteristic of cold, open ground conditions. A little way up the profile, these hardy species are replaced by insects acclimatized to the lusher ground cover of more temperate climates. This transition was radiocarbon dated to just less than 13,000 years ago. The same organic sediments also preserved the contemporary pollen rains, which might provide a second marker of environmental change. However, the pollen immediately around these warmth-loving insects was still derived from cold climate vegetation. Not until a further 25 cm of deposit were laid down did the warm-phase tree pollen appear, an accumulation that must have taken three centuries. There is a considerable time lag between the rapid flight of insects to a newly warm location, and the sluggish spread of a woodland community in response to exactly the same climatic transition. Such a time lag distances the slower elements of the ecosystem from equilibrium. Like a spinning top, their disequilibirum state can take them in unpredictable directions, repeatedly following a novel course. This helps explain why the pollen evidence from different isotope stages follow similar, but certainly not identical patterns. The difference between successive patterns of vegetation ebb and flow is particularly evident when the warm-period woodland is ebbing. The plants that flourish at this point in the cycle vary markedly between different ebbing episodes. These effects arise from responses that may be slow, but there are other features of the organization of the whole woodland ecosystem that are slower still. Perhaps the slowest of all to respond are the soils. There are still soils exposed on the surface of Britain which formed in desert conditions millions of years ago, and failed to modify their form in line with more recent soil development. The system has a lot of lags in it; they ebb and flow less in the manner of a marine tide than a slurry of treacle.[16]

The process of feeding itself can amplify disequilibrium, such that as we move up the food chain to herbivores and carnivores, the turbulence becomes yet more accentuated. Moderate fluctuations in the plant cover may lead to substantial fluctuations in the animal populations feeding upon it, and consequent turbulence in predator prey couplings higher in the food chain repeatedly lead to extinction. It is not simply a question of some tardy species lagging behind. In the intense competition of colonization, they may be too late to make their mark at all. As a result whole permutations, indeed whole communities of plants and animals, may get lost. If we look at the pollen rains that were falling in northerly regions when the world was at its chilliest, around 18,000 years ago, grass and heather pollen fall in proportions that are without parallel today. There seems to be a whole arrangement of vegetation missing from the modern map, and a highly significant one at that. Specialists of the period talk of 'arctic steppe' or 'mammoth step' to describe the vegetation on which great herds of animals, many of which we only know from their fossil bones, once grazed. The vegetation communities have since disappeared along with the herds that grazed upon them. The plants have not so much disappeared. They have just regrouped, in the helter-skelter of activity following fast climatic change. Arctic steppe is not alone.[17]

There is a form of pollen analysis that goes beyond tracking individual plant types through time, and tracks instead the whole suite of pollen types falling at any one episode. In this approach, analogues are sought among modern vegetation for plant communities that release a similar collective pollen rain to that found in ancient profiles. If we go back 15,000 years only, we find that no more than half of ancient pollen rains can be accounted for in this way. Taken at face value, the plant communities that we might have come across when the planet's temperatures were really changing are as likely to have disappeared as they are to have survived, and this in turn has implications for early human life and the food quest at palaeolithic Boxgrove.[18]

The evidence of changing global temperatures derived from coring through the seabed indicates a planet whose temperature is fluctuating and has always fluctuated. The underlying causes of those longer-term fluctuations lie in the physics of the solar system and the gravitational forces between planets. These create minor changes in the earth's orbit, and gentle oscillations in the degree of warming by the sun. In certain periods of the planet's history, the poles accumulate caps of ice, and these interfere with the gentle climatic oscillations, giving the temperature curve through time a more sharpened and jagged edge, with certain periods of especially rapid climate change. The last two million years, broadly corresponding to the lifetime of the human genus, is one such period; it is known as the Quaternary Epoch. We have increasing evidence of episodes of abrupt temperature change during the Quaternary Epoch, and also evidence that the world's biomes have had some problem keeping up.[19]

We can bring all this evidence together to draw some conclusions about the changing world of nature of which the big-game hunters were part. It would seem that the notion of timeless harmony is not just an illusion for the hunters themselves; it is also an illusion for the worlds of nature they inhabit. This is as true of the recent High Plains Indian as it was for the ancient Boxgrove hunters. Even as Clements was writing, there was evidence in existence that the prairie was not exactly timeless; indeed its existence was in part a consequence of the ecological actions of the Plains Indian themselves. Going back in time to the Boxgrove hunters, the frequency of extinction is, in itself, an indicator of the underlying disequilibrium of the natural environment, a disequilibrium we could extend to the period known as the Quaternary Epoch, broadly corresponding to the timescale of the genus *Homo* itself.

One evolutionary consequence of the jagged edge of the quaternary temperature curve was that fast response times have been favoured. This has encouraged the diversification of small short-lived organisms, and quaternary extinction has particularly affected larger animals, a category that includes our own genus. Early humans adapted to the jagged temperature curve, and the disequilibrium world it engendered, by moving in the opposite direction. Rather than getting smaller and

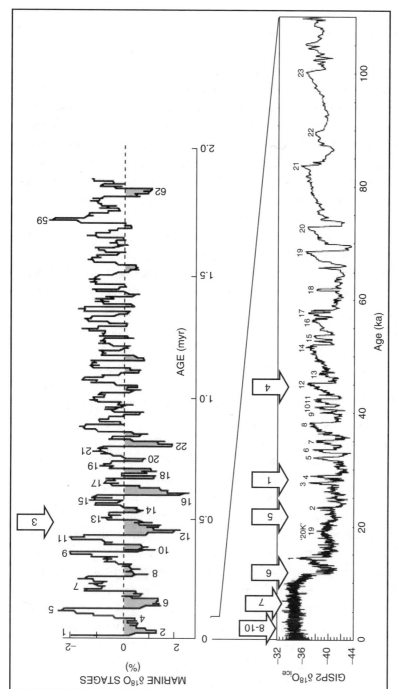

8. Ambient temperatures as reflected by oxygen isotope evidence ($\delta^{18}O$). The most recent 100,000 years has been charted through the Greenland Ice Sheet Project (GISP). The last two million years has been charted through the Ocean Drilling Programme (marine cores). Peaks to the left of the curve indicate cold periods, and peaks to the right, warm periods. The chronological position of the key case studies is indicated by their chapter number alongside.

speeding up their generation time, humans enlarged their feeding group to a sizeable cooperative community, ranging extensively across the landscape, and evolving a mental capacity to handle bigger slices of time in the form of memory. Rather than harmonizing with a timeless nature, humans have adapted to the constant potential for change, and that is what particularly marks out the human food quest. That ability to respond to change enabled their movement around distant and contrasting parts of the Old World, everywhere depending upon a particular, and quite unusual facility of sharing food on a very large scale, a scale which came from bringing down the largest animals in the landscape. During the Quaternary Epoch, the period when ice caps have given our planet a considerable thermal shake-up, the key to early human survival was to engage in our food quest in a very social way indeed, an engagement that has been captured in fine detail in a sand and gravel quarry at Boxgrove.

Returning to the opening narrative, the predators and prey have by and large disappeared from Britain and sometimes the planet. The wild horse itself has gone, as have the hyenas and lions, and of course *Homo heidelbergiensis* itself. The gulls are still flying up ahead, taking food to the air, but I have to admit they were conjectural. Indeed, humans as a whole are perfectly consistent with the general pattern for medium- and large-size animals in that the Quaternary Epoch has seen a fair amount of extinction. Here once again, the scale of our observation greatly affects the patterns we see. Looking back from the modern landscape, the oldest monuments we see around us are a few thousand years old at most. The style of hand-axe in use at Boxgrove persisted for more than a million years. The long epoch of hunter-gatherers understandably has a timeless feel about it. However, looking forward from the broader context of plant and animal evolution, the human line has a very short evolutionary history of about two million years. Some life forms have barely changed their structure in fifty times that interval. Within those few million years, all bar one of those human species has gone into extinction, a familiar fate for slow-living, large animals in the climatic hurly-burly of the Quaternary Epoch. Those that persisted into the most recent periods of all did so through food quests and patterns of food-sharing marked by versatility.

At Boxgrove, we already observe two key elements of that emergent versatility. First, we see an African genus a long way from 'home'.

The vast geographical range of the Acheulian hand-axe is testament to an ecological versatility that continues to mark the human genus. Second, we see that versatility in their social interaction. For all the remaining uncertainty about how they actually engaged and communicated, we are clearly looking at a relatively large number of individuals sharing an undoubtedly large supply of meat. The consumption of big game captures a theme that also continues to mark the human genus. Feeding is fundamentally a social phenomenon, bringing together human communities in a complex range of permutations. As humans evolved with larger brains still, the ecological and social complexities of the meal would similarly expand and diversify.

9. Imagined scene of Neanderthal life within the Abric Romaní rock shelter, Capellades in Spain.

4

FIRE, COOKING, AND GROWING A BRAIN

Capellades, Spain, 46,000 years ago

Ascending through the juniper scrub, laden with gathered deadwood and their share of the day's hunt, they made their way back. Carrying the fuel and the leg of wild horse across the fallen rocks at the mouth of the shelter, the warmth of the flames was a welcome sensation. They passed round the back of the fire, where two cousins sat together, one stroking the head of the other, resting on his lap, meticulously picking out dirt, and biting out fleas and lice. Their grandfather reclined in the shadows beyond the deerskin screen. On the far side of the screen, his daughter sat on a pinewood log feeding her newborn baby. At her other breast was her young child who enjoyed the comfort, even though he had been on solid foods for several months now. Sitting alongside them, the grandmother was out by the fire, squatting on a pinewood log, and doing what she did for hours on end—tending the flames, for ever turning and controlling the burning embers, occasionally reaching into her store-pit for more wood for the fire. One of the hunters added the deadwood bundle to her store-pit, settled down in his regular spot, and began chipping away at one of the nodules he kept in his own flint-store. Every now and then he tossed an unwanted flint fragment, or a hammerstone that was past its best, across to the other side of the flames.

The grandfather stirred to the smell of fresh cut horse meat mingling with the soothing aroma of pine resin from the fire. Such ancient teeth as had not already fallen out were so completely worn he found it difficult to work through raw flesh, let alone chew away at a marrow bone. *His elderly cohort skewered a small strip of meat onto her wooden poker and held it in the flames. He could suck on that awhile. She still preferred the taste of raw flesh, and her teeth were in good shape, but she too was holding more and more of her food in the flames.*

These days, the boys had been coming back to the shelter with the oddest things: lizards, tortoises, roots, and even awful shrivelled little seeds that could be shaken out of the autumn sward. Some of that stuff was impossible to eat raw and had to be left under a roof-drip until it softened. They became marginally edible, but other flavours drifted fleetingly through her consciousness, hazelnuts, walnuts, wild olives mingling with aftertaste of fat and blood.

One hunter was now fixing up a tripod of wooden sticks above the glowing embers of a small hearth over which the longer strips of meat filleted by a fellow hunter could be dried in the fire's heat. Some of the men's more distant kin were engaged in similar activities further along the valley sides. There were more prizes from this and other hunts, and other strips of meat drying in the flames. They formed a substantial gathering, settling in front of their deerskin shelters looking out across the drying meat and cooking tripods, the flames coming brighter as dusk fell. As they looked across to the flickering images, they created their own personal space by angling themselves in a way that avoided too much eye-contact. Instead of looking at each other, they looked out towards the flickering lights of the fire, and beyond to the valley, with the sound of hooves and rustling grass echoing in their mind, though no animals were in sight.

A T a distance of 45 kilometres north-west of the Catalunian city of Barcelona, a rock shelter perched above the Anoia River has trapped the fragments from which this narrative was assembled. Access to the river involves a steep descent of 90 metres down a limestone cliff. Two-thirds of the way down, the Abric Romaní shelter commands a view of the valley. Because of the way water moves through the limestone cliff, emerging as springs and roof drips, a considerable quantity of dissolved lime precipitates out in a variety of forms. One of these is a deposit called 'travertine'. It is the thick layers of this travertine that has engulfed the final traces of that meal above the river. Uranium series dating places that meal around 46,000 years ago.

That was a time when Spain, and Europe more generally, was inhabited by another species of early human, one distinguishable from both the *Homo heidelbergiensis* of Boxgrove, and the modern humans of today's world. The *Homo neanderthalis* community that made use of the cave on several occasions before and after that visit seem quite different from their predecessors at Boxgrove. There is a different tone to the cooperation that I have imagined, as most clearly displayed in the care of the grandfather. The cosy feel is further enhanced by home fires burning, and the cooked meal.

Around a century ago, archaeologists visited the rock shelter from which that narrative was fashioned, and excavated the top three metres of accumulation beneath the shelter's roof. Further excavations were commenced in the 1950s, and over the last twenty years have been continued with modern scientific methods. With the aid of boreholes penetrating even further than the excavations, close to 20 metres of accumulation have been charted within the shelter. These represent an accumulation over at least 30,000 years. At repeated levels within this sequence, flint and quartz tools are conserved. In the upper layers that Romaní himself excavated, the stone had been knapped to produce slender blades, the hallmark of the appearance in Europe of modern humans, our own species. These particular blades, dating to around 40,000 years ago, correspond to some of the very earliest traces of modern humans in Europe.[1]

Beneath these top layers, the lower sediments contain stone tools that have been fashioned in a different way. In contrast to the slender blades in the overlaying deposits, they have been fractured into angular cores and irregular flakes, often reworked to provide at least one serrated or 'denticulate' edge. This is a form of stoneworking we associate with Neanderthals, whose activities under this shelter have formed the focus of the more recent excavations. The 'stage directions' arising from these recent excavations are of high quality, on account of both the close attention to spatial mapping of artefacts and biological traces, and the effectiveness of the travertine seal. As it is excavated away, the hearths it engulfed so long ago return to view, clearly marked out by charred wood, charred bone, and in some cases flagstones. Between the hearths and the

10. Recent excavations at the Abric Romaní rock shelter, with deep accumulations of travertine visible in the exposed sections, and exposed areas of burning towards the lower left.

cave wall, clusters of flint debris came to light. They did not extend all the way to the cave wall, suggesting some barrier separating the busiest activity near the fire from the space next to the shelter. A comparable space, also associated with Neanderthals, has been excavated within the Grotte du Lazaret near Nice in France. It was interpreted as the traces of a tent-like structure made from skins anchored by stones. Back at Abric Romaní, big chunks of flint towards the shelter's opening suggest a 'toss-zone' away from their point of production.

Occasionally the travertine reveals something quite unusual. The brushing of loose particles from the surface exposes the boundaries of elongated shapes free of lime. Sometimes a scraping of the travertine platform would expose a complete void. The excavators had the foresight to make plaster casts of selected voids that could be examined back in the lab. From their overall shape it appeared these were pieces of wood, engulfed in the lime accumulation, and only rotting away after the lime had hardened, leaving their shape as an inverse impression or void. One such void corresponded to a 3.5 metre length of pine log, over half a metre in diameter along most of its length. The tree was too large to be growing in the shelter and had presumably been carried there. It is where I have imagined the three generations of mothers and children sitting. Another cluster of voids is interpreted as a collapsed tripod, over which I have speculated that strips of horse meat were arrayed. The horse leg and the flint blades used for its butchery are attested in a manner similar to that at the earlier site at Boxgrove. Occasionally the wood within the voids has not completely disappeared, sometime because it is partly charred, and sometimes because mineral replacement of the specimen has turned it into a kind of fossil. One such fragment was a juniper wood slab, which the archaeologists argued might have served as a form of plate. The animal data from the bone debris and the plant data from pollen inspired much of the specific reference to species, and the use of 'alternative' foods, such as small animals, pods, and grass seeds draws upon a range of different Neanderthal sites across Europe.[2]

A recurrent theme within the Abric Romaní deposits is fire. The travertine has captured the ashes, charcoal, and burnt earth of many hearths, of different shapes and sizes. Some are short-lived and soon abandoned; others are maintained for some time. Here and elsewhere, hearths, discrete reddened areas beneath lenses of charcoal and ash, sometimes together with laid 'hearth stones', are found within the caves and rock shelters in which Neanderthals left their flaked stone artefacts, and sometimes their own bones. These hearths provide clear evidence that Neanderthals could control fire, and fragments within the ashes provide circumstantial evidence that they could perform a radical transformation on their food, a transformation that Claude Lévi-Strauss regarded as one of the principal features that marked out humanity as something distinct and separate from the natural world. They could cook.

The earliest hearths in the world go two or three times as far back in time as the Abric Romaní deposit, and may go as far back as 180,000 years at Kalambo Falls in northern Zambia. There are a few contentious candidates that go back further still. While not all such hearths are directly associated with identified hominid remains, we can infer that, like ourselves, Neanderthals practised cooking. Some have speculated that the cooking goes even deeper into the human evolutionary line. There are, after all, traces of fire further back, in quite close association with early human activity. Even if the earlier 'hearths' are open to contention, fragments of ash, charcoal, and burnt bones certainly have been recovered from earlier deposits. In a number of African sites they are attested as far back as half a million years. At a small number of sites in Kenya, such as Chesowanja near Lake Baringo and the famous site of Koobi Fora on Lake Turkana, there are less direct traces in the form of burnt stones, baked clay, and reddened pieces of earth. These fragments of evidence are around one and a half million years old.[3]

We cannot be sure that these fires were actually lit by early humans. Close to the East African focus of human evolution, volcanic activity continuously creates natural fires, as do lightening strikes universally. It would appear that there has been a lot more fire in the world since the appearance of our genus *Homo*. This much we know from ocean drillings, whose more recent sediments display an increase in the microscopic fragments of charcoal, which drift from a fire as a component of smoke. The increasing amplitude of climatic and environmental change could simply have brought natural sources of fire more frequently into contact with more flammable types of vegetation, such as seasonally dry open scrub. We are less clear how much, and in what ways, humans interacted with the natural fires they encountered. If a natural fire is of sufficient intensity and duration to redden earth, it is also sufficient for cooking. There could certainly have been a period when fire was like wild honey, an occasional boon to be harvested and exploited whenever encountered, but not depended upon. They would not be alone in some opportunistic use of natural fires. Wildfires today attract birds of prey in search of small animals fleeing from the flames, and land-based carnivores will move in on those that failed to escape, and remain as ready-cooked meals, courtesy of nature. Subsequently the ashes are an attractive source of salt for herbivores and carnivores alike. If early hominids were exploiting natural fires, they were unlikely to have been alone.

Within the timescale of Neanderthals and modern humans, and in the context of both their sites, fire was clearly either transferred or initiated, and controlled. This much we can see from the existence of hearths.[4] Earlier than that, such species as *Homo erectus* clearly came into contact with fire, but whether these were controlled, natural, or the result of harvesting natural fires, is currently open to speculation. At whatever point fire did actually come under hominid control, the implications were enormous, for the environment, human society, human biology, and in the preparation of food.

Digestion outside the body

But what is cooking for? The entire animal kingdom appears to do perfectly well without it, and that includes our close relatives. We still enjoy a lot of raw foods, indeed elevate some of them to the status of luxury cuisine. Cooking in the analyses of social anthropologists such as Claude Lévi-Strauss and Mary Douglas resembles language. It is a form of narrative that marks out our 'culture' and our separation from 'nature'. It allows us to weave elaborate culinary stories with which to shape and consolidate our social worlds. If we look at what is going on in a material sense to food as it is exposed to cooking, we uncover a range of transformations, some with direct relevance to weaving that social narrative, some affecting the nature of the social group that can gather to eat, and furthermore affecting the nutritional quality of the food we eat.

Lévi-Strauss explored a contrast between two strands of culinary narrative in living societies, connected to roasting and boiling. Roasting was a form of *exocuisine*, literally 'outside cooking', in which the meat was open to the flames, much as the social gathering was open to guests. A roast is an extravagant, theatrical meal, in contrast to boiling, an enclosed, contained *endocuisine*, literally 'inside cooking'. Boiling and stewing was a cuisine for the home, to be shared within the family, and contained within a stewpot. In each case the culinary narrative and the social drama merged, themes to which we shall return in subsequent chapters.[5]

The content of the narrative are the colours, textures, and flavours of the food, in each case fashioned and modified by cooking. Among the material changes brought about by cooking, the most immediate to our senses is that it tantalizes the taste buds, and does this in various ways. First of all it sweetens food. This it does by breaking down long-chain carbohydrates and other related molecules to simpler sugars. Second, it generates a series of more complicated molecules by chemically linking carbohydrates and proteins, or at least the sugars and amino-acids of which they are constructed. One of these more complex creations is.

caramel. Others are known as 'Amadori products' named after the scientist who researched them, a suite of compounds that turn cooked food brown, and endow it with a crust and pleasant aroma. Third, certain forms of cooking can act like an artist's palette, forging a series of separate flavours into a culinary masterpiece. Taste and smell have clear evolutionary functions, guiding us as to which parts of the natural world to avoid, and which to consume, and in what balance. It is not entirely clear how much these ancient biological functions are being deceived by the art of cooking. We are certainly familiar with that possibility in commercial foods today, but since it is reasonable to suppose that cooking has been around throughout the existence of our own species, there has been time for some evolutionary harmonization to take place. However, the links between cooking flavours and nutritional benefit are easier to see in raw food than in cooked.[6]

A second material effect of cooking with clear social consequences is to tenderize meat, and generally soften food, by breaking down cell walls, and shortening molecules, and this affects the range of individuals who can share a meal. Softened food is notably of benefit to two groups, weaning infants and the elderly, and these are two groups that have a particular place in both Neanderthals and modern humans. Weaning is a protracted process in big-brained humans, placing demands on the transitional diet.[7] In many species, the elderly and infirm are not conspicuously in the picture, other than through dying as a consequence of the brutal rigours of natural selection. Examination of Neanderthal teeth and bones does not suggest they lived as long as ourselves; perhaps forty-five years would be a good lifespan. However, it also seems that the elderly and infirm had a place in Neanderthal communities much as they do in our own species, and that has allowed me to place a grandfather behind the screen at Abri Romaní, and reflect upon how he was fed.

What we know about the elderly and infirm among Neanderthals comes from a small number of illuminating individuals who we know through their fragmentary skeletons. The huge cave of Shanidar in Iraq, source of a number of key Neanderthal remains, yielded one of these. He was a male who had lived much, perhaps all, of his life with a withered arm and leg. In addition, he had recovered from serious injuries to both his foot and his head. He could only have stayed alive with the support of others from his group. A second individual, more directly related to the putative grandfather is an old Neanderthal man whose bones were recovered from the much smaller French cave of La-Chapelle-aux-Saints. This old man had lost a great number of his teeth. What is more, the bone around his toothless gums shows evidence of healing; he clearly lived for a fair while longer than he could comfortably chew.[8]

There are other ways to soften food that do not require cooking. The most straightforward is for a healthy adult to chew the mouthful first then pass it on, but if cooking is clearly in place for other reasons, then it may serve this purpose as well.

A third material consequence of cooking is to alter nutritional quality. The thermal breakdown of molecules does not simply soften food; it also causes those molecules to be rearranged, sometimes for the better in nutritional terms, sometimes for the worse. In the case of plant foods, cooking frequently performs the important task of breaking down toxic substances. Toxins are widespread in vegetation, and one of the principal means of a plant's natural defence against being eaten. Looking back to our evolutionary roots in Africa, our woodland-dwelling ancestors were confronted by a range of plant defences, including spines, thick skins, and hard woody coverings, They countered these by adept skills of timely dextrous unpacking. As they moved into more open habitats in which small herbaceous plants gained prominence, so did toxicity as a means of plant defence. The use of heat unquestionably opened up the possibilities of plant food consumption in such environments.

The situation is less clear with animal tissue. Going back as far as half a million years ago, the earliest burnt bone chips recovered may well have arisen from the shattered ends of a butchered joint left to barbecue in the intense heat of an open fire. This simple form of barbecue is clearly a major candidate for early cooking, and it is one in which toxins are likely to be created rather than removed. The culprits are the so-called Maillard reactions, the same family of reactions that generate those aromatic 'Amadori products' whose taste and texture so tempts our palate. While the tasty Amadori products are best generated at relatively low temperatures, the higher temperatures of direct exposure create compounds that some have argued may be harmful. This does not apply to all cooked meats by any means, but may be an issue with meat and fish exposed to high temperatures. With fish, seafood, and in particular the oils they contain, the situation is fairly clear. They make their broadest contribution to our nutritional needs when eaten fresh and raw.

However, even when cooking has a negative or mixed impact on overall nutritional quality, it can have a positive effect on energetic costs of consumption. Like every other bodily function, digestion burns up energy, and some foods require more energy than others, not just to masticate it in our mouths, but also to take it apart in our guts. Some potential foods would require as many, or more calories to digest than they actually yield to the consumer, and in many more, the profit margin is narrow. What cooking can do is greatly enhance that profit margin by taking care of much of the chemical disassembly of the food outside the body, and this, in some researchers' minds, is the key to its evolutionary advantages.

Balancing the machinery of the body

The most tangible evidence that human evolution has something to do with reducing the costs of digestion is the changing size of teeth on fossil remains. Following the whole sequence of hominid fossils through time from the early australopithecines to modern humans, the relative size of teeth tends to diminish. This is first evident around 1.5–2 million years ago, with the first skulls attributed to *Homo erectus*. Another major period of tooth reduction lies within the last 200,000 years. Alongside the fossil record of diminished tooth size, the modern physiological record of living mammals reveals a corresponding pattern in the organs of the gut. Not only are human teeth small in relation to overall body size, we also have a relatively small gut. Our bodily eating machinery has shrunk, just as another prominent organ of our body has grown, and this may be the clue to the whole process; shrinking guts may be to do with growing brains, and the average size of the Neanderthal brain is the biggest of them all.

One intriguing attempt to account for this pattern goes something like this. Different parts of the human body do different kinds of work within it, and also use up energy in doing so, energy which they acquire from sugar transported through the bloodstream. Some tissues once constructed, skin and tendons for example, have relatively low running costs in calorific terms. Other organs, for example the liver, gut, and brain, burn up a lot of energy. There is a limit to how big and active they can get, determined by how much food any animal can consume and release as sugar. By looking across the mammal kingdom, and measuring the mass of different organs, one can arrive at a mammalian norm. When we compare that norm with the respective masses in our own bodies, we discover that the modern human brain is two to three times as large as what would be predicted from looking at mammals as a group. A central feature of the evolution of humans has been increased brain size, so that comes as no surprise. What a consideration of the energy economy alerts us to is the need to balance the books in energy terms. With a brain that big, and consequently using up a lot of sugar, something else has got to be small. The two other 'big spenders' are the liver, that basically manages the chemical balance in the body, and the alimentary tract, or gut, the corridor down which food goes, in part making its way into the bloodstream to fuel the body. In humans, it is this latter organ that is performing the balancing act, down to almost half the size predicted from the mammalian norm.

So the flip side of a generously provisioned, massive brain seems to be a economically downsized gut. The liver, it seems, is doing too critical a job for cuts to be made. The economic nature of our own downsized gut is placed in perspective when compared with a prize cow, lazily turning grass leaves into beef. A cow's gut is big, and equipped with a suite of four specialist stomachs, one with an army of bacterial guest-workers that also need feeding. The grass can be chemically dismantled, almost in its entirety, and distributed through the bovine factory. Our own guts do a much feebler job of work, and are particularly thrown by the high cellulose content that is good at cleaning out our gut in a more or less untransformed state as 'fibre', but poor at meeting any nutritional needs. We cannot break it down to sugar.

The so-called 'expensive tissue hypothesis' proposes that possession of a big brain is plausible in energetic terms if not too strenuous a task is given to the necessarily smaller gut. Animal tissue, for example, simply does not have cellulose around its cell walls, and can supply energy and protein in a concentrated and unoccluded form. Another way to ease the workload on a downsized gut is to do some of the digestion outside the body, before the food has been ingested. Digestion is a chemical process in which large indigestible molecules are turned into small easily absorbed molecules, and can be achieved in a variety of ways including fermentation (essentially, getting yeasts and bacteria to do the job first) and heat. The hypothesis forges a biological connection between large brain size on the one hand, and on the other, easily digestible food, or food rendered easily digestible by such processes as heat. Their elegant argument mapped out the conceptual strands linking fire, cooking, and the brain.[9]

Brain capacities have now been measured or estimated for a broad range of hominid fossils, and it is possible to track key periods in which the brain substantially increased in size. Alongside these, although we cannot measure gut size from a fossil specimen, we can measure the reduction in tooth size, which may mark the easing of pressures on internal digestion. The two major periods of brain expansion in hominid evolution have been the emergence of the genus *Homo* itself, around 2 million years ago, and subsequently the emergence to the common ancestor of modern humans and Neanderthals, 300,000–400,000 years ago. If anything, the principal episodes of reduction of tooth size mentioned above lag a little, occurring with *Homo erectus*, 1.7–1.9 million years ago, and modern humans within the last 200,000 years. The second episode provides a good amount of support for the expensive tissue hypothesis. A surge in brain size coincides with the earliest evidence of ashes, burnt bone, and charcoal in conjunction with hominids, and the subsequent appearance of hearths coincides with tooth reduction in some lines. Evidence is far slighter for an earlier episode of cooking association with the brain expansion and tooth reduction of *Homo erectus*. But let us speculate on a broader notion of external digestion, starting with leaving foodstuffs for a while in the vicinity of volcanic deposits, the aftermath of a bush fire, or even under a scorching sun. These can each have a digestive effect on the tissue, as can leaving plant tissue around without intense heat.[10]

Wild acorns have formed a snack food in some parts of south-west Asia within living memory, but the local gatherers know that, if eaten from the tree they will be too toxic for consumption. However, if left on the ground for a while, natural fermentation will break down the toxins. The part-'rotted' acorns can then be eaten with little further modification.[11] Virtually nothing is known about the early exploitation of natural fermentation but acorns are among those plant foods for which indirect evidence of early hominid consumption have been gleaned. In many ways, making good use of the natural processes of germination and rotting requires the combination of good timing and natural history intelligence that we share with other great apes and so quite conceivably with early humans. When we today consume a diet of bread, beer, yogurt, tofu, and soy sauce, we are taking advantage of microbial breakdown, in other words a controlled form of rotting. In this context, we are 'detritus feeders' exploiting what may well be the most ancient form of external digestion of all.

Why big brains?

The cooking of food clearly requires both agile forelimbs, hands in other words, together with a brain that can steer those agile forelimbs through a multi-step task. From some of the more durable artefacts, elegant flint points, hafted with bitumen onto wooden shafts, for example, we know that the Neanderthal mind was capable of multi-step operations of this kind. A corollary of the expensive tissue hypothesis is that, not only did cooking require a certain amount of brainpower, but also brainpower required a certain amount of cooking. So which drove which? To answer that we need to consider what else the brain was doing.

The modern human brain is, amongst many other things, an instrument of social life, allowing us to recognize a fair few people, make conversation, keep in touch, and so on. In my own society, a lot of people have about 100–200 names on their Christmas card list, which is also the size that gives a local society or small primary school a certain sense of intimacy. It is a number that recurs in human social life, and not just in the Western world; it matches well the average group size of recent hunter-gatherer groups. Looking at other living primates there seems to be a correlation between familiar group size and the size of part of the brain known as the 'neo-cortex'. This is the outer, much folded, region of the brain that differentiates mammals from other vertebrates, and which has grown to a very substantial size in our own genus. Soft tissue, such as the neo-cortex, is not something we can directly measure in the fossil record, but there is a broad correlation between the volume of the neo-cortex and the volume of the entire brain, and another broad correlation between the size of the brain, and the brain cavity, which can be assessed from fossils. So by suitably enlarging the error bands, we can translate the size of the brain cavity of fossil hominids to their potential group size. Following this logic, the earliest hominids, the australopithecines, yield a set of figures broadly in line with other great apes, such as chimps, gorillas, and orang-utans. They all predict group sizes of 60–70. The equivalent figures for the earliest humans see an increase of predicted group size to 75–90. In *Homo erectus* this number climbs to 130. This may be the kind of group size in the background of the horse kill discussed in the preceding chapter. In Neanderthals and modern humans, the number climbs to 150 and beyond. From these data, we can begin to build an evolutionary trajectory leading to cooking.[12]

The story begins back in Africa towards the end of the Miocene Epoch (around 12 million years ago) when the rich equatorial woodland so important to primate evolution and ecology became vulnerable to climatic change. With rainfall diminishing, the woodlands fragmented, and the apes followed a diverse range of evolutionary paths through different habitats. Two million years ago, one genus of ape, *Homo* moved extensively across the open landscapes, where many animals' natural defences resided in their large size, and many plants' natural defences resided in their toxicity and texture. At certain points in their evolution, early humans breached both those lines of defence. The large animals could be dispatched with spears, stone tools, and social cohesion. The plants could be transformed into food by external digestion, through pulverization, rotting and fermentation, and exposure to heat. All these activities placed demands on intelligence and the brain, and, quite possibly, the most demanding of all was the imperative for social cohesion, requiring an expansion of the neo-cortex. This would only be possible with the reduction of another expensive organ, such as the gut. The link between brain complexity and external digestion produced the positive feedback loop that would make all this possible. The more effective external digestion became in reducing demands on the gut, the larger the potential size of the brain. Larger brains enable more elaborate technologies, including technologies of external digestion, taking the feedback loop through another, self-enhancing cycle.

We might envisage that early humans were adept at 'letting nature take its course' in terms of rotting, fermentation, sun baking, and parching, opportunistically extended to natural hot spots in volcanic regions and in the wake of bushfires. This would require little more than a propensity for curation, guarding, and returning to a spot. From around half a million years ago, fire harvesting might account for the appearance of charcoal, ashes, and burnt bone in conjunction with hominid locales. In the last 150,000 years, control of fire cave and rock-shelter hearths elevated controlled heat to a central place within the various means of external digestion as practised by hominids possessing the largest brain of all.

How to build a brain

Like any expensive organ, the building of a brain requires a lot of protein, a great deal of energy, and a good suite of nutrients and vitamins. In primates, this mostly happens through the highly efficient mechanism of the placenta, which takes from the mother's body whatever it needs and passes it on to the foetus. By the time the young primate is born, the great majority of its brain growth has been accomplished. Not so humans. In a real sense, humans are unusual in giving birth to 'babies'. Most mammals give birth to 'toddlers' able to take on some fairly grown-up tasks, such as limb coordination, within minutes of birth. Human babies have far more growing to do, and that includes the brain. It will take another eighteen months (till the point they became toddlers in fact) for them to catch up with their newborn primate cousins. So a large part of brain growth in humans depends on the mother's milk, and ultimately on the diet of a mother at a stage in her life in which she might be least able to compete for food.[13]

By the time of the much earlier meal at Boxgrove, the human brain had evolved to a sufficiently large size for this nutritional challenge to be an issue, leading us to explore the possibility that the father and other kin cooperated in supplying the needs of the young offspring. It was yet more of an issue with the large-brained Neanderthals who visited such sites as Abric Romani. Building a large brain was an issue of meeting nutritional needs not simply in terms of quantity, but also of quality, and of supplying some rather particular chemical ingredients.

Beyond the familiar materials listed above, a great deal of the brain is composed of fats, and some rather specific fats at that. One of the most common fatty acids in myelin is oleic acid, which is also the most abundant fatty acid in human milk and in our diet. Two other fats crucial to the optimal development of the brain and eyes are called DHA and AA respectively. DHA is furthermore the most abundant fat in the brain. These initials stand for the rather unwieldy 'docosahexaenoic acid' and 'arachidonic acid' respectively, which is why the acronyms are preferred for these and the other fats discussed below. Mother and child can manufacture both DHA and AA from two other fats, but these two source fats cannot be synthesized in the human body. They have to be consumed as part of the diet. For this reason they are referred to as 'essential fatty acids' (EFAs).[14]

EFAs have sometimes been described as 'nature's antifreeze'. That is because of their importance in keeping the flesh of cold ocean fish supple, however low the temperature drops. The oil from cold ocean fish is one of the best sources of EFAs around, and has a long-standing reputation as 'brain food'. In the plant world, they are also found in leafy vegetables and are widespread in oily seeds, such as walnut, hemp, and flax. Not only do we need EFAs for the growth of our brains, we need them in the right balance, and this has particular bearing on our consumption of meat.

The two types of EFAs are 'omega 3 EFAs' and 'omega 6 EFAs'. The numbers 3 and 6 refer to the internal arrangement of their chemical bonds. A mixed diet of meat, fish, and vegetables will tend to take care of this balance, but in a diet heavily weighted towards the meat of ruminant animals, the balance may weigh too heavily towards the omega 6 group. Not everything is known about how contemporary communities make up this balance at critical periods of brain growth, let alone those in distant prehistory. Some shattered seed fragments from the sediments within the Syrian cave of Doura could provide a clue. These seeds were the hard nutlets of a member of the borage family of plants, a family whose oily seeds are rich in EFAs. We can speculate about young Neanderthal mothers taking a hammerstone to gathered oil seeds, but even the meticulously recorded layers at Abric Romaní leave no evidence that that was happening. There is, however, one very visible source of fat offering a balanced package of EFAs, and that is the relatively soft oily fat of the horse.[15]

How 'focal' are the focal points?

Does this mean we have reached a critical moment in the form of the meal? Would Claude Lévi-Strauss and Mary Douglas, transported through time to these hearths, recognize something entirely familiar? And from this scene should we envisage the blossoming of culinary art and skill, structured family meals, and social discourse? Not necessarily; something about these earliest hearths raises questions. It has a lot to do with their spatial pattern within sites, or rather their lack of it.

There are a lot of hearths at Abric Romaní. Indeed, hearths are a familiar feature of sites of this period. In looking for patterning in hearths, we become aware that we do not just think of hearths as a source of fire. In modern contexts, they form something of a focal point within space. The word *focus* comes directly from the Latin for 'hearth' or 'fireplace'. Its other Latin usages include 'home' and 'family', revealing recurrent associations within our own species. They may not be directly transferable to Neanderthals. At Abric Romaní itself, if we edit out the voids left from the older excavations, the most recent plans give the impression that hearths had been laid all over the place. That is a pattern that can recur across a wide range of Neanderthal sites, leaving us with the impression that quite a lot of what we find could be explained by fairly ad hoc, individual action, creating a rather diverse range of different patterns in different sites. Such a range can be best interpreted as an overlay of relatively disconnected returns to a shelter to carry out a recurrent series of tasks, rather than a recurrent focal point of a communal hearth. This does not conflict with the evidence from Abric Romaní, indicating that some hearths were kept going for some time, or indeed that on some sites there was a zone for hearths and other zones free of hearths. We do not know how they started fires, but there would have clearly been an advantage in keeping at least some fires continuously burning. They do not, however, give the impression of forming a distinct focal point within the shelter.[16]

What kind of cooking?

Let us turn to the various burnt debris from Neanderthal and earlier hominid sites to establish what kinds of foods they were exposing to fire, and what effects it would have. First of all, the most widely attested fragments are chips of burnt bone, going back to fragments from the African sites of Olorgesailie, Swartskrans, and Cave of Hearths, around half a million years ago. One possibility to bear in mind is that these may be chips discarded from raw marrow consumption, and have little to do with cooking. However, if they do relate to cooking, then they are likely to be fragments from the end of a butchered bony joint. In the latter case, we can argue that the meat was roasted in a fairly fresh state. Given Africa's warm climate, and what we assume to lie within the techno-logical capacity of early humans, long-term storage of meat would most likely be through drying of fillets, and we know from butchery marks on the bones, that fillets were cut this far back in time. Storage on the bone in a warm climate is a fairly challenging and risky process; it would simply be too difficult to desiccate the bone, which in any case would waste the important marrow.[17]

If we assume that the chipped bones on early African sites were from fairly fresh meat, then the two benefits are the enjoyment of the taste, and the energy costs of digestion. In terms of nutritional quality, the outcome is probably negative, breaking down some thermally sensitive vitamins and lipids, and generating mildly toxic Maillard products on the barbecued surface.

As we move northwards and forwards in time, to some of the European Neanderthal sites, then the burnt bones of a wider range of animal turn up, including a scatter of smaller mammals, reptiles, amphi-bians, and birds. Two such sites in south-east Spain, Cueva Negra and Sima de las Palomas, have been especially prolific. At Cueva Negra, the bones of birds and tortoises are found in abundance, alongside more modest quantities of hedgehog, rabbit, frogs or toads, and a number of small rodents. Sima de las Palomas has a similar range and in addition, lizards. The big game consumed by early humans was made up of herbivorous animals. The innards of herbivores tend to be safe to consume in a very fresh and uncooked state. This range of smaller animals had a much wider diet, embracing carnivores, omnivores, insectivores, detritus feeders, and scavengers. These occupants of more distant parts of the food chain may have innards that are not as safe and tasty in the fresh state. Especially if they were gathered without a full awareness of each species' eating habits, cooking could indeed offer hygienic protection while experimenting with small prey of this kind.[18]

The situation is rather different with animals from the sea. In nutritional terms, these are most nutritious when consumed fresh, especially in view of their important contribution of EFAs, which are easily oxidized by heat. It may therefore come as some surprise to learn of the concentration of burnt mussel shells uncovered at a Neanderthal cave site on Gibralter. If we ask why they were cooking mussels 45,000 years ago in the Vanguard Cave, it may be they were simply opening the molluscs by exposing them to heat. It may also be that they just liked the taste, irrespective of the fact that the nutritional effect was either neutral or negative.[19]

The driving force of curiosity about taste may also explain some of the plant foods found on Neanderthal hearths. At Dederiyeh Cave in Syria, seeds of the hackberry plant, *Celtis* sp., were found. Different species of hackberry turn up in the Old World and the New at various stages of prehistory. They can be eaten and have certain nutritional benefits, but the Old World hackberry has very little flesh on it, and more likely served as a flavouring. In North America, the Apaches, Tohono, O'odham, Navaho, and Hualapai used it in this way, rather in the manner of peppercorns. Their presence at Dederiyeh may point to the importance of flavour in Neanderthal diet. With other plant foods, the chemistry of digestion could be the greater issue. One such example comes from Kebara Cave in Israel, where over 4,000 charred seeds were recovered from over twenty species, making it the richest Neanderthal plant food assemblage of all. Around 80 per cent of these were the seeds of small legumes, and there is some suggestion from the form of these seeds that they might have been unripe. This would certainly fit in with our picture of a timely wild harvest, not too soon before the seeds have started fattening, and not late enough for the seeds to become two hard and toxic, although exposing them to the fire would both soften the seeds and reduce their toxicity. Grass seeds are present, but only as a fraction of a per cent. Another cave site in Israel does preserve evidence of the collection of mature grass seed heads. Hearth

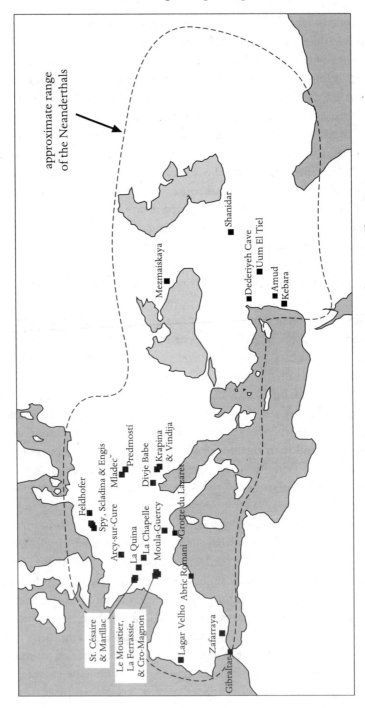

MAP 3. The Neanderthal world, indicating some key sites. Their European and West Asian range is indicated by a continuous line.

deposits at Amud Cave retain the minute phytoliths that are characteristic of those seed heads.[20]

Hearths were recurrent features of the Neanderthal rock shelter, providing warmth and protection, and an occasional accessory to the meal. Much food was consumed raw, but from time to time this was complemented by foods held in the fire for a while. The evidence suggests to me that the driving force was experimentation with flavour, and an attraction to those flavours might or might not coincide with any nutritional benefit. Indeed, the nutritional quality of the food was sometimes reduced. Apart from the rather haphazard relationship with nutritional quality, this occasional experimentation with cooking enabled three other things to happen. First, it broadened the Neanderthal niche to encompass a wider range of small animals and plants. Fire served to sterilize the flesh and guts of small animals with uncertain habits, and it broke down the toxins and inhibitors, 'nature's pesticides' in many plant foods. Second, it reduced the energy costs of digestion, dovetailing with a continued evolutionary trend towards big brain and simplified gut. Third, by softening the food, it opened possibilities for feeding slow-weaning infants, and the elderly, infirm, and toothless.

The care of the weak is a powerful component in the reconstruction of the sharing of food at Abric Romaní 46,000 years ago. Whether or not the engagement with fire involved more transient and solitary activities than the powerful and enduring focal points they constitute in modern humans, the notion of grandparents and the infirm sheltering behind skins in the back of the cave seems consistent with seating a bonded kin group along the transported pine log, and equipping them with a quite extensive 'social language'. Some observers would query the cast of the wooden tripod and especially the juniper wood 'plate', but those travertine 'pseudomorphs' must presumably indicate some working of wood. Their queries more reflect a range of views about what the mental capacity of Neanderthals actually was. Some have argued from their artefacts that they were unlikely to have been able to conceptualize the future, which is why I have given their reflections upon change through time a rather impressionistic feel. There is always, of course, the possibility that their very large brains possessed mental capacities that we do not possess, and thus would find it impossible to categorize, let alone discern.

The rock-shelter visits in context

As modern humans, however, we can do more than just half-close our eyes, and arrange our inferences in the space beneath a moist, dripping rock-shelter roof. We can also look through time, and often with a greater clarity than the diners we have inferred. Nothing is left of the uppermost levels in the shelter. Those had been dug away in their entirety. But beneath this void, the current excavators have left a section, along the eastern wall of the shelter, displaying the three metres of deposit through which they had dug. We can still see concretions of stalactite and stalagmite that eventually sealed in the archaeological levels. Beneath these are large chunks of travertine, tumbled from the roof. Traces of the moss and other plants that lived within the seeping lime-rich water can still be discerned, including the delicate fronds of the maidenhair fern that carpeted the moist and dripping rooves. These are embedded within layer upon layer of porous, friable lime-rich sediment, several metres deep. It is sediments such as these that have trapped and preserved our Neanderthal episode. Just near the base of this section is a large round circular feature, the fill of a borehole sunk by recent investigators, which demonstrated that these sediments went down another 12 ½ metres at least. From Uranium series dating we learn that the entire accumulation took around 30,000 years, from approximately 70,000 to 40,000 years ago.

As well as preserving the occasional Neanderthal visit, these travertine sediments also trapped the rains of pollen that were blown each year into the shelter. This pollen provides our most direct evidence of how our brief Neanderthal episode of shared consumption unfolded into the environ-mental dynamics on much longer timescales. The sequence preserves the kind of successional fluctuation envisaged by Frederick Clements and subsequently seen in a number of deep pollen sequences. There are colder phases, in which shallow open vegetation forms are prominent, grasses, steppe plants, and members of the thistle/daisy family. Between these are warmer episodes with signs of deeper woodland, with trees like oak, and either wild olive or a near relative. If we look closely at the oscillations between these two forms of plant cover, a pattern can be detected, and a pattern that is not unique to this particular region.[21]

Between around 70,000 and 60,000 years ago, there are sizeable oscillations between the colder and warmer episodes, each oscillation taking around 2,300 years. Through this period, the amplitude of the oscillation diminishes, as the general trend moves towards the colder extreme, and for the following ten millennia, the oscillations become more frequent, each one completed within a thousand years on average. It is towards the end of this period that the Neanderthal episode explored in this chapter took place. In the final ten millennia of the sequence, the sequence first moves into its coldest phase, with little sign of the woodland type, and then moves into a new protracted warm phase, at which point the available sequence ends.

Temperature can be directly studied over the same time period, from light and heavy oxygen isotopes measured from cores drilled through the seabed and into glaciers. A relatively high proportion of the heavier form of oxygen indicates relatively warm conditions at the time of deposition. If we line up the Abric Romaní pollen data with oxygen isotope data from, for example, the deep Greenland ice sheets, then the patterns match. Between 70,000 and 60,000 years ago there are big fluctuations, between 60,000 and 50,000 years ago, there are shallower fluctu-ations, becoming faster in turnover, then 5,000 years of sustained coolness, before a return to warmer conditions at the end of the sequence. The rock-shelter pollen is picking up fluctuations in the global climate. In other words, the Neanderthal community was hunting and foraging at time of relatively rapid climatic change. Not that a transition between moist deciduous woodland and cold open steppe would happen within a lifetime. Such a change would take a few centuries, even during the fastest oscillations. But as we saw in the previous chapter, fast climatic change can upset all sorts of balances, particularly those that relate to slow-growing woodland species, and large, long-lived animals. Various aspects of their ecology begin to lag behind the climate change, stranding some species, sending others in extinction, and reconfiguring food webs as a result. Some of the species in the pollen sequence seem to reflect a dynamic of this kind. Pine trees however seem to brave the fluctuations well, finding some niche or other in both the warm and cold periods, and defying expectations about how this genus might respond to temperature change.

As for the animals whose bones were found around and about the Neanderthal hearths, they display the mixed fate of large feeders at a time of change that was also seen half a million years ago at Boxgrove.

The other carnivore at the site was the Iberian lynx, which made it through and still clings on in small numbers today. Among the grazers, red deer are the real survivors, making it into the modern age in sizeable numbers. The Spanish ibex has done reasonably well. Wild horse and wild ox continued for some time but have now long since disappeared, and the narrow-nosed rhino was already in decline when those ancient hearths were alight. The other large feeder was the Neanderthal itself, a species that would persist in southern Spain for several millennia, declining fast after 30,000 years ago. Although it had taken an equatorial genus into some very northerly regions, the rapid temperature fluctuations described above sorely tested its viability. At the time of the food-sharing episode outlined in this chapter, Neanderthals had completed nine-tenths of their time on earth. As they diminished in numbers, a new species of human spread across Europe, a species which also entered the Anoia river valley and left its trace in levels of the Abric Romaní rock shelter. Along with the characteristic blades, the 'calling card' of our own species, a number of perforated shells and teeth were recovered from these upper layers, and an assemblage of perforated fish vertebrae. These pierced skeletal fragments may not be the most dramatic items ever to find their way onto a museum display, but their implications for the manner in which modern humans share food, the manner they interact generally, and indeed what was going on inside the modern human mind, are profound.

Opening up the cathedral of the mind

Pierced skeletal fragments, bones, shells, teeth, and ivory, have remained a recurrent feature of human material culture ever since. They are used now much as we imagine they were used 40,000 years ago, as beads to adorn the human body. At Abric Romaní, we know little of their precise context, but through subsequent millennia, they will reappear on buried skeletons, providing some indication of how they were used. Recurrently they will be strung together in necklaces and headgear of buried bodies, emphasizing the face and head, and sometimes arms, in other words, the body as communicator, as social person. If we return to the model of the early human mind explored in Chapter 3, it could be compared to a cathedral with individual chapels, in which distinct services were enacted. There were 'chapels' or domains of intelligence relating to nature, to physical materials, and to social engagement. Various aspects of the archaeological record suggest a level of separation between these. The pierced skeletal ornaments imply something new. Something taken from the world of nature, a shell, tooth or bone, is treated like a physical material, and pierced to assemble with similarly pierced items, and placed on the human body in a manner that clearly pertains to face-to-face encounter and social engagement. The pierced skeletal fragment is one among a whole series of transformations in the archaeological record that correspond to a new kind of humanity; the screens and chapel walls of the cathedral of the mind have been breeched: the interior is now open to multiple interconnections.[22]

Coming forward from the time of the Abric Romaní beads by 10,000–15,000 years, we capture some remarkably detailed images of the consequences of that revolution. A series of burials in Italian caves indicate how those pierced fragments might adorn a human body. The skeleton of one individual found at Arene Candide was wearing a bonnet, made up of hundreds of brown seashells of the genus *Cyclope neritea*. They were perforated, indicating how they had been laced together. Cowrie shells, sea urchins, and red deer canines had also been incorporated into the design. Dropping from the bonnet was a small ivory pendant, and what must have been a tassel adorned with more red deer canines and marine shells. The bodily adornment continued to the legs, where ornaments were found around the knees, and the chest, upon which engraved elk antlers had been laid. On this individual's left wrist was another ivory pendant and many more of the brown seashells. In their right hand they held a large flint blade.[23]

The stone blades in use by the communities who buried their dead at Arene Candide can be found across a wide stretch of Europe and parts of Asia, on sites for which archaeologists have invented the term 'Gravettian'. They can be found, for example, 750 km to the east of Arene Candide, at the Moravian sites with which this book opened. Here too, adorned skeletons have been recovered, and close by, the deep accumulations of wind-blown sediments have proven an ideal archaeological trap for the remnants of the hearths around which their living relatives shared food.[24]

We can catch a glimpse of fragments of life within that food-sharing circle; we have in plenty the remains of the food they were eating, scattered in and beyond the hearth, and some of the flint knives they used to cut their meat, and stone grinders used for plant food. From time to time, pierced beads of tooth or shell and fragments of red ochre have fallen to the ground, hinting at how those present had adorned their bodies. Just occasionally, a more dramatic artefact is left behind, the representation of a human form, fashioned in bone or clay, the earliest human models known. The ability to make them at all, and to pass that skill on, clearly points to the narrative, storytelling capability of the modern human mind. It hints at the free-flowing conversation that would resolve the tension inherent in close confrontation, allowing participants to share food in an intimate circle, face to face, a situation that for other mammals, even for their close cousins the Neanderthals, might constitute a quite threatening encounter. Claude Lévi-Strauss and Mary Douglas would have recognized a familiar scene, and begun to ask who was sitting where, to what gestures and manners they adhered, what recipes they learnt from their kin, and the stories they told. Their adorned faces, their beaded headgear and necklaces, were lit up by the shifting flames of fires that have left enduring traces within the Moravian silts. These are not the scattered ad hoc hearths we associate with Neanderthal sites, but hearths centrally placed, and returned to again and again. The durations of use and reuse are sometimes long enough for windblown sediments, the sands of time, to interleave with the lenses of reddened earth and charred remains. But the hearth retains its position, at the centre of the circle, within the enclosures and shelters of skin and bone, within the circle of adorned bodies in conversation and sharing food, the focal point.

A modern meal

We begin to see a manner of sharing food that recurs more than any other in our own species, modern humans. In the centre are food and warmth, and certain items of equipment, blades in particular, to assist in the food's consumption. The main tools of consumption however are hands. Encircling the food is an intimate group, whose seating depends on rank and gender according to a mutually understood code. Their bodies are embellished in a manner that reflects status, and they are deep in conversation. The stories they tell reach deep in space and time, and are richly infused with irony, humour, and hope. Around about them, other features of the space are embellished, their patterns directly or indirectly alluding to the same stories. Around the circle, other people are in motion, in different ways contributing to the sharing of food at the centre, occasionally retreating into alcoves and dark spaces for some ancillary activity.

The previous paragraph could have been written with mammoth bone shelters of Moravia in mind, or, with a great deal more poetic licence, to embellish the pierced fish-bones at the top of Amador Romaní's sequence. It was actually assembled while looking at an eighteenth-century Parisian sketch of the Café Procope that I was thinking of using in a later chapter of this book (Figure 32). It shows warm food being consumed primarily by hand. Around the plates of warm food are some of the eminent figures of the Enlightenment; Voltaire, Diderot, d'Alembert, La Harpe, and Condorcet. From their conversations spring many of the ideas that would go on to shape our own thoughts, about the future, the present, and the past. Around them, others are listening, watching, and carrying food to the kitchen. There are firm rules about gender and age shaping the gathering; this particular scene is exclusively adult and masculine. There were other sets of rules about age and gender in the distant past, rules that we can glimpse from burial practices such as those at Arene Candide. Among the mammoth bones of ancient Moravia and beneath the elegant ceilings of the Café Procope, the fusion of conversation and food-sharing that uniquely characterizes our species is the same. A close look at the traces from an earlier gathering among our closest relatives, the Neanderthals, gives some sense of the roots of that modern human pattern of behaviour, and simultaneously throws its most unusual features into sharp relief.

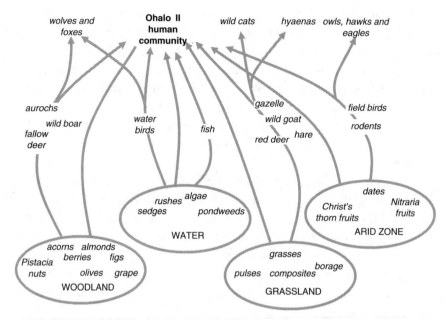

11. Food web inferred from the biological remains recovered from excavations at Ohalo II, Sea of Galilee, 23,000 years ago.

5

NAMING AND EATING

Lake Kinneret, Israel, circa 23,000 years ago

They spent less time looking towards the southern sky around this time of year. A couple of moons ago, when the Dog Star was rising over the high ridge that looked like an eagle—that's all everyone was doing, waiting for the big birds to come. It was a much loved time of year, when the worst chill went, and before the herbs had gone brown. And plump breast meat abounded at every gathering around the hearth. Each day they would wait silently at the water's edge, with net, bow, and arrow to catch a few more. Each night they told each other stories about the bird ancestors and gorged themselves for as long as it lasted on one bird after another. Now the stories and the flavours were both changing.

That's how it would be, season by season. For a couple of moons, the stories would be of the bird ancestors and the meat was plentiful. The next few moons, the stories would be of the waters and the sun, and baked fish and sprouted seeds would abound. Then they would return to the birds, as heads turned to the north. The rhythm of their lives from morning till night was the rhythm of the seasons. The moon and the Dog Star between them shaped the morning, noon, and night. It steered their course, towards the morning sun and the woods, the evening sun and the steppes, south or north along their sacred waters, and it shaped the food they shared around this hearth.

Down by the water's edge, a foraging party was returning, with heavy loads across their shoulders. It was hard work walking for miles along the broken woodland edge rhythmically beating at the sward to catch the ripening seeds. They spent a third of the year at this, two months in spring gathering seeds, and two months in autumn gathering fruits and nuts. It was hard work, but it was all hard work, gathering so many foods from so many places—each harvest took so much effort but seemed so small. Like the miniature beasts they captured and had slung across their shoulders together with their bows. The bigger beasts like the gazelle were great to feast on, but the gazelle hunts, like everything else here, was seasonal— they went when the old man said so.

His shelter was their first stop—they found him sorting out the last of the over-wintering provisions. They deposited their seed harvests in the appropriate hut, and looked across to the hearth to which two others were carrying pistachios and ground almonds. The weaver woman was already seated there, her headdress adorned with talons and falcon wings. The old man sent them to the water's edge with a bag of fish. They would have to be cleaned before approaching the hearth. They prepared the fish, washed themselves, and joined the rest of the group at the fire's edge to prepare the meal.

THE margin of a lake can be a goldmine for archaeologists, especially those interested in the preservation of food remains. It was the lowering of the Swiss Lakes in the middle of the nineteenth century that opened our eyes to the possibility of a 'bio-archaeology' in the first place. Just five years before Charles Darwin published his ground-breaking work on the dynamics of change in the living world, the Swiss lake-edge villages revealed a frozen episode of that change. Exceptionally low lake levels provided an opportunity for the commune of Meilen on Lake Zurich to build a harbour. Their construction trenches revealed ancient timber piles, the first of a whole series of dwellings to come to light, bordering the Alpine lakes from 3,000 to 6,000 years ago. In amongst the piles were finds of many kinds, including some of the first ancient plant foods ever encountered. With the new ideas that Darwin was about to bring to the world of science, the preserved hazelnuts, dried apples, spices, and grain crops could soon be analysed for marks of evolutionary change and 'domestication'.[1]

In the last few years a drop in water level has similarly affected the shores of the Lake Kinneret (the Sea of Galilee) in Israel. This time, the drop revealed an episode of food-sharing over four times as old as those around the Swiss Lakes.

Lake Kinneret's shores have changed a great deal over the 23,000 years since the meal portrayed above. The substantial fluctuations in climate that could be detected from the Greenland ice sheet, and from the pollen within the Abric Romaní rock shelter, had joined forces with the 'tectonic' movements of the earth's crust. These are the periodic heaving processes, that over tens of millions of years can build mountains and shift continents, and over thousands of years tilt and crack the earth and radically reorganize the pattern of rivers and lakes across the landscape. Such turbulent reorganization has left many scars across the landscape, in the form of dry lake beds and empty river channels, and deep gullies cut in just a few thousand years following the changing course of drainage.

Today, the Lake Kinneret (the Sea of Galilee) sits at the northern end of a gigantic tectonic scar across the earth's crust, the Rift Valley, which in turn connects them to the ancestral habitat of early humans in East Africa. It was this valley along which humans spread northward out of Africa, and it has remained an axis of migration, on a shorter, seasonal timescale, for many species ever since. In the millennia before the meal narrated above, the topography and drainage had substantially changed. There had been a much larger lake to the south of the site, and a river running not far from the actual site of the meal. At the time of the meal, Lake Kinneret was a smaller body of water. Later climatic and tectonic fluctuations have changed all that again, building the modern Jordan River to the south, and conveniently sealing the last episode of the ancient encampment under a protective coating of lake muds. Over the last decade, that encampment has been exposed once again, by a drop in water level and the work of the archaeologist's trowel.[2]

This drop in water revealed an expanse of light-coloured mud. Strolling along the water's edge, a local man noticed some dark stains on the surface of that mud. His report to the authorities instigated the excavations. Beneath those stains, their trowels revealed among the clearest evidence of Palaeolithic huts that we have, with bedding, food debris, and the bases of the branch superstructure found in place. Outside those huts a series of hearths was found, including one substantial cluster of overlapping hearths greater in size than the huts themselves. These hearths spread out north and south parallel to the lake's edge. On the east, towards the water's edge, a linear dump ran alongside the settlement. A few metres to the west, an individual lies buried, the old man featured in the above narrative.

He died aged around 40 years old after a fairly active life. That activity was revealed by the muscular attachments on the bones, which also showed various signs of mild disability, perhaps brought about by age and a hard life. That hard life had given his whole body a notable asymmetry, the more pronounced musculature evident on his right-hand side suggesting much experience of spear-throwing, or some similar physical activity. His shallow grave contained a small number of artefacts, such as the hammerstone placed between his knees. Behind his head was a gazelle bone, deliberately incised with a series of parallel marks. In terms of his biological identity, unlike the diners of previous chapters, there is no physical reason to suggest any significant difference from ourselves. He was anatomically a modern human, a member of *Homo sapiens sapiens.*[3]

Like so many features of the settlement, his grave follows the north–south alignment which also traced the migratory path of many of their prey, but his head was turned in a different direction. The front of his skull was pointed towards the east, allowing him to face the epicentre of human gathering, the largest hearth. Perhaps as subsequent generations gathered around the hearths for their meals, they included him, and other ancestors, among the diners. As with countless meals since among our own species, they would be telling stories over their food and drink, stories woven around the ancestors. Oral tradition would extend their collective consciousness to a time-span of generations, crossing centuries. Just as the growth of language and storytelling was stretching that social consciousness over longer timescales, the physical and biological environment was changing over ever shorter timescales. By now, the major climatic oscillations between warm and cool episodes had accelerated to a cycle of a thousand years, a mere geological moment, but still a human eternity, or perhaps not. Even within a single lifetime, warm–cool fluctuations that spanned a thousand years would leave their mark in an individual human memory. An old person would remember trees growing in a different place in their childhood, and birds migrating at different times, and different fish flourishing in the waters. Twenty to thirty thousand years ago, when planetary phenomena were accelerating climate change to a millennial cycle, so the rich storytelling of modern humans was extending collective memory beyond individual lifetimes and centuries. The two timescales were converging. It may well be that storytelling, and the conveyance of information across space and time, were key in human adaptation to this changing world. But to explore that more closely, let us focus upon the remains of meals from the Ohalo bank.[4]

Around the hearth

On either side of the largest hearth the archaeologists found a series of filled depressions, 3–4½ metres across, and bordered by a black line in the sediment, several centimetres thick. Careful sampling revealed that these black stripes resulted from charred plant material, some of it very finely fragmented. Under optical and scanning electron microscopes, this material was recognizable as burnt grass bedding, and burnt wood for the construction of an interwoven superstructure, made up of branches of tamarisk, pistacia, and oak. Inside, the shallow depressions contained the rich remains of past activities within what were perhaps the earliest known brushwood huts in the world.[5]

Elsewhere, there were other hearths across the site, and on the far side of the huts and hearths, a linear dump of some kind, also aligned north–south. Thanks to the conditions of preservation, and to the detailed research of archaeologists and scientists working on the project, this site conserves perhaps the richest record of the early meals of our own species.

Even bearing in mind our poor knowledge of plant foods among earlier humans, the Ohalo foods seem strikingly diverse in a number of ways. First, there seem to be an extensive gathering of hard seeds, in particular grass seeds and acorns. Second, there is a substantial presence of both birds and fishes among their prey. Taken together with the bones of large and small mammals, the Ohalo community was clearly making quite exhaustive use of each and every component of the landscape, from the arid open slopes grazed by gazelle and wild goat, to the parkland steppe from which both the grass seeds and acorns were taken, and the richer riverbanks, sources of herbs, fruits, wild boar, and wild cow. But

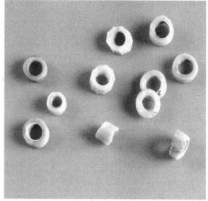

12. Finds from Ohalo II on the Sea of Galilee: a fragment of burnt, twisted fibre; Mediterranean Dentalium shells, finely cut into 1–2 mm slices for use as beads; charred grains of wild barley; fish vertebrae.

even beyond this land surface, the inhabitants made extensive use of the waters and sky on a scale unprecedented in earlier species of human. The list of food plants and animals ranges widely, with around twenty species of large and small mammals, sixteen families of birds, and several types of fish. Alongside these were more than 140 taxa of fruit and nut, seed and pulse. In addition there were plants gathered for craft, structural and medicinal use, and one of the craft activities has a fundamental importance to the food humans consume.[6]

The activity that made this massive expansion in food range possible has left its trace in one of the huts. In amongst the food remains were found three small fragments of charred fibre, each just a few millimetres long, testament to one of the fundamental differences between modern humans and other humans. These diminutive fragments of fibre provide evidence for an entirely new technology of food acquisition, one that on the surface appeared more benign than the spears and arrows and razor-sharp edges of the bloody hunt, yet would prove far more devastating in ecological terms. That novel technology was weaving.

Spinning a yarn

I use 'weaving' in a broad sense, to encompass a range of procedures, including spinning and basketry, in which combinations of interleaving and twisting transform strips of fibrous plant tissue into a wide variety of compound structures. The fibrous tissue that may be thus woven is very varied. The materials most easily available to the first weavers may have been reeds, rushes, and the fibrous innards of larger plants. Their stone blades were clearly well suited to splitting inner wood into thin slivers, and some blades display wear patterns consistent with woodworking. Some modern fibres require other processes of transformation, such as soaking or 'retting'. If the Ohalo community were aware of such possibilities they could also have woven fibres from a range of herbs around the site. In terms of the food quest alone, these technologies have allowed baskets to be made for harvesting seeds, fruits, nuts, and herbs. They also opened the way for the production of a whole array of lines, nets, weirs, and traps, with which to ensnare fish, birds, and small mammals. The same brushwood hut from which the three fibre fragments were recovered also contained a doubly notched basalt rock, one of a series of doubly notched pebbles from the site, interpreted as net-sinkers. The archaeologists suggest that these sinkers anchored a net in the shallow waters in which to trap fish of all kinds. Thousands of years earlier, the technology of fire had widened human usage of plant foods, so the technology of weaving now both extended the possibilities of plant gathering, and transformed human use of the waters and the skies as sources of food and materials.[7]

Weaving may have only been feasible in the context of the modern human mind. In the preceding chapters we have explored how the apparent straitjacket in earlier tool design might indicate that early human mentalities were qualitatively different from our own. Their thoughts were somehow compartmentalized such that boundaries were rarely breached. We now imagine that early human awareness of natural history was extensive; it had to be for them to move through such contrasting and challenging environments. But it was only with modern humans that we see the materials of natural history, such as bone and antler, being fashioned into complicated forms. The production of woven plant tissue may similarly depend upon the fluid interconnections of the modern mind.

Actual fragments of textile are rare in sites as old as these, but their impressions in clay are known from a number of sites across Europe and stretching back over 28,000 years, for example around the hearths buried beneath the Moravian sediments and discussed in the opening chapter. All these impressions are on small fragments, but when studied closely under a microscope reveal the variety of twisting and weaving techniques available to our ancestors, and perhaps particularly to the women.

One particular form of evidence for weaving is the so-called 'Venus figurine', recovered from those Moravian hills and elsewhere. A number of these small human models exist; some were sculpted naked, others to indicate woven headgear, belts, and bandeaux. A close inspection of these sculpted representations of weaving patterns reveals that the same care and intimate attention to detail applied to the weaving and to the representation of primary and secondary sexual characteristics on these modelled women. That might suggest that the women around the campfire were both the modellers and the weavers.[8]

Inside: an appropriate order of things

While we cannot probe directly into the ancient mind itself, we can see how conscious thought translated into action, and the creation of site plans and artefacts that we can actually scrutinize, thousands of years later, for example, in the arrangement of the early human world around the hearth. Those hearths may be rich in the debris of past meals, and give the initial impression of a disordered assembly of food refuse, but much closer scrutiny reveals a great deal of order. For example, some elements of food never reached the Ohalo hearths.

Consider the fish scales, or at least their absence. These are found on other archaeological sites, and indeed can provide a rich source of information about fish size and population structure. We would expect them to survive in these excellent preserving conditions, but they are absent. We must assume that the initial cleaning of the fish took place at the water's edge. The mammal bones also present a partial picture. From the cut-marks on the bones, we can infer that the major initial butchery, presumably including the release of blood, was conducted away from the hearths. Absences from the hearth of other elements of a potential diet are easy to overlook, because we also exclude them ourselves. These include insects, which could have provided a significant source of nutrition, and can survive reasonably well in lake deposits, but are not found here. A further dietary product that seems absent is faeces, presumably deposited beyond the settlement area. The absences give some indication of how space was ordered around the hearth. A list of substances kept away from the hearth emerges. It includes blood, faeces, insects, and fish entrails, substances that we too might wish to keep away from our dinner tables. In fact, because we would avoid the same things, we tend not to stop and ask why. Anthropologists of food who have asked why have come up with two kinds of explanations. Let us return to the seminal ideas of two key anthropologists introduced in the opening chapter, the 'biologically' inclined Marvin Harris, and the 'socially' inclined Mary Douglas.

The style of approach that Harris has taken to feeding behaviour would tend to emphasize hygiene and biological necessity; these materials may harbour disease and infection, and indeed this is an argument with significant evidence in its favour. Yet the relationship is approximate; there is no reason to think of insect meat as a general category to be any more or less risky than mammal meat. The disgust we would feel at being served a dish of insects is probably surpassed by what we would experience if confronted by a plate of fresh faeces, yet neither need be as great as risk to our health as a plate of meat that is beyond its best. The relation with biological hygiene is there, but is approximate. Like modern hygiene, ancient hygiene persisted because it was consistent with the needs of biological survival, and indeed contributed to meeting those needs. A reflection on our own feelings of relative repulsion towards, for example, insects, faeces, and stale meat, suggest that this is not, however, the whole story. They may have as much, or more, to do with social hygiene.

Mary Douglas was primarily interested in social hygiene. She explored its importance in ordering, placing, and excluding things and persons around the meal table and beyond, and in the process, coming to terms with the complex and mutable world around us, and creating within it an appropriate and sustainable order of things. Her central thesis was that in gathering together to share food in this intense, face-to-face interaction characteristic of modern humans, categories need to be clear and unambiguous. At Ohalo the social status of diners needs to be clearly indicated, for instance by the necklaces whose beads have occasionally fallen around the hearths, a status presumably mirrored in the less durable face make-up and clothing. Foods need to be recognizable and discrete and placed in a certain way, within spaces organized in a particular manner. Beyond the hearths and the dining circles lie other elements of categorization and order, and further away still, the unpredictable and ever-changing world of disorder. What is impure, transitional, or dangerous in the human body, such as death, sex, bodily fluids, and excreta, and what is impure, transitional, or dangerous in foods, such as blood, entrails, and ambiguously formed creatures, are relegated to an outer world, which is itself characterized by constant change and danger. The hearth is a place of order in which categories are clear and unchanging.[9]

Around the time Mary Douglas was formulating these ideas, Lévi-Strauss had been developing his much bolder model of food preparation, touched upon in the context of the Neanderthal hearths at Abric Romaní. In doing so, he hoped to discover an underlying structure of food preparation and sharing. If meals could be regarded as a series of narratives, each with its own storyline and sequence of episodes, then Lévi-Strauss wanted to identify the shared 'grammar' of those narratives, the underlying rules of construction they shared in common, universal grammar of the meal. His speculative grammar is expressed in the context of a culinary landscape. At the hearth or 'heart' of that landscape is an *endocuisine* or 'inside cooking' controlled by women, and feeding the immediate family gathered around. Recurrent themes of *endocuisine* include concavity, as for example in the concave cooking pot, containment, as in the safety of the protected home, and economy, in as the optimal of gathered and stored ingredients. The tempo of this *endocuisine* may be slow, seemingly timeless, and the mode of cooking is also slow, typically a stockpot gently simmering over a slow-burning fire that never extinguishes.

Outside the cosy and secure hearth lies the world of men, strangers, danger, and transition. In this part of the culinary landscape, men engage in the more primal practice of *exocuisine* or 'outside cooking', of exposing unenclosed food to the fire. Here they carve meat from the roast and offer it to strangers (guests). Recurrent themes of *exocuisine* are convexity, as in the joints of meat exposed to the fire and profligacy, the consumption and disposal of seemingly excessive quantities of food and drink. Such a culinary landscape may be further elaborated by drawing from Mary Douglas's ideas and cross-cultural observations. Drinks, narcotics, and fermentation perhaps belong somewhere on the outside, with the *exocuisine* and interaction with strangers/guests. Fermentation is a transitional state, and Douglas contrasted the secure certainties immediately around the hearth, with uncertainty and transition on the outside, where narcotics and fermented products may be joined by all manner of things connected to transition and danger, blood, death, sex, semen, insects, animals with the wrong hooves, fish with whiskers, and so on.[10]

Such a culinary landscape is more of a mind game, full of context-specific assumptions, a tool for thinking about the social logic of meals, rather than anything approaching a precise social grammar, and Lévi-Strauss himself presented it very much as a work in progress. Nonetheless, it does stimulate a few reflections upon, and indeed have resonances with, the shape of the meal we can reconstruct from the Ohalo bank. Here too, there is permanence, intimacy, and order close to the hearth, though the cooking containers are somewhere between speculative and non-existent. Death is not relegated to a far place, but, perhaps, blood, fish entrails, and faeces are.

Moving away from the large Ohalo hearth, we can certainly see fixity in the use of space, particularly by considering the location and contents of the different brushwood huts on either side of the hearth. In terms of location, these huts have a clear position in the world. Each hut lasted more than one generation of rebuilding. Careful excavation has revealed that one hut was periodically burnt down, but then re-erected on the same spot. Looking at the fixed location and arrangement of these huts, our immediate assumption would be that these are the sleeping quarters of subsections of the Ohalo community, and indeed, their organic contents include grass bedding. In addition to that, however, they were used for the storage and preparation of food. In one hut, for example, there is a stone 'anvil', from the fine crevices of which were prised the minute granules of starch from the grass seeds pulverized on the stone surface. If the food remains from these huts resulted from the needs of the different occupants, we would expect a fair bit of repetition between huts, corresponding to the full seasonal cycle of foods. Yet there are clear differences in the contents of different huts, in the deposition of plants, fish, mammals, and birds, and the artefacts associated with their treatment. The separate huts had distinct roles in the order of the settlement. Some were used for the processing of birds, others for the storage of acorns and dried fish. Some were for seed harvests from the northern slopes, another for plants gathered from the saline strip to the south. Materials were excluded from or admitted to the settlement area, where their storage, processing, and consumption are spatially ordered. I have speculated that the old man had some role in maintaining this order: checking things were in the right place and instructing younger members in their society's rules of purity and danger. My slender basis for elevating him to this status was the idea that the gazelle bone placed behind his head may have served as a lunar calendar. Such an implement would signify the ordering of the heavens above.[11]

The word 'ordering' may seem a little odd here; the heavens clearly order themselves, with little assistance from the occupants of our tiny planet, but in all human classifications of the world there is an element of putting nature in order, arranging it for our actions. Looking out from the hearth, the point of clarity and certainty, towards the outer world of flux and danger, which is nevertheless the source of food and sustenance, the skies at least would have offered a dependable regularity, and we have reason to suppose they recognized patterns in the skies, and their relationship with the seasonal availability of foods. Tying the food quest in with the changing night sky imposed an order to the human ecosystem, even when the unstable food web was deviating from the familiar pattern.

Within an earlier model of human progress, it was assumed this would not be the case, that knowledge of the night sky was something that was acquired, through the course of civilization, technology, and science. Far more recent hunter-gatherers than these were presumed to live in ignorance of such complexities of pattern. It was only quite recently that some attempt has been made to collate what such societies do know about the night sky. It transpires that if we really want to find a community that had difficulty finding, for example, Plaiades and the Dog Star in the sky, then we might have some difficulty looking outside the Western world. The best place to look was at home, amongst urban communities at the heart of civilization, but blinded at night by street lights.[12]

Indeed, those same modern urban communities may be a good place to look for people who can recognize less than a hundred plant species, another attribute once assumed to pertain to the 'primitive'. The expanding field of ethnobiology has increasingly challenged that. It is clear that communities remote from Western civilization have rich and complex taxonomies of nature.

In an ideal world, everything would happen with certainty and order to match that which they had created around the hearth. Just as the diners had a particular place in the social group, so the foods were cleaned, prepared, and arranged in the same way. Each type of bird would migrate from the north at a predictable time of year, and after a given number of months return from the south. The young gazelle would be easy prey in a certain season, and the grasses ripen in another season, and so on. All these certain patterns would match the equally certain changes in the night sky. In the real world, the shape of these cycles was in place, but the certainty less so.

In previous chapters we have repeatedly seen how the physical environment was in a state of long-term flux. The ecosystems it contained would similarly be shifting, populations would boom and bust, and on the biographical timescale, communities would need constantly to steer their way past famine and hardship, to ensure there were not days, weeks, or seasons without food. Their storytelling could relate the regularities of the ideal world, but could it connect with its uncertain changes in direction in such a way that would assist in the food quest?

To explore this in a society that is remote from the Western scientific world, the anthropologist Roy Rappaport has over a number of years given close thought to the ecological world of a community of New Guinea Highlanders called the Tsembaga Maring. The Maring had been engaging with a fast-changing world, the changes in their case propelled by the encroachment of global civilization and colonial control, but through an enduring approach to the classification and ordering of the world. Rappaport takes us through two dimensions in which that world was ordered, their approach to understanding and explanation, and their sequence of ritual practices within and across the years.[13]

He recorded several levels at which explanation and understanding worked. First there was the timeless world of sacred spirits. Next there was the cosmology connecting those spirits to tangible elements in the world. This in turn framed the next level of rules and restrictions of purity and danger that were major forces in the community's daily life. At another level, there were signals coming from the outside world requiring a response, for example a new offering of pigs to the spirits, and finally, there were the domains of the world to which all these explanations and understandings pertained.[14]

Rappaport, like many Western observers, distinguishes between two world-views in his anthropology. One is the realized world of the community under study, the 'emic' world, as it is sometimes known, of spirits, myths, and other stories. The other is the operational world, or 'etic' world, of scientific 'reality', explaining the biological processes actually taking place. However, some would argue that the scientific paradigm is just another emic view, taken as seriously in the modern Western world as other emic views are taken in their own societies. It is interesting to note how similar our scientific world-view is in structure to what Rappaport and Douglas have observed among very different societies. Take, for example, Rappaport's hierarchy of understanding. In the position of the spirits, science too has its own enduring unquestionable and untestable truths, for example that simple explanations are superior to complex ones, and general explanations are superior to contingent ones. At a second level, these truths connect with tangible data from our cosmologies, and from these flow principles of action and restriction in our daily practice. As in the Maring world, science also has its own procedures for responding to new data from the outside world, and fine tuning or revising its cosmology accordingly. Also like the Maring world, science has domains, such as 'ecology' to which these various themes apply, domains that can be subdivided, classified, and put in appropriate order.

The hierarchy of understanding that Rappaport observed among the Tsembaga Maring simultaneously allowed timeless truths, 'it has always been thus', and contingent action, 'quick change of plan needed', to coexist. This is how the communities, which had incidentally within living memory witnessed the spread of metal technology and new crops such as sweet potato and maize, changes of a truly radical economic nature, nevertheless seemed to Rappaport to be embedded in the timelessness of ancient rituals and social practices. Endurance and flexibility, timelessness and impermanence, sacred and profane, could be brought together within a single ambiguous narrative, stories about nature, culture, ancestors, and spirits that could be retold and reinterpreted to map freshly upon the perceived world and guide ecological action in the food quest.

His analysis of a very different modern society allows us to look back at our own society .to see a similar hierarchical structure in our own scientific world-view. That too is grounded in a series of untestable premisses that connect through evidence to our cosmology. We too have daily rules of practice and restrictions of behaviour that connect to that cosmology, and ways of responding to new evidence to fine tune, or even redraft it. We also classify the world according to various domains, to which the other levels of understanding apply.

At Ohalo, we can pick up fragments of their levels of understanding and making sense of the world, particularly in the rules and restrictions that govern what can come close to the hearth and what is kept away. Moreover, the domains of the world are evident from the way gathered food is organized within different huts and spaces. A careful comparison of the plant remains from two of the huts to the north of the largest hearth area revealed that harvests from different ecological zones were brought separately and stored and processed in different huts. Similarly the treatment and preparation of birds and fishes displayed distinctive spatial patterns. The Ohalo food web was categorized, partitioned, and organized into distinct compartments.[15]

Mary Douglas had observed that this manner of ordering and classification, at the same time as serving as a metaphor for larger, external worlds, sprang from intimate social gathering, and ultimately from the metaphor of the human body, the one thing we all share. Just as, within the Christian world, the body of Christ at the Last Supper, and on the cross, lent its form and essence to the structure of the communion meal and the physical church, so she observed the human body serving as metaphor for symbolic behaviour and structured action in other societies. The body, its different components, entrances, and exits could be classified, ordered, and delineated in a way that mapped onto how the shared meal was also classified, ordered, and delineated. The body, the meal, the hearth, and the house, then served as a model of how to order the outside world into compartments, categories, entrances, and exits.[16]

The same series of metaphors is put to work within Western science and our ecological study of the natural world. A social gathering of people is repeatedly employed as a metaphor for the structure of the external world of nature. That science of ecology organizes nature into 'communities', 'alliances', 'guilds', and understands their relationships in terms of 'symbiosis' (living together) and 'commensalism' (eating at the same table). Inside connects to outside through the manner in which we impose order on the world. The word 'ecology' itself literally means the 'logic of the household'. Let us turn to that logic, to see what it might reveal about the food quest on the Ohalo bank.[17]

Outside: nature's household logic

Ecology revolves around a series of models, assembled by the early twentieth-century pioneers of the new science, people like Frederick Clements, who developed the idea of plant 'succession' from his observations of the American prairie, and populated his plant communities with 'food chains' linking plants and animals together through their feeding patterns. These two models joined with a third to form the analytical framework of the new science of ecology. That third model was the 'geochemical cycle', the route of elements, such as carbon, oxygen, nitrogen, through food chains, soils, waters, and the air. These three models together constituted a ledger of materials (cycles), and energy (food chain), and a forward projection (succession) through which ecology the dynamics of its household could be understood. A scatter of food debris alone may be rich in qualitative detail, but does not quite get us as close as we would like to the ecological patterns of the past. They are greatly enhanced by adding another set of data, the evidence of isotopes.

'Isotopes' are forms of the same element that differ in weight. Each of the commonest elements in food has more than one stable isotope. There are light and heavy forms of carbon, nitrogen, and oxygen, for example. As elements move through the nutrient cycle, and calories move through the food chain, these light and heavy isotopes move in slightly different ways. If they get trapped, for example in the skeletons of the feeder, they may retain some record of how that feeder is placed within the ecosystem.

That, incidentally, is how the oxygen isotope 'thermometer', introduced in Chapter 3, works. The precise operation of the oxygen cycle, through biosphere, sea, and air, is sensitive to temperature. That is why an oxygen isotope balance, trapped in the body of a marine micro-organism, serves as a fossil record of past temperatures. Isotopes of nitrogen also reflect movement through food chains. By analysing the nitrogen isotope balance within a human or animal bone, we can place them at particular positions within that chain, their so-called 'trophic' position. This is how it works. Food consumption and digestion involve a fair amount of transformation between solid, liquid, and gaseous states. At each of these changes of state, or indeed any change in mobility at the molecular level, the distribution of light and heavy isotopes may also change. So, when we consume more protein than our bodies can handle, the protein is broken down and the nitrogenous breakdown products are excreted in liquid form, as urine. This will differentially remove the lighter nitrogen isotope, enhancing the level of heavier isotope remaining within the body. In other words, a combination of digestion and urination leads to an accumulation of heavier nitrogen isotopes in the growing body. We can follow that logic beyond the food chain to the larger cycles of carbon and nitrogen through land, river, sea, and air. These cycles incorporate repeated changes of state between solid, liquid, and gas, and changes of mobility within them, all with consequences for the differential movement of heavy and light isotopes. Something similar can be attempted with different elements that occur in small traces in bones, but which also accumulate in different ways in different parts of the food web. There are many other factors and variables the analyst needs to take into account, but if we manage to reach an understanding of these, we can use combinations of trace elements and isotope analysis to identify the predominant trophic positions of past humans, and indeed other species, within their food web. Moreover, we can distinguish patterns typical of aquatic food chains, which tend to be longer than terrestrial chains, and can recognize marine food chains through a characteristic fractionation of carbon. Drawing these indicators together, we can contrast modern humans, from the time of the Ohalo encampment, with their early human predecessors.[18]

In a recent study nine modern humans were sampled from sites in Russia, the Czech Republic, and Britain dating to between 26,000 and

20,000 years old, broadly contemporary with the encampment at the Ohalo bank. Five Neanderthals were sampled from sites in France, Belgium, and Croatia, dating to between 130,000 and 28,000 years ago. Taking the carbon and nitrogen data together, the isotope balance in the Neanderthal bones is similar to what has also been recorded in the wolves, cats, and hyenas. The five Neanderthals could be placed in their food chain at the trophic position of carnivores, terrestrial meat dominating their diet. No surprise given the evidence of animal bones, even though it does seem that Neanderthals were extending their range in comparison with the earliest humans. That extension of range is, however, much more evident in the modern human bones. The nitrogen balance has been shifted to a level that could be correlated with the high trophic position of fish. Again a result that resonates with the presence of fish bones at sites like Ohalo, but the value of the isotopes is that they provide a sense of scale. Fish were not just present in the modern human diet, they were significant resources. Similarly, seed and pods may have been part of the Neanderthal diet, but as a small complement to the principal diet of meat. The shift between the two corresponds to what has been describes as a 'broad spectrum revolution' in the human diet, a concept developed before the Ohalo site displayed its immense breadth in detail.[19]

Bringing all the evidence together, we can think of the rich Ohalo food web as a series of compartments. Those separate compartments were channelled to the Ohalo hearth through the distinct brushwood huts from different sections of the landscape, and by reference to the changing skies from different seasons in the year. Each channel through each ecological compartment no doubt involved its own technologies, of which we get a glimpse. The glimpses we do catch expose techniques that allow an entirely new engagement with nature in the course of the food quest. To understand how the Ohalo food quest may have engaged with the world at larger scales of space and time, we need to explore the dynamics of that novel, complex food web.

The multi-track food web of modern humans

The site yielded up not just a few fragments of woven net, and a series of stone net-sinkers, but also the bones of a wide range of fish and birds.

The majority of the caught fish were small, between 15 and 25 centimetres long. From these it is clear that the mesh size of their nets was also small, trapping old fish and young, of all species in the water. The bird cull is also extensive and seemingly indiscriminate. Moreover it comprises species at a variety of trophic levels, including grain feeders, fish feeders, omnivores, and even birds of prey. Like other humans, our own species is omnivorous, but the technologies of weaving and netting have extended and diversified the range of that omnivory, expecially within the novel feeding territories of the waters and the skies. That in itself may have implications for the stability of the food web of which they were part.

In the contemporary biosphere, there are over 100 well-documented food webs, in which each of the feeding links has been charted, and the entire web mapped, and subjected to ecological analysis. One thing that analysis has revealed is that omnivory plays only a modest role in these recorded food webs; omnivores tend to be isolated within webs made up primarily of more specific feeders.[20] This is one of a number of features demonstrating that these webs tend not to be 'overconnected', that is, criss-crossed with too many feeding connections. To explain this in more detail, let us imagine, for example, a rather absurd food web, composed only of humans, wolves, ravens, and berries, in which the first three customarily eat all other species in the web. That would be a food web in which the 'connectance' was 100 per cent, in other words, all potential connections between species correspond to actual feeding relationships. In the case of food webs in the real world, the measured connectance is considerably lower, often falling below 20 per cent. Higher than such figures and it seems the webs become unstable. This is the context in which omnivory plays only a modest role. It would seem that the behaviour of our own omnivorous species, which consumes significant quantities of food from many trophic levels, some of those food species themselves omnivorous, is perennially in danger of destabilizing the web of which we are part.[21]

The sources for that instability may be found through the mathematical modelling of feeding relationships that a number of ecologists have explored. It has long been established that such a model, even of a very simple feeding relationship, could be made to move away from equilibrium, to oscillation, and then to chaos.[22] If we connect a series of feeding relationships to each other, the network they form has an even greater tendency towards disequilibrium, as perturbations in one part of the network are freely communicated to others, which may themselves be near the margins of equilibrium. That is the 'castle of cards' effect that can throw species, especially those near the apex of the food web, into chaotic fluctuations, the kind of fluctuations that were recorded in detail in populations of Canadian lynx.[23] Nature tends to favour webs in which the connections are not too plentiful, loose webs in which perturbations do not amplify too easily across the entire food web. The inventiveness of the versatile modern human mind has always had the capacity to subvert that natural logic, and lead to excessive connectance within its food webs. In recent epochs, that is an unsurprising and familiar eventuality. Even in the earliest high-quality record of the modern human food quest, a capacity that may be in evidence from early records of the modern human food quest, some elements of that capacity are already in view.

A wide-ranging, intensive cull is indicated by the remains of fish and birds. It may also be inferred on land where, once again, the technology of weaving is implicated. Nets, traps, baskets, and strings remain inconspicuous in direct terms—just a few tiny fragments of cord or cord impression—but highly conspicuous in terms of their impact on the food web. At the outset of the evolution of early humans, blades and stones expanded the size of herbivore upon which earlier humans could feed. While evidence of plant diet remains fragmentary, isotope analysis on the European Neanderthals conforms with a wider picture from early humans derived from the trace elements in their bones. Such data as exists for early human bone each give strong carnivorous signals, placing early humans in their food web above large grazing animals. The weaving of sticks, stems, and fibres has changed everything for the Ohalo people, scattering them across a number of trophic positions. On the arid, open slopes they were primarily carnivores, preying on gazelle and wild goat. On the parkland steppe on the valley slopes, they occupy two levels in the food chain, feeding herbivorously on herbaceous seeds, acorns, and a variety of fruits and nuts, and carnivorously on wild cow, deer, and boar. At the water's edge, their position is more complex still. Among the fish and birds they capture and eat are omnivores, herbivores, carnivores, and top carnivores. The indiscriminate capture of prey across a number of trophic levels consequently enhances the number of cross-links in each compartment of the food web.

The overall 'depth' of the food web, in other words the length of the component feeding chains, also has implications for stability. In nature, feeding chains are not that long, especially on dry land. The simplest shallow ecosystems, such as grasslands and tundra, may just have three levels, primary producer, herbivore, and carnivore. Deep, woodland ecosystems may have more 'top carnivores' at the fourth level, and aquatic ecosystems may have one or two levels more. The predominant position of humans at Ohalo is in the second position (grass seeds and acorns), third position (gazelle), and fourth position (grebe), but some chains are longer still. If the recovered eagle bones indicate that its meat was among the meal, the eagle may in turn have eaten a small bird, say a coot, that fed on frogs amongst other things. The frogs in turn would have fed on insects, feeding on algae. That feeding chain has six links, and more or less marks the outer limit in chain length.

So within particular compartments of the human food web, there may have been a significant tendency towards instability, arising from trends that weaving and netting technologies facilitated towards extensive cull across a range of trophic levels, the humans' own omnivory combining with the omnivory of a number of species they eat. This, at a time when the climate, the physical landscape, and the ecosystems within it, were all in a state of flux would suggest that occasional food web collapses and prey scarcities may not have been unusual. How did such food webs persist?[24]

The first point to make is that they did not persist indefinitely—not at least in any particular place. The Ohalo community were by the shores of the lake for a number of generations; this much can be inferred from the rebuilding of the brush huts and the burial of the old man. However, much Palaeolithic data derives from sites that are far more transitory, and we usually do not know what happened to any of the communities whose traces in the archaeological record came to a close. Our species, nonetheless, has expanded and persisted, and persisted through diverse and widespread exploitation of the land, waters, and skies. Ohalo is not alone in displaying a very diverse food web. It is simply one of the best-documented sites of a whole series across the world that also display such a range. The recurrence of such sites during the millennia following the date of Ohalo has given rise to the concept of the 'broad spectrum revolution' in the quest for food mentioned earlier. There are various features that increase the chances that such food webs will persist, even in the context of wider environmental flux.

On the basis of modelling food webs mathematically, they would appear to grow in stability if they are partitioned, if barriers, across which perturbations are hindered from passing, are placed between different compartments of the web.[25] At Ohalo, such barriers may arise from the basic separation of regional and topographic units, a separation which is emphasized by the division of foods between the different brushwood huts.

In practice, the acorn harvest and the fish supply may each collapse in certain years. However, the ecological separation of their sources may lower the chances of their collapse in the same year—an obvious example, but one which may be applied to subdivision within the dry land or the waters. This compartmentation through space, and also across time, can be further enhanced to increasing the sheer breadth of the food web, an enhancement for which language and mobility are both key. By continually enlarging the range of ecosystems, the food web may be broadened to encompass different, relatively isolated compartments, the collapse of any one compartment having a diminished impact in the viability of the population at the apex of the food web. At their heart is the conversational circle around the sharing of food, that remarkable depository of information and engine of its transfer, which allows the food web to spread across space and time.

The demise of the Palaeolithic diet: a wrong turn in human history?

In addition to potential problems with ecological stability and resilience, does this novel human diet also bring problems of a nutritional kind? This has been the contention of a number of dieticians since the nineteenth century, including Dr Robert Atkins, whose advocacy of a high meat and fat consumption is still hotly debated. The general contention is that many foods in the modern human diet, including the world's top three food species in terms of output, wheat, rice, and maize, are not foods to which the human digestive system is adapted. These three are all grass seeds, and grass seeds are among the new foods captured in the Ohalo nets and baskets.[26] The list of dietary and disease problems that some would claim arise from diverting so radically from our Palaeolithic diet, dominated by animal flesh and fat, is long. The much-contested list includes micronutrient deficiency, gastro-intestinal and skin disorders, multiple sclerosis, Parkinson's disease, schizophrenia, and autism.[27]

Most advocates of a 'Palaeolithic diet' were writing at a time when the beginnings of agriculture seemed to be the point when seeds, and then other 'unnatural' foods first appeared in the diet, but now the Ohalo evidence has more than doubled their antiquity. That is still a very short period of evolutionary time for an unaccustomed feeder to adapt effectively to the battalion of chemical weaponry with which evolution has equipped plants to protect from predation of their cherished offspring, the seeds. Nonetheless, it is clear that evolution can progress on that short timescale; we have, for example, adapted partially to consumption of that other unusual foodstuff of modern nutrition, the milk of domestic animals.[28]

It is also the case that, since the time of weaving, nets, and baskets, and conversation around the hearth while sharing novel and unusual foods, the human species has, whatever the ecological and nutritional problems, expanded across the globe. Conversation and storytelling allow journeys to be described, remembered, and planned anew, journeys across new terrains with ideas for gathering new resources. They allow knowledge of new resources to be conserved and passed on. Quite critically, they build an understanding of the world not simply over large expanses of space, but also large stretches of time. Any one culture's understanding of the texture of the world through space and time may not easily translate between cultures, but within them serve to guide and inform new exploratory journeys into the world of nature. Early humans certainly expanded their range, and gradually reached some latitudes quite different than those of their evolutionary origin. However, both the pace and the scale of modern human movement across the latitudes were of different orders of magnitude.

By the time the necklace of fish bones had shed its beads in the Abric Romaní rock shelter, modern humans were not only in the Iberian peninsular, they were also in the Arctic Circle. A few thousand years earlier, the ancestors of both were still in the Rift Valley. The powers of wide-ranging, conversational language had propelled modern human action onto a quite novel range of food quests. With the conspicuously enduring, yet infinitely varied narratives of the storytelling sage, communities could surf the turbulent waves of environmental change through the web of fragile threads their novel strategies of food acquisition had forged. In this transformed relationship with nature, movement from one ecosystem to another, and the change from one food acquisition practice to another were not escape route options, they had become a core feature of the evolutionary strategy.

13. View of the sunken building and surrounding ancillary structures, exposed during excavations at Jerf-el-Ahmar.

6

AMONG STRANGERS

Jerf-el-Ahmar, Euphrates valley, Syria, 11,000 years ago

The afternoon sun dropped below the horizon, exposing the neighbouring hills to the pink light of dusk. Numerous houses came into view, terraced into each hillside. On the western hill, a group of mudbrick buildings formed an arc interrupted by the aromatic smoke from cooking pits, and clustered around the most impressive building of all. It seemed huge from the outside, it was certainly the biggest in the group, but as he descended into its shady interior, it shrunk to a more familiar size. A familiar size but an unusual form—he had entered a very angular space, angular walls, angular designs upon them. He was more used to gathering in a circle, where he could see everyone's faces, but there were more corners here. You would need to turn back and forth to meet the gaze of each person present, but in any case, attention was drawn straight ahead, to the senior woman, who was seated on a raised dais straight ahead in the most open part of the interior. He had learnt how he should behave as a visitor in one of these community houses. It was to the woman that the gift of shells was offered, brought many miles from the southern sea. These she accepted, and invited her visitor to sit and share food and drink.

Travellers often told disparaging stories about the food from this part of the river valley; it had a reputation for being a little monotonous. Like every community in the region, these people preyed upon the hillside herds, and took seed harvests from the grassy expanses, but they developed likings for particular plants and animals which they would eat again and again, day in, day out. What is more, even though they lived right above the river, the people in these parts did not much care for fish. The travellers that reserved their greatest disdain for the cuisine of the middle river communities were the ones accustomed to a varied diet of tasty fresh fish, for which no amount or variety of grass seeds could substitute. The visitor prepared himself to receive an uncertain meal with due gratitude.

It was not nearly as bad as he anticipated. He had caught the pleasant odour emanating from the cooking pit that was being opened outside the house. He was soon invited to taste the gamey joint of gazelle; with its side dish of almonds and wild pistacia nuts it was delicious. He knew those flavours well. The wild ass they brought next was a speciality of the region. He had also been eating the more bland and doughy ground seed mixes all his life, something you could see from his teeth, which were by now nearly worn back to the gums. But the seed cuisine here in the middle river proved to be quite interesting.

Alongside the familiar starchy mash, he was brought some lightly roasted seed-bearing stems. From time to time, another food was brought in, a dish of hot cracked seeds, and baked lentils. One particular food, the most unusual of all, was a cake with a distinctly spicy flavour. The different grains and seeds were typically prepared separately from one another, such that the visitor could often distinguish the different plants he was eating. He knew enough about these plants to be aware that he was eating seeds from different seasons in the same meals. This year's almonds for example, were not yet ready, but he had noticed last year's, still in store behind one of the partition walls. Indeed, much of the house was given over to storage, which was why the interior felt smaller than the house from the outside.

He had the opportunity later on to catch a glimpse of the source of these unusual foods. Climbing back up into the open, he looked beyond the inevitable cluster of curious eyes to survey the houses around him. In many ways they were far stranger to his eyes than any of the dishes he had tasted. His travels had allowed him to taste many regional cuisines, so many variations on the central themes of game, seeds, fruits, and, in some places at least, fish. Even in this middle river region alone, the actual form of this cuisine varied over quite short distances. The most surprising feature in his experience *of this settlement was not the food, interesting though it was, but the architecture around his meal. In all his travels he had seen nothing quite like it. He had offered his gift of shells, and accepted his food within the enclosing curve of the community house wall, but a curve that was dissected by partition walls. Looking now beyond that house, the entire settlement was chopped up by such partitions; many huts were built only of partitions; they had dispensed completely with the usual curved surround. He wondered what it was like to live within such spaces. Right adjacent to the central house was one such building. He could see straight into one of its small compartments, where a woman was kneeling, hard at work grinding away at the mustard seed to prepare the cake. She was just one among a busy working party of women and men, filling the room, and engaged in grinding, soaking, cooking, and washing, transforming and disguising their favoured seeds to create the unusual cuisine he had tasted, which was far less monotonous than his fellow travellers had conveyed.*

T HE building in his view burnt down around 11,000 years ago. Its daub walls collapsed and in the process captured the episode of food preparation leading up to narrative above. Those falling walls buried and sealed the fragments of food that the fire had charred, in amongst the equipment for its preparation. This small area, less than 8 square metres in extent, from the site of Jerf-el-Ahmar on the left bank of the Syrian Euphrates, provides a glimpse of a new dimension in the sharing of food.

The great Mesopotamian rivers, the Tigris and the Euphrates, like many rivers at this time, were carrying changing loads of water across a changeable landscape. Such was the climatic impermanence of the natural environment. At the same time, human features in the landscape were displaying a new level of permanence. That permanence is manifest in a new kind of site, a settlement mound or 'tell'. These are small artificial hillocks, the accumulation of generations of collapsed daub. A series of these tells can be seen along the rivers and plains of southwest Asia, sometimes quite conspicuous features, visible from afar. At the same time it was a landscape through which there was a considerable amount of human movement, over long distances.

The movement is revealed in some of the finds excavated from such sites, for example the 'tooth shells' of the genus *Dentalium* so favoured for bead-making, gathered from the Red Sea and travelling the full length of the Euphrates. It is revealed with even greater clarity by the finds of shiny blue-black obsidian, a volcanic glass much favoured for blades and other artefacts. Obsidian is a material whose chemistry can quite precisely connect these blades with their geological sources. Some of this obsidian has travelled vast distances across the landscape, such that routes of 'obsidian trade' can be mapped out from central Turkey across south-west Asia. But this landscape of permanence and mobility did not begin within urban societies; we do not imagine a scene of merchants, ports, inns, and taverns. Eleven thousand years ago, the communities along the Euphrates subsisted by hunting wild animals and gathering wild plants, much as they had for thousands of years. They lived in quite small communities, and their lives were relatively simple in material terms. They were now, however, putting down roots, and staying in the same place. In doing so, they were creating a fixed human landscape that enabled a new kind of mobility of travellers, over considerable distances. These new landscapes of permanence and mobility generated new kinds of social encounter, sometimes between complete strangers, and new settings for the sharing of food.

The settlements excavated on the twin hills at Jerf-el-Ahmar are examples of such permanent habitation. On each hill, a succession of building foundations have been superimposed, forming sequences of seven successive hamlets on the eastern hill, and six on the western hill. It is within the latter sequence that one particular collapsed building provides an insight into food-sharing in this new landscape of permanence and mobility.

A number of archaeological excavations along the Euphrates have been conducted in advance of dam construction. French and Syrian archaeologists had five years to expose and study the ancient settlements on these two hills at Jerf-el-Ahmar, before they were submerged beneath the Tishrine Dam. Working with them was George Willcox, who has conducted much of the archaeobotanical research along this part of the river. He had already sampled and floated many sediments from the site when the collapsed building came to light. Hundreds of those samples were rich in the grains of wild barley, in amongst the seeds of a wide range of annual plants, and occasionally some perennial nuts such as almond and pistacia. All these plants could grow wild along the chalky slopes around the settlement, with one proviso: a moister climate than today is needed for some of the species encountered to flourish, a reminder that, as we cross the millennia, climate and environment continue to change. Indeed, the Jerf settlers put down their roots above the banks of the Euphrates at the end of an episode of substantial climatic change, a point to which we shall return.[1]

In one room of the building, a careful removal of the collapsed mudbrick revealed a series of stone implements in their places of use around the room, a space of approximately three metres by two and a half. These implements comprised three limestone basins, one small limestone bowl, several pounding stones, two flat polished stone plates, and three long grinding stones or 'saddle querns', over which a kneeling individual would work an upper stone back and forth to prepare flour. Flint sickles were also recovered during the excavation. Under a microscope, a polish could be made out on their surfaces, consistent with the cutting of tough grass stems. Jerf was set in a landscape made up entirely of wild plants whose seeds would disperse freely when ripe, and consequently need no sickle to harvest. I have therefore tentatively connected this polish with the gathering of green heads, for consumption before they become brittle, when their seeds are still soft, or 'milk-ripe'. There is, however, little need to speculate too much on what plants were consumed and how they were prepared, as the plant remains from the room provide a rich body of more direct and solid evidence.[2]

Placing a grid over the exposed surface, the charred plant remains could be sampled and their densities plotted across the room, and in relationship with the various pieces of equipment. The most abundant remains Willcox recovered were barley seeds, which like all the seeds from this site were from wild plants. These seeds had been mostly broken up into fragments. Under the microscope, their inner surfaces, exposed by fracture, can clearly be seen to have swollen in the process of charring. This small observation informed him that he was looking at original breaks, purposely created before the fire. What had been found was 'cracked' or 'kibbled' barley. The broken seeds reached their greatest concentrations close to the limestone basins, suggesting they were cracked and then soaked, much in the manner that modern cereals are prepared today in this part of the world to prepare 'tabouleh' salad.

14. View of the 'kitchen' exposed at Jerf-el-Ahmar, with basins, working surfaces, and grinding stones left in place.

Alongside these, the characteristic lens-shaped seeds of wild lentil were recovered in significant numbers. Like the barley, they also concentrated around the stone basins, and in addition to this they clustered around the hearth. These lentils were presumably soaked and then cooked, following a long-standing procedure for preparing legumes. Looking through the samples from the grid squares over to the far side of the room, around where the saddle querns were found, concentrations of a different species showed up. They were of a large-seeded grass, either wild wheat or wild rye, it was not too easy to tell. These seeds were presumably being ground on the querns to flour, in the preparation of a porridge, dough, or bread. On one of the grinding stones or 'querns' fragments were recovered whose culinary preparation is clearer still.

Two charred seed cakes, each around the size of a small bun, were recovered intact, and fragments of similar cakes were recovered from elsewhere in the room. The seeds from which they had been prepared had been ground up, so were not easy to identify. However, with the help of a scanning electron microscope, traces of fragmented seed coat could be seen, and their surface cell patterns studied. These patterns had a perfect match with seeds of the mustard family.

This diverse range of foods and methods of preparation were further complemented by some tasty nuts, wild almond and wild pistacia, other flavours from caper and mallow, a few other grasses and legumes and a wild relative of buckwheat. Looking back another 12,000 years further, to the earlier encampment at Ohalo, we can place this varied diet in the context of a long tradition in which a wide range of seeds played an important role in the diet of our ancestors, but there are also differences. At both sites, the gathered seeds were taken to designated places for storage and preparation before the meal, but in different ways. At Ohalo, the different *harvests*, each of them diverse, were separated for storage in different brushwood huts. At Jerf they had separated a narrower range of individual *species*, and subjected those species to a series of separate culinary transformations. By cracking, soaking, grinding, moulding, and heating, a series of favoured plants, in which grasses and legumes played starring roles, were transformed from their often bland original state, and disguised to find more interesting and mysterious culinary creations.

Culinary theatre

That small room, less than 8 square metres, was a busy, crowded space. It gives the general impression of serving another unit, rather than being self-contained. One such candidate is its near neighbour, the largest building in the group, a sunken round building in which the narrative above has been set. The excavators suggest it served as a community space, and draw a parallel with a particular structure found recurrently on the recently abandoned Anasazi villages of North America. These deserted villages recurrently have a submerged circular structure within them. As they are much more recent, we know something of their use. They were nodes within the Anasazi network, places where people would be brought together for ceremonial purposes. They were embedded within their own village architecture of partitions, and laid out according to certain astronomical alignments. They were also similarly constructed from place to place.[3]

Extremely similar buildings to the sunken Jerf building have been uncovered in other house clusters in the region. One has been exposed on the eastern hill at Jerf, and another a short way downstream from Jerf, at the tell of Mureybet.[4] Around the Mureybet house, the contents of cooking pits have been closely studied, and I have 'borrowed' them to enhance my own narrative. What seems clear from the organization of activities across space at both Mureybet and Jerf-el Ahmar is that culinary preparation happens in one place, and the transformed creation is taken to a second venue for consumption. An enduring feature of food-sharing among our own species, as we have explored in the preceding chapter, is the conversational circle of the familiar group around the hearth, the focal point of food preparation at the centre of the social action. At these sites, the logic of the central hearth has been broken, the focal point has been taken from the conversational circle and transferred to a separate enclosed space. The room that had been so meticulously sampled at Jerf-el-Ahmar may well be the oldest known 'kitchen'.

In the modern world we are so familiar with the idea of the kitchen as a separate room from the dining space, it is easy to forget that not all food preparation works in that way. Indeed, across the full diversity of contexts of human food-sharing in the present and past, the prevailing pattern has probably been to prepare food in the centre of the conversational circle, and a wide variety of dishes, both elaborate and simple, can be prepared in that manner. It is only certain societies in certain circumstances that chose to remove the preparation of food to an ancillary space, to conceal its transformation from the eyes and senses of the diners.

Looking at food in far more recent societies of Asia and Europe, the anthropologist Jack Goody has drawn our attention to an axis of food-sharing, between the *basse cuisine* of ordinary family meals, and a differentiated *haute cuisine* amongst diners of status, a status that may be both preserved and discretely contested in the drama of this distinct form of meal. *Basse cuisine* is homely and familiar, often combining ingredients the diners themselves have raised in their fields. *Haute cuisine* involves a large element of theatre, display, and disguise, prestigious ingredients and exotic flavourings hinting at distant, almost mythical regions. Not all kitchens are found in prestigious places, but a separate place of preparation does serve well as an ante-room to culinary drama, maximizing the element of surprise and mystery. Today, we are used to kitchens in much lowlier, homelier contexts, but even here, they remain places where food is transformed and disguised in order to impress. Moreover, even in the lowliest of homes, the separation of spaces for the preparation and consumption of food typically reveals much about status and differentiation. There will typically be a distinction of gender or age in who is in the kitchen and in the dining space. In larger establishments, these will be compounded by distinctions of rank and servitude. The concept of a kitchen is not identical with the concept of an *haute cuisine*; the two can exist independently. However they have several themes in common, in relation to theatre, disguise, and differentiation of roles and status.[5]

Different people

Some sense of that differentiation around the time of Jerf-el-Ahmar can be gained from turning our attentions downstream, to another early site in the Euphrates valley, the tell site of Abu Hureyra.[6] A study of human remains from excavation at this site has revealed a great deal about daily life. The recurrent daily activities that subject their bodies to sustained stress show up in the way the joints have developed, and as signs of arthritis. The state of spines, shoulders, hips, and knees provided clear evidence that a lot of lifting and carrying was going on. The upper vertebrae in certain cases had grown to a toughened, modified shape, a growth response that could be equated with carrying heavy loads on the head. I have modelled the woman that our traveller saw working away at the saddle quern on a composite of various women whose bones had been recovered from the site.

Although muscle tissue rarely survives, the muscle attachments can frequently be discerned on ancient bones. The upper-arm bones from one woman had especially well-developed muscle attachments; they had been put to hard work. The thigh bones of another were curved and the region around the knee arthritic. This woman had spent much time kneeling, with her toes tucked beneath her; her toe bones were deformed and her foot joints arthritic. The most disconcerting stress would probably be on their lower backs; deformation and compression of the last dorsal vertebra may be observed as a consequence. We can see in these bones the long and recurrent labour that gave shape both to growth of these women's bodies and their weary decline. We can envisage individuals kneeling for many hours, driving their bodies backwards and forwards, pivoting alternately around the knee and hip joints. Their arms were stretched out ahead, and their forearms bent inwards towards the body. This is precisely what our traveller saw over the kitchen quernstone. In other times, and in other parts of the world, kitchens had been the domain of men, servants, professionals, or slaves. The meticulous study of the bones from Abu Hureyra indicates that in the ancient Euphrates valley at least, a very significant role in food preparation was played by women. All this evidence of back-breaking women's work raises the question of what the men were up to.[7]

In the earlier chapters of this book, the different roles that males and females played in the acquisition and sharing of food followed a delicately balanced logic of bartering, scrounging, threatening, and cooperation over the support of the young. Quite central to that logic was the balance between two things; the central role of females in raising and nourishing their big-brained offspring, and the central role of males in hunting down rather large animals laden with nutritious flesh. That balance shifted significantly when modern humans developed weaving and basketry, technologies that greatly enhanced the potential to gather fish, birds, and seeds, technologies where men had no intrinsic physiological advantage over women.

If we extend the kind of analyses applied at Abu Hureyra to skeletons from earlier periods in south-west Asia, an admittedly small sample displays a pronounced difference between the sexes. A number of males have been found with very robust long bones, and other features consistent with spear-throwing. By the time of Abu Hureyra, these lifelong hunters are disappearing from the skeletal record, a trend that is quite consistent with the food remains, the state of human teeth, and the isotope signatures within human bones, which in different ways reflect various aspects of the shift away from the male arena of big game hunting, a shift that has been in progress since early in the expansion of modern humans across the world.[8]

Let us return to the question of what the men were actually contributing to life at Abu Hureyra. They were certainly carrying loads, as were the women, and they were squatting with feet flat on the ground, as were the women. I wonder whether it crossed their minds as they squatted in contemplation that, with game hunting diminishing in importance, their communities did not actually need quite as many men around to fulfil biological needs of survival and reproduction. In much later, grain-based farming societies, the fate of males 'surplus to requirement' became a significant issue in many places and different stages of history. Their migration to new territories became an influential driving force in the peopling of the modern world. The start of that process might be traced right back to the early decline in the place of big-game hunting in the food quest, and the consequent shift in balance between men's and women's work.

Different places

Our traveller might indeed be one such 'exported' male, shifting his efforts from the food quest itself to the mobilization of objects of status across the landscape. The only bits of his body I have borrowed from Abu Hureyra are his worn-down teeth. What he brings to the narrative are his experience of the interconnections between the different permanently settled communities on his path. We have more direct evidence of how far shells and stone objects were moving across the landscape than of the people who carried them for parts of that journey. That knowledge is gradually being assembled through trace element and isotopic analysis of bones.[9] Following the artefact evidence, however, we can imagine the world of at least certain individuals spanning the Red Sea in the south, the Jordan River and the middle Euphrates in the north, and the Cappadocian obsidian sources in the north-west.[10] This would have been a journeying landscape of enormous diversity, of lush riverine woodland and barren desert, of craggy mountain regions and flat open steppes. Journeys across these would have taken the traveller through many different communities, living and sharing food in many different ways. The charred seeds and bones left among the ruins of those settlements to be recovered later by archaeologists reflect some considerable diversity of regional traditions in cuisine. So in Jerf, wild ass meat was commonly consumed but rarely eaten in the southern Levant.

Gazelle was eaten everywhere. Over even shorter distances the variation could be seen, say, between Jerf and Mureybet, less than two days' walk from each other, but with noticeably distinct foods.[11]

The actual settlements along the traveller's path would also have varied greatly in structure and style; in some places the tents of wandering nomads, in other places permanent, enduring houses made from mortared mudbrick, in other places still, houses of stone. In one form or another, the round or oval house enclosing a sunken floor within would have been something he was familiar with from a number of his journeys. The excavator at Mureybet speculated that those early sunken oval structures, those oldest permanent 'houses', were pits that captured the even older idea of a cave or rock shelter in constructed mud and stone. As in the cave or rock shelter, close kin gathered in these early houses around the hearth, where food was prepared and shared among an intimate group.[12]

From the outside, the oval house on the western hill at Jerf-el-Ahmar offers a similar prospect, if on a more substantial scale. Like many buildings he would have entered, it had a sunken floor, but once on the inside, the grammar of space would have seemed unusual. However familiar the gently curved exterior, the building's angular interior would seem novel and unusual. The angles are produced by a series of interior partitions, the excavators presume for storage. The effect of these interior walls would be to reduce the size of the space, endow it with more angles and complexity, and emphasize the third dimension of height. The interior was reached down a flight of steps to where, straight ahead, he faced an elevated bench or dais. This room, with its angular and differentiated internal spaces, and presentation from outside of transformed and disguised foods has a different feel to it from the hearth-centred conversational circle. That angular drama, that deviation from a homely circle, evokes the notion of novel kinds of social encounter. We know from other traces in the archaeological record that new encounters were taking place.

People were clearly moving around the landscape, and encountering strangers as a matter of course. However, theirs was a world that lacked the cities, towns and entrepôts where strangers meet, and which provide facilities for people to eat, drink, rest, and sleep among those they have never met. Outside the mercantile foci of the modern world, a meeting with a traveller is not so casual an affair. Thousands of years before such foci even existed, those meetings would have had something of a formal, ritual structure to them. Someone in each community would see it as their role to receive the stranger, and embark upon a particular set of gestures, courtesies, and offerings to which both host and guest would adhere. In his influential essay, *The Gift*, the anthropologist Marcel Mauss explored how such engagements unfolded in living societies around the three central obligations, to give, to receive, and to reciprocate, obligations that regulated social encounters, and forged bonds between travellers and the local communities through which they passed. The Jerf-el-Ahmar kitchen came into being along the course of some very ancient journeys, journeys carrying shells, obsidiaṅ, and other less arch-aeologically visible goods besides, eleven thousand years ago.[13]

As one of those journeyers, our own particular traveller ascended from the oval house and looked back towards the kitchen and surround-ing buildings, the strange angular partitions would seem to be every-where. Several of those neighbouring buildings were completely angular, inside and out, including the building in which the foods were prepared.

The first impression of this 'architecture of partitions' may well have an element of novelty and strangeness comparable with first sight of a high-rise block in more recent times. One obvious question in the minds of such observers is 'how did they do that?', and indeed rectangular housing, like high-rise building, involves aspects of technological innov-ation, in particular a form of cross-linking walls built at right angles. This question is quickly succeeded, and soon overtaken by another, 'what is life like in that? How can it be possible to do the things we are used to do in such a space?' Thirty years ago, the prehistorian Kent Flannery put his mind to working out the meaning of this change from curved to angular living spaces. Looking at extant examples in the ethnographic record and following the logic of rectangular architecture, he suggested that it was all about the need for additions and extension. A single rectangular house could bring together parents and children, and in time a third generation. The less extendable round buildings were cells within a larger kin group. In other words, rectangular building was about the emergence of the nuclear family. More recently, Jacques Cauvin has explored the idea that this change is to do with a fundamental change in mental attitude, in cosmology and the shape of the world.[14]

The driver of the change does not have to be unitary. It is true that the spaces in which we find ourselves shape and influence our activities, but do not determine them. They provide a grammar, but we write the scripts, indeed, different scripts on different days in the same building. If we step back from connecting round and rectangular housing with specific ways of life, and think instead of the common structures or 'grammars' that shape a diverse range of ways of life, there are several general observations we can make.

First of all, a curved wall encloses, whereas a straight wall divides, and this is very clear from the pattern of walls at Jerf. One can indeed assemble straight walls to form an enclosure, or in certain circumstances, divide a space with a curved wall, but even here, partition and enclosure are emphasized by such modifications. Second, a curved wall tends to fix the scale of a space, whereas the boxed plan of a rectangular building can be indefinitely extended by annexing new rectangles. Third, an individual can find a wider range of niches within an angular space in which to stand or sit. A rectangle has long sides, short sides and corners, places than the light reaches in a different way, places in which others have to turn to meet your eyes. In a round house, around a circular hearth or round table, it is at least possible for everyone to place themselves in equivalent position and for everyone to remain in view. An angular space lends itself to differentiation, a theme that can be taken into the third dimension of elevation, through differences in the level of the floor and side benches. Even without the upper part of the large central house at Jerf, a differentiation of levels is apparent, of *going down* into the house, and *looking up* towards the person on the dais opposite.

A grammar of curved and rectilinear space that could be endlessly followed, subverted, and reinvented might be shaped around a series of oppositions: between curved space and angular space; between inclusiveness and subdivision; between containment or stability and growth or expansion; and between equality and differentiation. It was quite an unusual departure from the age-old sunken oval house, something that Jacques Cauvin connected to the constructed cave of ancestral hunters. But one need not be one of these ancient hunters to remember the old style. The changes at Jerf in the grammar of space were happening fast, within a lifetime.

Memories of a changing world

While many human communities preserve a collective memory of gradual change through storytelling and oral tradition, our traveller would have had a real sense of change through his own lifetime, and not just in the way they built houses. He may have directly sensed the longer-term rumbles in the turbulent world of nature around him.

These natural rumbles could well have been most evident in the instability of rivers and run-off. Some of the settlements he may have visited in the southern Levant were protected by defensive walls. These walls were first interpreted by archaeologists as being for defence against other humans. Modern studies suggest that the threat for which they were constructed was the possibility of flash floods and mud slides. Many settlements of this period were situated beside alluvial fans, and the river systems are known to have been actively changing, a symptom of wider change in the natural environment.

An imprint of the rapid changes in the environment of the time are preserved in the sequences of pollen trapped in ancient lake deposits across the region. Such lake deposits are not that common, but a comparison of dated pollen records from the few that do exist provides an interesting impression of changing vegetation patterns across time and space. Such a comparison would suggest that, in the general region around the middle and upper Euphrates, the pace of change was so fast that boundaries between different vegetation types could move by more than two kilometres in a single decade. A favoured plant that was growing all around the threshold of a child's house at the start of their life might be a day's walk away at the end of their life, on account of the pace of global climate change. It may be that the oldest inhabitants at Jerf could remember when the twisted stems of the shrubby wooden stems that grew in a certain kind of steppe were an ideal source of fuel for the cooking pits. But those woody plants had greatly diminished, and were now being replaced with a grassy steppe better suited as a source of food rather than fuel. Individual memories, even more so the conversations between young and old, would preserve narratives of windstorms and torrential downpours, rivers running dry or changing their course, woodlands shrinking and seasons coming earlier or later.[15]

Looking at pollen from further afield, extracted from cores drilled in Europe, America, and New Zealand, we can place these changes at the very end of a striking fluctuation in the Quaternary Epoch. In the European diagrams, where it was first spotted, a key signal marking the fluctuation is a peak in the distinctively sculptured pollen from the small white flowers of a low, downy perennial called mountain avens. Its Latin name is *Dryas octopetala*. Today it can be found in cool mountain refuges, but in much colder periods, it can spread more widely into lower altitudes. In pollen sequences it consequently serves as a marker for very cool episodes. In cores spanning the period since the last ice age, two peaks of *Dryas* pollen may be found at levels a little way above the glacial maximum. These levels have been named the 'Older Dryas' and 'Younger Dryas' climatic episodes respectively. The Younger Dryas lasted from around 13,000 years ago up to the time in which Jerf-el-Ahmar was settled. As this cool period came to an abrupt end, it left planet earth once more in considerable flux; the temperature was changing dramatically, ice caps were melting apace, and rivers radically reworking their beds. As the cold-loving *Dryas octopetala* retreated to its mountain refuges, other plants radically altered their ranges, and many of the animals in their food chain followed. In many an earlier fluctuation, humans had followed suit with the rest of the food chain, but this is not what happened in the world through which our traveller was moving. He visited many settlements that were resolutely immobile, settlements whose lives were far longer than his. He could return after many a long journey to be hosted and fed once again and exchange gifts. True, there seemed to be some radical rethinking of architectural design, but as the rivers shifted and the landscape changed, they stayed put.[16]

The ecological demands of staying still

In many ways, it was the permanence of settlements that facilitated the movement of long-distance travellers and the artefacts they carried with them. In the absence of fixed settlements, nomadic people can certainly cover vast distances in their lifetimes, but of necessity following quite constrained patterns of movement encapsulated in storytelling and oral tradition. The fixed points of permanent settlement, together with a shared understanding of the protocol of offering food and shelter to the traveller, create a series of 'nodes' or meeting points across which journeys can vary, a new more fluid form of mobility, a mobility traced in the long journeys travelled by shells and worked obsidian, exotic items that play a central role in the giving of gifts, the maintenance of networks, and the establishment of status. But permanence of settlement within a fluctuating environment places significant demands on the quest for food. By expanding our view from Jerf-el-Ahmar to other sites in the middle Euphrates valley, and stepping back to look at a few thousand years in time, we can gain some insight into how such communities ensured they still had food to share with each other and passing travellers.

A number of sites of this general period have been subjected to modern excavation along a 100-kilometre stretch of the middle Euphrates valley. The seeds and bones recovered from them provide much insight into how their food quest proceeded during and after the Younger Dryas. A wide range of wild animals was hunted, including gazelles, horses, asses, deer, sheep, cattle, and boar. A far wider range of wild plants was collected from woodlands, woodland edges, and the open steppe, running into hundreds of species. If we look through time at this diverse range, we do see species decline and disappear from the settlement deposits, but we also see a fair degree of persistence in the food quest. Overall, the greater variation in what is eaten remains the variation between sites, where local differences in topography and soil type favour different resources. Within the enduring settlements, there is a strong trend towards conservatism in the overall range of foods consumed. Each community clearly had generations of experience of how best to capture these wild foods. We can see the technology of capture directly in the refinement of flint blades and arrowheads, and speculate on an equivalent refinement in strings, nets, baskets, and traps. Amongst the vast range of plant foods gathered, a growing emphasis can be seen on selected species, which receive special attention. In a changing climate, there are traces of evidence that some communities were making some attempts to 'fix' the seasons in which their favoured foods thrived.[17]

One of the consequences of a climate change after the Younger Dryas was that highly seasonal stands, from which many of the annual seeds in the diet derived, were being engulfed by different forms of vegetation that could put on growth for a larger part of the year. Both at Jerf-el-Ahmar, and at some neighbouring sites, a marked shift in the species lists towards annual plants that can tolerate disturbed ground suggests that action was being taken to resist that process. Invading perennials were being cleared and ground broken around favoured plants, in order to retain the seasonality their community had known for generations. The annual grass seeds and legumes, for example, would be encouraged by any action that preserved soil moisture in the growing season, and that suppressed the growth of competing perennials in the rest of the year. There are many ways this might be achieved, especially on a small 'garden' scale, and indeed, their predecessors may have been doing such things for thousands of years. In the centuries following our traveller's visit to the oval house at Jerf, this trend towards environmental conservation makes its mark on the archaeobotanical record. Securing the settlements in space seems to be linked with securing the food chain in a changing world, something that involved sharpening the focus of attention onto particular species.

A mobile food chain

Returning to the kitchen at Jerf-el-Ahmar it was not just seeds that emerged from the floor deposits, but also some fragments of the stems of the seed heads. In wild plants, evolution has fashioned those seed heads to fragment readily on ripening, in order that the seeds have the best chance of avoiding predators and dispersing to find a new niche in the soil for the next generation. Through the microscope lens the clean, natural breaks along the stem are clearly visible. Just very occasionally, a fragment is found in which the stems are tough. In samples from other sites that are a thousand years younger, most fragments are from tough, non-fracturing stems. These are not from plants that can reproduce easily in the wild. Their seed heads remain intact and vulnerable to predation, unless one key predator assists in their planting and germination. They are 'domesticated' plants, the foundations of modern global agriculture. These domesticated plants are found in more recent assemblages in the middle Euphrates region. One recurrent domesticate is a now unfamiliar species of wheat, called 'emmer wheat'. If we were to go in search of the wild ancestor of this crop, we would be best advised to follow the obsidian routes south, to where another group of early permanent settlements have come to light.[18]

In these southern sites, one of the early domesticates is another unusual species of wheat, called 'einkorn', and remarkably, the pattern is reversed. To go in search of the ancestor of einkorn, we would follow the obsidian route north. There has been an apparent swap over in the earliest episode of the transformed, domesticated plants; wild einkorn in the north, and wild emmer in the south, followed by domesticated einkorn in the south, and domesticated emmer in the north. A number of other early crops, such as chickpea, flax, bean, and figs also seem to 'move around' in an interesting way. What these new domesticates are tracking are food chains on the move. At the time of our traveller's visit to Jerf-el-Ahmar, the things we can know were moving far across the landscape are the small, precious, easy-to-carry items, for prestigious weapons and personal ornamentation. From around 10,000 years ago, people are moving with other things besides. They were travelling not just to exchange goods but to settle down, taking with them plants, animals, weapons, ideas about building styles, and beliefs about nature, the world, and what lies beyond.[19]

The seeds they took with them included their favoured wheat and barley, whose growth they had been nurturing for many generations. Indeed, they may have been sowing them as well; the tell-tale evolutionary shift to a tough, non-fracturing stem might only be expected when plant populations become isolated, in other words when their carers migrate beyond the ancestral range of these plants. They were clearly dependent on the human predators once in their new homes. Alongside a seed supply of their favoured grasses, they were travelling with goats, a rather easier animal to control and tether than some of the beasts their ancestors had hunted. They also travelled with weapons, skilfully fashioned points, and blades of razor-sharp stone. Their most conspicuous footprint was their architecture of partitions, that novel use of space that seemed so strange to our traveller, but was subsequently to become commonplace, indeed, to spread with farming across continents. The Mureybet excavator, Jacques Cauvin, has delved further into the material evidence from their settlements, and in particular their imagery and treatment of the dead. He argues that as well as taking their sources of food, weapons, and architectural styles with them, they also spread their beliefs about the world, and their cults of the head, the woman, and the bull.[20]

The new mobile food chain that travelled with these migrants displayed great evolutionary fitness, in that it has not stopped multiplying, even over a subsequent 10,000 years. In the first millennium of expansion, numbers of settlements proliferated and so did their geographical range. The sizes of individual settlements grew and the architecture of partitions diversified. The range of both plants and animals travelling in domesticated form diversified. In subsequent millennia the mobile food chain multiplied and spread eastwards into Asia and westwards into Europe. However, it did not spread by bulldozing flat the opposition, but by leapfrogging from favoured site to favoured site, where the mobile food chain could find an ideal niche, each new settlement taking with it many elements of the food chain, the styles and the beliefs of its parent communities. In the right ecological setting, the mobile food chain would flourish and support new generations, including a proportion of surplus males who would embark on new journeys of migration.[21]

The idea that the new ecology of farming was propelled by a widespread export of males may find some support from the quite separate study of modern human genes. In the past two decades our understanding of the diversity in those genes has mushroomed, and different researchers have attempted to relate that diversity to patterns in the human past. In a pioneering study of human genetic diversity, a series of well-known genetic traits such as the various blood-groups was mapped and argument put forward that many of the spatial variations could be explained by the spread of agricultural communities. In Europe, for example, the variation in blood-group genetics could be in large part resolved in terms of a south-east–north-west trend across the continent, broadly mirroring the direction of farming spread. It seemed that our ancestry across Europe was largely an ancestry of migrating farmers. This conclusion, however, was quickly exposed to challenge from a separate group who looked for spatial patterns across Europe from another genetic system, called mitochondrial DNA. They came to a rather different conclusion: that the majority of our modern European ancestry can be explained in terms of much older hunter-gatherers, and that farming travelled as an idea, with just a modest movement of accompanying migrant farmers. Further research looking at more recently charted genetic systems has come up with new geographical patterns. They have shown that different patterns of mobility can be detected within the male and female lines, indicating a difference in mobility between men and women.[22]

The geneticists are still debating the finer details of each other's arguments, and the field is constantly being enhanced by new data. In the meantime, there is one potential explanation of the differences in inference outlined above. If we look at the conflicting data sets, one favours a substantial movement of people with the spread of farming, and derives from expressed genes on the 'ordinary' chromosomes (those which exclude the sex-linked x and y chromosomes). These ordinary chromosomes hold genes inherited from both parents. The other data set, for which a contrasting inference has been offered, is the one data set that relates to our purely maternal inheritance, the mitochondrial DNA. If we were to imagine a spread of migrant pioneer farmers that had a rather stronger male element to it, with a tendency to marry local women, we would expect the genetic data to differ in the way that they do. A long history of exporting males may have been captured in our genes.

Looking back

With 11,000 years' hindsight, we can look back to the cramped kitchen on the western hill at Jerf-el-Ahmar, and place its bars of mustard seed cake, its lentil stew, and kibbled barley somewhere close to a transition with profound implications for all human ecology and society, implications that continue to shape our lives, our health and welfare, social structures and technologies, our engagement with the natural world, and even the pattern of our genes. Last century, Vere Gordon Childe captured this momentous change is his phrase the 'Neolithic revolution', the passage from the control of humanity by nature to the control of nature by humanity. In Childe's time one could still talk of transitions from savagery to civilization, but we more modestly talk of a change from foraging to farming, but in looking at the modern world around us, that transition to farming has had a massive impact. How might this have felt for the traveller to Jerf, or the woman he saw bent over her quernstone?[23]

Childe saw his revolution as a radical move from wandering free and living for the moment to settling down and planning ahead, a permanence accompanied by the different mobility of trade and exchange. The domestication of plants and animals was part of a composite package, bringing together fixed, permanent settlement, craft activities such as pottery production, storage and movement of goods, and an expansive population, taming the wilderness and opening it up to cultivation. We have the advantage over Childe not simply in having far more evidence, but also a series of radiocarbon dates to attach to that evidence. Those carbon dates have certainly put the brakes on his revolution, scattering those different elements to different centuries, sometimes different millennia. It now seems that many of these changes were too gradual for the participants to actually notice. Our traveller would have had little sense of the transition to fixed permanent settlement and the opening up of long-distance networks for shell and obsidian. Those developments were deep in the distant past, far beyond that range of oral tradition and folk memory. The woman at the quernstone would have had no knowledge of pottery production or the rolling back of the wilderness in order to carpet it with arable fields. These were not to come about until thousands of years into the future. Her grandchildren might spend a lot more time among the grass and legume stands than she, attending to those stands in ways that might have seemed excessive to her. It would be her very distant offspring who noticed that the flint sickles their ancestors had used for generations were needed more and more in the harvest as the seed heads seemed to be changing their form.

So the transformation in the food quest that seems in retrospect to have been revolutionary, to many the most important transformation in human history, might not have been the most obvious and immediate transformation experienced by those who lived through it. Ecological change was indeed taking place with considerable pace, sufficient to impinge on a lifetime's memory, and certainly enough to make life hard, something clear from the human bones recovered from these sites. But changes of an even more immediate nature were taking place in the patterns of social encounters, patterns we can now pick up in the form of their settlement space and the traces of the travellers who moved through them. Since Childe first wrote of a Neolithic revolution, our understanding of the massive environmental changes underpinning the transition have improved, and so have the more local and immediate changes in social encounter, and the first changes we see in the pattern of the archaeological record, permanence of settlement and long-distance mobility of exotic goods, are to do with changing patterns of social encounter. A growing awareness of the importance of social encounter in food-sharing has shifted our thoughts and attention from the ordinary 'meal' to the special 'feast'.

The meal and the feast

The boundary between a 'meal' and a 'feast' is an illusive one. The distinction alludes to a number of things, such as frequency and scale. A meal is an intimate, everyday sort of thing, whereas a feast takes place on special occasions, with people we do not see all the time. Some might argue that our everyday meals served a predominantly functional role of meeting our biological needs, whereas feasts were more important as rituals of social reproduction, but that is hard to square either with Mary Douglas's observations of the social dynamics of some very 'ordinary' family dinners, or Marvin Harris's observations of the calorific and nutritional importance of some large-scale feasts. Perhaps a more interesting, if equally fragile, contrast is between the supportive, *pro-social* tenor of an intimate meal, and the competitive, perhaps even *antisocial* tenor of a feast. It may seem slightly odd to link the word antisocial, with the eminently social gathering of a feast, but it serves to highlight the subtext of rank, differentiation, and competitive change in status associated with feasting, in stark contrast with that fundamental and widespread pro-social food-sharing between close kin, and particularly parent and child. There is no doubt that, bringing our fictional traveller down into the restricted angular well of the central house, placing him opposite the occupier of the spacious dais, and feeding him with foods prepared in a separate building, it is easy to arrive at a sense of differentiation between participants, a sense encouraged by the grammar of space infusing the entire settlement, and the theatre of cooking as a process of disguise and illusion. Such a distance and competitive tension may have been quite critical at the time of Childe's great transition.

Thinking about feasting may allow us to draw a distinction between two broad types of hunter-gatherer community. One is something like the Boxgrove horse hunters of Chapter 3, seeking out long-lived, slow-growing prey, and following that prey through the landscape, the seasons, and longer fluctuations. The other is more like the hunter-gatherers of south-west Asia, staying in one place and harvesting a much wider range of short-lived plants and animals from land, sea, and sky, often in lush environments. The latter may be more able to accumulate and store food in quantity, and then translate that food into status and power by competitive feasting. Looking worldwide at the times and places domestication did and did not happen, at which species were taken into domestication when, it has been argued that competitive feasting might be the key to understanding how this major revolution in human ecology and society was propelled forward.[24]

Returning to Jerf-el-Ahmar, the traveller and the woman at the quern-stone have been brought to life as far as fragments of evidence and imagination allow, and the senior woman in the community house mentioned in brief. Following through Hayden's analysis, it may be that we have left some of the key players out. The woman is working hard to transform the gathered foods that will be offered and displayed, the traveller is the focus of the offer and bringer of ornaments of prestige. But the whole performance is being watched by people in the corners and alcoves, sometimes out of the line of sight. This is another key theme of culinary theatre, and one which will recur; diners are present both as consumers and as spectators. In a changing world of social competitions, it is perhaps to impress these people in the shadows that the workers in the world's oldest kitchen must suitably prepare the meal, and the ritual of sharing food must be appropriately performed.

15. The skull of a young adult, exposed during the excavation of the main enclosure at Hambledon Hill.

7

SEASONS OF THE FEAST

Dorset, southern England, c.3500 BC

The trees had put on a lot of growth since they had last gathered on this spot. They would soon be cleared once more, both to provide fire for the roasts, and to expose their own ancestral family plot for the ritual of redigging. The hill was a place of transition, where woodland, scrub, and clearance were juxtaposed, as were life and death. In the midst of this changing patchwork landscape of trees, scrub, and glades, were the resting places of the dead, striking monuments of earth, in which the deceased relatives rested, both the ancestral humans and the ancestral cattle, family members whose presence would be acknowledged at the feast. There was also an element of uncertainty, perhaps even danger on the hilltop, not simply on account of wild animals that might take advantage of the woody cover and the large influx of food, but also on account of the other humans travelling to the hill, with whom relations were not always benign.

The feast that was about to unfold was not a familiar sharing of food among intimates. There were intimate kin groups who would each gather around their own family plot and set about the ritual business of clearing and digging, but alongside them would be other kin groups, some familiar, others relative strangers. It was a place where marriage partners could be sought, but it was also by no means unknown for hostilities and violence to break out at large gatherings such as these. There was much eating to be done, particularly of the beloved beef, roasted on an open fire. There was also much drinking—generally of beer but occasionally of some more exotic concoction to transport the inner spirit. Tensions would in this way be alleviated, and relative strangers would reaffirm old bonds and secure them anew.

One such kin group had a substantial offering to be made at this particular feast. While others would bring sacks of hazelnuts, dried fruits or grain, others the carcass of a young lamb, they were honouring a much revered matriarch from their own line, and for that would be slaughtering two of their precious cattle. Their cows were as much part of their kin group as they were. As children, they moved straight from drinking their mother's milk to milk from the cows with whom they lived and died. Flesh would be taken from their bones respectfully, just as it would be cut from human bones respectfully, and accepting an offer of their meat was a token of bonds that linked the relative strangers who had gathered from across the landscape on this hilltop—bonds that would be remembered during some subsequent season of festivity.

Nature in transition

O N a sinuous spur of chalk downland overlooking the modern meadows and hedgerows of southern England, a series of impressive earthworks forms a defensive ring around the spur's summit. These earthworks were erected over 2,000 years ago around an Iron Age hilltop village. A less conspicuous linear earthwork, twice as old as the defensive ring, forms a linear feature along the central crest. This was a place of the dead, the remains of one of two 'long barrows' on the hill, earthen monuments to ancestors erected by some of Britain's earliest farmers. Those same farmers created a series of hollows across the hill, repeatedly dug and backfilled over time. The repeated gaps between these hollows seemed to past antiquaries to resemble causeways, and they described sites of this kind as 'causewayed enclosures'. While we still use that description as a term of convenience, archaeology has shown these supposed causeways to be less key to the site than the hollows on either side. These hollows yield rich evidence of a novel form of gathering to share food. Recuts into those hollows sometimes contained the bones of up to three cattle, as well as smaller species. The state of these bones, some remaining in articulation, suggest that they had been recently slaughtered and consumed. The cattle alone would have yielded over 700 kg of meat, offal, and fat—enough to feed hundreds of people. These buried bones leave plentiful traces of the consumption of large amounts of food, but not consumption close to their homes and their hearths. Like other causewayed enclosures across Britain, Hambledon Hill lies on the boundaries of the living, boundaries in both space and time. Now that it has been subjected to detailed archaeological analysis, we can begin to understand how these early meals on the periphery forged a connection between the societies and natural worlds within.[1]

Surprisingly, much of the general scene on Hambledon Hill almost 5,000 years ago comes from a rather unremarkable animal, the snail. Its shells are plentiful in and around this Dorset hilltop. Here, as in large stretches of southern England, the predominant subsoil is chalk, providing an ideal environment for snails to inhabit, and ideal sediments to conserve their shells after their death. Each of the sediments excavated from the hill contained a fair number of these shells. The oddly shaped hollows that were arrayed in roughly concentric circles across the hilltop each had snail shells within its various layers of backfill. The two long earthen mounds which were the most conspicuous repositories for the bones of the dead, also sealed ancient land surfaces beneath them. The snails that inhabited these land surfaces were sealed in with them. Snail shells were similarly trapped in sediments accumulating within dry valleys in the general vicinity of the hill itself. Samples were sieved, sorted, and the shell fragments identified, and the resulting species lists revealed a great deal about the overall landscape, the hilltop itself, and the context of the various feasts that took place during its use.[2]

Given the density of archaeological features on the hilltop, the two long burial chambers and all the irregular ditches laid out in concentric rows, we might at first think of a fairly open landscape, but the snail shells from within the fills of those ditches tell another story. Snail species of grassland and open ground are rare in these assemblages, and by contrast, the most plentiful species are those that feed within the kind of leaf litter that would be found below woodland. There are also a number of other, specifically woodland species, and even one that prefers types of woodland which are relatively undisturbed by humans. One sample did, however, contain a higher proportion of open ground species, reflecting perhaps a clearance, but the prevailing picture from the snails is of woody vegetation on the hill, a picture that recurs on sites of this kind and date across the country. The consumption of large quantities of beef we infer from the bones was not taking place in open land at the centre of the human dwelling space. It was taking place at a peripheral place that was continuously tumbling down to its natural wooded state.

If vegetation kept regenerating, this would suggest feasting visits that were intermittent. Animal remains of another sort reveal something of the frequency of those intermittent visits to the hill. In this case it is the vertebrates rather than the invertebrates that are particularly informative. Take for example the jawbones recovered from a series of young lambs from the site. In a number of these young jaws, the teeth had not yet erupted. Those that had erupted showed different degrees of wear. A pattern found repeatedly was of jawbones in which not even the first molar had erupted. These animals had lived a very short time indeed, and were culled in the same spring season in which they were born. Slightly older jaws with erupted first molars also displayed a moderate amount of wear, enough to put their death at the previous summer or autumn. Older animals cannot be aged with such precision, and so it is from these young jawbones that we get an impression of two seasons in which parts of this wooded hill were temporarily cleared for the sharing of food. Another set of bones, the human bones, reveal another recurrent feature of these peripheral, seasonal meals in wooded places.[3]

Life in transition

Hambledon Hill has been described as 'death island' on the edge of the 'ocean' of barrows on the neighbouring grasslands of Cranborne Chase.[4] Fifteen human skulls were excavated from different parts of the hill, and half of these had been placed in a formal manner at the bottom of the hollows. The majority were buried without their lower jaw, and a few retained traces of cut-marks indicating where the flesh had been removed. Other human bones from around the site display much evidence through cut-marks of defleshing and cleaning, and all these features come together to suggest consumption of human flesh, curated bones, or possibly both. The bones were not just in these hollows, they were also in the elongated barrows of earth that crowned the hill. The ancestors were as much in motion on this hill as the living—possibly more so.[5]

The commonest species among all the bones on the hill was cattle, and their bones too not surprisingly display cut-marks from butchery. As with the humans, they also show signs of quite formal deposition. A similar association may be discerned between cattle and people in the contemporary series of long barrows running along a second range of limestone hills in southern England, the Cotswold hills. Human and cattle bones from these barrows had repeatedly received similar treatment. Cattle bones are burnt where human bones are burnt, are articulated where human bones are articulated, and dis-articulated where human bones are dis-articulated. It seemed that the family group comprised both humans and cattle, and the birth or death of either was a significant event, as was the consumption of either's meat. Like the trees that grew on the family plot, the ancestors were participants in the feast, perhaps the ancestral cattle too.[6]

What were these mysterious yet abundant meals about? What can be gleaned from the filled-in hollows that are their most direct testimony? Now that many of those backfilled hollows have been excavated and their contents analysed, we can infer that they represent repeated cycles of digging and immediate backfilling, probably in conjunction with the clearance of associated woodland. The backfilling repeatedly incorporates some kind of offering of food to the ancestors, together with the fresh and abundant debris of food for consumption by the living. The repeated returns to that particular spot, to celebrate rites of passage and to feast, linked that plot to a family tree alongside other plots and other family trees. At the base of many such a fill within these hollows we see evidence of that ancestral homage, in the form of a carefully deposited human skull.

There is much about Hambledon Hill that is resonant of what Claude Lévi-Strauss and Mary Douglas associated with activities on the periphery. The periphery was a place of transition, altered states, sexual liaison, death, and danger, where close kin and relative strangers from far and wide intermittently meet and share roasts and fermented drink so characteristic of what Lévi-Strauss describes as *exocuisine* or 'outside cooking'. It was not a place where people lived out their daily lives, not where their home fires were kept burning, but instead a place to assemble on special occasions; birth, maturation, marriage, and death, occasions of social and biological transition. The feasts in these places were about building larger communities of people and livestock, forging a common identity beyond the bounds of any individual hearth. They are points connecting with different networks, networks that reached far out into societies and landscapes beyond.

The close bond between humans and cattle was significant. These were farming communities, managers of a mobile food web that had travelled across the entire continent. The backfill from the hollows provides much evidence for other elements of that mobile food web. Quantities of wheat and barley, sacks of hazelnuts, even grapes, were brought to the site, sometimes to be burnt whole, as food for the ancestors, perhaps.[7] In those same hollows, and indeed all across the entire site, fragments were recovered of a novel form of artefact that has retained its intimate association with the meal ever since.

Containers of moulded clay

To track down the origins of this new artefact, we need briefly to turn our attention from the western edge of the Old World to the East, where a tranquil setting between wooded hills at a river's edge in southern China takes us to the earliest known examples. A mound of shells marks a point where early foragers gathered over many seasons to prepare their food. In amongst the shell debris are some fragments of fired clay, formed into the shape of vessels. The shells in which they were buried have been carbon dated, suggesting that the pots are around 20,000 years old. It may be that the date will need to be adjusted forward slightly, in relation to possible limestone contamination. However, the shell mound at Liushou Dalong-tan Liyuzui is just one of a group of sites in China and Japan with dates for pottery between 15,000 and 20,000 years old.[8] A few thousand years earlier, hunters of Moravia in Central Europe had been fashioning clay into figures of humans and animals, but over the far side of the Old World, fired clay was being used to make vessels. While our planet's temperature was dropping to a glacial low, the first clay pots were being fashioned along

16. Fragments of one of the world's oldest pottery containers, an estimated 17,000 years old, recovered from the Yuchanyan site in Hunan Province, China.

the waterways and woodland edges of mainland China. The precise use of these early pots remains a matter for investigation, but they certainly allow a novel range of culinary possibilities, extending the range of foodstuffs from the solid to the liquid and semi-liquid. This new range included soups, stews, beverages, and sauces, in the preparation of which flavours could be mixed and concocted in quite different ways, corresponding to Lévi-Strauss's enclosed and economic *endocuisine* or 'inside cooking'.

Pottery made a much later appearance in western Asia, not figuring large until the growth of farming communities was well under way, but by the time of its spread across temperate Europe, farming was almost invariably accompanied by the use of pottery. In comparing the great range of forms of pottery vessel among early foragers and farmers, another feature of their use becomes clear. Not only are they ideal for holding drinks and fluid foods, they can also be marked with a range of designs, designs that recur across regions. Just as the feasts of early farmers and foragers can serve to build communities, pottery provides an ideal surface over which communal identity can be inscribed through characteristic design.

The pottery fragments from Hambledon Hill came from round bowls with a simple curved rim and lugs for handles. A modest style, but distinctive enough to place it within a geographical spread of similar vessels that spans 300 km across south-west England. Communities travelling across this landscape would recognize a number of familiar signs as they assembled at these meeting places on the periphery. The pots are simply the most durable material items to record these cultural styles. Those same pots also reflect how, within such assemblies, the community is composed of quite small groups. From the curvature of the rim fragments, it could be deduced that the vessels were not big enough to feed extensive groups. A diameter of 30 cm would represent quite a large bowl. In fact, a great number of the vessels were very small indeed; a third of the measurable rims indicated a diameter of 6–12 cm. Perhaps 'cups' is a better description than bowls. In a gathering that brought people together from landscapes spanning several days' walk, the larger bowls, like the fragmented hollows themselves, suggest an *endocuisine* bringing together small groups, and much of the consumption was as individuals. These same small groups and individuals were simultaneously bound together within their larger social networks reflected in the style rather than the diameter of their pots, and through the *exocuisine* of hundreds of kilos of shared meat.[9]

Looking inside the pots

Most pottery studies in archaeology have focused their attention on the outside of the pots. This is where surface design may help us delineate cultural communities across space and time. It is only in the last few decades that archaeologists have paid much more attention to the insides, and the possibility of finding traces of what they once held. Like most early pots, the cups and bowls from Hambledon Hill were unglazed, leaving many microscopic channels in their matt surfaces to trap small samples of what was placed within them. Some of the most persistent traces are the fats, oils, and waxes, a group whose collective chemical name is 'lipids'. Lipid chemistry is such that these trapped signatures can last indefinitely. It is quite possible that the majority of unglazed pots retain some lipid trace of their contents, and some of these lipids can be linked to particular species, enabling us to read a lipid signature from an ancient pot as 'cabbage', 'olive oil', or 'cow' for example. A particular feature of the way an organism works enables us to go yet one step further than 'cow'. We have seen how light and heavy versions of the same element, 'isotopes' as they are known, can be used as monitors of the food web and trophic positions within it.[10] With the appropriate element, we can sometimes even chart the movement from organ to organ. In a female mammal, meat and milk fractionate their oxygen isotopes differently. These are the isotopes we have encountered in Chapter 3, used to construct a geological 'thermometer', a tracker of climate change. Within the mammal body, those same isotopes show up differently between meat and milk.

Measuring this sorting effect with precision and care has allowed the recognition of milk or milk products in early pottery. Indeed, traces of milk have been found in pots along the Danube basin associated with some of the earliest farming in Central Europe, over 7,000 years ago. Two thousand years further on, characteristic milk lipids have been repeatedly found in the fabric of the pots of Britain's first farmers. On some sites, the proportion of pots with a dairy signature may reach 50 or even 80 per cent of all pots examined. At Hambledon Hill too, the dairy signature was widespread. However much milk was flowing in their farming lives, it seems implausible that they could have brought vast quantities of fresh milk to their hilltop seasonal feast, and more likely either it travelled in fermented form, or that the milk was used as a primer to seal the inner unglazed surface, in preparation for some other beverage or fluid.[11]

We can thus assemble a range of foods together with these small cups and bowls: hazelnuts and cereal grains, the meat from pig, sheep, red deer, roe deer, and wild cows. Dominating the whole picture is milk and beef from their much-valued domesticated cattle. While some bones have been cracked open for marrow, the general absence of signs of burning or dog-gnawing indicates that meat was cut from the skeleton, and then the bones disposed of as an integral part of the ritual cycle of digging and backfilling. These traces tell us something about what they did eat, but we can also glean evidence of what they did not, which is more informative than one might first imagine.

Avoiding food

Hambledon Hill rises between two rivers, which they no doubt followed on their way to the coast to gather large beach pebbles for use as hammerstones. A most suitable opportunity for fowling and fishing perhaps, yet bird bones are relatively few, and fish bones are absent. There are many reasons why the rather delicate bones of some birds and certainly fish might not be detected; they might not survive, or even if they did survive, may not always be spotted during excavation. However, the absence of fish resonates with another set of skeletal remains. As we have seen, the human bones at the bottom of the pits had lost their flesh well before the ceremony described above. That defleshing, however, has helped preserve another type of protein, the collagen within the bones themselves, rendering them ideal material for isotopic analysis.

In a study that used the same isotopes described in Chapter 5 to compare Neanderthals with early modern humans in the study, the isotope signature in the bones of fifty-one individuals was compared with those from three control populations, first those who had eaten large quantities of fish, second those for whom marine resources made up around half the diet, and finally for those acquiring their food entirely from the land. All the Hambledon samples lay outside that range. There was no overlap whatsoever. This suggested that the absence of fish from the excavated bones was not an accident. Even with such easy access along rivers to the coast, they were not eating fish.[12]

Not eating readily available foods is a topic that has intrigued anthropologists studying food. Any community, exposed to a vast array of non-toxic potential foodstuffs, rich in proteins, carbohydrates, fats, and vitamins, will reject at least some of it. My own society is still pretty squeamish about terrestrial arthropods, insects, woodlice, grubs, and so on, at the same time as regarding their aquatic cousins, crabs, lobsters, crayfish, etc., as great delicacies. This particular 'taboo' is so deeply rooted that we have forgotten from whence it came, and certainly forget to note when such prehistoric societies as those around the Ohalo campfire seem to share that taboo. In other strategies of food avoidance, the meaning is not so deeply buried; our refusal to eat certain categories of perfectly edible food marks us out as belonging to one particular community, and definitely not belonging to another, foreign community, which in turn is characterized by the despicable practice of consuming that same foul foodstuff with relish. At the feast, the sharing of food simultaneously builds an 'in-group' and excludes an 'out-group'.

Food avoidance is repeatedly a strategy for demarcating communities, establishing who belongs and who does not, who is friend and who is foe. It is an aspect of that classification, of 'putting the world in order', whose roots could be discerned around the campfire at Ohalo, where foods and food waste were separated around, away from the fire, around the fire, and within brushwood huts. However, whereas the organization of space around the intimate meal serves to order and acknowledge the close kin group, the family, the definition of the larger group requires different, more portable markers, some of which leave traces for the archaeologist, others which do not. Many aspects of body decoration, for example, may not last, but through research such as that done at Hambledon Hill, food avoidance strategies may become evident, within the early farming society being observed, and among ourselves, the observers. We may infer that the Hambledon Hill community avoided eating fish; they may even have expressed distaste and disgust at the idea. By the same token, we might ourselves have uneasy feelings about those defleshing cuts visible on so many of the human bones. Taking the flesh off a bone does not necessarily imply consumption of that flesh, but the state of the human bones from the site has posed the question: were the visitors to the hill eating each other?

The community's ultimate boundary

Cannibalism has intrigued Western authors for centuries, and has been explored and analysed from countless different perspectives. One thing that is clear from observations of the many instances in which it is practised is that a common theme in cannibalism seems to elude us. Some communities eat the people they hate, others eat a portion of those they have loved. Some do it for purely symbolic reasons, others because human meat tastes good. Even the definitions are vaguer than might be expected. We in the West are clear that the *Fore* people of New Guinea were practising cannibalism when they ate the brains of newly departed relatives. If we travel to another part of the same island however, we might meet the Umeda people who are equally clear that we in the West practise cannibalism when we chew our fingernails or suck a bleeding finger. On reflection, it is probably easier to say something coherent and uniform about *non-cannibals* as a group. Non-cannibals by and large find the consumption of human tissue (however they define it) repulsive, and something that foreign people, extremely foreign people, do. The ancient classical authors placed cannibals on the far periphery of the civilized world, not as far as the monsters and human/animal hybrids, but further than most. Non-cannibalism is a very pronounced form of food avoidance strategy, one that remains active in Western society, as a way of marking the boundary of the entire civilized world and separating it from the barbaric hinterland beyond.[13]

We may conjecture that the Hambledon Hill community delineated themselves in a rather different way. The parallels in the treatment and deposition of human and cattle bones suggest they were both part of an 'in-group' treated with respect in life and in death, and their flesh consumed with respect. The 'out-group' were fish eaters, and just as many ethnic clashes are between groups that are genetically close, the genetic relationship between the fish eaters and the fish avoiders may not have been that distant.

Across the North Sea from Britain, fish are far more in evidence, in a most intriguing way at the Danish site of Dragsholm, where three bodies were interred within a few metres of each other, around the time of the cattle feast on Hambeldon Hill, a cluster that it has been suggested might correspond to 'a man and his wives'. If this was the correct interpretation, then it was a household in which gender came conspicuously to the meal table. The carbon isotope measurements of the man are substantially different from those of the women, the man's being far 'meatier' and the women's far 'fishier'. Feeding prescriptions and food avoidance are not just employed to delineate communities and ethnic groups, but also to separate people by class, age, and gender. It may be that these bones are in any case not entirely contemporary—their carbon dates are also a little offset, but viewed on a coarser scale, they may be emblematic of a deeper dynamic, rooted in the manner in which farming spread across Europe.[14]

Denmark is notable for a coastal fishing foraging tradition that persists long after most Europeans were heavily agricultural. Its coast has a series of middens, large mounds composed of the debris of marine, coastal, and inland food resources that continue in use from the last glacial maximum through to a time when agriculture is widespread in Britain and mainland Europe. Other coastlines, including the British coastline, probably have similar middens, but ones that now lie beneath the sea. It is only in regions of geological 'uplift' we would expect to find them exposed, and there, in Denmark, Scotland, Brittany, and Portugal they can indeed be found, monuments to a way of life that farming successively replaced. However, it was also the practitioners of this way of life that contributed a large genetic input into subsequent farming communities, predominantly through the female line. Whether the Dragsholm bodies are actual contemporaries, or just near contempories, they highlight an ecological difference between two intermarrying groups that certainly was a widespread occurrence, one that occurred in the context of some inter-community tension. The isotopic shift from fish to meat is a pronounced one, and some have argued against a strict avoidance strategy on the grounds of a clear overlap in time and space between fish eaters and fish avoiders. However, it is precisely that overlap that strengthens the avoidance argument. Taboos and avoidance strategies exist to draw boundaries separating a remembered or partially visible 'out-group', not one that is lost in the mists of time.

The closer two cultural groups get to each other, the more strongly they will typically emphasize their difference. The manner in which they affirm their identity and difference, be it through dress, hairstyle, behaviour, feasting, or food avoidance, will often be amplified. As farming spread across Europe, in the closest observed contacts between farmers and foragers, for example along the Danube, in the Baltic region, and in Brittany, the foragers with whom they came into contact made considerable use of aquatic resources. In the growing entanglement of human networks that unfolded with the expansion of farming, definitions of who belonged to which community needed an imposed clarity, not actually justified by their melting-pot origins. In this world of changing places and seasonal encounters, who were these newly forged and reforged communities, who gathered together to share food on a scale much greater than the intimate family?

Who were the feasters?

We can start by asking certain questions about the bodily evidence of their skeletal remains on Hambledon Hill. The same isotope studies that suggested an avoidance of fish allowed levels of meat consumption to be assessed and, in an admittedly small sample, the women seemed to be getting more meat than the men. They also constitute the commonest category of skulls that are kept or 'curated' for some significant period after death. A further indication of a potentially powerful female role is that they are equally likely to suffer injury in armed conflict as their husbands and brothers.

A wide-ranging study of contemporary skeletal remains from around Britain has indicated a great deal of physical injury. From the skulls alone, it would appear that almost one in ten, both men and women, had experienced head injury during their lives. The commonest injury results in a skull depression inflicted by a heavy blow on the left side of the head, what might be anticipated from face-to-face combat between right-handed men and women. Around a third of those wounds were fatal. Others lived to fight again. One man went to his grave with the recovered head wounds of three separate, serious injuries.[15]

We might suggest a large community of small matriarchal bands, collecting together on a wooded hill to honour the ancestors and add shape to their altered landscape. By and large, the maternally inherited DNA of people still alive in Britain carries a strong pre-agricultural signal. It is true of many people alive today that their maternal ancestors foraged in localities quite often within a few hundred kilometres of where they live thousands of years on. The women of Hambledon Hill were that much closer in time to their fishing/gathering/hunting ancestry, an ancestry that may have retained a significant imprint on their stories, beliefs, and traditions. Nonetheless, it seems that the fishing heritage was now negated in the context of the new culture being forged, in which we see a stronger element associated with men.

As was discussed in the previous chapter, there is an argument that paternally inherited DNA generally carries a signal we can relate to pioneer farmers, and domesticated cattle and crops, together with a cult of the death and the skull, may have travelled with them. In time their monuments become quite substantial features in the landscape, such as the earthen long barrows they constructed for their dead.

We see evidence of conflict and of violence, and of a politics of gender. However, neither the causewayed camps nor the long barrows bear the stamp of a figure that has often been associated with monument construction, the authoritarian leader. Careful excavation of both monument types has revealed that their overall unity of form breaks down to a series of smaller piecemeal constructions. It does not seem from the incidence of head wounds that the small bands that came together in this collective enterprise were always on the best of terms, and we have found no trace of the dictatorial palace or high-status individual burial. So what brought them away from their familiar hearths, their small gatherings of close kin to share food around the fire, to gather together on the uncertain periphery, to share food and drink with friend, foe, and stranger?

The scenario looks unusual, unfamiliar, in need of explanation, only when looking forward in time, from within the intimate, pro-social meals shared among familiar diners grouped around the earliest conversational circles of all. Visitors from the periphery, bearing gifts of shells and exotic stones, had certainly joined such meals, but great feasts on the periphery itself were less in evidence. There is some evidence that these peripheral feasts arose both among the farming communities whose extent across Europe had been growing, and among the fisher foragers with whom they came in contact. Some of the shell middens along the Brittany coast, for example, have been interpreted as foci for elaborate feasts. Indeed, we may assume that meetings, exchanges, and marriage transactions between such different communities required that both sides had some sense of the logic of a peripheral feast at which strangers were not unusual. They need not be directly linked with agriculture; it has been suggested that these shell middens on the coasts of Brittany were places of funerary feasting.[16]

Looking backwards from the present, peripheral feasts, knitting different communities on different scales, are commonplace. Some of them require some elaborate hierarchical superstructure, such as is not discernible at Hambledon Hill, but others do not. Take for example the practice of *tesgüinada*, that forms a central part of the cycle of life of the Rarámuri people of Mexico.

Tesgüinada literally means 'beer party', an opportunity to consume large quantities of the maize beer (*tesgüino*) to whose preparation the average Rarámuri family will devote almost 100 kilos of their annual maize harvest, enough for around 500 litres of beer. Anyone with enough beer at their disposal could initiate a *tesgüinada*—there was no need for a single conspicuous authority. They were initiated in relation to a common enterprise, a piece of building work, a curing ritual, or a seasonal religious celebration, for example. The attraction of a feast would then draw people from scattered settlements in the region. By coming and partaking, they would tacitly engage themselves in extended networks of shared endebtedness and labour. A combination of humour, entertainment, and alcohol would soften the route to engaging with relative strangers, surmounting tensions and hostilities. Not surprisingly, a *tesgüinada* is well suited to finding marriage partners. The *tesgüinada* is far from unique. Similar beer feasts were in use among the Samia people of western Kenya, the Sebei of Uganda, and the Fur of Sudan. Here, beer-drinking brings people together for such tasks as mining or large-scale agriculture, again outside any conspicuous structures of authoritarian control.[17]

A landscape of constant regeneration

What happened when it was time for the Hambledon Hill feasting parties to return home, and what precisely was 'home' like? These things are rather less easy to explore than the feast itself. The landscape around the hill has been scoured for the telltale flint debris that might mark the valley settlements. They do not seem easy to find. The dry valleys neighbouring the hill have been probed for evidence of the erosion patterns that accompany a sustained human presence. Such patterns as are found seem to belong to a much later epoch. The feasters' return home is decidedly discreet.

We can tell a great deal from what they brought with them to the hilltop. Their cattle, pigs, sheep, and goats must have grazed somewhere;

the isotopic signal from their bones suggests they grazed a combination of wooded and open land. The woods are still important as a source of deer, wild cow, wild boar, and hazelnuts, but there must also have been open plots in which to raise their cereal crops. Another way of finding these illusive communities who did not disturb the earth in a manner that archaeologists can easily detect is to look for their impact on vegetation. This can be attempted by returning to the ancient pollen rains trapped in peat bogs and lake sediments that we have encountered in the context of studying climate change. Human impact in recent times shows up as a substantial drop in the proportion of tree pollen. Nevertheless, sequences from the time of Hambledon Hill suggest that most of the trees are still in place. Within this wooded landscape, human action shows up not as a wholesale removal of woodland, but by the appearance within it of patches of distinctive vegetation, and in particular the plants known as 'weeds'.

Weeds are plants that can withstand a physical attack on their soil, the kind of attack inflicted by glaciers, avalanches, and human farmers. From a few centuries before the hollows at Hambledon Hill were dug and refilled, at the time of the earliest traces of visits to the hilltop, weeds appear within sequences of pollen recovered from bogs and lake muds that had accumulated during that period. These weeds had tracked the passage of the mobile farming food chain across Europe, following the hoe and the ard[18] as it broke up soil, and showing up as fairly small numbers of pollen grains on the corer's microscope slide.[19]

On either side of those few pollen grains on the slide are a much larger number of grains belonging to woodland species. Some of the trees were more sensitive to the farmers in their midst than others. Pollen of the elm gets more scarce around this time. Nevetheless, much of the structure of the vegetation remains intact. Just as Hambledon Hill moves through endless cycles of clearance and regeneration, so the landscape all around continually returns to woodland, even with the clearances in its midst.

In many ways, the 'family plots' marked out by repeatedly infilled hollows on Hambledon Hill formed a microcosm of the entire landscape. The kin group gathered for a while, cleared vegetation, organized a plot of earth, pursued their social practices, and then left the plot to grow back to a prior state. They returned to places where the same cycle was enacted, albeit on a tempo that was slower, but had sufficient pace for the cycles to merge in millennial pollen sequences. Some very finely sampled sequences have picked up the oscillations between open and wooded ground, but this requires samples that discriminate pollen rains of a few decades or less. Sequences with less resolution give the general impression of continuing woodland, just as the snail shells from Hambledon Hill gave the general impression of a continuously wooded hilltop.[20]

An in-between world

Looking both to the recent and distant past, human ecology seems to fall fairly and squarely into two modes, modes that fall either side of Childe's Neolithic Revolution. In one mode, food is procured in a responsive relationship with nature, by hunting, gathering, and foraging. In the other mode, food is produced by controlling nature, through farming. Communities past and present are placed in one mode or the other, one side or other of Childe's revolutionary transition. We have various ways of dealing with evidence of societies which do not quite fit. Those with a lot of domesticated species, but a notable minority of wild resources might be farmers, backing up a poor year's harvest with occasional famine. Those using a lot of wild species but just a few domesticates may either be 'experimenting' with agriculture, or trading with their farming neighbours. However, in the period of time between the appearance of the first domesticates in Europe around 8,000 years ago, and their arrival in the northerly isles of Britain around 5,000 years ago, the great majority of sites are mixed in some form or other. True, there are clusters close to either extreme, but sites can be found during this period at more or less each point on the spectrum between 100 per cent domesticates and 100 per cent wild resources. Could it be that a mixed hunter/forager/farmer way of life was far more than an intermediate or transitional form, and instead a stable and sustainable way of life? Or indeed that mixture and uncertain boundaries are normal and expected features of a system characterized by the marked expansion of interconnecting networks?

Our tendency to think in terms of a simple sharp split between hunter-gatherers and farmers comes largely from looking at societies that survived long enough to be observed in the present and recent past. On the one hand we have a vast population of farmers now dominating the global ecosystem, and along the margins and in remote regions a small and decreasing number of hunter-gatherer societies, particularly in the equatorial and polar regions. After 10,000 years of agricultural expansionism, it is hardly surprising that those hunter societies that do survive are ecologically and geographically remote. The more mixed and proximal ways of life would have shifted to full farming long since. When looking at early communities that leave traces of both domesticated and wild resources, particularly within the temperate zone, we are looking at communities whose ecology is not easily paralleled within the ethnographic record; they engaged with nature in a different way, unconstrained by our modern taxonomies and dichotomies. At their seasonal festivities on Hambledon Hill, the food they brought to share with their ancestors might be a sack of grain or a harvest of hazelnuts; it might be the carcass of a domestic lamb or a wild deer. All these have left their trace within the backfilled holes. Most intriguing of all is a fruit that may have made a longer journey than most.

So surprising was the find of a single grape pip within the backfill of one of the hollows that the excavators had that pip individually carbon dated. Like other dates from accompanying material in the same feature, its date places it within an early period of feasting on the hilltop. The find was further confirmed by the recovery of a piece of charred vine wood from the site. Grapes from this particular period are few in number, and barely feature at all in northern Europe. The closest parallels are from a site in southern France called La Poujade. It seems most plausible that they travelled long distances, as exotic fruits of some value. They may have travelled on the stem, which explains the charred vine wood found at Hambeldon Hill, perhaps dried as raisins. However, it is interesting to note that the other characteristically Mediterranean crop to reach Britain by this early period is the opium poppy, so perhaps the significance of these long-distance imports was their narcotic potential, wine and opium at the feast.[21]

The Hambledon grape pip was carefully measured and compared with modern wild and domesticated forms. Like the pips from La Poujade, its size and shape place it in an intermediate position between modern domestic and wild forms, an ambiguity that is emblematic of the prevailing relationship between people and nature at the time. What is perhaps more significant about the presence of grapes is not the precise status of its human predators as gatherers or farmers, but that it was brought from a place separated by a distance across space to be shared with ancestors who were similarly separated across time. These feasts on the periphery built networks across space and time that underpinned both their ecological and social lives. Those networks can also be seen in many of the artefacts brought to the site. There are pots from the far south-west of Britain and from the Jurassic ridge to the north. The polished stone axes at the site have been sourced to Cornwall, Wales, and the Lake District in the north-west of England. Two fine axes of nephrite and jadeite were picked up from the surface of the site. These had travelled from mainland Europe.[22]

Farmers within a multi-track web

While the pottery and stone axes describe an intricate and extensive social network, what of the ecological network described by the bio-logical evidence? Setting aside for a moment considerations of quantity, the food web we can reconstruct displays a certain degree of diversity at each level, but greatly reduced in comparison with foraging sites that make extensive use of birds and fish. At each level are both wild and domesticated species, including some taxa we may be uncertain where to place. At the base of the food web, both clearings for crops and woodland are significant loci of primary production. Two types of barley and emmer wheat were raised within the clearings, which provided sustenance not just for the humans, but also for the cattle and the pigs. This much we can infer from isotopic study, which can be applied to animal as well as human bone. The pigs were found to be towards the vegetarian end of the spectrum, which suggests fattening up on grain and other crops, rather than being left to forage omnivorously in the wild. However, the bones of at least one of the cattle carried an isotopic signal suggesting woodland foraging, and reminding us of the importance of this plentiful resource.[23]

The most conspicuous woodland resource is the hazelnut, which, as in most early farming sites in northern Europe, is widespread in the assemblages and evident in plenty. We might also think of grapes as belonging to the woodland edge. At the next trophic level up, the woods support the much-consumed red deer and roe deer. Cattle, pig, and possibly goat, grazed in both wooded and open areas, and the latter also provided grazing for the sheep. At the top of the food chain are a range of carnivores, omnivores, and carrion feeders, including foxes, badgers, pine martens, carrion crows, and rooks. There were most likely wolves and bears around, and of course dogs and humans. The overall structure of a food web such as this is very similar to stable food webs in nature, with numerous pathways for energy flow, and not too many interconnections between different pathways, much as was the case at Ohalo. The human feeding strategy was presumably opportunistic, and in particular, seasonally opportunistic. As had been the case in middle latitudes since at least that early encampment at Ohalo, it is likely that the human diets changed from season to season. In this manner, they contrast both with contemporary farmers practising complex storage technologies, and with contemporary hunter gatherers, either foragers from the non-seasonal equatorial regions, or hunters from the circumpolar regions. They may have had more in common with the early hunter-gatherers around the Ohalo campsite in their intensely seasonal lifestyles.

Turning to quantities, the isotopic data indicate that human diet was rich in meat, and the bones indicate that a great deal of this meat was beef.[24] This points to the importance of the species with which the community is most intimately associated, the cow, with which they lived together and died together. In each case, we see clear evidence that the flesh was taken from the bones and the milk consumed. We also know from other contemporary sites in Britain and Europe that they worked together on the land to prepare the soil for barley and wheat.

Underneath the long earthen burial monuments used by these societies, excavation has occasionally revealed evidence beneath those monuments of how they worked the land. The land surface exposed beneath one such barrow in Wiltshire in southern England was criss-crossed with the marks of a heavily wooden implement that had been dragged through the ground. These cultivation marks were created more than 5,000 years ago by trained cattle pulling a wooden 'ard'.[25]

Within those hidden plots, cloistered within a continuous wildwood, a food-web dynamic is coming into being. Connections are multiplying as strands are interwoven in new ways. Elements are transferred from one trophic level to another, manure and energy is forging links up and down the food chain, the consumption of wool and milk by humans, and of anything left over by pigs and dogs. This daily food quest is quite different from the intermittent hilltop binge. While the latter intermittent activity has left a clear physical mark in the landscape, the former, daily activity is almost impossible to find. Between these discrete hilltop episodes of burning, burial, digging, drinking, fighting, and feasting, they slip back into the wooded landscape, into which they merge with only the slightest trace.

As we saw in the context of Ohalo, a key feature of sustainable food webs in nature is that they are relatively loosely interconnected. Energy can move quite independently down different pathways, limiting the knock-on effects on the various perturbations that are a normal part of our changeable quaternary worlds. This has been integral to the food webs of modern humans since their spread across the world, and a key feature of their broad diets. It is also integral to early farming communities that retain many pathways through the 'wild' elements of their food web. We can see in Hambledon Hill evidence of ways in which that looseness of interconnection was beginning to be compromised.

In seasons of the feast, small communities from all through the wooded landscape made their way to the revered hilltop, the place of their ancestors. They travelled with their cattle, livestock, and sacks of nuts, fruits, and grain, more speculatively cheeses and beer. How much they gave and how much they received was interwoven with the stages of life within each kin group, whether there were rites of passage to celebrate or over which to grieve. They were coming together to the node of a vast social and ecological network. They recognized their more distant kinsmen at the feast by avoidance of certain foods, and through portable signs, body adornment, tools, weapons, and pots, but there was still occasional tension and inter-group violence.[26] This social tension was mirrored by certain elements of ecological tension, shifts in the balance of the woodland and the decline in a few vulnerable species. Nevertheless, they were still sharing food within loosely connected, multi-track food webs, which had proved both successful and sustainable, making far less of an impact upon the global ecosystem than a rather different pattern of food web that was to follow.

17. Imagined view of the throne room (megaron) and its ceremonial hearth, from the Mycenaean palace at Pylos in Greece.

8

HIERARCHY AND THE FOOD CHAIN

Messenia, southern Greece, c.1200 BC (recounted c.800 BC)

But as the sun was rising from the fair sea into the firmament of heaven to shed light on mortals and immortals, they reached Pylos the city of Neleus. Now the people of Pylos were gathered on the sea shore to offer sacrifice of black bulls to Neptune lord of the Earthquake. There were nine guilds with five hundred men in each, and there were nine bulls to each guild. As they were eating the inward meats and burning the thigh bones [on the embers] in the name of Neptune, Telemachus and his crew arrived, furled their sails, brought their ship to anchor, and went ashore.

Minerva led the way and Telemachus followed her. Presently she said, 'Telemachus, you must not be in the least shy or nervous; you have taken this voyage to try and find out where your father is buried and how he came by his end; so go straight up to Nestor that we may see what he has got to tell us. Beg of him to speak the truth, and he will tell no lies, for he is an excellent person.'

'But how, Mentor,' replied Telemachus, 'dare I go up to Nestor, and how am I to address him? I have never yet been used to holding long conversations with people, and am ashamed to begin questioning one who is so much older than myself.'

'Some things, Telemachus,' answered Minerva, 'will be suggested to you by your own instinct, and heaven will prompt you further; for I am assured that the gods have been with you from the time of your birth until now.'

She then went quickly on, and Telemachus followed in her steps till they reached the place where the guilds of the Pylian people were assembled. There they found Nestor sitting with his sons, while his company round him were busy getting dinner ready, and putting pieces of meat on to the spits while other pieces were cooking. When they saw the strangers they crowded round them, took them by the hand and bade them take their places. Nestor's son Pisistratus at once offered his hand to each of them, and seated them on some soft sheepskins that were lying on the sands near his father and his brother Thrasymedes. Then he gave them their portions of the inward meats and poured wine for them into a golden cup, handing it to Minerva first, and saluting her at the same time.

'Offer a prayer, sir,' said he, 'to King Neptune, for it is his feast that you are joining; when you have duly prayed and made your drink-offering, pass the cup to your friend that he may do so also. I doubt not that he too lifts his hands in prayer, for man cannot live without God in the world. Still he is younger than you are, and is much of an age with myself, so I will give you the precedence.'

As he spoke he handed her the cup. Minerva thought it very right and proper of him to have given it to herself first; she accordingly began praying heartily to Neptune. 'O thou,' she cried, 'that encirclest the earth, vouchsafe to grant the prayers of thy servants that call upon thee. More especially we pray thee send down thy grace on Nestor and on his sons; thereafter also make the rest of the Pylian people some handsome return for the goodly hecatomb they are offering you. Lastly, grant Telemachus and myself a happy issue, in respect of the matter that has brought us in our to Pylos.'

When she had thus made an end of praying, she handed the cup to Telemachus and he prayed likewise. By and by, when the outer meats were roasted and had been taken off the spits, the carvers gave every man his portion and they all made an excellent dinner. As soon as they had had enough to eat and drink, Nestor, knight of Gerene, began to speak.

'Now,' said he, 'that our guests have done their dinner, it will be best to ask them who they are.'

(*Odyssey*, Book 3, trans. Samuel Butler[1])

In search of an epic

NESTOR's feast was echoing through the thoughts of Cincinatti archaeologist, Carl Blegen, while he travelled through the fertile olive groves of the south-west coast of Greece in the spring of 1939. The villagers he met on the way were eager to show him the ruins and antiquities in their farmland. He was not the first archaeologist to come that way. A few of them were old enough to remember when the pioneer excavator of Troy, Heinrich Schliemann, visited their villages on a similar quest. Back in the previous century he had collected some pottery fragments from beside a coastal lagoon in a place that had come to be known as the 'Cave of Nestor'. The fragments he found displayed some similarities with pots also found at the famous site of Mycenae around 130 km to the north-east. In the ensuing decades, a series of excavations had unearthed elite burials in the same region, furnished with fine vases and items of gold. As Blegen talked with the villagers sixty-three years after Schliemann's first visit, he hoped to go one step further than interesting pottery and elite burials. His aim was to get close to one of the characters named in Homer's *Odyssey*, an elderly statesman in the league that the king of Mycenae, Agamemnon, headed against Priam, king of Troy. This statesman was also host to the feast narrated above, the fabled King Nestor.[2]

Looking for stories beneath the ground is always an uncertain task, with rich findings on the way, but the invariable conclusion that the story does not exist there. Its true home is instead the conversational circle above ground, around the real or metaphorical campfire, or alternatively as words carefully arranged on a page. It is there that a selection of real people and real events are woven into a storyline, whose other threads draw from other episodes, real and imaginary. In searching for Homer's *Odyssey* beneath our feet, Schliemann had certainly found some extraordinary artefacts and structures from what he thought was Priam's Troy, but which we now believe belong to a much earlier epoch. He may have been closer to the target with Agamemnon's Mycenae, and his efforts certainly inspired generations of Mycenean scholars. Carl Blegen continued Schliemann's work at Troy, before turning his attentions to the region around the Cave of Nestor where those early pots had been found, in the hope of finding the core of Nestor's kingdom, his magnificent palace.

Finding a plausible location of fragments from the *Odyssey* is not a straightforward matter. My own particular interest in doing so is to get closer to a particular pattern of sharing food depicted in the narrative that had some considerable consequences for the way society and ecology interacted in later prehistory. The eighth-century Greek poet we know as Homer was separated from the stories he narrated by half a millennium, and his tales interweave a tapestry of strands from the intervening centuries; much is refashioned, fictionalized, and enlarged, and much is lost. Homer may not have been that certain where the Pylos of which he spoke was located. The first-century geographer Strabo despaired at the task of deciding on the true Pylos from its many contenders on the coast of southern Greece, commenting, 'There is a Pylos before Pylos, and yet another.' When two millennia later, the Ottoman Empire retreated in from Messenia, a Turkish town was renamed Pylos, basically on little more than a hunch. It was just inland from modern-day Pylos that Carl Blegen, his colleagues, and the local villagers climbed to a peaceful olive grove on a hill called Englianos, to a plateau with commanding views over the valley and westwards towards the Ionian Sea. They selected this place as the most promising spot, and sought permission to lay down some exploratory trenches in between the olive trees. By mid-morning of the very first day of their excavation, the team was dramatically rewarded.

The soil of the olive grove was thinly covering the eroded footings of a series of stone walls, each of over a metre in thickness. From fragments of wall plaster recovered close to these footings, it was clear those walls bore elaborate paintings. But the most memorable finds of that profitable morning's digging were five clay tablets, inscribed with a text which, though undecipherable, matched a text that had previously been unearthed at the Cretan palace at Knossos. The excavator of that site, Sir Arthur Evans, had christened the text 'Linear B'.[3] Over the following month, another seven long thin trenches were laid out across the hill to establish the extent of the structure: substantial walls were encountered right across the hilltop. At the southern end of his very first trench, yet more of the inscribed clay tablets came to light within a small

18. A view along the axis of the throne room (megaron) at the Mycenaean palace at Pylos.

walled space. They now had over 600 tablets, and fragments of tablets, inscribed with the mysterious text.

Those first discoveries were interrupted by the Second World War, and Blegen had to wait another thirteen years to resume his work within the olive grove. During that war, a young code-breaker named John Chadwick would acquire the skills he could later transfer from decrypting military messages to that ancient script on the tablets. He was one of a number intrigued by the script, including a young architect named Michael Ventris. They both grappled with the script in the early post-war years, but there were too few of the clay tablets around to make significant progress. That is until Blegen returned to Pylos. In May 1952, he led a joint Greek–American team to embark upon excavating the site in full. In this first season, they exposed a lavish room with a large and ornate central hearth, 4 metres across, with footings for four columns around its base, and to one side, the footing for a throne. They returned to the small walled space that had produced the earlier tablets. It proved to be a pair of rooms, and close to 500 further inscribed tablets were recovered. One of these, when the lime had been cleaned off, proved critical in bringing to conclusion the deciphering efforts of Ventris and Chadwick; Linear B was a way of writing Greek. Its decipherment unlocked a vast body of new information about many aspects of Aegean society in the second millennium BC, including the provisions for their lavish feasts. Linear B had proven to be a script for transcribing Greek language, used to record quantities of oil, wine, grain, and flavourings. They additionally recorded many categories of worker, official, and priest. Among these were *hegetai* (counts), *lawegatai* (generals), and at the apex of the social order the *Wanax* (chief or king). On a single tablet, the *Wanax* might commission the equivalent of a thousand kilos of meat and grain together with a few hundred litres of wine. The two rooms in which so many of these clay tablets had been found were described as 'archive' rooms, offices devoted to some sort of tax collection and accountancy. Offerings would come from far and wide, and from many levels of society. The clay tablets made mention of heralds, fullers, potters, weavers, even slaves making offerings.[4]

A decade later, archaeological investigation had extensively probed and fully exposed the site. It is still possible today to walk among the rooms, between the eroded footings of the walls, walls that collectively span around 100 metres in each direction. A walk from the southern exterior to the throne room takes the visitor past the two small archive rooms on the left, through the palace entrance vestibule or 'propylon', then a courtyard, and beyond that a porch and another vestibule, before finally approaching the hearth and its adjacent throne. All around are smaller rooms, and beyond them, a series of storerooms with massive storage jars set into the ground.

A cluster of the smaller rooms, directly to the west of the throne room itself was instrumental in turning the excavators' attention to feasting and drinking. These five rooms between them contained a collapsed mass of around 6,500 ceramic vessels. Some had fallen directly from their position in stacks, and others in a manner that they had hung together, by a cord through their handles. An occasional black stripe in the deposits bore witness to a burnt shelf, evidence of the catastrophic fire that had engulfed this palace, bringing the store of its vessels of consumption crashing to the floor. Well over 3,000 of the vessels among those heaped upon the demolished pantry floors were of a particular kind reminiscent of the feast described in Homer's texts.[5]

19. Kylikes and assorted pots recovered during excavation of Room 20 at the Mycenaean palace at Pylos.

Hierarchy and protocol

In Homer's account of Nestor's feast, Pisistratus passed a wine cup to Minerva, and she onto Telemachus in turn. The commonest vessel in the cluster of pantries adjoining the throne was an elegant stem goblet, a 'kylix', with two handles on opposing sides of the rim, ideal for passing from hand to hand down a line of feasters. While the position of the handles made these cups ideal for sharing, another aspect of their design, the fabric of which they were made, served to highlight the divisions in society. The thousands of stored kylikes were of a fine clay. Pisistratus' cup was of gold. Blegen's team did recover several fragments of gold and silver, which might well have derived from damaged goblets, including eleven pieces clearly from the rim of a cup and its handle. These were recovered from the throne room itself.

There were many more kylikes recovered from the excavations, and variation in quality was a recurrent theme. The precious metal cups from the throne room and the fine clay kylikes from the adjacent pantries contrasted with a series of coarser clay kylikes from a different pantry, serving a courtyard some way from the throne room itself. The lowest-quality kylikes were found outside the southern entrance and beyond the archive rooms, where the village communities (*damoi*) gathered in vast numbers on the slopes stretching down to the bay. What they heard or sensed of the inner celebrations we cannot know, but it seems highly likely they saw little with their own eyes. They might get to the archive room to deliver their tribute and have their donation duly recorded, and there they might gain their closest contact with the heart of the feast.[6]

Food for the gods

Only after a terminal catastrophe do archaeologists have the good fortune to recover things in the place of their last use. In a site that continued in use, free of calamity, all of the organic remains and most of the pottery would end up on the manure heap and from there be scattered across the fields, but the same fire that left the pantry contents collapsed in recognizable heaps preserved final moments throughout the palace. The archive rooms are prime examples. In one corner was a massive storage jar, perhaps a depository for small tribute in the form of oil. The jar was found smashed, and it was probably the burning oil it released that cooked the inscribed clay tablets in the archive to the durable hardened state in which they were found. It also preserved a cluster of miniature kylikes together with a considerable heap of burnt animal bones.

As was typical for an archaeologist of the mid-twentieth century, Blegen was so taken by the architecture and the Linear B tablets that he did what many of his contemporaries also did, and put the bones in storage. Indeed we are lucky they got this far; many digs of this time took a decidedly cavalier attitude to the less glamorous of their findings. Almost half a century later, a series of dusty boxes was rediscovered in a small museum a little further inland from the Hill of Englianos. Within those boxes were the food bones Blegen had recovered from his excavations at Pylos. They were in a burnt and fragmented state, but nevertheless retained much information about the nature of the feasting before the final palace fire.[7]

As we have seen at the much earlier site of Boxgrove, meat bones are often recovered from archaeological sites in a state of highly informative damage. They are broken, sliced into, boiled, burnt, and gnawed. It is by looking carefully at this damage that we can work back to the sequence of transformations to which the animal's carcass was subjected. At this site the skeletal elements were found in a rather particular combination. Most of the skeleton was completely missing, and the elements that were present were burnt, and fragmented. By looking closely at the breakage patterns, it was clear that before fragmentation, the bones had been burnt whole. They were the jawbones and upper limb bones of cattle. The limb bones might have provided an excellent source of marrow and soup stock, but not these. Each bore cut-marks at either end, corresponding to where the muscle could be detached, but had been burnt as entire bones, after their flesh had been removed, and not simply scorched in the final destructive fire. The jawbones also displayed a series of cut-marks, consistent with skinning, dismembering, and filleting. Further excavations across the site complemented this unusual assemblage with five other 'special' assemblages, also of selected elements of the cow skeleton, unbroken but with cut-marks, and burnt. Each of these special assemblages corresponded to somewhere between five and eleven cattle, and two of these assemblages also included deer bones, in a similar state. The boxes of bones that had been gathering dust in the small museum were thus decoded by bio-archaeological methods as the residue of around six separate feasts, at which bones were offered to a chosen god by feeding them to a fire, and also providing thousands of kilos of meat for the mortals. Generations of Mycenean archaeology had filled many a museum store, and the Pylos bones were not the only ones waiting for scientific analysis. Around the same time that modern methods of analysis were being brought to those dusty boxes of bones, others were thinking about doing the same with the richest and most plentiful remains from sites like these, the pots.

Vessels in plenty

The kylikes were among many different kinds of small and large vessels recovered from the palace. Stored in the pantries closest to the throne room were large numbers of bowls, cups, and dippers. Other pantries contained jugs and flagons, large two-handled bowls or 'kraters', and a series of characteristic three-legged cooking pots.

The notion that these vessels might retain some remnant of their contents is almost as old as Mycenean archaeology itself. A century ago, a certain A. H. Gill reported on his examination of the contents of a Mycenean vase found in Egypt. His bold suggestion that it contacted oil of coconut has somewhat receded in plausibility now that we believe coconut reached Egypt in the early nineteenth century AD. We now have the means to reach more robust scientific identifications, but that does not mean they are free of speculation or opinion. Like the object of its study, residue analysis can involve a complex and surprising cocktail, mixing hard data analysis, assumption, conjecture, and guesswork. A range of chemical methods can now detect fragments of molecules in tiny quantities, as we have seen from the detection of milk in the Hambledon pots. Those studies were conducted on freshly excavated sherds of pottery. When working with pots excavated some time back, there follows a complicated quest to ensure that the molecules detected have nothing to do with the hand cream, suntan lotion, or insect repellent of the excavator, or indeed the plastic bag in which the potsherds were packed, long before the excavators were aware of the future possibilities of archaeological science.

Once these extraneous possibilities have been contained, there remains the uncertain task of rebuilding fragments of molecules into whole molecules, and then wondering from where in the vast range of living plant and animal species those molecules might have derived.

During the 1990s a series of specialists nonetheless set to the task of making sense of the rich legacy of excavations of the Aegean world. Some fairly romantic names entered the scientific literature, such as King Midas, whose supposed tomb in central Turkey was the subject of one study of funerary feasting vessels. The chemistry of the residues within was taken to indicate lamb or goat in a spicy stew with lentils, washed down with an alcoholic beverage. Closer to the world of Mycenean Pylos, the same scientist examined a series of conical cups from Minoan Crete. A trace of pine resin, a hint of calcium oxalate, and a smear of beeswax, found within the same cup might correspond to resinated wine, barley beer, and honey. This mixture in turn might be taken to match the Homeric *kykeon*, a beverage served up to the same Nestor during the battle of Troy.[8]

Over the last decade, kylikes, cups, flagons, craters, storage jars, and cooking pots from a range of sites in Mycenean Greece and the parallel 'Minoan' culture from the island of Crete have been borrowed from museum shelves and storerooms and tiny samples of their fabric taken for a range of different analyses by different scientists, with the aim of establishing the use of a large sample of vessels of the forms found in abundance at sites like Pylos, Mycenae, and the palaces of Minoan Crete. Their results revealed a series of recurrent themes, themes that connected as much, possibly more, to drink and intoxication as they did to food and sustenance.[9]

There was indeed some evidence for food and sustenance; those three-legged cooking pots, which to modern eyes would look ideal for a modest stew, clearly, in some circumstances, were used for precisely that. One such pot from Mycenean Thebes retained lipids characteristic of meat, olive oil, and cereal, for example. However, if that were their only use, we would certainly expect them to end up with a strong signature of cooking fats, and that is not invariably the case.

Another tripod cooking pot, this time from Mycenae itself, was rich in organic molecular traces. It was one of a number of cooking pots retaining traces of dissolved pine resin, consistent with a wine in the style of retzina. More direct evidence that wine was involved come from traces of a fermentation by-product, tartaric acid, and the general scarcity of fats among the residues. There were other interesting molecules besides, including two forms of a family of molecules called ketones.

This particular pairing of traces is of interest as only three plants are known to produce this combination, of which one is restricted to Chile. The other two plants are hops and rue, both narcotic plants of which the latter is deemed more likely on geographical grounds. This pot seems to have been used to prepare an alcoholic infusion of some kind. The chemistry of other tripod pot residues suggests it is not alone.[10]

A Bronze Age feast

These various strands of evidence do not bring us direct to Telamachus or Minerva, but instead to a series of final feasts around the hill above Pylos, where the *Wanax* had his palace. They were the kind of feast that went on to inform the narrative of the *Odyssey*, and also to a widespread style of sharing food that wove society and nature into a single network in many parts of the later prehistoric world. Here is how the Pylos feasts may have unfolded. Village communities would arrive from all over the region to feast around the palace of the *Wanax*, bringing with them contributions according to their wealth and status. Their status would also determine how close they arrived to the centre of the action. The vast majority of the thousands so assembled would gather on the hill slopes between the palace and the sea, in sight of the buildings of the complex, but not directly of what went on inside. Senior members of the various groups would gather in one of several courtyard areas, each of which had its own viewing platform, and serving pantries from which the drinking cups would be passed around. A massive wine store held provisions to keep these cups flowing, and cooking pots and basins available in plenty to infuse the wine with exotic flavourings. The cattle, together with a few captured deer, were taken through a sequence of entrance chambers, courtyards, and ante-rooms to the principal throne room. Here they were slaughtered and the flesh removed from their bones. Tongues and selected leg bones were roasted in the burning hearth to feed the gods. All those within earshot would listen for the toasts, and raise their drinks accordingly. Only the most elite diners, passing their gold and silver kylikes of wine, witnessed this stage directly, but the lesser diners would get to see the bones. They would be taken to be displayed in a small room closer to the outside courtyards, where a wider range of feasters could pass by and observe. Competitive feasting had always tempered participation with a certain amount of spectacle. At Pylos, the spectators were in the vast majority; to some extent everyone was a spectator apart from the gods themselves.

It would appear that there were diners everywhere, passing cups from hand to hand, but not always the same type of cup. In the throne room itself, gold and silver chalices would change hands. Between the entrance and the throne room, other groups of diners would be found, drinking from cups of lesser quality. Another courtyard to the west of the main palace building hosted yet more drinkers, and there were further groups that did not make it into the palace proper, but gathered in celebratory clusters outside. Both in the architecture and the different qualities of kylix, the material record gives us a clear indication of rank, and the inscriptions upon the clay tablets allow us to attach names to a few of those ranks. As heads would swim under the influence of alcohol, the air would thicken with other odours and perfumes, some adding to the intoxicating effect of the flavoured wine.[11]

At the end of the corridors is a large space with a substantial hearth at its centre, around which the community gathered to share food and drink. Each had their place, and there was one position marked out for the senior diner. On the far side of the conversational circle of diners lay a series of ancillary spaces, each one allocated a particular function in relation to servicing the meal, and on walls around the gathering were images of the animals to be culled for the feast. This description is as apt for the throne room at the heart of the Pylos complex as it would have been for any number of gatherings to share food including those gatherings five times as ancient on the shores of Galilee at Ohalo, or ten times as ancient in the first European meals to be shared by modern humans. The great throne room at the heart of the palace may be grand, and removed from view of the vast majority of diners, but its grammar of space has endured from much earlier and simpler places of gathering. It is looking beyond the hearth and beyond the room itself when a novel pattern of spaces is seen.

The earlier views beyond the intimate conversational circle looked directly out to the periphery, across the transition from culture to nature. The separation of the throne room from its natural periphery is much greater; it is a cultural space within other cultural spaces, which in turn are enclosed within more cultural boundaries still. A truly elaborate series of routes separates the inside from the outside, constraining access through courtyards, vestibules, pantries, storerooms, lobbies, and entranceways. To move from the throne room to the exterior, a minimum of five spaces must be traversed.

Redistribution, hierarchy, and time

Although they are separated by 1,000 years and the breadth of Europe, the feasts at Hambledon Hill and Pylos have a great deal in common. In each case, we imagine that beef and drink figure centrally in the occasional gatherings of small communities from far and wide, and there is a clear ritual theme to both. There may be strong resonances in terms of content, but significant differences in terms of structure and hierarchy. At Pylos hierarchy inhabits every feature, from the different qualities of kylix, to the compartmentalization of space. The spaces in which the Hambledon feast was enacted were transient and cyclical, repeatedly returning to nature. The spaces in which the Pylos feast was enacted are more fixed and enduring. As well as spaces for feasting, they incorporate spaces for large-scale storage, a clue to the different way these feasts articulated with contemporary society. In the previous chapter's discussion of the 'work-feast' that seemed an appropriate analogue for Hambledon Hill, the emphasis is on the pooling of labour for an immediate task at hand, a building project or healing ritual, for example, for which a plentiful supply of food and drink serves as a magnet to gather feasters from far and wide. At Pylos, the vast quantities of food and drink may have a more enduring role in the social cycle. They are not simply consumed in the feast but given in tribute, to higher authorities, kings, generals, priests, and gods, to be stored and passed on at a later point in time. Each village community which brings its produce to the palace in times of plenty may also receive support and protection in times of need. The Pylos feast may thus fit better with a 'redistributive feast', binding the community with a sense of indebtedness to their *Wanax* and ultimately to their gods.

In the feast, the *Wanax* reaffirmed his authority as a figurehead who when times were bad could support his people, finding food from somewhere to ease famines and the like. The payback for such occasions was the constant supply of tribute to the *Wanax* to be centrally stored, dipped into for lavish feasts, to feed retinues of palace staff, and to supply to indebted bondmen at times of hardship. Ideally the lands of bonded families would be sufficiently extensive for hardship to fall in different places at different times, such that the palace simply becomes a conduit for sharing. Clearly, widespread harvest failures were much more of a problem, and tested the palaces' powers of long-term storage.

The *Wanax* occupied the pinnacle of a hierarchical social pyramid, bringing together several thousand people, with the lowliest at the base, and the various roles described on the Linear B tables arrayed on different gradations up the social pyramid. Subsistence goods would move up and down the pyramid, with a sufficiently ample 'top slice' at the apex for the *Wanax* and his higher-ranked associates to exchange food for other services. These would include craftworkers manufacturing pottery, textiles, furniture, chariots, and arms, and fashioning leather, wood, bronze, and gold, things for which access at lower ranks in society would be extremely limited. It would also allow those at the apex to engage in long-distance exchange, acquiring such prestigious goods as metal, textiles, perfume, oils, and fine wines. It would also support a population of scribes and accountants, using the novel technology of writing to control all this exchange and indebtedness. Such a structure of linked 'conical' societies, internally held together by redistribution, and externally by warfare and trade, is celebrated and reaffirmed in lavish feasts such as this, and leaves a range of signatures in the archaeological record.

These signatures include a differentiation between access to goods, according to rank. In other words, the higher-ranked individuals do not simply have more of the commonplace things, they also have different, distinctive things, and some of those items come from beyond the lands over whose people they hold sway. Their centres of redistribution are widely separated, an indication of the large number of families indebted to them, many of whom they may hardly recognize, although they share a mutual understanding of respective rank. Those centres of redistribution may have significant capacity for central storage. In the wider region around Pylos, many smaller contemporary sites are known, whose variations in size form a pattern around Pylos itself, describing a subordinate territory extending tens of kilometres across the landscape. These were the dispersed *damoi* which travelled to Pylos to pay tribute and receive protection around the focus of the redistributive feast.[12]

Resonances can also be seen with one of the earliest surviving depictions of an elaborate feast, around 5,000 years old. The 'Standard of Ur' was a wooden box excavated from the royal Babylonian tombs from Ur in the Chaldees. The box had been richly decorated on all sides with a mosaic of shell, lapis lazuli, and pink limestone. One one side of the box, these mosaics form a picture organized into three rows. In the top row, an elite figure sits with his court of six fellow diners, each raising a drinking cup. They are attended to by servants and musicians. In the lower two rows, provisions in abundance are being brought to the banquet. They include cattle, a flock of goats, bundles of fish, and heavy packages, perhaps of grains and fruits.[13]

Descriptions of what could be interpreted as redistributive feasts recur across the eastern Mediterranean and beyond in such early narratives as the *Odyssey*, the *Iliad*, and the Bible. Rather like Homer's epics, the earlier part of the Bible is believed to be a compilation in the first millennium BC of stories relating in large part to the preceding millennium. The Book of Genesis is a story of Joseph in Egypt that seems to describe such a redistributive system in action. Joseph interprets one of Pharaoh's dreams as predicting seven good harvests followed by seven years of famine. His advice is to impose a levy of a fifth part of the harvest for the next seven years, in order that stored grain could be redistributed in the subsequent seven. An attractive logic, with a sting in the tail for the Egyptian farmers. When the seven years of famine came, Joseph, now Pharaoh's right-hand man, intended to *sell* the grain back to the famished farmers who produced it, thus reducing them to debt bondage and slavery, and transferring all land and livestock to Pharaoh's ownership. Redistribution may in principle serve as a collective means to smoothe environmental fluctuations, but it may also in practice lend itself ideally to appropriation and accumulation at the centre.[14]

The potency of small hard seeds

The most prominent features in early feasting narratives may be opulent surroundings, and wine and food that is also plentiful and opulent, and the

20. The 'Standard of Ur', a wooden box from Sir Leonard Woolley's excavations of the Royal Babylonian tombs at Ur in the Chaldees, showing the side that depicts a prestigious feast held 5,000 years ago.

opulent food may have certain recurrent elements, particularly large roasts. Behind these conspicuous elements of the feast, the heart of the redistributive network depends on a different kind of resource, one that is easily taxable, controllable, and above all storable. One particular component of the feast lent itself exceedingly well to that purpose, the small hard seeds that assisted early humans in their spread beyond Africa, which became domesticated as 'grain crops', and would form the basis of transition within expansive hierarchical societies.

Among the hundreds of seeds and fruits gathered by early modern humans, the relatively small number that travelled with the mobile farming food web are notable for their ease of storage. The entire seed head of grasses, for example, can be dried and stored intact, and the digestible proportion of the dried seed head is very high; it constitutes a very compact and transportable store of starch and other nutrients. It would be wrong to think that the domestication of these grasses to generate 'cereals' immediately created the uniform expanses that we know as arable fields today. The earliest plots were probably much more like gardens, with closely tended, mixed plantings, nestling within diverse landscapes in which the existing vegetation remained prominent, much as we discern around sites like Hambledon Hill. Domesticated cereals have been around for at least ten thousand years. The prairie-like landscapes of arable fields that dominate much of the world today leave archaeological traces for only half that time. However, in the third and second millennia BC, just as redistributive feasts are becoming a recurrent feature of architecturally lavish sites, evidence of such landscapes appears in many forms. It is in this period that yields the first archaeological records of permanent field systems and constructed cropping terraces. Across these same regions evidence of the physical remains of field irrigation systems recurs.[15]

Up until this period, agriculture had generally made its impact on pollen curves as a perturbation, a reconfiguration of existing tree species, and a proliferation of hitherto rare species that could tolerate soil disturbance. From the third and second millennia, the pollen records the wholesale loss of trees and expansion of herbaceous vegetation on a hitherto unprecedented scale. In buried soils and dated profiles of valley-bottom accumulation, we discover the consequences of this new phase of engagement with nature. Each creation and each reorganization of a continuous landscape of fixed fields has a massive impact on soil stability, and is marked by wholesale erosion into the valleys. Soil destabilization can also occur *in situ*, with the loss of nutrients from the surface layers to leave the upper layers starved, and the lower layers impeded by an encrusted mineral pan, such as underlie many northland heathlands today. Destabilization of the water cycle through irrigation can further impact the soils by enhancing their salt concentrations to levels toxic to plant life. The traces of all these effects can be found at various places during the third and second millennia BC. We can even find descriptions of these new prairie-like agrarian landscapes in some of the oldest texts in the world.[16]

The same mounds of Ur that yielded one of the very oldest depictions of a redistributive feast also produced clay tablets bearing Sumerian text, rich in information about agrarian landscapes of the third millennium BC. They record fields' dimensions, which are large, and well suited to the teams of animals that are also recorded working those fields. We read also of their varied yield potential, the farmers and officials with which they were associated, and the narrow range of arable crops grown within them. The temple officials of the Third Dynasty looked out across the uniform expanse of barley that accounted for an estimated 98 per cent of land under cultivation. This emphasis on one cereal, barley, in the texts is reinforced by repeated finds of charred barley seeds from excavations throughout the arid regions of south-west Asia.[17]

The emphasis upon barley in the Sumerian texts is mirrored in the following millennium by an emphasis upon wheat in the Linear B texts, leading us to ask whether these vast, controlled, enclosed, and monotonous arable landscapes are a creation of redistributive feasting, or at least of the hierarchical order that perpetuates itself through the medium of these feasts. The individual farming family may well have been better off cultivating their allotments with a diverse cropping system, supported by wild resources from woodland, marsh, and river. The move to prairie-style arable fields and mono-cropping may connect those families to a larger system that provides protection and support, but may also engender a pronounced need for such protection, through an increased dependence on a smaller number of crops.

From the point of view of a hierarchical order, cereal monoculture lends itself to centralized control. Fixed fields are far more conspicuous than shifting garden plots. Their product is more measurable, transport-able, and storable, and the palatial centres retain much evidence of that storage. Pylos has vast storerooms and magazines, and silos, storage jars, and protected spaces within central sites are widespread features of human landscapes of the third and second millennia BC. The Pylos clay tablets record the considerable quantities of grain, olive oil, and wine that was exacted from the population of the region as tribute for the palace, and its royal and religious occupants. The landscape around is organized into arable fields to supply their needs, and in among them, groves of olives and vineyards. Both oil and grape had been exploited for a thousand years before the heyday of Mycenean civilization, but it is only during the second millennium BC that the pollen record of the eastern Mediterranean reveals the kind of pollen peaks we would associate with orchard arboriculture on a large scale.[18] This landscape of extraction and centralized redistribution stretched right across the Mycenean world, north as far as Thessaly. A little further north still, centralized storage is still a feature of the landscape, including one of the most important storage assemblages of all. 400 km north of Pylos is one such set of storerooms, in use around 1350 BC. Like so many sites of these periods, these storerooms suffered a devastating fire, once again catastrophic for the contemporary community but a boon to future archaeologists. In this case, the fire produced one of the best-preserved assemblages of charred grains in Europe.

The storerooms close up

The second millennium village at Assiros in Macedonia superficially displays much in contrast with the magnificent Mycenean sites further south. In place of the open, lavishly decorated courtyards of the southern palaces, Assiros was a warren of narrow passageways between close-packed walls of mudbrick, a site considerably more modest than Pylos, but also a centre for the storage of the harvests of its hinterland. Along those passageways and within those walls, some rooms were packed with stored goods, including massive earthenware bins filled with grain. They had been lost in the fire, and simply covered over to prepare a new floor. In the process, these burnt harvests remained in place, available for scrutiny when the ruined village was finally excavated.

The harvests belonged to four species of wheat, together with barley, broomcorn millet, and bitter vetch. Many of these crops occupied separate bins, presumably grown separately in fixed monocultural arable fields. There may, however, be some evidence of mixed planting; two of the wheat species, emmer and spelt, were stored as mixtures. Just beyond the edge of the Mycenean world, the site's scale and general organization suggested to the excavators that it was part way between collective storage for cooperating families, and a collection suggestive of central control. The landscape from which the produce was derived was part way between a mixed cropping and a monocultural landscape. It was estimated that the excavated storerooms held around 5,000 litres of grain, enough to feed twenty people for a whole year—a valuable buffer against the fluctuations of nature for a small community, and lending itself easily to centralized control of the agrarian landscape beyond.[19]

Looking out and looking in[20]

Let us, for a moment, go right back in time and place ourselves at the shore of the Sea of Galilee 23,000 years ago in front of the Ohalo encampment and compare the views looking out and looking in. Looking out across the lake, valley, and hill slopes beyond, a world of nature comes into view that was complex and changeable, changing on a whole series of overlapping timescales or 'tempos'. By 'tempo' we mean something akin to rhythm—the pace at which a system returns to a starting point of some sort. There are a series of rather obvious tempos in nature, such as daily, seasonal, and annual tempos. Then there are slower tempos, about which we are increasingly learning, tempos affecting vegetation regeneration, weather, and climate. Society too operates on a range of different tempos, and, as Mary Douglas observed, marks those different tempos with patterns of sharing food. Looking inwards to where that food was shared, the Ohalo community space was visibly ordered and familiarized, a place of security and stability. There was a place for the hearths, and a series of activities appropriate for the hearth-side. There were other places for brushwood huts with different harvests designated to each one. The people within the ordered and secure world around the hearth could constantly respond and adapt to the multiple tempos of the outside world, readjusting their food quest, from day to day if necessary, to track the complex changes and multiple tempos of nature.[21]

If we come forward in time and cross the European continent to the landscape around Hambledon Hill in the third millennium BC, the world of nature retains its complexity and multiple timescales, even though the mobile food web of agriculture has been nested within it. The Hambledon feasters looked outwards across a rich mosaic, an intricate overlay of multiple tempos within a transitional world. Their agricultural plots reflected both an annual/seasonal tempo and a longer tempo somewhere between long fallow and abandonment. The surrounding woodland had its own cycles of regeneration resonating with the very long lives of its principal trees. Produce from the forest followed a range of tempos; everything from hazelnuts and acorns, to deer and boar underwent sharp year-to-year fluctuations, as a normal consequence of the multiple tempos of a wildwood. Looking inwards, their cultural tempos around the feast seemed also to be lengthening, with strong allusions to ancestry and the dead all around them on the hilltop.

In many places during the third and second millennia BC, the balance of tempos, looking out and looking in, underwent a change that was quite subtle and yet profound in its consequences for our species' engagement with nature. For most of the human past, the tempos and cycles of nature have been multiple, complex, and long. Successive human cultures adapted to that complexity by operating on faster, simpler tempos. Through time, the spatial and temporal complexity of culture increased, while the parallel complexity of nature was reduced by human action. At different times in different places, the balance of relative complexity shifted. Nature was subjected to neat organization within clear partitions of space, the wild clearly separated from the cultivated, and cultivation being organized into neat rows and plots of single crops. That controlled world of nature was brought more and more into the rhythm of the annual cycle of determinate seasons. By contrast it was culture that displayed an enhanced complexity, mystery, transition, and a multitude of overlapping tempos stretching out to the timeless endurance of the gods.

Coming back to the Aegean world of the second millennium BC, the views outwards and inwards have been thus reversed. Looking outwards from sites like Assiros in the north, and Pylos in the south, the multiple tempos of nature have been regularized; nature has been partitioned into fixed units of space and time. Space is marked out by field boundaries and terrace walls that are permanent. Within them the soil is similarly regimented into orderly rows by hoe and ard. The cultivation of broom-corn millet at Assiros indicates that the flow of water must have been similarly controlled; this is a crop that needs seasonal irrigation in a Mediterranean environment. More and more species growing in these fields have been brought into the annual routine of predictable seasons. Looking outwards across the hinterland of this palace complex, a once wooded landscape has been simplified and partitioned into fields. Within each field, the crops are few in number; there may be interplanting of cereals and fruit crops, or simply one crop alone. In contrast to the overlapping multiple tempos of a woodland ecology, the tempo of this landscape is overwhelmingly annual. Grain crops, cereals and legumes, come to the fore. Even the vigorous pruning of tree crops and autumn cull of spring-born animals would have pressed this longer-lived species into an annual routine.

Turning round and looking inwards at the entrance to the palace at Pylos, the view is rich in mystery and complexity. Somewhere in the heart of the site is an ornate throne room which, for all its decoration and grandeur displays precisely the same organization of space as the Ohalo encampment, with a community gathered in a conversational circle around a hearth to share food and drink in the context of decorated bodies and constructed spaces. Obscuring our view of that age-old arrangement is an elaborate penumbra of over a hundred rooms, inter-spersed with inner courts and complex interconnecting passages. This complex of rooms mirrors the complexity of contemporary society, and its constellation of constituted roles and ranks. What we see from the outside is food for the gods, brought out for display to the masses. The mystery and grandeur of the palace alludes to powerful men, kingly lineages, priestly traditions, eternal deities, and the multiple tempos from which they impinge on ordinary lives. The archive rooms at the entrance to the palace serve as a reminder that the routinized world of nature now had to track the needs of that complex world of culture. By managing the balance of their activities, year by year, the farmers, the fields, and their produce would need to follow the changing demands of that complex core, demands for vast quantities of grain, wine, oils, and livestock, recorded as palace offerings on the inscribed clay tablets in the archive rooms.

Tempos, boundaries, and influence

Tempos of change are important in understanding how boundaries are established between different entities, and then in understanding interactions between entities differentiated in this way. We often define, and sometimes recognize a boundary in terms of an abrupt change in tempo. To take an example of the seemingly uniform oceans, we may be persuaded that they are actually made up of superimposed layers, moving at different speeds and directions, those shifts in tempo creating boundaries between layers. We need no persuasion at all to recognize the ocean as distinct from the shore, because the difference in tempos of mobility is that much more abrupt and pronounced. A similar argument can be applied to subdividing two categories of grassland, whereas the distinction between grassland and woodland (essentially a difference in the tempo of growth) is that much more self-evident. All around us are entities, microscopic and macroscopic, that are bounded by abrupt changes in tempo. Cultural entities within a natural world are examples of that.[22]

Where such entities coexist, their response to each other depends upon their respective tempos; by tracking its changes, the entity operating on a faster tempo harmonizes with the slower. This is the essence of evolutionary adaptation; a species harmonizes with its environment through the 'tracking' process of natural selection. Species that respond at slow tempos are able to track environments that are relatively stable. We have seen from the jagged edge of the palaeotemperature curve for the last two million years that it is a period in which the dynamic of nature is overlaid with yet greater temporal complexity and rapid environmental change, generally encouraging the spread of fast-growing herbs and small animals which can respond quickly by virtue of their brief life cycles. A number of woodland species and larger animals whose populations respond more slowly to change have not fared so well, an exception being the large mammal whose massive brain responds with unusual speed.[23]

For the majority of our species' existence, we have looked out from our hearths to those multiple tempos of nature, tracking them through our considerable ability to quickly reshape our activities and to redefine our notion of food according to what is available. In the landscape around Pylos, nothing has changed to affect the essential mechanism of adaptation, but the balance of tempos has reversed. The natural world has largely been fashioned and moulded into an annual tempo; within the monocultural expanses, even the livestock and perennial crops have been coerced within the annual agricultural routine. By contrast, human societies often emphasize their identity with allusions to slow tempo, such as the permanence of monumental architecture, kings, and gods. The changed gradient of tempos is such that the direction of influence and response has reversed; it is now the orchestrated landscape of nature's resources that adapts to the deep time complexity of the human culture.

This was not a sudden change. For thousands of years, human societies had been alluding to deep time, most typically by including their ancestors in social gatherings, and also in giving certain places in the landscape meaning and permanence. For thousands of years, parts of the environment had been enclosed and forced within the seasonal and annual cycles of their cultivation plots. But the gradient of tempos goes one way or the other, and influence and response follow that gradient. At a certain point, the gradient moves through zero and those directions reverse. In the context of other significant changes in the modern human food quest, this might be placed alongside the emergence of weaving technologies and the domestication of mobile food webs, in terms of its impact. Indeed, it is from this point that we perceive nature as being vulnerable to damage. It is from the third and second millennia BC that evidence for environmental degradation, in the form of woodland collapse, soil erosion, and salinification, become far more commonplace. That trend towards instability may be linked to the impact of these changes upon the form of our food webs.

One-track webs

Five thousand years ago and before, the food webs of modern humans were typically diverse and composed of multiple compartments. In this way they follow the patterns displayed by other well-studied food webs encountered in nature. Ecologists have analysed the food-web structures of a number of living foraging and fishing communities. They have many, relatively independent, feeding pathways along which energy can flow. Such loosely connected, multi-track food webs are found across the natural world. The communities around Pylos may well have fitted within a rather different form of food web, one that departed from this structure, and also as a consequence, departed from stability.[24]

The creation of clear boundaries between a wilderness beyond, and an ordered agrarian landscape within, entails an aspiration for there to be a single top predator at the apex of the food web we control, ourselves. They become 'one-track webs', at least in intent, and to varying extents, in reality. Hunter-gatherers, foragers, and fishers, and earlier generations of farmers, coexisted with a range of other predators. The relationship between them varied greatly, sometimes completely hostile, sometimes competitive, and sometimes cooperative. In doing so, whatever the relationship, they conformed to a widespread model of multi-track webs in nature. One-track webs are different; if the broader regularities of pattern in multi-track food web apply, we would not necessarily expect a stable outcome.

What these regularities are about are shape and interconnection. The regularity in shape is captured by an alternative term for the food web, the 'ecological pyramid'. At successively higher trophic levels, the number of species decreases. This has been clear from early observation of food webs. What recent detailed survey has shown is that the rate of decrease tends to fall within certain bounds. Nature is not populated by excessively tall thin, and short fat ecological pyramids; instead there is a trend towards a stable proportionate state. So far as we can tell, one-track webs conform with this. They may be composed of a rather smaller number of species, but when plant foods, herbivores, and carnivores are arranged according to feeding relationships, they form an 'ecological pyramid' that is fairly typical in shape. That brings us to the second regularity of interconnections.

Interconnections are links within the food web where one species directly influences another, most commonly by eating it. In natural food webs, the number of such connections is small, relative to the number of species involved. Such webs are 'loosely connected' and therein lies their resilience. Any external disturbance or ecological calamity may disrupt one branch within the web, but the chances of a 'knock-on' disruption of other parts of the web are limited by loose connectance. The situation in a one-track web is quite different. The number of species is relatively low, and the number of linkages relatively high. Outside disturbances and calamities are easily transmitted from one part of the web to another; the entire system is consequently fragile.[25]

Much of this can be modelled and predicted mathematically. It is also discernable from fairly straightforward observations of one-track webs in action. It is easy to see how they do become highly interconnected, for example through the feeding of food waste and surplus milk products to pigs, the use of animal traction and manure to raise crop yields, and other such forms of farmyard economy. We can also see repeated tendencies for energy pathways to diversify, in spite of the intentions and best efforts of the farmer. They diversify through the proliferation of weeds, diseases, and vermin, for example, and in the process tend towards more stable, if undesirable, food webs. In relegating the 'wild' to the wilderness, and erecting boundaries between it and the controlled and structured agrarian landscape, farming communities intensified their battles against nature, and against the mathematic logic of food-web dynamics. There is some skeletal evidence that pre-agricultural foragers were less prone to disease organisms,[26] and archaeobotanical evidence that the division between crops and weeds was less clear in the early stage of mobile food webs. With the generation of a clear partition between external nature, and bounded one-track webs, the battles against disease, weeds, and vermin intensified, and have remained intense ever since.

The limits of cultivation

The kind of one-track webs we see documented in the third millennium BC, Sumerian texts, detected from the granaries, and inscribed tablets of the second millennium BC Aegean, and infer from the contemporary north European proliferation of permanent land allotment, are still all around us today. They make up a vast expanse of the earth's biosphere. They are so familiar to us that they become our automatic model for agricultural landscapes in the past. We struggle to visualize the landscapes of the first farmers, which all bio-archaeological evidence suggests was quite different. In evolutionary terms, it is clearly successful; it has not only survived, but also multiplied and expanded. Paradoxically, in terms of food-web dynamics it is intrinsically unstable; we see much evidence for that instability in the form of destabilized systems of soil and vegetation in the prehistoric record. How can we square that circle? One way may be through the social complexity at its core.

In the redistributive system described in the Book of Genesis the argument put by Joseph to those from whom dues were required was that there would be seven good years, and seven of famine. It is not impossible to store grains for that long, but neither is it at all easy. It is generally more feasible to redistribute food across space rather than time. If the Pharaoh's realm encompassed a number of different regions, but critically regions that were isolated in climatic and environmental terms, then a rich harvest in one area could serve to compensate for a failed harvest in another. Inasmuch as the regional ecologies are isolated, that system might be effective. The ecological logic is that the food web becomes broken up into bounded compartments, thus replicating pathways and consequently reducing the connectedness of the web overall.

Other forms of compartmentation within one-track webs may have the dynamic effect of breaking up internal linkages, and those ameliorating these webs' instability. Fixed fields and rotation systems are also forms of compartmentation in space and time. It all depends on how much the barriers created across space and time serve as barriers to ecological interaction. It may, however, be that stability is not what these one-track webs are about—at least, not stability at each and every scale.

The biblically recorded fates of Pharaoh and the Egyptian farmers were not identical in material terms. It is quite possible, even typical, for the stability of a system at a larger scale to be independent of the individual stabilities of its component subsystems on which it ultimately depends. That is the nature of systems of all kinds; stability is scale-dependant in both space and time. If we were able to view the ancient Aegean landscape from the air, we might see patterns in the landscape separating fertile valley bottoms from olive-clad slopes, and grazing uplands, of a very stable and enduring nature, harmonizing with topography and climate. Descending for a closer view, the valley bottoms and slopes would disaggregate into separate fields and terraces, and the changing fates of particular communities may become more evident in the patchwork, fluctuating according to weather, local histories, and personal fates. Closer still, the grazing animals and their tending farmers can be individually discerned in all the complexity of their daily changing lives. But it is not simply a question of the smaller the spatial scale, the greater the temporal complexity. In other systems, the reverse may be true, or the complexity may move back and forth between scales. However, in the particular case of the one-track web, in which the food web has a single apex, then a simple relationship between stability and scale is part of the implicit *modus operandi,* and one celebrated and reaffirmed in the feast of redistribution. In Mycenean Greece, we can follow that apex up through the ranks of society to the ruling *Wanax,* and beyond to the supreme deities, all of whom partake in the feast.

21. A dining scene from the wall paintings at Pompeii, displaying the rectilinear
arrangement of diners in the Roman style.

9
EATING IN ORDER TO BE

Colchester, southern England, c.AD 45

He made his way unsteadily along the side passage, still clasping a dish of some identified concoction. The outside air was a relief—it might clear his head a little, and in any case he needed the break. It was so important that he made the right impression—how often was he ever going to get that chance to dine in the Tribune's house again?—Nonetheless, it was hard going, both physically and emotionally. The physical side was troubling him most now—all that exotically flavoured meat, whenever was it going to stop? And fish that looked like snakes, and others of the strangest shapes imaginable.

This last thought hurried his pace to the door to the latrine. Turning speedily into the darkened room, he hardly made eye-contact with his companions before occupying the one free seat. He glanced momentarily at the glamorous brooches that marked them out as of rather higher status than he. He certainly made no attempt to join their conversation, which any case he couldn't quite follow. He hadn't imagined his Latin was that bad—indeed, he had to use it every day since his promotion, but sorting a few soldiers out was one thing, following drunken Italians in full flow was quite another.

The ache returned. He was not yet aware that his problem didn't so much derive from the stuffed intestines he'd bravely consumed, or even those wizened sticky fruits that the little boats brought up the River Colne in great jarloads. He was unknowingly sharing these treats with a fast growing population of whipworms, currently taking vigorous exercise in his alimentary tract. Slumping a little, his thoughts returned to the warm sunshine of his distant birthplace, and to the more comforting meals of his childhood. For a brief moment the strong stench of cess gave way in his mind to that distant smell of moist thatch and chickpea stew, and to recaptured thoughts of a space between earthen walls, family, and a slow burning fire. He pulled himself back to the moment and rose up. Since those soothing chickpea stews, a great deal had happened that he preferred not to recall, and in any case, he needed to rejoin the companion who had secured his invitation to this strange and elaborate feast. He might have trouble following the conversation, but that didn't mean he couldn't still make an impression.

In a gloomy underground car park beneath a shopping centre in eastern England, we can look up to an empty space where the unfortunate incident imagined above lay entombed for the best part of two millennia. The car park is in the town of Colchester in southern England, hewn out of the subsoil in the 1970s after a 'rescue excavation' had been carried out. The local archaeological unit was used to Roman remains turning up all the time; modern Colchester was built over the site of a legionary fortress on the northern periphery of the Roman Empire in the middle of the first century AD. Enough of Roman Colchester's outline survives in the modern town for the team to work out that the car park was being excavated through the foundations of one of a row of larger houses within the fortress, almost certainly the house of a 'tribune', a high-ranking officer, probably a young man being groomed for high office in the civilian world.[1]

The excavation of the tribune's house was carried out in advance of the development of the shopping centre. In one corner of the house they exposed the ground plan of a small room, dominated by a deep, timber-lined pit. We can only speculate on the seating arrangements over that pit. Beneath those uncertain seats, the evidence gains in solidity. Two to three metres down into the latrine pit, past the traces of the wooden lining that became increasing clear, one of bio-archaeology's great prizes came to light. The diggers had recovered 'coprolite', the formal term for fossil faeces.

The word coprolite derives from the Greek *copros* and *lithos*, or faecal 'stone'. The stone refers to the mineralization of the ancient faeces;

22. The pit beneath the latrine of the Tribune's house at Roman
Colchester during excavation.

they are found encrusted and rendered soil by an infusion of calcium
phosphate, which gives them a light-brown colour. The calcium derives
from lime in the surrounding sediment, and the phosphate from the high
phosphate content of the faeces itself. The actual form coprolites can
take varies, as a consequence of the considerable variation of dietary
input featured throughout this book. Sometimes they may retain a
recognizable shape, but quite commonly they collapse into layers of a
more anonymous kind. Here at the legionary fortress, the coprolite from
the tribune's latrine was described as 'pale buff in colour with an open
porous structure including fragments of plant material . . . formed as flat
irregular sheets within the pit fill'. After careful lifting, those ancient
faecal fragments were softened and broke up in hydrochloric acid,
yielding a solution of dark brown hue, within which lingered the insol-
uble residue of some ancient repast. There were the microscopic fragments of silica, known as 'phytoliths', the least digestible part of plant
food. Other small fragments of tissue were still intact. They could be
identified under the microscope as pieces of cereal bran. Alongside these

fragments, the minute eggs of the *Trichuris* nematode were spotted, an intestinal parasite more commonly known as the whipworm.[2]

The bulk samples taken from the fill of the latrine also included seeds of figs, raspberries, grapes, and elderberries, fragments of bones of some of the animals consumed: cattle, sheep or goat, pig, hare, and the birds, mostly domestic fowl, with some duck and goose. Careful sieving would add fish to this list, eel, herring, mackerel, and, rather surprisingly, stickleback. Anyone who has seen the vicious spines on this particular fish will wonder how it found its way into a latrine. It may have come in with some of the broken tableware that was also dumped in the loo, some very delicate fragments of eggshell ware imported from Italy. Perhaps we are catching a glimpse of culinary theatre, discretely rejected and disposed of?[3]

In refuse deposits of this period in other parts of the fortress at Colchester, flotation and sieving has further enriched this list, with increasingly exotic elements. Figs and grapes are not the only fruits to have travelled as far as the Italian tableware. Other deposits within the fortress produced mulberry pips, walnut shells, olive stones, and even the charred remains of dates, the most exotic item of all, with some of the flesh still visibly attached. This residue of a diverse and novel table is further enhanced by shells of chicken egg, and of mussels, oysters, scallops, and cockles. The contrast with the staple fare of that time was immense. What were these meals about, in the otherwise bare and functional setting of a military fortress?[4]

The ends of empire

The British Isles may have seemed chilly and rainy to its military occupiers, but they were very far from the most extreme landscapes touched by the expansion of Rome. The meals enjoyed on the best tables within the Roman fort could be read as a map of its political influence. From the cool British north came raspberries and hare, and fish from the adjacent oceans; from the estuarine lowlands around the North Sea came eels, and from the lush grasslands of temperate Europe came beef. Figs, grapes, and wine arrived from the Mediterranean, and most exotic of all, dates from the south-eastern limits of empire, bordering the desert. In this respect, their meals are similar to the meals enjoyed at the heart of later imperial powers of Europe, which similarly mapped out their global conquests through their food, giving particular prominence to exotic spices and beverages, which not infrequently travelled from colonies on the far side of the planet. If we trace the Colchester date stones back across the empire of Rome to their source, we reach the south and east margins of the Mediterranean Sea, and the arid, sun-drenched regions of south-west Asia. Beyond those even, there are Roman forts in regions too arid for anything to grow, and to which all food must have been imported from some distance.

One such string of forts runs for around 170 kilometres from the Nile valley, some way north of the ancient site of Luxor, to the shores of the Red Sea. They are arranged along two Roman roads, perhaps a day's march from each other, crossing Egypt's Eastern Desert, a parched mountainous expanse traversed by a thin population of Bedouin shepherds. Each road leads to an ancient stoneworking settlement. One road leads to Mons Claudianus, the other road to Mons Porphyrites. The very fine stone quarried from these sites was dressed on site and exported vast distances. They can still be seen in Rome today, for example in the form of the columns that grace the Pantheon. Imperfect columns that fractured before completion remain in the desert close to their source, ominous memorials to the memory of the workers whose prodigious efforts did not always bear the required fruit. We can reflect with awe on the formidable task of shaping such columns under the blistering heat and then transporting them to the heart of the empire. Archaeobotanist Marijke Van der Veen was keen to learn how they undertook the basic, but equally challenging task of feeding themselves.

Ancient writers had spoken of the harsh living conditions that slaves, prisoners, and conscripts endured at these sites, leading her to speculate on some fairly grim meals. The terrain, the heat, and the isolation of these sites made it fairly difficult to reach, let alone dig these sites, but once excavation began, those same environmental features served well. The sites were encountered in a marvellous state of preservation, clearly visible from some distance, with nothing in this barren land-scape to disturb them. Within their planned military outlines, the footings of huts, storehouses, and middens could be seen. The arid conditions also greatly favour the preservation of food debris. In middens, and in abandoned huts within the quarry settlement, Van der Veen recovered a mass of food plant debris. Working her way meticulously through this material, she was increasingly surprised by its make-up.

As might be expected, there were fair numbers of cereals and pulses, heavy to move, but the most compact and transportable foodstuffs of all. There were also oilseeds, such as sesame and safflower, and nuts such as walnut and almond, adding flavour and variety, and still easily moved around. Yet more flavour is added by fourteen species of spices and herbs, including coriander, dill, anise, basil, and fenugreek. The list becomes increasingly interesting when we move to fruits. Date, olive, grape, and fig are among eighteen fruits identified, which also include pomegranate, mulberry, and watermelon. Least expected of all were the green vegetables, including cabbage, chicory, cress, and lettuce.[5]

Like the northern meal with which this chapter opens, their meals were also arranged around a fusion of Roman and local meat. In both places, the Roman favourites of pork, oysters, and chicken were enjoyed. In the north of the empire they were consumed alongside the traditional beef, and here in the south with donkey and camel. This ample desert fare was further complemented by a wide variety of fish imported from the Red Sea.[6]

Who was eating in such splendour? A clue comes from numerous fragments of pottery, found amongst the refuse, that have been used as writing tablets. These 'ostraca', as they are known, add some important details to the plant list, for example recording the importation of bread and wine, and alluding to gardens and the importation of manure, accounting for the presence of fresh vegetables. But they also allude to the types of people at these sites. They were clearly employing paid labour, including skilled stoneworkers, masons, smiths, and quarrymen. We also learn about their wages and, significantly, how substantially their wages varied from one class of worker to another. We can imagine such pronounced differences were conspicuously displayed in the manner of sharing food.[7]

On both the northern and southern extremes of empire, archaeology is revealing some surprisingly luxurious lists of ingredients in what seem rather stark military contexts, and in regions where the meals were traditionally rather simpler. A deeper sense of what this luxurious eating was about is gained by moving from the periphery of the empire to its heart.

Power dining on a different kind of frontier

In Rome, two decades after this chapter's opening meal, we encounter a rather Byronic figure who briefly drifted through the court of Nero. His name was Titus Petronius Niger, and he carried the title of the emperor's *arbiter elegantiae*, in other words, his personal style guru. When it came to that vast population of aspirants of simple origin who yearned to climb the ranks of *Romanitas*, of which our opening fictional character having trouble at the meal and on the toilet is a rather modest example, Petronius' snobbery and acerbic wit found its natural target. He wrote a parody entitled the *Satyricon*, and fragments of the text have survived. In those fragments of fiction we can read about a freed slave who has fast become fabulously wealthy, the owner of vast lands, and who has planned the most elaborate of funerary monuments. Wealthy he may be, but in Petronius' eyes the freed slave Trimalchio remains a *parvenu*, an object of ridicule who no amount of newly acquired wealth can free from his native coarseness, coarseness that will forever distinguish Trimalchio, at least in Petronius' mind, from the latter's refined circle. The poor man's aspirations are most easily ridiculed by observing the excesses and pretensions on display at the dinner party he throws.[8]

The passage within the *Satyricon* entitled 'Dinner with Trimalchio' is a lively description of perfumed fools, old wine, abused slaves, and theatrical cuisine. A collection of lavishly attired social aspirants recline upon couches, their cups filled, hands washed, and nails manicured by an assortment of attendant boys. It is a hard task to condense the absurd drama to a menu, but for the sake of comparison, here it is:

Dinner with Trimalchio: Menu

hors d'oeuvres

———————— ⸙ ————————

An ass of Corinthian bronze with two panniers,
white olives on one side and black on the other

———————— ⸙ ————————

Dormice sprinkled with honey and poppy seed

———————— ⸙ ————————

Steaming hot sausages, on a silver gridiron with
damsons and pomegranate seeds underneath.

———————— ⸙ ————————

Mock peahens' eggs (pastry shell containing
small fowl seasoned with yolk and pepper)

———————— ⸙ ————————

A goose, two mullets and a honeycomb, with bread
Celestial arrangement of plump fowls, sows' udders,
and hare

———————— ⸙ ————————

Peppered fish

———————— ⸙ ————————

Zodiacal arrangement of chickpeas, beef steak,
testicles and kidneys, figs, cheesecake, sea-scorpion,
sea bream, lobster

———————— ⸙ ————————

Wild boar dressed with baskets of Syrian and Theban dates.

———————— ⸙ ————————

Drinks:

Mead

Wine Vintage : FALERNIAN CONSUL OPIMIUS C.30 BC

Even in bleak military settings ranging from the wet chilly north to the scorched arid south, we could start assembling the food remains from either remote location into a reasonably exotic and elaborate menu. Within the fairly unadorned spaces of these army compounds, meal tables were being set with the same colourful array of elegant plates, bowls and cups, some rich red, others charcoal black, or an elegant grey. Upon these plates would be servings of meat, eggs, fowl, and fish, adorned with exotic fruits and flavourings, elaborately presented along with white bread loaves and abundant wine. Not necessarily a feast of *Satyricon* proportions, but when compared either with what was eaten a few years previously in any part of the empire's periphery, or indeed in the homelands of many of the troops now stationed along its length, a striking departure, and a new kind of meal. It was novel in terms of its diversity and sheer geographical scale, but it was also novel in relation to transforming the diners, their relationship to their environment, and to each other.

If we venture a little way outside the British fort, or back in time in the lives of those diners, meals would instead comprise a reasonably healthy, if somewhat monotonous, mix of a wide variety of cereals and grain legumes, together with mutton or lamb. Such had been the familiar daily diet for some centuries across a large expanse of Europe. On special occasions in the temperate regions north of the Alps, this simple fare was complemented by consumption of beef in quantity, washed down with beer and mead. Steak and alcohol had been the mark of a good party since at least the days of Hambledon Hill. Within the fortress excavations at Colchester, some malted barley, ready for brewing, was recovered near to the barracks of the ordinary soldiers.[9] Against the background of this culinary pattern, these imported fruits and strange seafoods would have seemed most exotic to many who observed them and even those who partook of them. Mutton, pork, and beef would have all been familiar, but it is clear from the proportions of animal bones that much more pork is being consumed, a clear reflection of Roman taste.

Like all parodies, the *Satyricon* can only raise a laugh among Petronius' effete circle if the absurdist images have some resonance with real lives. Out on the fringes of empire, archaeology captures a few fragments of those real lives, and individuals reaching for a new or improved identity through the manner in which they share food. Earlier cuisines explored in this book consolidated communities around the hearth at the heart of the cultural landscape. The sharing of food reaffirmed those communities, giving ever greater substance to the difference between them and others. Even the feasts at Hambledon Hill and Pylos, while taking farmers away from their homes and hearths, brought them to the focus of their own community's landscape. In contrast to this, elaborate Roman dining typically had its impact *at* boundaries, actively shifting those boundaries and in this way redefining who was, and who was not, one of the gang. These could be boundaries of status; Roman hosts often brought a client or protégé to their meal table, to further develop their relationship. They could be boundaries between rich and poor, freeman and slave, as parodied in the *Satyricon*. They could alternatively be geographical and cultural boundaries as at the military frontier of empire. In a society of unprecedented scale and ethnic mix, sharing food played a key role in the process of *becoming* Roman. *Romanitas* is rather like a growing network of cultural connections, first spreading by trade and exchange, then by military conquest and political consolidation. At the many stages within the expansion of that network, strangers from contrasting backgrounds and cultures would meet, and gather together to share food or drink. In doing so, they both transformed themselves, and transformed the network of which they were part.[10]

Because sites like Colchester have a rich archaeological record we can come very close indeed to such food-sharing occasions, even to the private movements of one particular diner. We can also step back from the day of his discomfort to see how such food-sharing can unfold, on greater scales of space and time, to impact, not just upon military/urban culture and consumption, but also in a fundamental way on the nature of the wider community and landscape and the manner of their food production.

An aspiring diner

To capture a sense of cultural ambiguity and social arrival that characterized this style of dining, I have imagined the visitor to the Tribune's latrine to be a Thracian whose Latin was not entirely fluent. This is totally speculative but not that implausible; we know from military records that Thracians made up one of the largest ethnic groups within the camp at Colchester. Most were of fairly low rank, but at least one gravestone indicates that they too could start climbing the ranks of military office. Indeed, the unprecedented scale of Roman expansion owed a great deal to the relative ease with which the conquered, whatever cultures they were born into, and whatever languages they spoke, could join with their conquerors, and in a relatively short space of time become Roman, in a similar manner that a polyglot community of nineteenth-century European émigrés could become American. In the heart of the Roman Empire, meals very commonly mixed social rank, and the meal played a critical part in advancement towards their goals. On the empire's periphery, a corollary of mixed rank and status must have been a fair range of language abilities. The remarkable wax writing tablets from the waterlogged fort at Vindolanda upon Hadrian's Wall bear witness to the fluency and literacy of at least some ordinary soldiers, but others would presumably have struggled.[11]

By taking one such Thracian legionary to the dinner party, and from thence for a brief interlude to the latrine, which leaves the most enduring record of the meal, a drama unfolds that is the inverse of Trimalchio's own feast, as portrayed by Titus Petronius in his satire. At the latter, Petronius has two rather effete poets arrive at the dinner party of a ludicrously wealthy social aspirant, to whom they will always feel greatly superior. In my invented drama, however, it is a rather low-ranking individual who secures an invitation to the house of someone who is comfortably superior. The tribune may well have been quite aristocratic, or if not that, then certainly scaling a far classier and more elevated greasy pole than the one upon which our diner is struggling to maintain his grip. Their lives constitute two inverse dramas, presenting different views of a common theme in the sharing of food upon the frontier, a frontier that may be geographical, social, or cultural, or some combination of all three. In this context, the sharing of food and drink operates on the periphery of a social cohort, shifting the boundary between an 'in-group' and an 'out-group', such that some of the latter may transform themselves into the former.[12]

Such feasts serve as marketplaces of social capital. Some of the participants know and care for each other, but others may be strangers. All, however, will come away with some sense of whether or not they have had a profitable time, but in social, rather than pecuniary terms. Rather like the ordinary market, the various participants may in principle all come away satisfied, and with an enhanced personal sense of their own status. Again, like an ordinary market, their investment may not pay off. Nonetheless, the shared enthusiasm for the general principle can elevate this particular form of meal to a lead position in the cultural dynamic. In this context, it may be worth bringing our two poets from Trimalchio's residence all the way north to chilly Camulodunum (the contemporary name for the town of Roman Colchester) to see what they make of our own diner. They would no doubt make fun of his rudimentary Latin, and might wonder whether he would be better advised to stick to his Thracian 'black bread' back home, rather than the more refined white bread that was clearly testing his unrefined bowels. They would mock the assortment of physical attributes they regarded as gross in a typically Thracian sort of way. Their cultural background would endow them with an ample language of ethnic hostility from which carefully to fashion delightful witticisms.

This was an empire, and a time, in which social movement could be very fluid. A century later, the emperor was an African with a Syrian wife, whose sister scarcely spoke Latin and whose citizens followed numerous different religions.[13] Nonetheless, the archetype of 'foreignness' is prominent in perceptions of the time and must have greatly shaped the sharing of food and drinks with strangers and those of different rank. To get some sense of contemporary ideas about 'foreignness', we can follow the son-in-law of one of Britannia's conquerors on his literary journey northwards, in his *Germania*. This account is in part drawn from the personal travels of Cornelius Tacitus, in part drawn from accounts by others, merchants, soldiers, and the like, and in part from a traditional understanding of what foreigners are like. In his account, written in the first century AD, we can see a contrast with our own modern racial stereotypes that emphasize skin colour and religious affiliation, for example. The recurrent features of foreignness in Tacitus' writing are notably fluid and, in principle, mutable. One such mutable mark of foreignness is hairstyle; the Chatti were hairy and bearded, and only cut their hair after they had killed. The Suebi dressed their hair on the side and bound it up into a tight knot. We very occasionally recover a preserved coiffure from archaeological deposits. Much more frequently, we recover the hairpins with which it was held in place. Many of them slipped out to be later recovered by archaeologists at sites like Camulodunum. Tacitus makes occasional reference to such things as squalor, bravery, and earth worship, but nothing that might be regarded as biologically fixed. There are also allusions to a confusion between male and female roles. The Gauls, though once powerful, were now effeminate. The Cherusi, once brave, were now cowardly. Among the Sitones, the women ruled the men. Ethnic identity seems to have been generally more fluid; people could adopt a new identity, allowing the empire to expand. In this novel transformation, a prime rite of passage was the sharing of food and drink the Roman way.[14]

An emphasis on mutable ethnic signals reminds us of the much greater ethnic mobility in Europe in the first millennium AD than that in the second. Individuals were not as bound by birth, belief, or language as they might be in more recent times. Very many people changed sides quite dramatically and died with a different ethnic identity from that into which they were born. In this dynamic, the meal adopts a very primary place in cultural transition. That is borne out clearly by the archaeological evidence of Roman expansion. Hot on the heels of the military presence came new kinds of food and new styles of eating. In that sense, the Camulodunum evidence is typical of a much wider picture. However, it is not the earliest form of consumption to spread north.

Before the main course, a drink

Between two modern gardens a couple of kilometres to the west of the legionary fortress lies a mound of earth, partly obscured by trees. In 1924 this mound, the Lexden Tumulus, yielded another exceptional find. A wide range of luxury items was unearthed that clearly marked the burial of an individual of high rank. There were fragments of silver and gold that had quite likely been woven into clothing. Alongside them lay the metal parts of fine vessels, pedestals, stools, and a chest. There were small pieces of chain mail, and the studs, buckles, and hinges with which they would be held together. The deceased presumably had the status of an elite warrior. Other artefacts in the burial give an indication of cultural association, but an indication that is ambiguous. Several of the finds indicate a prominent member of late Iron Age elite, but one piece has a quite different date of manufacture. It is the head of a copper alloy axe, whose style places it much earlier, not simply a few generations earlier, but back in the preceding millennium. This local elite warrior was buried in traditional local style, together with an heirloom that had been in their tribe for at least 1,000 years, a clear signal of power and status within a long-standing indigenous cultural tradition.[15]

Yet at the same time as making this strong allusion to the ancestral past, this assembly of grave goods simultaneously points in another direction. Alongside these functional items and the curated heirloom are a series of ornaments with the style of the fast-expanding empire in the south. The most striking of these was a medallion of silver, prepared from a cast of a coin of the Roman Emperor Augustus. While in essence a member of the traditional elite, this warrior had some rather nice trinkets with which to display a certain worldliness. But these trinkets are dwarfed, in volume at least, by another allusion to cultural contact with the south. This local elite warrior was buried with at least seventeen large clay flagons (amphorae) of Mediterranean wine.

Vast quantities of exotic alcohol, or at least allusions to its consumption, are a widespread feature of the tribal elite that was ultimately consumed by the northerly expansion of the Roman world. Some of the most spectacular are the elaborately decorated and massive bronze punchbowls found in elite burials around Burgundy. In some cases, these massive containers filled with wine could lighten the heads of a thousand or more people. Wine and wine-drinking equipment had been travelling from central Italy up the Rhine for seven centuries before it reached the Colchester grave.[16]

Even further than the wine itself travelled the glamorous *idea* of wine. Within a few years of our tribune's feast, a noblewoman was laid to rest on the Danish island of Lolland. Although Lolland was several hundred kilometres beyond the empire's limit, the noblewoman's lavish jewellery and several imported Roman glasses and bronze vessels bore witness to her worldliness and wealth. One of those bronze vessels conserved a residue of its contents. Within that residue, fragments of cranberry, of cowberry, barley, and bog myrtle could be discerned. This could well have been the drink to which Tacitus refers. With marked distaste, he

23. Drinking equipment from an elite burial of the first century BC at Goeblingen-Nospelt in Luxemburg, including amphorae used to transport Roman wine.

described a drink made of cereal grain, forged to a certain resemblance with wine.

Such evidence seem to put wine at the vanguard of the northerly spread of Mediterranean culture, and there are other cases, possibly before, and most certainly since, when the consumption of some psycho-active substance, such as alcohol, tobacco, or opium, has been a notable feature of the contact zone between cultures. It is also at the vanguard of contact zones on a more intimate scale. In many societies, the very first gesture of the host when welcoming their guest is to offer them a small preparation of alcohol, or whatever psycho-active substance their society permits. Sharing a drink, or a pipe, also forms a basis of making contact with those for whom insufficient intimacy has been established to share a meal. It could have played quite a critical role in this respect at both Hambledon and Pylos. Even before we feel comfortable about sharing food for the body, we feel able to share food for the mind.

As aspiring north Europeans gathered along the very modern water-side entrepôts and in emerging markets, over a flagon of wine, real or fake, they were not just changing their drinking habits; they were also adjusting their styles of presentation, not just in their hairstyles, but in the presentation of their entire body. They were by no means the first generation to carry manicuring equipment with them, but we do see an increase in the loss of personal tweezers for archaeologists to rediscover. Their grandparents' sheepskins and linen shawls had been fastened with a discreet and much-valued bronze brooch. They did the same, but their brooches had become larger and flashier, their varied design more easily discerned by their fellow drinkers. Just as, over 30,000 years earlier, diners came to the very first conversational circles around the hearth adorned with necklaces of shell and bone, so these Iron Age drinkers came to the wine cauldron bedecked in brooches, bracelets, necklaces, and rings in their ears, and upon their manicured fingers and toes.[17]

A more traditional hearth

For several generations, elite nobles and their clients, traders and artisans had gathered together along these frontiers of consumption, to conduct their business and share food and drink. First they gathered in riverside entrepôts that had grown up from the Mediterranean, across Gaul and on to Britannia. As these trading routes were followed and captured in military conquest, they gathered in and around Roman forts, and subsequently in the towns that grew up around them. All the while, the great majority of the population lived a different sort of life.

Not far from the centres of cross-cultural contact were a great number of rural settlements that seem to continue without any clear seismic change. These sites correspond to the countless farming families who produced a large part of what was consumed. Their farms can be found in the near vicinity of Camulodunum, and indeed all over Britannia, marked out by less-enduring traces, but traces nevertheless that come unequivocally into view from the air, as cropmarks. They are the compounds and hamlets in which 95 per cent or more of the population lived. In this particular region of Europe, they are made up of round or oval house plans, together with paddocks, ditches, fences, and palisades.

Fragments of neither amphora nor wine cup grace the rubbish tips of these humble settlements. Figs and dates are nowhere to be seen in their storage pits or among the ashes of their hearths. Instead those ashes are characterized by the chaff of the staple cereal crops they had farmed for centuries.[18]

Over other parts Europe, the remains of farms away from the main axes of cross-continental networking can be recovered, and the ashes of their hearths habitually bear witness to the grain harvest, and the immense amount of work involved in threshing, de-husking, winnowing, sieving, and storing. We get the clear impression that, at the time a wave of exotic cuisine was transporting Roman culture across the map, the expanses over which it travelled were in large part given over to a more prosaic arable production. A very wide range of grains crops were grown, including species and varieties of wheat, barley, millets, rye and oats, beans, peas, and other pulses that are hard to find among today's harvest. Among the ashes we also find the charred seeds of their field weeds, the silent monitors of past environments. Among them are weeds characteristic of damp and nutrient-starved soils. These landscapes had borne centuries of exploitation. From these ancient fields, the vast majority of the population gathered their harvest of grains and pulses that made up the bulk of their diet. Around the arable fields grazed the sheep, cattle, and pig that would occasionally be slaughtered to supplement the meal. From here they would bring their harvests and meats to clusters of roundhouses at the heart of these intensely worked landscapes.

Even though a rectangular architecture of partitions, whose beginnings were seen at Jerf-el-Ahmar, had come to characterize farming communities all over the mainland for thousands of years, the people of Europe's north-western isles had continued to share drink or food in the round. Their circular buildings, of wattle, daub, and thatch, came in many sizes, and were often clustered into a hamlet, or bounded compound. From legal codes that survive in Ireland and Wales from just a few centuries later, we learn of five-generation extended families, bonding together a great-grandfather and all his descendants.[19] The scale of these hamlets and compounds would fit well with such groups, and is believed to have been the norm in across what came to be the Roman province of Britannia. In the heart of these compounds, parents, children, grandchildren, first and second cousins, uncles and aunts gathered, according to gender and age, to collectively carry out their farming chores. Stories of the feasting habits of the northern Celts were described by a Greek author named Poseidonius. He records tales of bloodshed and gallantry, of prominent men engaged in conspicuous display. Here is how he sets the scene:

> When several dine together, they sit in a circle; but the mightiest among them, distinguished above the others for skill in war, or family connections, or wealth, sits in the middle, like a chorus-leader. Beside him is the host, and next on either side the others according to their respective ranks. Men-at-arms, carrying oblong shields, stand close behind them, while their bodyguards, seated in a circle directly opposite, share in the feast like their masters. The attendants serve the drink in vessels resembling our spouted cups, either of clay or silver. Similar also are the platters which they have for serving food; but others use bronze platters, others still, baskets of wood or plaited wicker. The liquor drunk in the houses of the rich is wine brought from Italy and the country round Marseilles, and is unmixed; though sometimes a little water is added. But among the needier inhabitants a beer is drunk made from wheat, with honey added; the masses drink it plain. It is called corma. They sip a little, not more than a small cupful, from the same cup, but they do it rather frequently. The slave carries the drink round from left to right and from right to left; this is the way in which they are served. They make obeisance to the gods, also, turning towards the right.
>
> (Athenaeus, *Deipnosophistae* IV. 151–2)[20]

The elite had access to Mediterranean wine dispensed from silver flagons. But even the beer-drinking lower ranks of these traditional communities on the periphery of empire had been nodding to new trends. Even on the more modest farmsteads, more brooches were being worn, and the occasional piece of imported tableware brought out to impress visitors. Who knows, perhaps they were also squeezing a few red berries to add a fashionable hue to their home-brewed beer.

One thing we do notice from the broken pottery retrieved from this period, is that consumption becomes increasingly individual, with a growing prominence of cups and plates of a size suited to the individual diner. The formal constraints of the extended family arranged around the hearth to receive and welcome the stranger were being relaxed.

Individuals from different families and societies were meeting to share food and drink in smaller groups. New trading settlements were growing up along river valleys across Europe, where such individuals could gather, negotiate, and exchange goods. The agents of this change, the travellers, traders, and purveyors of jewellery and exotic goods moved across a rich cultural mosaic on the periphery of empire, whose variety is captured in the writings of Cornelius Tacitus. Like a much earlier generation of travellers moving across Europe with the first elements of a farming economy, they would often find themselves in an architecture of partitions, new rectangular buildings closer to the trade routes, further from the long-established settlements, and in angular contrast to these intimate home circles of the north-west. Rectangular buildings and rectilinear spaces come to be seen on the sites where these new forms of exchange take place, and these spaces accommodate new styles and patterns of sharing food and drink.[21]

One particular rectilinear style would come to accommodate the classic Roman dining arrangement. Within urbane dining rooms, three couches would be placed at right angles, corner to corner, with up to three reclining diners on each. The fourth side was open, a stage to the other three for the display of foods and entertainments. Many depictions of this arrangement survive, and in some villas, the plans of such dining rooms was preserved in the design of the floor mosaic, or even in fixed stone couches. For all the heights to which the splendour of the cuisine rose, a lot of Roman meals were small-scale affairs. In contrast to the extended families of the north, the traditional Roman family was nuclear, composed of the paterfamilias, his one wife, their children and slaves, and dining was often in quite small groups.[22]

Community and network

Two complementary but contrasting ways in which people make contact with one another are thus expressed in the manner of sharing food and drink. The first is 'community', bringing together extended connections of kinship and land, the land of the 'ancestors'. The food a community shares has a clear ecological relationship with that land; the balance between grains, vegetables, and fruit, meat, fish, and fowl, reflects the balance and soil and water resources in the local region, the ancestral lands. The food is simple, and shared relatively equitably between the dining kin, reaffirming a sense of timeless community and security within its established bounds. The second principle is the 'network' along which relative strangers can move and meet to exchange goods and ideas. Such a network is an open rather than a closed system, an ever-expanding tree whose outer branches grow to take that same network further and further. The food shared along the branches of this network is ostentatiously laced with the exotic allusions to distant regions and the network's sheer scale. The food is complex, and dining is competitive, frequently bringing strangers together in unequal negotiation. Through sharing food and drink they reposition themselves in social and cultural terms. In a later historical period, the meals with the 'community' and the 'network' broadly correspond to the *basse cuisine* of the peasantry, and the *haute cuisine* of Europe's elite network of royal households.[23] On the eve of Rome's expansion, those networks were initially more modest in scale, propelled by modest boats carrying merchants and travellers, and in a subsequent episode, the military. From Britannia, they would bring corn, cattle, silver, hunting dogs, and slaves.[24] A single slave may have been worth a whole amphora of Mediterranean wine. The network of Roman influence and expansion would decorate its elite tables with exotica spanning the known world. A wide array of southern treats would follow military expansion north of the Alps; pomegranates, almonds, melons, and peaches have all been found. Perhaps their furthest reach of all is traced by a very small, wrinkled, dried fruit with a hot spicy taste. Black peppercorns have been found on three sites in Britannia and several more in Central Europe. Their remains can be traced to the Roman port of Berenike in Egypt, to where they entered the imperial network, a network that had taken them all the way to the northern frontiers of empire from their distant place of origin. They had been gathered from the wild forests of the Malabar coast in southern India.[25]

Anatomy of a network

All around the empire, and perhaps especially on its social and geographical frontiers, people were eating and drinking in manners that both celebrated the vast network of which they were part, and ensuring that its outer branches continued to grow. At the very tips of these growing branches, we see narcotic substances and exotic flavourings. At a certain distance they are followed by a elaborate cuisine and a new manner of dining. Stepping back, and viewing those frontiers from a greater distance still, these exotica fall into place within a range of either features of consumption and display, such that the Roman style of living and being leaves substantial traces all over Europe, traces in clothing and personal adornment, decoration, house construction, and the layout of settlements, towns, and landscapes. 'Romanization' leaves a powerful imprint all over the empire that Rome controlled, and that imprint is at its most emphatic in culinary, artistic, and architectural styles of consumption.

Beneath the surface of consumption

What about production? How did this massively influential, continent-wide network transform the food quest itself, and the source of supply to these new elaborate tables? The picture here is more complex, and to get some sense of that complexity, we can bring Petronius' fictional poets to another part of Britannia, to the house of another extravagant consumer in the Roman style.

For this northern province, the palace of Fishbourne, close to the coast of southern England, is magnificent indeed. Its excavator, Barry Cunliffe, speculated that it was the seat of one of the sharpest locals to do deals with imperial Rome, a tribal leader of whom Tacitus records: 'Certain states were handed over to king Cogidumnus—he has remained continuously loyal to our own times—according to the old and long-received principle of Roman policy, which employs kings as tools of enslavement' (Tacitus, *Agricola* 14. 1).[26] Such a principle paid off handsomely for this particular local leader, who celebrated his achievements in a display of fabulous consumption in the Roman style. By AD 80, the palace had suites of rooms, colonnades, tiled roofs, mosaic floors, and painted walls, all arranged around a most impressive formal garden. Our visiting poets would no doubt peruse the 150-metre frontage with their customary caustic disdain. On passing through the entrance, they might also get a little lost.[27]

Back in Rome, the houses of the elite followed a particular structure, a predictable arrangement of rooms and spaces. The view from this large garden was superficially similar, but actually quite different. All the trappings of urbane architecture were there, but the large interior garden was essentially a vast compound, with a series of doors opening off it leading to separate structural units of the palace. In central position, the most impressive rooms of all were entered from the far part of the garden opposite the entrance. Another structure that had been given a rather surprising prominence in this far part of the garden was a large bakery. The whole layout may have confused these poets from foreign parts, but would conversely be a rather familiar grammar of space for the region's local inhabitants. They would be perfectly familiar with entering a large enclosed compound with separate doorways opening onto it, including those of working buildings, and going across to the main house opposite the entrance. The compounds they knew from old would have been built from wood and clay, and be round rather than rectilinear, but the use of space was broadly the same.[28]

The landlord at Fishbourne provides an extreme and conspicuous case of consumption on the frontier. His parents before him would have been familiar with drinking wine in the Mediterranean style and trading for fine pots and ornaments from the Roman world. In the early days of his own political success, he went further and shared elaborate meals in rectangular spaces according to the Roman way. His first timber palace on the site has as one of its prominent features a bath-house, indicating that as he shared food and drink in Roman style, he and his guests also attended to their bodies in the Roman style. As he consolidated his political success in later years, his houses and compounds were all completely clothed in Roman style, and he was keen that visitors cast their eyes on his Roman bakery and other mod cons. However, not far beneath the surface, he remained a collaborating local tribal leader, in Tacitus' words, a useful tool for enslavement.

Perhaps for that reason, the consumption of food and drink at the frontier did not immediately connect with a changed food quest around the frontier. As far as we can tell, many methods of farming and land management stayed the same. Not that they were at all bad; the empire did not succeed in reaching anywhere in which a harvest surplus could not be extracted. Indeed, the limits of an available surplus are probably what determined the final limits of the empire itself. For centuries, new woodlands had been cleared for cultivation, and they continued to be cleared. A wide range of cereals and legumes had been grown, and continued to be grown using the same methods that had been used for centuries. Fishbourne may have had a kitchen garden, but there is no evidence from the archaeobotany that early Roman Britain saw an intensification of horticulture. The whole idea of creating a formal artificial garden was new to the north, but with an emphasis on design and decoration rather than function.[29]

There is, however, one area in which this new generation of peripheral consumers did transform the production, as well as the consumption of food. They were by nature importers of exotica, exploiting the vast networks of exchange that they also sustained and spread, moving an enormous range of items, building materials, metal, and glass, and exotic foods on an unprecedented scale. They were also expert at the technologies of importing and exporting, and moving things over long distances in large quantities. One consequence was that there was a lot more metal around, and they very quickly used iron to make large cutting knives to harvest and manage hay.[30]

For an ordinary farmer of the time iron was precious, and would be restricted to tools little bigger than a penknife, enough to harvest leafy branches for feed, but inadequate for harvesting the far more luscious grasslands. The new, wealthy consumer could afford to fashion long hay sickles, and in the process create a new form of vegetation, hay meadows, for repeated summer cutting. We even find waterlogged clumps of hay in some early Roman wells. Quite a significant contribution to the food quest had probably not been directly related to styles of consumption drawn from the Mediterranean south. The Roman favourites of pork, chicken, and oysters, are little augmented by the maintenance of hay meadows. This novel ecological product of metal technology, the hay meadow, was of more relevance in the sustenance of those essentially northern symbols of prestige and wealth, horses and cattle.[31]

After Cogidubnus' death, the palace continues as a theatre of consumption in the Roman style for many generations, continuing to reflect the changing fashions of the Roman world without impinging too much on the production of food by the enslaved wider populace. After many episodes of rebuilding and extension, the palace was finally destroyed by a fire in the later part of the third century AD, and for some reason abandoned as a charred ruin. Around the ashes of Fishbourne, the imperial networks of contact are also in fragments. The nodes of that network, the regional administrative capitals, were in decline, and even the divinity of the emperor at the epicentre of the network had long since been challenged. Britannia was effectively controlled by breakaway leaders. As the province's foremost palace of consumption collapsed, the rationale and ideology behind that consumption was also in a state of collapse. A culinary celebration on the far tips of the most expansive branches in the network would no longer have had the same resonance and meaning it had in the network's youth. And yet, when we shift our attention from the consumption of food to its production, the roofs of Fishbourne palace of consumption finally fell at the dawn of a new era of innovation in the food quest. It was a dawn that broke, not in the crumbling core of empire, but on its periphery.[32]

As the network collapsed, and people looked to their more local regional contacts, a great deal of wealth moved from the towns out into the countryside, and it was an urbane wealth, used to a wide range of transactions and contacts, but now more directly concerned with the productivity of the land. A certain sector of society built and lived in the Roman style, which was by now hardly 'Roman' any more; it had been around in Britannia for almost 300 years. Their villas were often more modest, but it was their farms that were particularly interesting. They certainly did have market gardens, and grew a range of vegetables, spices, and herbs, and fruit crops, and some had vineyards. Out in their fields, they grew a range of crops, including the species that has become the major food source of the human species in calorific terms, bread wheat. This species had been around for thousands of years, though only as a minor crop in the north. However, as Rome's control over the north waned, it ascended to premier position in the food quest, an ascent to which we shall return in a future chapter.

Their rich harvests they gathered in with enormous scythes, with blades of two metres in length. They used far more metal in their farming equipment than any of their predecessors, most notably in one particular tool that, like bread wheat, has gone on to conquer much of the planet. Their predecessors prepared their soils with digging sticks, hoes, and ards, highly effective tools, the best adapted for many a terrain.

For the deep-soiled lowlands, however, soil cultivation had been revolutionized by a piece of equipment that could dig deep, lift whole landscapes of soils and turn them upside down. To operate, it required substantial trained animal power, and the north Europeans were experts in the raising of cattle and horses. It required an appropriately shaped board to lift and mould heavy weights of soil. In front of that 'mouldboard', the incision had to be made in the soil with a blade so heavy that it was difficult to lift. A single one of these cutters or 'coulters' required the same weight of metal that might have been in the ownership of several villages a generation earlier.[33]

The lavish frontier consumption had run its course, the imperial divinity at its core consigned to history with the conversion of a fourth-century emperor to Christianity, a religion that specifically precluded his own divine status. By the time of the Emperor Constantine, citizens of his empire lived, farmed, and shared meals in a quite different way from the forefathers who had extended Roman culture further, and more emphatically, than any previous cultural formation. At the vanguard of that expansion was, first of all a way of sharing drink, followed shortly after by an elaborate and theatrical manner of sharing food.

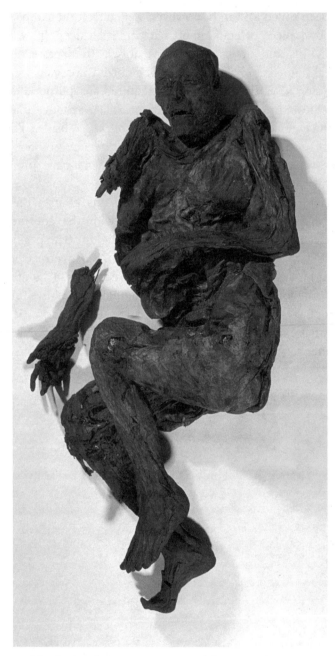

24. The body of a woman, preserved for around 2,000 years within a Danish bog at Huldremose.

10

FAR FROM THE HEARTH

Huldremose, north Denmark c.2,000 years ago

Dusk was falling and an evening mist was softening all the lines. A widow picked up the hem of her tartan dress, and stepped cautiously towards the water's edge. She really should return home, the fens were dangerous at night, especially now so many people were hungry and ready to resort to desperate measures. Passing close to an empty nest, her mind skipped back a few months when she had gathered a good many eggs, but that season had gone and other foods must be found.

The water's edge was a good place to forage. The past month she had been trudging forth, field after field, alongside the other widows, picking up tailcorn and anything else she could find for her meagre stewpot. The way they harvested these days, there wasn't much left on the ground, but the farmer down by the river could still afford to be picky, and left a fair bit of tailcorn rye and spurrey in his stubble. She had managed to gather a meagre harvest of both, and it was a small quantity of soup prepared from them that was inadequately filling her stomach at that precise moment. She tightened her bonnet and pulled her lambskin closer around her shoulders in the hope that warmth might ease her hunger.

Her own mother before her had known good years and bad, and equipped her with much knowledge about different sources of food in the landscape, ancient knowledge that the widow now used to scan the water and its edge. From her she had learnt about roots and rhizomes that could be pulled up and roasted, reed stems that could be nipped and marked, to collect a sticky sugar harvest the next day, of a wide range of leaves that could flavour the stew. But each thing had its own season, and now the season of seed-set was underway. She would soon be gathering hazelnuts and fruits of the forest, and if it was to be a good year for acorns, then she could leach them too, but you could never tell with acorns. Anyway this was all in the future, and she was hungry now, and gathering the smaller earlier seeds was hard enough when gleaning the field, it was even harder here by the fen. She went down the banks to seek out the rambling red stems of knotgrass. She'd have to thrash masses of the stuff against the ground to get a few seeds out, but they tasted good when you accumulated a decent harvest. She turned to look for the floating manna grass, whose sweetness attracted everyone.

Thoughts drifted back to happier days with fuller stomachs, bashing down the weft on her loom with the warmth of the hearth on her back, and the smell of fresh barley straw and animal sweat drifting along the smoke-filled eaves and mingling with the pork legs hung to dry. She was drawn back to the present moment by the sight of one of her favourite plants. Her mother had taught her a great deal about those big, plate-like leaves on the water. Every part of the plant could be used for something, a lot of it for medicine. The leaves were good for infections and different parts of the roots could serve for different maladies. She remembered, with a tinge of regret, her mother explaining how to use the rootstock to delay pregnancy. But right now, it was the fleshy fruits in view that caught her attention. The hard brown seeds within could be turned to popcorn in the fire and make a tasty snack. With these thoughts in mind, she strode, perhaps a little too boldly, in the direction of the waterlilies, without noticing the rustle of other footsteps among the reeds.

WE know a great deal about the manner of that unfortunate woman's death, if not the motive. For some reason or other, her legs were badly lacerated and an axe blow had almost completely severed her right arm, before she was plunged into the Huldremose (Huldre Fen) in north Denmark, round about 2,000 years ago. The whole episode was thankfully brief, or so it would seem from the body's unusually complete preservation, indicating a speedy transition from life to the airless depths of the cool dark water. There, she joined a large and unsettling archive of 'bog bodies', corpses that became consumed in growing peat, in a manner that severely arrests their decay.

With no grave to mark their untimely departure from this world, they remain in anonymity until some future turf cutter, seeking peat for fuel or fertilizer exposes their darkened bodies once again. At this point they are given rather severe geographical names, 'Tollund Man', 'Grauballe Man', and 'Windeby Girl' that attach them to their final places of rest. They form quite a mixture, rich and poor, young and old, some the victims of either crime or punishment, others perhaps sacrificed to the gods. The thing that binds them is not so much a single shared fate, as the attributes of peat, either as the 'quick-setting concrete' of your run-of-the-mill Iron Age gangster, or as an engulfing feature of the sacred watery places, revered for many centuries in northern Europe. It is the Huldremose woman's uncollapsed ribcage that suggests immersion was immediate, and that no prolonged ritual was involved. Her body was clothed, her long tartan skirt over a lambskin underskirt, lambskin shawl, and tartan cap. The woven cloth would have been fine when new, but at the time of her death, times may have been hard.[1]

She also joins a special group among bog bodies, in which more is preserved than simply bodily tissue and clothing. Preservation of peat results from a number of factors, first and foremost the scarcity of oxygen, an element upon which many decay processes depend. This oxygen-free pickling process is enhanced by a property bog moss has of sponging up all the soil nutrients, again something decay organisms need, and 'tanning', and therefore toughening, the outer tissues. Even in these circumstances, certain bacteria can operate, and operate on many of the softer internal organs. What these particular bacteria cannot break down is the newly toughened 'external' tissues, which are those tissues on the outside of the body, and the gut. Even when liver, lungs, kidneys, etc. have failed to survive, what might remain is the gut, and of more importance, the gut's contents.[2]

She was rediscovered in 1879, when a peat cutter's blade accidentally severed her hand. Her body was lifted and carried on a stretcher to a nearby barn, where she was cleaned and undressed (the men dutifully leaving the room at this point). Her clothes were washed and hung to dry, and her body reburied in a the local churchyard. She was soon to be disinterred at the request of the Museum of Nordic Antiquities in Copenhagen, and after a few further journeys ended up in storage in the nearby Museum of Anatomy. Here she lay forgotten for many decades until archaeologists rediscovered her for the second time, armed with a new set of analytical techniques. Interest focused on the most enduring of the internal organs, the gut. Careful dissection yielded two small samples, each less than a gramme in weight, which could then be rehydrated in distilled water, sieved, and inspected under the microscope. Much of the material was heavily fragmented, but their cellular patterns remained intact, even on very small pieces. From these small fragments of cereal bran could be discerned, and some could be recognized as belonging to rye. Alongside these were occasional finds of indeterminate grasses and some charcoal fragments. Rather rarer were fragments of animal tissue, grit, and the seeds of a wild persicaria and a plant called 'gold of pleasure'. Alongside all these was a plant normally thought of as a weed, but which in this woman's gut was at least as abundant in fragmentary form as the 'crop plant' rye. It seems as though this woman's last meal was, in modern terms, 'weedy'.[3]

In that respect, she is not alone. North Europe's bog bodies are not a uniform selection of individuals. One of Britain's best-studied examples, 'Lindow Man', was someone who had his nails manicured and supped on freshly baked bread.[4] Over the waters in Denmark, another kind of gut content is more widely attested. Two of the first bog bodies to have their gut contents scrutinized were 'Tollund Man' and 'Grauballe Man'. They did indeed contain several types of barley, wheat, rye, and oats, but alongside those cereals were the seeds of numerous weeds, including fathen, corn spurrey, and knotgrass, along with pale persicaria, redshank, black bindweed, violet, and greater plantain amongst others. Another gut, that of 'Borremose Man', analysed shortly after, contained a predominance of knotgrass, spurrey, and fathen. Two popular archaeologists on the then youthful medium of television were served up a weedy broth based on these stomach contents, and one was heard to remark afterwards that, with meals like that, perhaps they had thrown themselves into the bog. Tastes change, but it seems unlikely these meals were ever *haute cuisine*.[5]

They need not have constituted as awful a meal as they did on that occasion. A number of the weeds fall into the Polygonaceae family and are close relatives of buckwheat. Persicaria, knotgrass, and black bindweed if appropriately prepared compete with the best Japanese *soba* (the noodle prepared from buckwheat, a close relative of these 'weeds').

Similarly, the various grass seeds could make a perfectly reasonable cereal-like flour, and fathen and its relatives in the Chenopodiaceae would have been both tasty and nutritious, and good sources of iron and Vitamin B. A number of chenopods were cultivated for their leaves and seeds in pre-Columbian America, and one of these, quinoa, remains a significant crop in the southern continent. The problem with eating their weedy relatives is not so much what they taste like or how nutritious they are, but the enormous amount of time and effort needed to arrive at a very modest harvest. Gatherers of weeds would often fail to satisfy their hunger.

The woman from the Huldremose lived on the periphery of the world explored in the preceding chapter, but a very different kind of periphery. For every wine-enriched elite diner, there were many who struggled to find enough food. She may have filled her stomach by 'gleaning' the harvest of others. Many societies have allowed unfortunates among the community to search through the stubble for whatever might be edible. This might include the debris of the main crop, those grains that fell and got trampled into the ground, or escaped the scythe at the corner of the field. There may be weedy grasses, not favoured by the farmer, but whose seeds make reasonable flour, and there may be other weeds of the field, such as corn spurry and fathen, that could form a meagre if nutritious harvest.

The best known gleaner of all is the Moabite widow Ruth, presumed to have lived in the early first millennium BC, and whose story is narrated in her own book within the Bible. An ancient Israelite legal tradition permitted foreigners, widows, and the poor to follow the harvesters in order to glean tail-corn and whatever remained after the main harvest, a tradition to which Ruth resorted when left poverty-stricken by the death of her husband. She travelled with her mother-in-law to Bethlehem at the start of the barley harvest, where she followed in the path of the reapers, gleaning and gathering amongst the sheaths they had bound. It turned out to be a rich harvest. The strict rules of segregation of the sexes were necessarily relaxed in the fields at harvest time. As well as gathering a handsome harvest of barley tail-corn, she also caught the attention of a future husband, a liaison that reached an agreeable conclusion later that night at the threshing floor.[6]

Boundaries become blurred. We start by imagining two clear categories of people, the farmers and the paupers, two clear categories of resource, crop and weed, and two distinct episodes for food collection, harvest and gleaning. Each of these distinctions may be called into question.

Take, for example, the farmer and the pauper. These are not two distinct classes, but two states, between which many, if not most, rural families would have moved back and forth on a number of different occasions in their living memory. The expansion of one-track food webs emphasized the distinction between the hierarchical core and the small-scale peasant farmers who produced their food. Indeed, it was the existence of the network connecting the core with their producers that allowed farming communities to exist in smaller communities than their ancestors, even as small as an individual nuclear family. All communities this small are, however, vulnerable to a series of major fluctuations. They are first of all vulnerable to political fluctuations in the hierarchical core they support. They are furthermore vulnerable to environmental fluctuations; to recover from one or two bad harvests may take many years. On top of these things, they are vulnerable to their own demography. The balance between elderly and young can quickly shift to a group whose size falls below optimum levels for productivity and reproduction. Such imbalances can also add to difficulties of acquiring marriage partners, a further vulnerability of rural communities. For Ruth, prosperity went down and up according to marital fate. I have drawn from the contrast between the fine weave on the woman's skirt and headgear to the contents of her stomach to suggest a downturn in fortunes, perhaps through widowhood. Indeed the rather odd mixture of tartan cloth and lambskin that is attested by the material remains might suggest a chequered history of affluence.

In the context of such routine experience of changing fortunes, many farmers may have adapted their approach to single-crop, square-field agriculture to provide them with a greater range of options through the years. One approach may be to rely on crop mixtures rather than single crops. What is anathema to today's mechanized harvesting methods opens up to a range of possibilities in a hand-harvested field, especially when the harvesting tool is not a great deal larger than a penknife. As we have noted in the previous chapter, metal was a precious commodity in prehistory, prominent in elite display, but used sparingly in day-to-day farming. Metal sickles were short, as were the flint blades that preceded them. The prehistoric harvester moved slowly through the field, grabbing handfuls of 'ears' or grain clusters, using the blade to release each handful from the straw. If there was more than one thing growing, and at different heights, then the harvest could still be managed. Among the pithoi stacked in the Assiros storehouse explored in Chapter 8 were stores of the harvest of one such mixture, a 'maslin' of emmer and spelt wheats. Many of the late prehistoric crop assemblages of northern Europe appeared to be even more mixed than that, and mixtures of one kind or another would have been a commonplace sight. The mixing of crops spreads many things. It certainly spread the risk. In a maslin mixture of wheat and rye, for example, in good years, the wheat would flourish, in poorer years there would be more rye in the harvest, but there would always be something to eat. As well as spreading the height of the harvest, it would also spread the season. The slow operation of ear-gathering would have involved several trips through the ripening sward, a smooth progression from 'harvest' to 'gleaning'.

Such a development of the notion of a 'field' seems to have extended yet further, not just blurring the distinction between harvest and gleaning, but also that between crop and weed. There are certain plants we now think of as 'weeds' that figure rather too prominently in archaeological assemblages to be simply discarded as a waste product. One of these is the corn spurry in the stomach of the woman who died at Huldremose. She had not eaten so much a medley of the countless weed species that we would anticipate to be available to a gleaner as the seeds of two plants, rye and spurrey, and a lesser scatter of others. Other archaeological assemblages, principally from hearths and rubbish pits rather than stomachs, feature other single species as prominent contributors. Examples include the long seeds of brome grass (*Bromus* spp.) and the iron and vitamin rich seeds of fathen (*Chenopodium album*). These last two have continued to be consumed into recent times. Brome grass seeds were still being ground and eaten by Danish rye farmers in the early twentieth century. It was this wild species that flourished in their fields in years when the rye harvest itself was extremely meagre—so why not substitute one grass seed for another? Seeds of *Chenopodium* and its relatives are also widely consumed, particularly in the New World, where quinoa grows as the highest-altitude grain crop anywhere in the world. Indigenous American communities cultivated other species, and there is probably a full continuum between this genus as a 'weed' and a 'crop' to be found in the archaeological record.[7]

So rather than the clear bipolar landscape of affluence and poverty envisioned in my opening fiction, of neat monocultural fields around the homestead where full stomachs reposed around a roaring hearth, and the poor grubbing around anxiously in the fen edge beyond, the culti-vated field was more unusual to our modern eyes. We could envisage instead plots of land that were certainly sown from a particular stock of seedcorn, often a maslin mixture to hedge against poorer years. After these plots had been tended and brought to maturity, quite possibly everything in them was treated as a resource, not just the progeny of what was sown, but also the other plants the deities and spirits had decided would grow there. Even the small mammals that ran from their harvest home would have been captured for the stewpot. The seed harvest, whose proportions would vary from year to year, would itself be the basis of next year's seedcorn. Some farmers would instigate a quite intensive seed-cleaning programme between harvest and resowing, and we can find the debris of such cleaning activities on many later prehis-toric sites. Others would not, and the composition of the seedcorn would fluctuate widely. I remember hearing some first-hand observations of oilseed cultivation in west-central Asia. In different parts of this region, three plants could often be observed in varying mixtures. They were linseed (*Linum usitatissum*), 'false flax' (*Camelina sativa*), and roquette (*Eruca sativa*). It was not always possible to establish which were the intended crops, and which were the weeds, and indeed, the gathered seedstock often contained all three. What was repeatedly clear was that the local farmers, whatever they actually sowed, out of necessity made use of whatever grew up in the plots, not just for the valuable oilseed, but also for leaves, the fibre in the stems, and so on. The European's questions about crops and weeds were not so much unanswerable as slightly irrelevant.

This chapter and the previous one explore two distinct but broadly contemporary worlds of consumption in different parts of northern Europe. Consumption in the previous chapter was based upon the extraction of dues from communities of farmers. Indeed the expansion of the Roman Empire depended on the likes of Cogidubnus, local leaders who would serve as 'tools of enslavement', extractors of local surplus. They aimed to control one-track food webs in which production occurred within clear, visible compartments, following determinate seasons. Fixed fields and collective threshing floors suited them well. For the global collection of dues, it did not matter too much if some farmers went under, so long as a majority produced a taxable harvest.

The farmers themselves had different interests. They were less interested in maximizing a surplus that someone else would extract, and more interested in staying alive from year to year. The more diffuse and mobile their food web, the more locally buffered it is in the face of environmental fluctuations, and the less easy it may be for an extractive elite to take dues. Livestock can be moved from place to place when the taxman calls. A field is not so easy to hide, but the size of its harvest may be difficult to establish. Systems of agrarian taxation have often involved controlling a key stage in crop-processing, such as the threshing floor or the mill, such that the actual of the size of their harvest is less a matter of speculation and debate. All this favours single-crop harvests and one-track food webs. They suit elites who receive their grain as tax or tribute, but render the individual farmers much more vulnerable to environmental hazards and fluctuations. Of course that same vulnerability serves to enhance dependency on the extractive elite. Each poor harvest or farm failure offers another series of routes into servitude and debt-bondage. It would often have been far more in the individual farmer's long-term interest to retain an internal diversity and broad, multi-track food web.

The best studied stomach from an English bog body comes from a mature man, variously known as 'Lindow Man', 'Lindow II', and 'Pete Marsh', interred in peat after a violent death approximately 2,000 years ago. He could have been a contemporary of the woman from Huldremose. His gut contents have been subjected to a variety of scientific analyses, including electron spin resonance, a method that allows us to determinate the temperature at which something has been cooked. His last meal seems to have been dominated by an unleavened loaf or griddle cake, quickly cooked over a hot alder wood fire, and prepared from a finely ground flour of one or two 'regular' cereals. A few grains of mistletoe pollen may encourage us to weave druidic tales around his final mouthful. However that mouthful remains, not to mince words, a piece of bread. Two Dutch bog bodies, from Zweelo and Assen respectively, also had cereal-rich last meals, with little in the way of weeds. Alongside these are a wide range of other individuals, many from Denmark, the richest source of bog bodies, which had last meals that might be described as wild or 'weedy'.[8]

Among the recurrent weedy foods are spurry, wild grasses, and the wild relatives of the crop buckwheat (docks, persicaria, knotgrass, and black bindweed) and quinoa (fathen). Two bodies from the German sites at Dätgen and Kayhausen also contained wild radish seeds and wild apple pips. The stomach of the woman at Huldremose who introduced this chapter contained quantities of spurrey and rye. This mixture was still used for bread by very poor farmers from the Brejning region of Denmark into historic times. In the opening fiction, I have imagined that she had encountered poverty through widowhood, and was an unfortunate within her own community; we have moved to the possibility that she was an ordinary member of her community, practising a form of plant husbandry that allowed for periods of want in everyone's life. Either way, I placed her on the edge of a world that would come to dominate hers, in which most fertile areas are partitioned off into rectilinear, monocultural blocks geared up to the extraction and control of surplus crops. Implicit in that marginal position is another tradition of knowledge of plant life on which she can draw, and which I, not very adventurously, attributed to her own mother.[9]

Gathering such fruits of the land as hazelnuts, and the rich array of woodland berries, involves fast response and the ability to get there before other species, in other words knowledge of seasonality. Other resources involve a knowledge of the hidden parts of plants, such as underground roots and tubers, and how to grub them up. The environment would have supported pignut, the roots of beet, and acorns, from which they would have leached the harmful alkaloids.

Within the tamed landscape, the boundaries between domesticated and wild species were often blurred. It was rich in plants that had one use or another. At one end were the plants which were greatly valued and cared for, such as the large-seeded, high-yielding cereals and pulses. At the other end were useless or even counter-productive plants which cultivation, weeding, and seed-cleaning aimed at removing. In between lay a variety of others that were edible, sometimes of great value as medicinal or nutritional supplements, and which were variously used or avoided according to a host of factors, including cultural choice, economic necessity, and environmental fluctuation. Much the same can be said of the animals. At one end were the carefully tended cattle, sheep, and goats, and at the other pests and vermin. In the middle are a range of animals such as rabbits, hares, and other field rodents that occupy the same ambiguous position as edible weeds. While the division between an animal that is wild and one that is tended may seem clearer than in the case of places, there are several historically attested strategies of managing, for example pigs, horses, and rabbits that can be regarded as intermediate. Feral pigs can be let loose in woodland to be as free as their wild relatives, and feral horses can roam the marsh and plain. In each case they can be lured or rounded up on a semi-seasonal basis, not that far removed from corralling wild animals.

Many would place their fellow humans along the same spectrum. At one end of the spectrum were the most refined and elite individuals who like the Lindow Man picked up crusty white rolls with his manicured fingers. At the other end were the eternal poor, and those who were down on their luck, who could well be eating weeds. Their fates leave marks on their skeletons. We have seen in previous chapters how teeth and bones contain many clues of how well they ate. They also contain clues of how badly they ate.

Skeletal misfortune

A number of the bog bodies themselves retain their chequered nutritional histories within the structure of their bones. When a young growing person receives insufficient food, the bone growth can be arrested, leading to an accumulation of calcium at the zone of arrested growth. If the diet recovers, and bone growth restarts, the opaque, so-called 'Harris line' remains as testimony to the episode of hardship. A bog body recovered from Aschbroeken in northern Holland had developed Harris lines when he was around 9 or 10 years old, and his bones display several cycles of recovery and subsequent malnutrition after that. At the end of the tibiae from the Windeby Girl, eleven separate cycles of

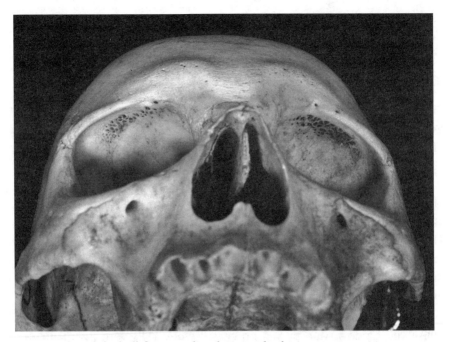

25. An adult skull from medieval Spain, displaying porous regions, termed 'cribia orbitalia' in the roof of the eye sockets. These are commonly a sign of anaemia.

calcification of this kind are visible. She only lived until her teens, suggesting she may have experienced serious nutritional stress every hard year of her brief life.[10]

For all the lavish consumption we see in the archaeological record of feasting, life was tough for most of the people much of the time, and hunger was commonplace. Going back to the early farming communities congregating around Hambledon Hill in southern England, almost 5,000 years ago, there is a seeming contradiction between the bones of animals and those of humans. The animal bones suggest meat in plenty, whole cattle slaughtered for a single feast, yielding considerable quantities of nutritious meat. Yet the skulls of 15 per cent of the humans recovered from the same site suggest they did not consume enough animal protein in their lives. In the eye sockets of eleven of the seventy-five skulls, the bone is more porous than normal, one of the symptoms of anaemia, an illness related to an insufficiency of iron.[11] The principal sources of iron in our diet are red meat, legumes, and shellfish, all foods we know our hunter-gatherer ancestors consumed, but which diminished in diets dominated by domesticated grass seeds. Cereals in fact actually inhibit the uptake of iron.[12]

In the early 1980s, a group of anthropologists gathered in New York to review the evidence for worldwide health in prehistory. A vast body of skeletal information was collated. Data was presented and compared from Asia, Africa, Europe, and America spanning the last 30,000 years, and the results challenged one of the most deep-seated assumptions about the human past. Throughout the history of archaeology, there has tended to be an implicit inference that, by actively changing society and inventing new technologies, past communities were improving their lot. Judging from the skeletal evidence, one of the major innovative transformations in our past did not seem to be doing much for our general health. The skeletal evidence from hunter-gatherers has left virtually no evidence behind of chronic or severe nutritional stress or disease. Prehistoric farming communities, however, were different. We find repeated evidence of illnesses linked to dietary stress. Moreover, the stature of early farmers had recurrently diminished from that of their hunter-gatherer predecessors. The conference organizers concluded that the appearance of farming brought not only population growth, but also recurrent poverty and hunger.[13]

Farming populations grew much faster than those of mobile hunter-gatherers. That is what propelled them across the world. This may be a successful trait in evolutionary terms, but has encompassed much hardship in human terms. Outside the relatively safe haven of modern Western medicine, high rates of reproduction are dangerous for women. In many prehistoric skeletal populations a peak of female deaths around the age of reproduction highlights the costs of childbirth. Moreover, infant mortality has been typically very high in the past, with around 50 per cent of children surviving to adulthood. Those that did live frequently bore the traces of childhood malnourishment in their teeth and bones.

If we look closely at someone living today who has a history of childhood malnourishment, we can sometimes see pits or grooves running horizontally along their teeth. These grooves often have a strong association with poor nourishment, lowing resistance to infection,

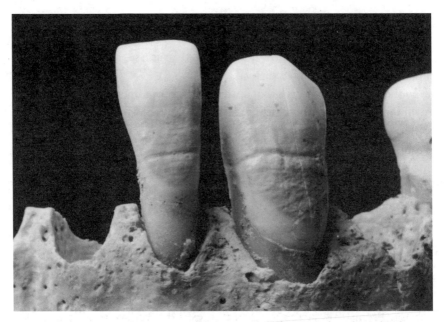

26. The incisor and canine of a young adult from medieval England, displaying prominent horizontal grooves termed 'enamel hypoplasia', which often have a strong association with poor nourishment in early life.

particularly in the period of growth directly after weaning. Those same dental defects show up in archaeological teeth and serve as a guide to the likelihood of malnourishment at different times in the past. Returning to the seventy-five individuals from Hambledon Hill, just two displayed this form of dental defect. This actually is not a bad figure. There were other scattered dental hints that diet was not universally optimal, caries, abscesses, a build up of calculus, and tooth loss, but only among a relatively limited number of individuals. Indeed, even the 15 per cent levels of anaemia are not as high as they might be. Just 30 km from Hambledon Hill at Poundbury is a cemetery half as old with over 1,400 burials, mostly of late Roman date. A full 28 per cent of these skulls display symptoms of anaemia in their eye sockets.[14]

Indeed, the evidence from Hambledon Hill, like other evidence from this early episode of farming, leads us to question whether the negative impact of a cereal-dominated diet had fully taken hold in the manner that it seemed to in other early agricultural communities. It was a question that many at the New York conference asked. They concluded that the apparent negative effects of agriculture appeared only gradually after the first sign of domesticates. We are reminded that those early farmers were part of a multi-track food web, in which domesticated plants and animals were just part of a many-stranded web that also involved a lot of woodland and wild resources. The situation is rather different when we move from the multi-track webs of early farming to the one-track webs of the hierarchical human ecosystems that replaced them.

As Hambledon Hill declined as a seasonal focus for dispersed communities, the landscape that superseded it accrued many of the physical characters of one-track webs: enduring clearances, fixed partitions within the landscape, and new kinds of burial indicative of elaborate hierarchy. In the two millennia following the demise of these early farming foci, the human skeletal remains also change.

The skeletal evidence from the British Isles offers valuable evidence for the prehistory of diet and health. When data are compared for the range 4000 to 2500 BC, broadly corresponding to earlier farmers within multi-track webs, with that from 2600–800 BC, broadly corresponding with later farmers within one-track webs, the contrasts are striking. Those porous eye sockets that result from anaemia are over twice as prevalent in the later group as in the earlier. A similar increase is seen in the prevalence of some other oral diseases which show up on the bone. The increase is even greater in other markers of dietary stress at different stages of life. The dental defects that serve as markers of deficiencies during childhood are over ten times more prevalent in the later group than the earlier. Among adults tooth loss is also ten times as prevalent in the later group. It would seem that, as communities got tied into one-track food webs, nutritional difficulties became a more significant issue for young and old alike. These markers all fluctuated in subsequent millennia, without returning to the low values of early prehistory.[15]

Patterns like this can be found in other parts of Europe and the Mediterranean. For the New York conference, the eastern Mediterranean material was gathered together and interpreted as a whole. This allowed a contrast to be seen between a very healthy looking hunter-gatherer population 30,000 to 9,000 years ago, and the rather mixed fates of the communities that followed. Throughout prehistory, the stature of men and women, a broad measure of nutrition, dropped by almost

10 per cent, and at the same time, tooth lesions of one kind or another doubled or tripled. Once again, the major changes do not come immediately domesticated plants and animals are in use, but in the later context of one-track food webs and hierarchical societies. The second millennium BC skeletons from the east Mediterranean could be subdivided according to burial custom, a valuable proxy for social status. Such a division allowed the health of ordinary people to be compared with the health of those given the most elaborate of burials. The ordinary people turned out to have five times as many dental lesions as their ruler, and to be 4 per cent shorter. An average Bronze Age male farmer from the east Mediterranean would stand at around 167 cm (5 ft 6 in) in height, 6 cm shorter than his ruler, and 10 cm shorter than his hunting ancestors.[16]

Fluctuations and differences are intrinsic elements of one-track food webs. The intrinsic structure of these narrow, highly interconnected webs itself tends towards instability, while the complex cultural core is seen as buffering and stabilizing its component ecological compartments. Variation in ecological fate is both the product and the rationale of one-track webs. That variation could be detected between different communities and between men and woman. For much of British prehistory, men seem more vulnerable than women to nutritional stress. In the centuries between the lives of biblical Ruth in Israel and of the woman from Hudremose in Denmark, however, the dental evidence from British sites coincidentally suggests that the tables were turned; women were more likely to suffer nutritionally than men.[17]

The precise causes of such patterns may remain beyond our grasp, and the samples are small and may be biased in ways we cannot always know. However, the general theme of internal difference within society shows up, not just in the incidence of traces of under-eating, but also of over-eating. While, at the end of prehistory, nutritional difficulties become more conspicuous among women, the strains of an ample diet show up in a small number of men.

In the same Dorset cemetery in which 28 per cent of the skulls display the marks of anaemia in their eye sockets, a much smaller group, around 1 per cent, display a different form of pathology. The spinal vertebrae, and some of the joints, are fused by an abnormal growth of bone that has the outward appearance of flowing candlewax. This pathology, prevalent among older, obese, and diabetic men, has the cumbersome name of 'diffuse idiopathic skeletal hyperostosis', abbreviated to DISH. From the British record, a single man with this illness is known among the earliest farmers, and a further three from later prehistory. The eleven sufferers from Poundbury are among twenty-three men of Roman Britain recorded with DISH. Inflammation and pain in the toes may also be connected with indulgence. Good living is not the only way to encourage the illness called gout, but its appearance in Britain during Roman times is interesting. Five of the Poundbury skeletons display its symptoms; three of these are men and two are women.[18]

As each of the gourmands of the Roman world uncomfortably moved their stiff backs, ample bellies, and aching legs to the next grand dinner, whole communities of farming families across the continent of Europe ate simpler fare, drawn from within the one-track webs that forged the invisible connection between their own productive work and their local elite. Many of them struggled at different stages in their lives, and many of them transformed their own food quest to adapt to their changing fortunes. They may have been forced to eat the oxen that had pulled their ard, and returned to cultivation with the hoe. A shortage of manure may have left their soils undernourished, and infested with weeds, which then became the source of their diet, and they would mix spurry, knotgrass, and fathen seeds into their flour. This they would complement with wild roots, acorns, and whatever small game they could catch. Desolate widows and paupers would wander to forage and glean. They were escaping the one-track webs which had in any case left them marginalized, and were re-engaging with multi-track webs that faintly echoed the more abundant food-webs of their distant ancestors. Beyond the monumental residues of extensive settlement, fortification, elaborate burials, fields, and roads, fragments of their various changing fates have left scattered fragments of a more unusual archaeological form.

27. The *fractio panis*, painted between 1600 and 1800 years ago on the walls of an underground chapel in the catacomb of Priscilla in Rome. A group of diners recline on a *stibadium* with loaves and fishes in the foreground.

11

THE STOMACH AND THE SOUL

Moreaucourt, Picardie, c. AD 1372

A full pound weight of bread shall be sufficient per day, whether there be one meal or a midday and an evening meal. If they are to eat in the evening a third part of this pound should be kept back by the cellarer, to be served at this meal. But should it happen that heavier work has been done, it shall be in the abbot's judgement and power to add a supplement if expedient, avoiding above all over-eating so that indigestion never overtake a monk. Nothing indeed is so unsuited to any Christian as over-eating, as the Lord says: TAKE HEED TO YOURSELVES LEST YOUR HEARTS BE OVERBUR-DENED WITH SELF-INDULGENCE. The same amount should not be served to boys under age, but less than to their elders: frugality shall be observed in everything. Except for the very weak sick all shall together abstain from eating the flesh of four-footed animals.

Each one has his own gift from God, one in this way, and another in that; and therefore it is with some misgiving that we are deciding the amount which others are to eat and drink. Nevertheless, looking at the weakness of the infirm, we believe that a hemina [approx. $\frac{1}{4}$ litre] of wine per day is enough for each. But let those to whom God gives the endurance to abstain know that they will each receive his own reward. But if the needs of the place or the work or the summer heat demand more it shall lie with the superior's judgement; he shall take care in all circumstances that neither stupefaction nor drunkenness creep in. Although we read that wine is absolutely not for monks, but because in our times that cannot be brought home to

monks, let us at least agree on this—not to drink to stupefaction, but
more temperately, because wine makes apostates, even of the wise.
(extract from the *Rule of Benedict, chapters 39 and 40, translated*
by the monks of Glenstall Abbey)

ALONG the River Somme, the ruins of Moreaucourt Priory still stand a little way west of Amiens in Picardie. It suffered badly in the fourteenth century at the rampaging hands of the English, but the surviving fragments have recently undergone restoration. Its grounds were also excavated in the 1970s and 1980s, and a series of rooms exposed of the Priory that one Aleaume of Amiens established for the Sisters of Christ in the later twelfth century. We assume that in addition to the inscribed stones and broken vessels that the archaeologists recovered in plenty, the original priory would have held copies of the rules of fathers and masters of the Christian Church, successive interpretations of the proper monastic life, drawn from life of Christ himself as well as other biblical figures. The most durable and influential of these interpretations was the rule of a sixth-century Italian monk, whose taught at the monastery at Monte Casino south of Rome, but which would carry Christianity across Europe over several subsequent centuries. By the time the priory had been ransacked, the *Rule of Benedict* was already eight centuries old, yet it remained one of the more prominent texts guiding priory life, directly guiding around 37,000 lives within monastic institutions that by now spanned Europe. In addition to the ordinary men and women of Christ, the Benedictine Order had by the fourteenth century included twenty emperors, ten empresses, forty-seven kings, fifty queens, 15,000 bishops and twenty-four popes. Its influence spread far beyond the cloister walls. Perhaps surprisingly for a text that repeatedly alluded to frugality and abstinence, it prescribed a simple meal that would in time eclipse the expansive nature of even those theatrical frontier meals of imperial Rome.[1]

Certain elements of this simple meal have made a more substantial impact on the global ecosystem than any other meal featured in this book. In the forefront of that impact was one particular cereal that lent itself to the production of a certain style of bread. But let us not imagine that St Benedict's guidance was followed to the letter in every Benedictine institution in Christendom. That much was clear from the contents of the priory kitchen at Moreaucourt.

28. View of the ruins of Moreaucourt Priory, Picardie, France.

The floor of the kitchen exposed by excavation was about 6 metres square, and in its centre was a large circular hearth. In the corner of the room was a well, which late in its life had accumulated the evidence for the prioress's relaxed attitude to food. Animal bones from the site were meticulously and systematically studied, care taken to record even the smallest bone fragments caught in fine sieves. Even a much cruder analysis, however, could not have failed to miss the plentiful bones of four-footed animals discarded in the well, bearing the cut-marks of the removal for flesh for consumption. The commonest meat bones were pork, followed by beef and then mutton, and, in addition, they were evidently catching a lot of rabbits for the pot. Whether or not a large number of the priory's communion qualified as being 'very weak', it is perfectly clear from the food remains on a wide variety of monastic sites across Europe that holy men and women found enough latitude in Benedict's rule to adjust his prescription quite considerably. What is also clear nonetheless is that they followed Benedict's prescription of a strict routine, through the day, the week, the seasons, and the year, and that routine provided many occasions to follow the theme of abstinence, at certain times within the cycle by a complete fast, at other times by selective abstinence. The more elaborate and extensive this agenda of selective fasting became, the more emphasis was placed upon those sources of meat that lacked the problematic quartet of limbs.

The priory well was rich in evidence of meat that would thus qualify. The admittedly crude measure of bone fragment number puts chicken in second place behind pork. Numerous goose bones were recovered alongside a few of woodpigeon. At two points within the well's fill were rich deposits of cockle shells. Food from the water was also indicated by shells of mussel and snail, along with a scatter of fish bones, bearing witness to cod, plaice, whiting, gurnard, herring, and pike. There were some other finds within the well that had a great deal to do with fish—these were fragments of charcoal; sizeable pieces of oak and beech, and much narrower slivers of hazel and willow. To understand what these might have to do with fish, we need to look beyond the well to the systematic sieving of the deposits on the floor into which that well had been set, and from which it eventually received refuse.

The well was one of a series of conspicuous features excavated on the priory kitchen floor. The other was a central circular platform, and within it, the traces of burning indicating a hearth. The entire deposit that lay immediately on the surface of the kitchen floor was sieved at a mesh of 1.5 mm, and the resulting assemblage of bone fragments was as rich as the fill of the disused well. However, it was a very different assemblage from the latter. Nine-tenths of the tiny fragments across the floor were bones of fish. Of those fish bones that could be identified, 15 per cent were of eel, but three-quarters were of herring. Against the background of the diverse meat diet discernible from the well's contents, some intensive activity was going on within the kitchen itself, with its focus upon the circular platform. This much was evident from the extremely high concentrations of bone forming a penumbra immediately around the platform, and including a few intact, articulated fish tails.

In the reconstruction of many instances of food-sharing in this book dating right back to Boxgrove, bio-archaeologists have made a great deal of what is there and what is missing to reconstruct how people were actually preparing their food, an approach we can explore in fine detail in something with a complicated skeleton. On other sites across the region of Picardie, it has proven possible to discern activities such as fish-gutting

29. Imagined view of the fish smoking room at Moreaucourt Priory, reconstructed from detailed bio-archaeological evidence.

and preparations from the presence and absence of bones from different parts of a fish's anatomy.[2] Here at Moreaucourt, all portions of the skeleton were well represented pointing to intensive treatment of the whole fish. The kitchen was operating as a smokery, with herrings and eels threaded onto thin wands of hazel and willow, and suspended above a fire to be infused with the smoke of beech and oakwood. We get a fragmentary hint of the scale of this operation from a document dated 13 October 1351 indicating that Moreaucourt was receiving, from a single source, an annual donation of 5,000 herrings.[3] The priory devotees would be able to immerse themselves in the abstinence and austerity of a frequent succession of festivals and fasts with a healthy supply of kippers.

By the era of the Moreaucourt Priory the central importance of fish in the culinary thread of the Christian liturgical calendar was making a profound impact, not just in monastic refectories, but also in the land-scape, the waterways, and the wider ecosystem. A little way to the west of the priory ruins, the River Somme deviates from its general natural meander to run absolutely straight for around 2 kilometres. A perusal of early maps and documents suggests a construction early in the thirteenth century, a few decades after the establishment of the priory, and probably instigated by the same man, Aleaume of Amiens. While this stretch in itself was probably not for fishing, it is clearly part of a system of intensive water management that typifies medieval monastic landscapes. Monasteries established from this time forward would excavate a com-plex series of waterways around their buildings, supplying clean water for drinking, and a more abundant supply for cleansing and drainage. The drinking water would ideally come from a spring, but the main supply could come from diverting and canalizing a river or stream. A series of channels, drains, sluices, and hatches would guide the water through the various living and working sections of the monastery, the water gathering in the main drain after its domestic work was done. From there, its flow would continue to sustain the monastery, through irrigating gardens, driving fulling mills and corn mills, and supplying fishponds.[4]

The fragmentary fish skeletons and vestiges of a controlled waterway are fleshed out by an illuminating document. In 1179, a chancellor of the Roman Church drafted the 'Bulle de Moreaucourt', copies of which sur-vive, detailing the allocations of land and goods to the recent monastic foundation at Moreaucourt. It talks of tithes from many sources, of gifts and donations. Prominent among these are fields and vineyards, and measures of grain and wine. There is in addition water for the working of a mill, a fish pond with its own sluice gate, a fishery with a capacity for 2,000 eels, and all the fishing along the river, between the neighbouring villages of Flixecourt and L'Étoile.[5]

Monastic fisheries leave a significant trace across the European landscape, the arrays of rectangular ponds often surviving as earthworks within riverine woodland and water meadows. The productivity of medieval fish farming was clearly immense, but nevertheless insufficient to meet the continuous demand for legless meat. This much is clear from similar analyses of a whole series of sites in the landscape around Moreaucourt.

Moreaucourt is only 15 kilometres from the coast; it is hardly surprising that marine fish figure so prominently. Looking further inland, to skeletal data from other sites, we can see a longer-term dynamic which explains the needs to manage inland waterways in the intensive manner evident from ponded enclosures and canalized rivers. It seems quite likely that the natural productivity of the terrestrial waterways had been feeling the pressure of the meal table.

The bones of the eels alluded to in the 'Bulle de Moreaucourt' have been recovered in plenty. They have been found not just among the priory ruins, but in a series of sites across northern France, which together give some idea of the environmental impact of the Christian community's demand for fish. Between the ninth and the thirteenth centuries, the consumption of fish reflects the local waters in a fairly straightforward manner. At sites near the coast, marine fish are prominent, whereas further inland, freshwater fish, first eels and then carp, stand out as the commonest remains. This all changes during the fourteenth century, and the final Moreaucourt kitchen is emblematic of that change. Herrings and flatfish have by now overtaken the freshwater fish on inland sites. By the fifteenth century, herrings are everywhere the most frequent fish among the archaeological debris. However elaborate and intensive the inland medieval fisheries, they could not keep pace with the demand and the changing possibilities of inland transport.[6]

If the spread of Christian dining had a highly conspicuous impact upon the aquatic phase of the European ecosystem, its impact upon the terrestrial ecosystem was equally profound, and in the very long term, more influential. The zoological study at Moreaucourt may be complemented by some sense of the plants they were consuming, by reference to another medieval settlement, around 40 km to the south-east, at a place called Dury Le Moulin.

Today the location is marked by a piece of public art. In advance of its erection, a rescue dig was mounted over an area of one hectare, providing a prime example of how good archaeological science may be combined with the pressures and urgency of modern development. Archaeological features across the whole hectare were mapped in detail, and the contents of ditches, pits, and postholes studied for animal bones, plant remains, human bones, pottery, and the whole contextualized within a survey of relevant documentary evidence. Today's *Route nationale* passing, by way of Dury Le Moulin, south of Amiens to Beauvais, follows the path of Roman military road. A length of this road was exposed during the rescue dig. Over the centuries that followed the road's construction, a series of timber houses would appear from time to time, leaving postholes, ditches, and pits, the standard legacy of early vernacular housing, either side of the enduring routeway. By the end of the seventh century AD, such houses constitute a settlement named 'Dury', worthy of brief mention in a couple of contemporary documents. By the time of the Moreaucourt kitchen 40 km to the north-west, Dury is in the record as also being in ecclesiatical ownership, this time with Amiens Cathedral as landlord. In the intervening period, the excavations at Dury Le Moulin give some indication of what the rural lay population was eating. They too were eating fish, although the conditions of preservation of fish bone in the site were greatly inferior to those at Moreaucourt. Around 44 kilo of animal bones were recovered from the excavation and examined; they were consuming the flesh of a variety of species, including goose, chicken, mutton, and horse. However, their favoured source of meat was beef.[7]

Around half the bones recovered were from cattle. From the wear on their surviving teeth, the principal age of cull could be calculated at between two and four years of age. Around half the herd would have been culled by this age. This is a familiar figure, broadly similar to the age results from cattle at Hambledon Hill, almost 4,000 years earlier. It corresponds to an optimal period of growth for meat production. However, around a third of the bones are from much older cattle, going to the slaughter at between 6 and 9 years of age. At other contemporary sites in the region, they are even older, 10 years and more. This age range is less common in prehistoric populations, and suggests some other reason for keeping these animals alive, long past their age of optimal meat productivity. One possibility is that they have been trained to work in pairs and perhaps larger groups, to pull carts and other heavy equipment, such as the plough.

The hard work of such trained animals can be tracked down in the plant remains that were studied from the site. The charred seeds of crops and weeds found in pits, ditches, and postholes at Dury reveal a pattern that is hardly unusual in the broader historic context, but nevertheless marks one of the quietest, yet most significant revolutions in the global history of food production, a revolution that connects those older cattle with a novel access to metal goods and a changing balance of crops. Traces of that new way of farming can be found among the weed seeds from Dury, particularly those belonging to a pretty pink flower called corn cockle, and one of a number of weeds in the daisy family called stinking mayweed. Those same species also turn up on the penumbra of the shrinking Roman Empire a few centuries earlier, when this revolution got under way. This was a time when wealth in the north of the empire was being transferred from the nodes and axes of the imperial network to the rural landscape.[8]

European communities north of the Alps had had a long tradition of living and working with cattle; they knew well how to raise them and train them. The imperial network had transformed their relationship with metalworking and metal supply. What was once a material of elite display had become increasingly accessible to well-to-do farmers who could put it to functional uses. The combination of cattle power and metal technology opened the way to cultivate the land in an entirely different way. For thousands of years, a small wooden tool, the ard, had scratched through the lighter, loamy soils. The mouldboard plough and its team of trained cattle could now turn whole landscapes upside down, driving through even the deep heavy clays of the lowlands. In doing so, they created much deeper arable soils into which more fertilizer could be fed. They also waged a far tougher battle against weeds than the lighter ards they gradually superseded.

A number of weed species went into decline, making way for others than were better adapted to this new brand of human onslaught upon their soils. We can find the charred seeds of those weeds among buried household ashes, silently charting the changing methods of agriculture. Prominent among the new weeds of the heavy plough are cockle, may-weed, and charlock. The earliest writings on weeds, that appeared during the lifetime of Moreaucourt Priory, highlight them as among the most noxious weeds of the field. Their presence at farms of the later Roman Empire, and then at later sites like Dury reflects the rise to prominence of this new technology. It appears on several medieval manuscripts: a team of two, four, or more oxen, yoked together and clearly working hard, dragging a wheeled heavy plough behind them, with coulter and share cutting deep into the soil.[9]

At the focus of this new technology were two crops that had now risen to prominence, rye, and bread wheat. Their charred grain is found alongside the weed seeds in the pits, ditches, and postholes at Dury. These two crops had been encountered north of the Alps for thousands of years, but only as a minor trace among other species. They increase in number in the same late Roman farms that yield the plough weeds, and at Dury are the most abundant crops of all, much as they continue to be in medieval Europe as a whole. They are both crops that respond well to intensive working of the soil.[10]

One of them, bread wheat, the most abundant species in the Dury assemblages, is also in calorific terms the foremost food source of the world's human population today. Each year, the yield of its grain now exceeds half a billion tonnes. It would seem to suit human needs rather well, and has been around and widespread for several thousand years. Rather surprisingly, therefore, it is only in the last 1,500 years that it peaked as the favoured grain crop and overtook all others. What was the change that laid the staple foundation of the world's modern diet; what was happening in the first millennium to shift a food plant that for thousands of years had been just one of a range of crops, and often a minor crop, to centre stage?

The world's favourite food

The modern science of botany gathers a number of different cereals and wild grasses within the single genus *Triticum* or 'wheat'. Earlier authors emphasized a finer range of divisions, reflecting the wide diversity of the crops so assembled, in terms of growing patterns, flavour, texture, and cooking qualities. The Latin word *triticum* seems to have related to crops we now call 'naked wheats', in which the ripe grain falls easily from the ear. Bread wheat is the most abundant of these naked wheats today. *Triticum* was seen as distinct from *far*, the Latin word that corresponds with our hulled wheats, in particular emmer and spelt. In these crops, the grains are held tightly in the chaff, which offers them partial protection from predation and the elements. From the first spread of agriculture across Europe, *far* was in the vanguard, and now, over 6,000 years later, the place of *far* was being taken by *triticum*. The explanation used to be a simple one—progress. Bread wheat yielded better than so-called 'primitive' wheats, and was easier to process, because of the looseness of the grain in the ear, rendering it easier to harvest. It was not an explanation that stood up to close scrutiny. Growing experiments have shown that, if fertilizer were available, emmer and spelt could yield far in excess of recorded medieval yields of bread wheat, and if fertilizer was not adequately available, they would all yield poorly, bread wheat probably worse.[11] The processing argument was never that persuasive, for two reasons; first, technologies were certainly available, and still are, to release hulled grain; and secondly, the naked wheats had been available for thousands of years, but were not extensively taken up on this basis. Convincing reasons for this late shift in preference have to be sought elsewhere, and an important clue lies in the geographical patterning of its take-up.

Dury Le Moulin is not alone in displaying a predominance of these two grain crops. During the ninth and tenth centuries, a number of sites in the region are marked by a large proportion of bread wheat, and a significant presence of rye. Indeed, the same is true across much of Western Europe at this time in the second half of the first millennium AD. Early in that millennium, the record of charred grain typically displays a diversity of seed crops in each place, optimizing and ensuring against bad years by mixing the grain repertoire. During the fourth and fifth centuries, the two minor crops, bread wheat and rye, come into their own on some farms, bread wheat to the west of the Rhine, and rye to the east. It seems to be the imperial lines along the Rhine that mark the divide, and yet it is a divide that persists and intensifies as the empire retracts.

Bread wheat becomes more and more common to the west, and rye becomes increasing abundant on the east, spreading further eastwards and northwards in the ensuing centuries. Later in the first millennium, fragments of narrative allude to the connections these crops have, not with ecological constraints and needs, but instead with the symbolism of the gods. In Eastern Europe, the Slavs paid homage to a pantheon of gods. Central to the agricultural cycle was Jaryla or Herovit, God of the fields. Jaryla matured, died and was reborn every year, according to the agricultural seasons. He was depicted as a handsome young man, in a white cloak and with a coronet of flowers on his head. He rode upon a white horse, carrying in his hand a sheaf of rye. Their neighbours in Western Europe paid homage to a single God, and his son Christ, whose body was represented by a baked product of bread wheat. By the later part of the first millennium, the black bread of rye and the white bread of wheat embodied pagan and Christian Europe.[12]

Why should crops connect with cultural rather than ecological boundaries? In today's world of 'national cuisines' we are very familiar with the idea that they do, but the roots of our species' early ecological success lay in the ease with which we could track complex environments, switching with ease between the different species that ebbed and flowed along with the sharpest of fluctuations in the Quaternary environment. The wide range of cereals and pulses cultivated across Europe 2,000 years ago preserves some of that flexibility, the pattern of their use following fluctuations in local soils and ecology. Around 1,500 years ago, the patterns change, as is particularly evident from bread wheat and rye. The crops seem first to map out the ghost of the Roman Empire, and then follow the boundary between pagan and Christian Europe. What is it about these crops that may connect, less with what was going in our stomachs than in our minds and souls?

Artistry of the loaf

We can approach that question by thinking of bread less as a source of nutrition, and more as a cultural object, an artefact. In some respects the flour ground from grass seeds as early as 23,000 years ago at Ohalo has similarities with the clay harvested from the earth a few thousand years earlier in Moravia. Both could be mixed with water, moulded and shaped, and offered to the fire. We are very used to the idea that the designs of the fired clay objects so produced are mirrors of culture; indeed, we define whole prehistoric 'cultures' by reference to their pottery. Just as different clays mixed with different tempering agents produce different kinds of ceramic, so different flours, combined with different ingredients, create different kinds and shapes of loaf.

Some of the best conserved archaeological loaves were recovered from the ruins of Pompeii, engulfed by the ashes of Vesuvius in AD 79. The eruption entombed the town's bakeries, and several of its last production of loaves. They are formed as *artes quadrati*, round loaves shaped with a knife into four, sometimes eight segments. They are designed to be broken and shared amongst a group of diners. In their form they ·represent the assembled 'company' (literally, from the Latin *cum panis* 'together with bread'), a metaphor for the food-sharing community and the individuals within it. The metaphor recurs in classical poetry. The comic poet Demetrius plays with the word *Artos*, both a personal name and a word for 'loaf' as 'a pleasant host, large in that country, and white'. A generous host and a generous loaf are praised for their volume and hue. The Macedonian poet Antiphanes asks 'how could a man of gentle breeding ever leave this roof, when he sees these white-bodied loaves crowding the furnace in close ranks, and when he sees, too, how they have changed their shape in the oven—deft imitations made by Attic skill, which Thearon taught his countrymen?' (Thearon was a legendary baker.) In contrast to those accolades to white bodies, edible and human, grey, black, and dirty coloured breads were increasingly associated with foreigners and paupers; in the fourth century BC the comic poet Plato described a particular group of large dirty untidy loaves as 'Cilicians' (Cilicia occupied a southern part of what is now Turkey).[13]

By this time, the bread baker's art was already thousands of years old. We get an early glimpse of it in the images and models of the Egyptian tombs of the third and second millennia BC. They depict how, in these early bakers' workshops, dough of emmer wheat and barley was mixed with sweeteners and spices, kneaded and fashioned into geometric shapes, rolls, and more elaborate shapes such as human forms.[14] It is from a much later resident of Egypt, who hailed from the Nile delta at Naucratis around AD 200, that we begin to gain a detailed insight into this diversity of the baker's creations. In a lengthy series of books on the culture of eating, drawing upon several centuries of earlier writings, Athenaeus describes a vast number of different loaves, more than seventy from the Greek mainland alone. They could be made from barley, rye, spelt, millet, flavoured with sesame, poppy seed, cheese, or spices, and their texture adjusted with oil, suet, or lard. They were fashioned into a host of shapes, into twisted plaits, a flat disc, a wafer, a flower, or a mushroom, a body or a breast. The interest in these artefacts was not confined to texture and shape; there was a very clear interest in colour, and from at least as early as the fifth century BC, a particular delight in loaves that were white.[15]

In certain eastern Mediterranean traditions, the whiteness of the flour represented the pure and wholesome home, a purity that could be corrupted by the dark forces of fermentation from leaven, or yeast, from beyond the home. This drama of purity and sin is captured in Paul's letter to the Corinthians, and also in the Jewish symbolism of unleavened bread. It is a drama to which one particular species of cereal lends itself, yielding the whitest of flours, and a dough that responds most actively to yeast by raising and growing into a light and airy loaf. While the species that were gathered under the Latin term *far* (emmer and spelt) can be fashioned into perfectly nutritious and tasty loaves, even when made from refined flour the colours range between yellow and grey, and they do not rise as high as loaves made from the refined flour of bread wheat. In many languages, the whiteness was sufficiently important to give the species its name. The word 'wheat', which originally referred to this particular species, itself signifies 'white' as do the similar words for bread wheat in German, Frisian, Gothic, and Norse.

The black loaves of rye to the east and the white loaves and bread wheat to the west, were not just food; they were also artefacts, and marked a clear cultural divide between two large regions of Europe. One of these artefacts, the white loaf, would expand yet further over the coming centuries, across the Old World and New. Its own cultural roots brought together two contrasting traditions within Europe and the eastern Mediterranean. One of these traditions had grown in the well-to-do households of the Roman world, the other in the world of the underdog and outcast.

A pastoral setting

The *artes quadrati*, recovered from the Pompeian bakeries, recur in frescos painted on the walls of that doomed town. They also appear in relief on later Roman stone coffins, and frescos on the walls of early Christian catacombs. Such illustrations display a softer, simpler meal than the lavish theatrical feasts enjoyed on imperial frontiers, both geographical and social. The latter were theatrical meals with disguised ingredients, consumed in angular places, often bringing strangers together to eat and enjoy some spectacle. From very early in the Roman Empire, while meals along social and geographical frontiers were gaining in theatricality, this more relaxed and collective form of eating in the round was also known in the more socially secure heartlands. Varro talks of eating in the round, and from the first century AD, poets make reference to curved cushions, stuffed with foliage or *stibades*. But it is from the late second and third centuries these cushions or *stibadia* are widely known.[16]

The cushions do not require a formal architectural space; indeed the entire manner of eating is ideally suited to a pastoral picnic, an erosion of the boundary between community and network, between the rustic and urbane. These later Roman meals in the round did not necessarily involve the loss of pomp, rank, and protocol. Diners had a particular seating arrangement, with pride of place at the ends of the semicircle. There was a protocol of reclining, always on the left arm with the right hand free to pick up food from the shared dish, and the fingers used in particular ways for particular foodstuffs. The meals were not necessarily simple; lavish menus were still prepared in the best houses, and served in a particular order; commencing with a *gustatio* of roots, vegetables, fish, and eggs, moving on to a whole series of main dishes, and finishing with *bellaria* of sweets, nuts, and fresh fruit. We can, however, see a clear distance from the highly decorated and disguised, meat-rich feasts of the social and geographical frontier. In the depictions of a meal in frescos, mosaics, and stone carvings from the late empire, the emphasis moves increasingly towards a small number of central elements. In contrast to the early imperial emphasis on small, individual servings, they depict larger vessels, from which food and drink may be shared. In the food and drink in question, certain items recur, in particular, wine, fish, and bread.[17]

In the barren desert

While the landed families of the late Roman Empire were comfortably sharing food and drink from large African bowls, a quite different approach to food was emerging in Africa itself, one also centred around bread. Travellers in the deserts of Egypt and Sinai might encounter devout, solitary individuals, eating very little of anything. They converged upon sites that tradition had associated with biblical stories of the Exodus out of Egypt, sites like Mount Sinai. Here, they lived out lives of extreme austerity in shelters and caves. They did have bread, but what little they had they reserved for a meal that transcended the bounds of earthly pleasures.

One such individual was a simple Egyptian farmer called Anthony, who rejected urbane life and escaped to the sand dunes, only to be pursued by the sophisticates of the city of Alexandria in search of a touch of holiness and enlightenment. After repeated attempts to escape attention and find solitude, he eventually set up a community of solitaries near Memphis, a site that remains the Monastery of St Anthony today. Many desert solitaries of the fourth century would survive on water and a few dates, or other fruits. Bread would feature centrally in their lives, but only in one special context. Each Sunday morning after they had gathered with other solitaries for a night of prayer, they would remember and repeat Christ's Last Supper and, through their one piece of weekly bread, enter into communion with their God. According to three of the four gospels, that Last Supper was itself a meal of commemoration, in remembrance of events held to have occurred a thousand years earlier. On the eve of their escape from Egyptian bondage, the Israelites gathered to roast a lamb whole, and speedily bake unleavened bread. The lamb's blood was smeared on the doorposts, in order that God would recognize that Israelites dwelt in that house, and pass over it on his purge against the Egyptian first-born.[18]

The Passover meal and Last Supper embrace a millennial tradition of the simple, hasty or meal meal, shared by the poor, the enslaved, and the outcast, beyond the gaze of worldly rulers and despots, and bringing the diners closer to their true Lord. The Bible alludes to others in this tradition, for example the unidentified manna from heaven on which the Israelites fed in their forty years of desert wandering. The solitary hermits were taking that tradition to its extreme. They returned to sites on the traditional Exodus route and constructed rudimentary living cells. Here they would approach starvation in order to intensify that most intimate of all conversational circles, communion with God.

On an island in the waters of the Nile, a community of these devotees left their isolation to live together under the guidance of a leader, a native of Memphis and veteran of the Roman army named Pachomius. His community on the Isle of Tabennisi has left traces of a very early 'monastic rule', a template for devout living that guided monks towards that divine conversational circle with God. Pachomius' rule prescribed that, on two days of the week, Wednesdays and Fridays, there would be no food at all. On other days, two meals would be served, the second very sparse. Some monks ate only a single food at each meal, sometimes just a small piece of bread. For some, even the presence of other mortals around the table disrupted the intimacy of the divine communion. They made do with a little water, salt, and bread, brought to their cell.[19]

By the end of his life in the middle of the fourth century, Pachomius had several monasteries of men and women, who combined their frugality and devotion with a fair bit of industry and trade. His was a tough rule, and in the subsequent centuries new rules were drafted, softening the edges and allowing a little more worldly indulgence, propelling a rich monastic history of cycles of relaxation and returns to austerity, that continued with different orders throughout the Middle Ages. A century or so after Pachomius, another rule is known from a monastic community near Jericho. Gerasimus' rule allowed its solitary monks to consume bread, dates, and water throughout the week, and after Holy Communion on Sundays, some cooked food and wine.[20]

A merger of traditions

During the course of the empire, Christianity shifted from being a religion of the outsider, to one of great popularity among the underdogs of society, to being a religion attractive to the well-to-do, and the two traditions of sharing food with bread in central position merged. We can get a glimpse of this merger on the walls of a small underground chapel in the early Christian catacomb of Priscilla in Rome.

On the walls of that chapel is a fresco, painted between 1,600 and 1,800 years ago, depicting seven diners, reclining on a *stibadium*. In the foreground are two large ceramic dishes, one bearing bread, the other fish. Alongside stands a two-handled cup. It is clear from the image that the diners are reaching into the same dishes, which are large because the food is being shared, much as the cup has two handles in order that it may be passed from hand to hand. They recline, not in the rectilinear arrangement of the lavish meal, but around a curved cushion. One of the diners is engaged in an action that has lent the fresco its adopted name, *fractio panis*; this diner is depicted breaking the bread.[21]

If this was the sacred meal, it had been detached in style from the Jewish Passover, and given a pastoral Roman flavour. Some would argue this happened early on; the Gospel according to St John already makes that separation. Several images from the fifth century onwards represent the Last Supper as a pastoral Roman meal in the round, reclining over a *stibadium*. Along with the bread *artes quadrati*, and shared cups of wine, a central plate of fish is repeatedly shown, a favourite of the Roman meal and now a symbol of Christ. Such images bring together the production of bread wheat and wine, traditional dining in the Roman pastoral style, and communion with God. These three strands come together in one person's life, author of the most influential 'Rule' of all.

Around AD 480, a rich and noble family gave birth to a boy near Spoleto in central Italy. He would become known as the father of Western monasticism. By his middle age, he had spent half his life as a well-to-do Roman youth familiar with civilized life in the large estates, and the other half as a cave-dwelling solitary monk. In the early sixth century, he founded a series of monastic communities at Subiaco, near Rome, and subsequently the famous abbey at Monte Cassino, the community that would serve as a model for monasteries throughout Europe over the coming centuries, and would play a central role in all aspects of society, spiritual and mundane, across the Christian world. Those two halves of Benedict's life reflect the different strands of influence upon the Christian meal. His rule dictates a life considerably less austere than the prescriptions of his desert predecessors. Rather than austerity, his emphasis is upon moderation. The monks could feast on ample bread, wine, fish, and fruits of the garden, and even then, there were escape clauses to permit further relaxation, and transform monasticism into something that could spread with speed and vigour. Within a century of his death, the rule of Benedict was widely accepted as far north as England. By the eighth century, the Benedictine order took the frontier of Christendom to Germany and from there, eastwards and northwards, transforming not only people's spiritual lives, but also their worldly and cultural lives, and their engagement with the land.[22]

The cross, the book and the plough

In AD 1220, Pope Honorius III wrote of the conversation of the Baltic pagans in the following terms:

> The hardness of the hearts of the Livonian pagans, like a vast desert land, has been been watered by the showers of divine grace and cultivated by the ploughshare of holy preaching, the seed of the lord is blessedly shooting up into a crop, nay, the lands are already white for the harvest.[23]

His writing followed a long tradition that connected spiritual enlightment with clearance and the ploughshare. Where once the pagans to which the text refers had engaged in a relatively diverse multi-track web, drawing upon the resources of woodland, field, marsh, and water, the lords and prelates of thirteenth-century Europe set in motion on the peripheries of their realms a quite distinct dynamic. Large rectangular fields spread out around planned settlements, fortifications, and ecclesiastical institutions. Their plots were sizeable enough to accommodate team-drawn heavy ploughs, and would bring forth a uniform harvest comprising a small range of arable crops. Central among those crops was the white harvest of bread wheat, a species that followed Christianity eastwards and northwards across Europe. Non-revenue-producing resources were in this way transformed 'into a fountain of corn and silver'. It is a transformation that the historian Robert Bartlett has described as 'cerealization'.[24]

The monastic expansion is sometimes described as the evangelism of cross, book and plough, alluding to the simultaneous transformations in spirituality, learning, and the food quest that seemed to attach to the monastic advance. In fact the depth of those transformations can be queried. We may get the impression from contemporary Christian sources that the north-eastern pagans were more or less foragers. The hard evidence reveals that centuries before conversion, cereal cultivation had been established as far north as the Arctic Circle. However, the crop raised in the Lofoten islands off the north of Norway was barley, not the favoured cereal of white bread loaves. There is also some confusion about the actual novelty of the plough outside the world of Christendom. Contemporary authors draw a distinction between a heavier German plough and a lighter Slavic plough. However, some of the earliest evidence for the heavy mouldboard plough comes from northern sites that lie beyond the limits of both Christendom and the Roman Empire. The heavy ploughs of which the texts spoke were primarily ploughshares of the soul.[25]

The symbolism of wine and bread, together with the potency of the plough, real and metaphorical, has followed Christianity across the world. The Norseman Leifr Eiriksson is reputed to have been the first European to encounter the American mainland, in the year 1000. According to one account, this recent Christian convert had drifted off course from a mission to convert the Greenlanders. On his newly found shore he is said to have seen 'fields of self-sown wheat' and a country 'rich with grapes and timber'. Timber and wild vines there certainly were, but wheat is not native to America, and one wonders whether this is not a symbolic allusion to the potential of further evangelism, a potential realized a few centuries later by the Spanish conquistadores.[26]

Columbus's voyages to the New World opened the way for an unprecedented exchange, not just in cultural, but quite profoundly in ecological terms. The Europeans brought horses, cattle, and pigs to America, and transformed landscapes and economies as a consequence. They also brought bananas, sugar, cotton, rice, indigo, and yams. A number of these would feature prominently in landscapes of plantations and slavery. They took back with them tobacco, potatoes, chocolate, tomatoes, some varieties of beans, and turkeys, each of which would become deeply embedded in a variety of European meals. The 'Columbian Exchange' affected many other species besides, including a range of useful plants and animals, alongside a range of weeds and wild species and catastrophic diseases. This momentous melting pot of global ecology also allowed the exchange of the principle grass seeds upon which meals on either side of the Atlantic had been based.[27]

On his second voyage to the New World, Columbus took a range of seeds for planting, including chickpeas, melons, onions, vegetables, fruits, and sugar cane, in addition, the two central elements of Christian life, seeds of grape and grains of bread wheat. Neither of these latter two crops took immediately to the new continent. They are both fairly particular in their demands, and on arguments of cost-effectiveness should probably have been dropped from the conquistadores' battery of new crops. So close were they to the Christian Spanish soul, however, that they persisted and eventually found New World environments where these crops would take and thrive. Forty years after Columbus first set sail, there were extensive wheat fields in Mexico. By the second half of the sixteenth century, there were wheat fields across South America, and along the coastal valleys of Peru and Chile, orchards of olive and wine. That century had witnessed a lively discourse within Spain on the issue of 'lawfulness' in the New World, its lands and its people. The conquistadores were conveying that law, moving across new territories with cross, sword, and plough, not to mention a range of diseases. Together, these arms of conquest left a substantial legacy in term of an extensive network of churches, a much reduced and impoverished Amerindian population, and vast landscapes of vineyards and wheat fields.[28]

On the face of it, the two-way exchange of resources might have featured a symmetrical interchange between the major cereal of Europe, bread wheat, and the major cereal of America, maize. While wheat unquestionably travelled with the Christian conquerors, the Amerindian communities did not adopt it with enthusiasm. They saw no virtues in wheat that could justify a movement away from maize, another grass seed with deep symbolic meaning for its consumers. Neither did maize become established on any significant scale in the European continent as a whole. It was only beyond the Old World borders of Christendom, for example in China, that large expanses of maize took hold. In the Italian language, this native American crop is still known as 'grain of the Turks', *granturco*, a name that is completely anomalous in terms of conventional geography, but might have a clearer meaning within a landscape of religious distinctions. The true Columbian exchange was not so much for wheat as a crop, but for white bread as an artefact steeped in ideology. The nature of that exchange is captured in essence in an artefact housed within a Spanish cathedral.

White for gold

All the regions of the globe have contributed their fruits and abundance to adorn and enrich this quarter part of the world, which we Spaniards found so poor and destitute of the plants and animals most necessary to nourish and give service to mankind, howsoever prosperous and abundant the mineral resources of gold and silver.

(Bernabé Cobo, seventeenth century)[29]

The city of Toledo, 70 km south of Madrid, was the destination for a fair amount of the gold that followed Columbus' path. Fifteen kilos of this gold was combined with over 180 kilos of silver to create an elaborate flourish of metalwork over 12 feet high. The Monstrance of Toledo is adorned with emeralds, pearls, and 260 statuettes, one of the largest being fashioned from the American gold. But these are all peripheral ornaments, the supporting cast to the true centrepiece. That role is taken by a small circular disc of white, wheaten bread, the essence of the body of Christ, the host.[30]

The Monstrance of Toledo marks a pinnacle in the elevation of white bread as an artefact. What began as a meal broken down to its simplest form was now an elaborate extravagance, centred upon a small wafer of white bread. The extent of its identity with Christ's own body had once been a matter for vigorous theological debate, and now the wafer or 'host' had become an object of veneration in itself, attracting a mythology of its own. Stories were told of it being raised aloft in medieval churches, and of parishioners crying out for it to be raised higher still. It was said that some would attend mass simply to catch sight of the elevation and consecration of the host, rushing from church to church to catch as many consecrations as possible, for there were many monstrances, displaying many such thin wafers of wheaten bread. Some had seen the central wafer of bread oozing drops of blood, others had watched as it adopted human form before their very eyes. When the thirteenth-century nun Wilbergis took the host into her cell to help her avoid sexual temptation, it transformed itself into a beautiful baby and proceeded to recite the Song of Songs.[31] In a convent in seventeenth-century Burgundy, Marguertie Marie Alacoque was in devout prayer before the sacrament. As she prayed, Jesus appeared before her, presenting his heart on a flaming throne, surrounded by thorns and mounted by a cross. Her ecstasy on beholding the 'Sacred Heart' of Jesus is celebrated by the Society of the Dames du Sacré Coeur dedicated to its veneration. One of its convents' most eminent alumni is the anthropologist Mary Douglas.[32]

The power of bread has taken many forms in many episodes of an originally east Mediterranean tradition that travelled with the Roman Empire, and then with Christianity across the world. The dominance of bread wheat within our modern food chain as the major calorific source of our species has been driven by bread as an artefact, rich in meaning, as much as wheat as a source of nutrition, rich in calories. If a committee of agronomists were assembled to advise on an ideal crop with which to colonize the world, they might well select barley, which uniquely combines relative hardiness with considerable adaptability. It has been cultivated from the tropical latitudes to the Arctic Circle, and from montane heights to saline coastal flats. There is nothing nutritionally problematic about porridge, barley bread, or beer.[33]

By comparison, bread wheat is a rather fussy crop, and has only flourished in the context of water and nutrient management, and the heavy plough. A number of generations of 'bread wheat evangelists' have toiled hard and with much suffering to establish it far from home. The final generations who completed the conquest of the New World by bread wheat were among these. As the mid-west settlers of the late nineteenth and early twentieth centuries took their wheat grain into ever more arid and sparse regions of the prairie, the ecological risks grew. Each day each family started by speaking to their God, asking him to provide their daily bread and forgive their sins. Each morning they cleared new land with the belief that 'rain would follow the plough'; as the share sliced through the sod, it would lure the water from the sky.

Their persistence was greeted in the 1930s by the tragedy of the dust-bowl, when the fine soil from their fields took to the air in monumental clouds of dust.[34]

By the middle of the twentieth century, bread wheat has taken its conquest to its final territories, north and south in the New World, across the vast expanses of New South Wales in Australia. The two major world crops, bread wheat and rice, now describe the two major economic power blocs of the world, the Western Bloc and East Asia. Bread wheat in the West, and rice and the East, have each become far more than a source of nutrition for the body. In a range of different cultural contexts, both plants have become rich in symbolic meaning, and served as important elements of religious practice, and marks of cultural identity. In pre-Columbian America, much the same could be said of their New World counterpart, maize.[35]

A wooden table within the late medieval refectory at Moreaucourt was laid with smoked fish, garden vegetables, loaves of bread, and wine. This quietly shared meal embodied the society and landscape around it on various scales. First of all it reflected the monastic community itself, its abbess and nuns, and the gardens, fisheries, and fields which they tended, and the smokery and mills they worked. On a larger scale, it reflected a transformation of the ecosystem. The waters of the Seine, as with many other rivers across Europe, are woven through gardens, water meadows, fishponds, and strings of mills, their energies fully tapped and their produce harvested to the full. The heavy demand for fish extends that wholesale transformation from the rivers to the sea. Around the waterways were garden plots and vineyards, and long fields, deeply ploughed, bringing forth the white harvest. On a yet larger scale still, it reflects a transformation in society, the fruits of the garden, loaves and fishes, bread and wine all alluding to earlier meals that bind a millennial tradition of belief and ideology, an ideology that would transform the world. In the vanguard of that transformation were a constellation of words and ideas, economic and political forces. Also in the vanguard were the food quest and the shared meal, the mouldboard plough and the loaf of wheaten bread.

30. An early advert for Swanson TV dinners.

12

A GLOBAL FOOD WEB

Portland, Oregon, AD 1954

My mother was always intrigued by consumer innovations during the postwar years. And by 1954, when the new meals made their debut, speed and convenience were becoming dominant themes in American culture.

Gerry Thomas is the man who thought up the dinners. He says the TV label was a way to make the product seem trendy and cool, by linking it to the explosive popularity of the new electronic medium.

Again, I confess: My family did eat many evening meals in our living room while watching television.

For a variety of reasons that are too complicated to explain here, the dining room table was usually piled high with junk mail and old newspapers. But at least we were watching quality programs such as the Huntley–Brinkley Report ('Good night, Chet.' 'Good night, David. And good night from NBC News.') In my opinion, what made TV dinners so appealing was the tray.

Aluminum was a product of space-age technology. I could easily imagine myself staring at the carefully measured portions of food while hurtling toward the rings of Saturn in the cockpit of a mighty star cruiser. TV dinners also gave kids the incredible option of eating the apple crisp dessert before the main course.

At this point, I must also comment on the other towering achievement in Swanson history, the chicken pot pie. There was always a moment of uncertainty that I enjoyed immensely as the pies emerged from the oven. Should I eat mine out of the aluminum tub, or flip it over onto a plate so it resembled a small, golden igloo?

Chicken was the best flavor, turkey was so-so, and beef was discouraging. The beef gravy had a dark, sludgy appearance, like the dredgings from our local yacht harbor. Sorry, Swanson, but you can't expect us frozen-food gourmets to swallow everything with a smile.

I sometimes wonder what happened to the old trays. My mother washed and saved every one of them while explaining, 'We can use these for other things.' I have an uneasy feeling they all ended up in a landfill.

(Jeffrey Shaffer in the *Christian Science Monitor,* Friday 16 April 1999)

FLYING into New Jersey's Newark airport, you may catch a glimpse of the highest geographical feature along the whole 1,500-mile stretch of seaboard between Florida and Maine. It is a man-made structure, twenty-five times the size of the Great Pyramid of Khufu at Giza, forty times bigger than the Temple of the Sun at Teotihuacan, and around the same volume as the Great Wall of China. At an estimated 2.9 billion cubic feet, the Fresh Kills Landfill Site may well be among the largest man-made structures in the history of the world. On 4 July 2001, a special ceremony, led by New York's then Mayor Rudolph Giuliani, sealed its future status as a 'tranquil and pastoral area, one with rolling green hills and marshlands. A place that teems with birds, animals and water life. A place that Staten Islanders, indeed all New Yorkers will one day visit in large numbers. In short, Fresh Kills will likely evolve into the one of the most attractive areas in this region and a jewel in the City's crown of world-class parks.' It is moreover the final resting place for large numbers of the TV-shaped aluminium trays that jogged Jeffrey Shaffer's memory.

The landfill was near the beginning of its life, a mere infant of five years old, when Gerry Thomas thought up the Swanson TV dinner. Now in monstrous middle age, its last refuse delivery has passed through its portals, through gates that Mayor Giuliani has padlocked to herald a more serene episode in its old age. A few years back, the grand old monument was subjected to investigative surgery by Bill Rathje, an archaeologist from Tucson, Arizona. Rathje is a leading figure

31. Professor William Rathje, archaeologist of the present,
on the Fresh Kills landfill site, Staten Island, New York.

in the archaeology of the present, and has directed a number of landfill excavations. His scientific approach is essentially the same as that of his colleagues working on more distant epochs, drawing on stratigraphy, typology, sampling, and laboratory analysis. He has to be somewhat more stringent on the Health and Safety front, and some of his methods are fine tuned for his particular material. So, for example, when several of the sites featured in this book were excavated with trowel and brush, Rathje found a 1,300 lb bucket auger of high tensile steel more suited to his particular circumstances, especially when boring to depths of 30 metres or more.[1]

As his mining derrick directs the spinning augur deep into the arch-aeological layers, its vicious teeth ripping through anything from rotten food to car axles, so a treasury of artefacts from increasingly distant epochs is brought to the surface. Prominent among them emerges the standard fare of excavation: fragmented building materials, functional containers, craft materials, and items to decorate and adorn the body, food remains, and food containers. A few things mark this out as belonging to a recent epoch, a range of new, exotic substances unknown to the ancients, such as plastic and aluminium, and a greater diversity and quantity of toiletries and medical materials, than even the body-conscious diner of classical Rome might discard. But these are not the type fossil of these modern archaeological deposits. The type fossil, which is deposited in truly massive quantities, is text.

Shaffer's commendable environmental concern was directed to the wrong part of his sitting room. True, the aluminum trays are there in the tip, as are their many descendants and relatives in the fast-food industry. Many of us would assume that a sizeable proportion of such landfills as Fresh Kills might be attributable to this material. Yet we would be wrong. Rathje's data indicate that less then 1 per cent of the volume derives from such material. Turning away from the food tray to the dining table, the real culprit comes into view. Newspaper, mail, telephone books, and the many other sources of paper in modern society account for around 40 per cent of the various landfill profiles he has excavated. Within this bulk, a full third is entirely composed of newspaper.

From the invention of the printing press, the industrious production of text has transformed our lives in every way, not least in the central theme of this book, the way we eat. Text immerses us in personalities, events, bills of record, and accountancy, and in particular timescales of human agency. In this final chapter I draw considerably upon that wealth of text, or to be more precise, in the work of anthropologists and historians who have done so, but I shall aim to retain the viewpoint of an archaeologist, treating text as just one of many forms of archaeological fragment, albeit with unusual powers to reveal and deceive, alongside the material evidence, of food, food containers, tools, bodily adornment, architecture, and landscape that constitute the conventional archaeological fare. I shall also retain an approach adopted throughout this book of moving through very different scales of space and time to observe and reflect upon particular meals, their contexts and their consequences. Such an approach takes me in a different direction from certain food historians who have viewed the fast-food industry as a quite radical departure, or even disaster, in the wake of the demise of traditional formal eating. It is as if the most treasured ancient ritual of the gathering in a conversational circle to share food 'died' at some point during the later twentieth century, displaced by an antisocial, commercial jungle.[2] It leads me instead to a conclusion that meals as social campfires are still very much alive, and in fact a greater diversity of styles of campfire are on offer in the modern age than ever before, and that this has much to do with the proliferation of text. The major transformation that accompanied that abundance of text is that in several of those campfires, first the hearth and then the diners themselves have become increasingly virtual.

But let us return to the archaeology of the present, and to Bill Rathje's excavation of vast quantities of paper. One of his notable findings was that the paper in municipal dumps did not show much sign of breaking down. Indeed many newspapers could still be read, providing his team with an important dating technique. Way down into each mound, the technique continues to work with a precision normally undreamt of by archaeologists. A discoloured fragment announces 'Apollo orbits the Moon' (30 July 1971). Further still comes the message 'Customs men bar hippies to cut Mexican dope flow' (18 October 1967). Peeling back a page that announces the detonation of a hydrogen bomb on the Bikini Atoll (1 March 1954), an advertisement proclaims 'Now Dad's an expert at "frying up" a chicken dinner!' A proud father beams from above a deliciously frilly apron, carrying two steaming Swanson chicken dinners to his happy children. The paper fragments are still quite warm—they were piping hot when they first re-emerged. It is the heat that is generated, along with the airlessness, which accounts for the surprisingly good preservation of these items.[3]

The Swanson adverts from the 1950s do not depict couch potatoes glued to the silver screen, but instead snatched rendezvous at the kitchen table to refuel, punctuating hectic, exciting lives. 'How to make dinner...and the double feature too' explains one helpfully. At 98 cents they were not cheap; that was the price of seven loaves of bread. They would have appealed to an aspiring consumer, even if the reality was closer to Shaffer's galactic daydreams in front of the black and white screen.[4]

As father of teenage children, I am not a total stranger to those family discussions about where to eat dinner. Perhaps it is the archaeologist in me that is especially keen to retain that conversational circle around the rock-shelter campfire, with the meal between us and nice pictures on the wall behind. The alternative proposal to eat in a row, gazing ahead at the flickering, flame-like images, is perhaps too reminiscent of the Neanderthal world beneath the gently dripping roofline at Abric Romaní. But the more we probed into Shaffer's remembered moment, the more a different interpretation arose. All that talk of rings of Saturn and Star cruisers conveyed a real flavour of post-war modernity, and what about that television programme?

The programme he called to mind, which first appeared when the Swanson brand was just a couple of years old, was a show that only lasted for fifteen minutes. Its form, however, set an entirely new trend in broadcasts. Up until then, they had typically comprised compilations of newsreel fragments, and authoritative voice-overs. What Schaffer saw instead was something live, which the veteran reporter Walter Cronkite recalled 'came at us like an express train'. Unaided by fragments of badly shot film, two men were conversing live about world news across a distance of 350 km. The screen would switch back and forth between Chet Huntley in New York and David Brinkley in Washington, DC. With texts piled up behind him closely documenting global and cultural narratives, starship cruisers weaving their mysterious journeys through the night sky, Jeffrey Schaffer was indeed sitting around a conversational circle, but it was a circle which spanned the state. Huntley and Brinkley's 350 km conversation was encircled by a constellation of identical aluminium trays, with identical meals, all eagerly consumed as the stories spiralled in narrative wonder and horror.

Perhaps fifteen minutes is long enough to bolt down a meal, but let us suppose, especially with all that playing around with the chicken pot pie, that Jeffrey's dinner lasted a little longer than that. A quick web search calls up the highest rated programmes of October 1956, and at number one, the memorable sit-com, *I Love Lucy*.

There were several family sit-coms in the 1950s, generally serving as relatively unchallenging dramas of light entertainment. They offered a kind of stress-free mirror, reflecting the aspirations of the TV diners with the comfortable safety valve of light humour. The most popular of all was striking in several respects, most notably that it was fronted by a very funny woman. Neither onscreen nor off could Lucille Ball be described as simply an unchallenging source of mild laughs. Looking back, her work can more clearly be seen in the context of the post-war reconfiguration of the nuclear family and in particular a woman's place within it. She mounted a number of battles with television's establishment, not least over her real-life pregnancy in 1952. It seems the concept of a model television family did not sit comfortably with basic elements of the human reproductive cycle, a mismatch underlined by the habitual segregation of TV husbands and wives to separate beds. Not only did Ball visibly transgress this rule in real life, her co-perpetrator, her real life husband, Desi Arnaz, was also her husband on screen. It all seemed too close to the bone and the TV company wanted to take the show off the air. Ball fought to continue even as far as the 'Lucy Goes to the Hospital' show on 19 January 1953. As real life and drama converged on that most precious moment in the inseparable fusion of social person and biological organism, a gigantic conversational circle of spellbound participants, dinners on their lap, rose to 54 million people.[5]

Choosing between campfires

These diners had not really turned their back on the ritual sharing of food around the age-old conversational circle. They had instead left one campfire to join another. The wooden dining room table first designed for the nuclear family with its paterfamilias at the head had been requisitioned for the storage of text, while a virtual circle had opened up around a vast telecommunicative network. While it may have felt as if an age-old tradition was being cast aside, the traditional table at the back of the room was itself an alternative new 'campfire' invented just a century earlier. The designated dining room with its central table and chairs was absent from any ordinary family house until well into the nineteenth century. For centuries before that, first in Europe and then in the houses of colonial settlers, the main room and its furniture in ordinary dwellings served multiple purposes, and tables and chairs put to use or set to one side as needs dictated. The specific setting aside of a 'dining room', its central wooden table and arranged chairs forever waiting for the next family meal, was a product of the newly emancipated voting man, as suffrage and male democracy spread across the nineteenth century Western world. His predecessors had had the occasional opportunity to observe a grand feast where a bishop, duke, or king might sit at the head of the gathering. Now, with the power to choose his own leaders, he could sit at the head of his own table, even hold his own 'dinner parties'. For that he needed to recreate anew an assembly of space, material objects, and gestures in a renewed ritual of sharing food.[6]

At the centre was, in place of a hearth, a wooden table where table cloth and hot food would be placed in readiness for a meal. Along the table's edges, the equipment necessary for polite consumption would be arrayed. These comprised plates, bowls, glasses, napkins, knives, spoons, and forks. Adjacent to the table's edge, the chairs would be positioned, with father and mother's chair at opposite ends on the longer axis. Beyond all of this lay the ancillary spaces of food preparation. Around the eating enclosure, there would be figurative decoration on the walls, both in hung pictures and increasingly by the application of fashionable wallpaper. Beyond that basic structure, the material culture could endlessly proliferate, with vases, flowers, candlesticks, and sideboards, and the gestural behaviour of 'table manners' even more so. The gastronomic theatre of a Renaissance feast had needed to be large and loud enough to be visible to everyone in the banqueting hall, including spectators on the margin. In the very confined space of a domestic dinner party, that theatre would reduce in scale, acted out in the precise and rule-bound choreographies of knife, fork, spoon, napkin, and tasteful conversation. This whole ritual had been actively constructed, with the helpful guidance of a series of widely available guides to etiquette, during the course of the nineteenth century as an emphatic departure from campfires of the past. Just a century later, that novel campfire was being challenged by a virtual alternative, and along with that, the paterfamilias and nuclear family was also shifting from certainty to option.

The TV dinner itself was a component in the reconfiguration of the nuclear family, and the roles and expectations of its members. The dinner's ease and speed of preparation opened up new possibilities for how the woman of the house could schedule her time and interact with husband and children. While a real Lucille Ball buzzed hectically and humorously through a fictional family life, so a make-belief Sue Swanson (dreamed up by the advertising people) reassured real-life housewives that they need not feel guilty about not cooking home-made meals for their families. The modern meal would be speedily and conveniently prepared in a space-age kitchen, with extensive refrigeration, electric ovens, toasters, griddles, and coffee-makers. Only the very wealthiest of 'homemakers' (a term that was beginning to replace 'housewife') would have persuaded her husband to purchase a Radarange, which employed a microwave technology. Even though the price had fallen by over half in recent years, they still cost well over a thousand dollars, four months' salary on average in 1956. It would be another decade before microwave ovens become commonplace in the kitchen, seeming to complete our emancipation from the toils and commitment that had arisen from our multi-millennial relationship with food and fire.[7]

With half a century's hindsight, we can see this revolution as a more complex affair, which has liberated some, and ensnared others. The quest for freedom from some constraining core circle, to explore ever new and more exciting possibilities on the peripheral network seems to characterize our modern, commercial world. For men in particular, there is nothing new about that, all part of the recurring theme of core and periphery, community and network. For European women, the situation is more novel, but not confined to the last half-century. Several of the themes within the TV dinner arise from another set of meals, which go back beyond the domestic dining-room table. The competition between a real conversational circle and a virtual campfire, and many of the social transformations that accompanied it, can be found among the world of European merchants, entrepreneurs, and travellers, the emerging middle classes who would come to wrest power from the *ancien régime* in eighteenth-century Europe.

Tavern, restaurant, and coffee house

The constraining campfires from which new generations of traders and travellers wished to escape were found within a range of eating houses, inns, and taverns, which punctuated journeys into the network of inter-national trade. Until the eighteenth century, those travellers would expect to eat at such establishments seated alongside the locals, at the table of their host, the *table d'hôte*, at a specified hour. Meals were shared from a common pot, and if you were late to the table, or slow on the uptake, there might not be much left. These tables were part of ordinary working life, and in earlier times when travel had been relatively rare, were very much a normal community meal, at which diners were familiar with each other and their places in local society. As industry and commerce grew, the increasing number of travellers hankered after something different. One example was the recorder of regional farming practices, Arthur Young. He expressed irritation at how fast the food disappeared around a French *table d'hôte*; moreover, he did not think much of French peasant manners. The popular writer Louis Sébastien Mercier described the typical clientele as cormorants and vultures. This was class elitism rather than ethnic hostility. In an age of growing capitalism, many of the new travelling classes were not only complaining about the awful food available in inns and eating houses; they were getting more than a little snooty about sitting alongside local peasants. But in one city at least, relief was at hand.[8]

In Paris, there were establishments where one could sit alone, with one's own table. While television was far into the future, the visitor to a Parisian 'restaurant' could bury his head in text. Sometimes that would be newspapers, and sometimes another newspaper-like text, the *carte*, literally the 'map' of a surreal culinary universe that spoke of oysters from Cancale, ducks from Rouen, and cheese from Chester. The impli-cation was that such delights were accessible at any time, during the day or night, according to the individual client's choosing and command. Freedom from the daily routine was a prominent feature of the early Parisian restaurant. The ability to visit them at any time was secured by prolonged legal battle against closure hour regulations in the 1770s and 1780s. The theatre, the tavern, and the cook shop had to close in the evening, but the restaurant could stay open all night. Once free from the external constraints of an imposed schedule, the restaurant client's control over schedule was ensured by the presence of large, elaborate, and conspicuously placed clocks. The pioneer restaurant reviewer, Alexandre Grimod de la Reynière, not only offered advice on matters of taste in food, but also on suitable clocks for the dining room.[9]

Another feature that was prominent in the post-Revolution restaurant, rather as it would also feature two centuries later with the Swanson TV dinner, was a reduction in the importance of an alpha male at the meal. By default, the absent male in post-Revolution Paris was the king, a figure who had in earlier epochs offered the general public repeated opportunities to watch him dining, a practice of consumptive display undertaken not just by monarchs, but also by dukes, lords, bishops, and so on. Meals across the full social range had one senior man or other at the head, all the way down from the king's *grand couvert* to the *table'd'hôte* of a lowly rural inn. Turning from those grand palaces and traditional inns to the novel ambience of the restaurant, some were exceedingly rich in pomp and grandeur, but if we looked around for the principal seat with alpha male enthroned, we would look in vain. Instead we would see a multiplicity of diners, disappearing into a virtual assembly, an illusion created by two simple artefacts, the mirror and the candle. A major expense of an early Parisian restaurant was the massive mirrors surrounding the guests, with which the flickering flames at each table created an endless universe of virtual, egalitarian diners. Alongside the absence of an alpha male, the collective gathering was notable for the presence of a number of unattached women. Some travelling diners were left aghast at the brazenness of it all. Others (or possibly the same diners in different mood) viewed the female presence at restaurants with delight.[10]

A sweet smell of sedition

Not for the first time, a new frontier in food for the body had been preceded by an equivalent frontier in food for the mind. A full century before elite Parisians were restoring their bodies in the novel fashion of the *salle du restaurateur*, an emergent class was refreshing its soul with a new narcotic from the East.

32. An eighteenth-century scene at the Café Procope in Paris, depicting
Voltaire, Diderot, d'Alembert, La Harpe, and Condorcet gathered around
a table, sharing food, drink, and wise words.

The city coffee houses of seventeenth-century Europe adopted a
number of features of the future restaurant, in particular a retreat from
the peasant workers of the tavern to a virtual campfire of books,
pamphlets, and ultimately newspapers. The 'grave and wholesome
liquor' was supped by merchants, travellers, politicians, and intellectuals
reposing between bookshelves, mirrors, and gilt-framed pictures. The
coffee houses were nodes along international networks of text exchange.
Clients had their mail sent there, and gathered around the beverage to
debate the issues of the day. Business was conducted in coffee houses,
and newsletters circulated. Lectures were held, on topics ranging widely
between literature, medicine, and science. Exhibits were displayed and
experiments undertaken. On the premises of the Grecian coffee house in
London, Edmund Halley and Isaac Newton carried out the scientific
dissection of a dolphin. Such establishments as Miles's coffee house in
London and the Café Procope and Café de Foy in Paris were crucibles of
discussion, debate, democracy, and radical politics. It was in the Café de
Foy that Camille de Moulins called the citizens to arms on the eve of the
French Revolution.[11]

For all the stark contrasts between the café, the restaurant, and the TV dinner, they seem bound together by themes of text, science, and individual freedom. Future archaeologists, who from a greater distance in time will view the modern industrial age as a whole, will note the rise of glass and metal as appropriate containers for food. The great pioneer of airtight preservation in jars and cans was Nicolas Appert, whose career was launched by solving Napoleon Bonaparte's problem of how to keep his troops fed without fresh food. Those archaeologists of the future will be particularly struck by the proliferation of disposed vessels of pottery, metal, glass, paper, or plastic, for *individual* servings, and a greatly diminished loss/breakage rate of larger vessels. The archaeological record offers a reasonably good sequence of discarded footwear, which will no doubt chart the greater frequency of women 'going out', a trend also mirrored in the novel material culture of first the bicycle and subsequently motorized transport and mobile phones. Once future archaeologists see fit to delve deeply into the biological traces, they may find another, initially surprising feature connecting the post-Revolution restaurant with the TV dinner. Between the flashy mirrors of the former, and within the aluminium tray of the latter, for all the modernity of the context, the actual contained meals are deeply infused with nostalgia.

Let us first consider the TV dinner. The aluminium tray may have propelled Schaffer on a journey through Saturn's rings but its contents harked back to another age. The creator of Swanson dinners recalls its origins in the functionalist terms that sit well with the modernist ideology of the age. He begins his story with 520,000 pounds of surplus turkey, moving backwards and forwards from coast to coast in ten refrigerated railroad cars, awaiting an idea of what to do with them. At a certain point he came across a batch of metal trays destined to carry meals skyward (in aeroplanes rather than spacecraft), which triggered in his mind a possible solution—turkey plus tray equals product, but with one key refinement: 'Necessity was the mother of invention. I had just spent five years in World War II, eating off mess gear, and no matter what you got, it became stew because it all ran together.'[12]

Where was the problem? This was the Space Age, and real astronauts were eating out of what looked like toothpaste tubes. What an opportunity to fit out those shiny trays with an exciting collection of gleaming tubes and geometric pills, issuing the perfect, nutritionally balanced ration. Thomas wisely judged that the revolution had a better chance by hinting backwards to a more traditional recipe. Devising a way to subdivide the tray into three separate components, a design modification that must clearly have had significant cost implications, he drew inspiration from a recipe that was already three centuries old.

Modernity and nostalgia

our Governour sent foure men on fowling, that so we might after a more speciall manner reioyce together, after we had gathered the fruit of our labors; they foure in one day killed as much fowle, as with a little helpe beside, served the Company almost a weeke, at which time amongst other Recreations, we exercised our Armes, many of the Indians coming amongst vs, and among the rest their greatest King Massasoyt, with some nintie men, whom for three dayes we entertained and feasted.

(Edward Winslow, 11 December 1621)[13]

The precise composition of the first Thanksgiving meal is the topic of much discussion and scholarship, but a general outline will serve here. In essence, after an extremely tough journey from England, and then a long period moored just off the shore of the New World, four of the only five surviving women on the *Mayflower* brought their European culinary skills to bear on the first year's successful harvest in their newly adopted homelands. In combination with wild fowl, acquired as outlined above, and whatever remained in the stocks of the *Mayflower* itself, such as dried pulses and grain, they turned their harvest into this most celebrated of meals. While most Americans would choose to celebrate Thanksgiving with a more ample feast than the contents of the aluminium tray, that is essentially the structure of the first TV dinner—a New World crop (sweet potato), indigenous fowl (turkey), and pulses from the ship's store (peas), all prepared in the European culinary fashion (cooked separately and then served with stuffing and gravy). The turkey dinner, which both looked forward to a bright shining future and alluded back to America's founding fathers, remained the most popular of all the Swanson range. The Thanksgiving meal is a quintessentially American occasion, and is served up simultaneously across the United States, by decree of a string of Governors and Presidents. Even if we have a sketchy idea of the meal, its ingredients, and accompanying ritual, the meal and the nation are easily equated.

Geography, region, and nation were also central themes in the post-Revolution restaurant. In 1808, the Parisian diner could open up Grimod de la Reynière's newly published *Carte gastronomique de la France*, in which his country was mapped out according to its 'regional cuisine'. Elsewhere he had counselled on the style of clock which would allow sophisticated diners to keep control over time; his gastronomique map enabled a similar command over space. In subsequent years, the satirical magazine *La Charivari* would muse: 'Under the Republic and the Empire, our victories enlarge the maps (*cartes*) of France, but today they have no influence except on the menus (*cartes*) of restaurateurs.'[14]

Regional and national cuisines

The anthropologist Jack Goody has explored the long history of *basse cuisine* (the fare of peasants) and *haute cuisine* (the fare of the elite) in European society, stretching back into the hierarchical societies of pre-history. The two forms of cuisine have tended to describe two distinct patterns on the continental map of food. The *basse cuisine* presents a pattern that on this large scale is essentially ecological. Europe split into stripes, in which the montane and sharply seasonal Mediterranean, the wet but fertile lowlands of temperate latitudes, and the frosty, maritime north each displayed its own themes in the ecology of food acquisition. Over the last 1,500 years, that ecological pattern has been overlain by the prescriptions and prohibitions of organized religion. The *basse cuisine* in most communities was a familiar mix of cereal and garden products, such fish and meat as available and acceptable, and the same species recurred according to the two principal drivers of ecology and religion. *Basse cuisine* was a constant negotiation between these two forces. Superimposed upon this *basse cuisine* were the meals of an elite network.[15]

Haute cuisine overlays a pattern that is essentially social and political. The theatrical cuisine of Rome describes its imperial borders as much as its core, with a penumbra of wine consumption beyond those borders.

There is an apocryphal and largely discredited story that connects origins of regal *haute cuisine* to the arranged marriage in 1533 between Catherine di Medici and Henry Duc d'Orléans. Catherine is said to have brought her kitchen staff from Italy to France, and with them a cornucopia of notions about light sauces, custards, table manners, and truffles from which French *haute cuisine* was soon to spring. However apocryphal, the story captures a truth in the way a style of eating moved through marriage and contact in the elite monarchic network of pre-Revolution Europe, such that courts throughout the continent employed similar French cooks practising similar styles of cuisine. As is typical of the meals of the network/periphery, these meals were increasingly elaborated and their ingredients disguised, particularly through the now famous sauces, and increasingly framed within the most exotic, intricate, and showy display. It was from this world of monarchic domination and excess that the Pilgrim Fathers were keen to escape. A stream of marital liaisons between royal houses across Europe would form a complex network of conduits through which fashion, manners, and culinary practice could flow. By the time of the *Mayflower*'s voyage, the elites of Italy, France, Britain, and Spain all enjoyed an opulent cosmopolitan fare, the culinary manifestation of a world against which the migrating puritans reacted.

These various patterns can be discerned quite distinctly in the bio-archaeological record, but they leave no residual pattern that requires recourse to nationhood to explain. But from the time of the *Mayflower*, and more particularly the French Revolution, the shared meal became a significant instrument for crafting nationhood. From various reassemblies of *haute cuisine* and *basse cuisine*, the post-Revolution maps/menus of Paris and subsequently Europe somehow crafted 'regions' and 'nations', and left a legacy of regional and national cuisines that still informs our patterns of eating. The countless descendants of the TV dinner that fill supermarket shelves today are primarily classified according to national cuisine. French and Italian takeaways are now accompanied by Indian, Chinese, Thai, and so on.

Italian meals offer one example of the inventive potential of the exercise. Consider a recipe that starts from the ancient Chinese practice of working dough into long thin worm-like forms and immersing them in boiling water. Shift from the Old World to the New to gather a bright red fruit from the valleys of South America, and then bring them all together with beef raised in European valleys, and some Mediterranean herbs and vegetables, the result is the typical *Italian* meal of Spaghetti Bolognese. Alternatively, let us take a tour of south-east Asia, stopping off at the Spice Islands for cinnamon, cloves, and nutmeg, move on to the Asian mainland for sugar and ginger, stop off in the east Mediterranean to collect some dates, nuts, and figs, butter, and suet, then make the transatlantic journey to pick up some cornstarch, then we are clearly making preparations for a traditional *English* dessert to follow the yuletide consumption of an American bird. National cuisine tells a story, or interweaves a constellation of different stories, about mercantile enterprise, an empire over which the sun never sets, and many other things besides. That has been so since the first stories in the conversational circle around the hearth, but in the age of text, those stories become minutely accessible. The narratives are about who we are (native peasant meals), who we are not (in ethnic and religious terms), our power in the world (global ingredients), and our aspirations (*haute cuisine*). However modern and cosmopolitan we become, we choose to keep these stories in mind, so that even a space-age concept like the Swanson TV dinner harks back to the Renaissance and the bloody period of nation-building that followed.

New stories may be assembled at a whim, and the pioneers of Parisian menu-drafting were nothing if not whimsical. Given what we know of eighteenth-century English dining, *nouvelle cuisine à la mode anglaise* is particularly intriguing. Other stories may be direct and transparent. Dining out in Amsterdam will often take us to a *Rijstafel*, a meal that unabashedly parades an episode in the Dutch colonial past central to the European palate. In scattered locations from the Indian Ocean to the islands of south-east Asia, a range of tropical plants produced alkaloids much prized as flavours among the elite of the from Europe to China. Cargoes of cloves, nutmegs, mace, and cinnamon, and hundreds of tons of pepper left the region in a vibrant medieval trade involving many nationalities and many levels of trader. The capture of much of this trade by the Dutch East India Company, and a subsequent period of Dutch colonialism, has transferred those same spices to the modern restaurants of Amsterdam in the form of *Rijstafel*. As an alternative to the colonial periphery, we may choose instead to celebrate the peasant core, and dine on *hutspot*, a simple meal that for ever evokes the Dutch people's own resistance to domination by the empire of Spain, in 1574, when the city of Leiden managed to survive a lengthy siege, and relief is said to have come in the form of this simple meal. The *hutspot* is one of many European peasant hotpots, combining whatever vegetables and legumes were available with the stock of the most available bones, together with lower-quality meat. *L'estouffat de boeuf*, Italian Minestrone, and Lancashire hotpot have become established as regional recipes among many others, their ingredients fixed in text, classified on menu sheets, and quantified in cookbooks. Before eating became such a textual matter, the hotpots of Europe described a series of continua, interrupted in places by ecological barriers and religious prescription.[16]

The whole compendium of culinary storytelling within menus, cookbooks, reviews, and gastronomic almanacs wove a rich thread of nostalgia through the modernity of the new virtual campfire. That same interweaving of nostalgia and modernity characterizes the TV dinner and its various descendants. However, this has also been the age of choice between 'campfires'. The astronaut's scientifically constructed meals of pills and pastes is not entirely without precedent; in fact a whole tradition of modernist scientific food burgeoned alongside nostalgic national cuisine, with roots once again in the restaurant.

Efficient circulation and science

Another myth of food history accounts the emergence of the Parisian restaurant in terms of redeployment of *haute cuisine* chefs, no longer needed by their former employers once the Revolution had relieved them of their heads. The cultural historian Rebecca Spang has looked beneath that myth to the Parisian restaurateurs who were in business a quarter of a century before aristocrats formed a queue in front of the guillotine. A pioneer in these pre-Revolutionary establishments was an endlessly inventive champion of global economy and scientific ideas, Roze de Chantoiseau. His variously flawed projects included a proposed system of credit-based commerce and an almanac of traders, each aimed to enhance the circulation of goods within a modern global economy. Circulation was not only important for worldly goods, but also for the body. A fast evolving science of health stressed the interplay between circulation, respiration, and digestion, an interplay of which the refined and sensitive elite needed to take especial care. To serve these needs, Chantoiseau launched his most enduring project. His almanac of traders advertised a new Parisian facility, the *salon de restaurateur*. The sensitive and 'weak chested' could come to these salons to be 'restored'. For this, they needed to sit alone and in peace, gently sipping a scientifically prepared extract of meat described as a *'restaurant'*.[17]

If there had been astronauts during the eighteenth century or earlier, they would certainly have carried a good supply of these *restaurants*, or *bouillons* as we would describe them today, into space. An early *restaurant* is recorded as deriving from the glass kettle of a fifteenth-century alchemist, in which the concentrated essence of a fresh capon was prepared, enhanced by the addition of metallic gold and any gemstones that are to hand. The concept persisted as the purest scientific essence of meat, rarefied and separated from the courser solids we are accustomed to consume. To give some idea of how pure this essence was, a later recipe employed four to five pounds of veal, a quarter of ham, a fowl, mixed with beef marrow, onions, and parsnips to distil one quart of fluid.

The scientific nature of these fluids mirrored the mechanistic terms in which the refined and modern client of the *salle du restaurateur* viewed his world. Back on his estate, gardeners would be hard at work unblocking the nozzles of his elegant fountains to ensure the orderly circulation of water through complex, geometric gardens. Here in the *salle*, a chemical extract of meat was doing something similar for his own internal circulation.

At the end of the eighteenth century, Lazzaro Spallanzani extended that control over the invisible world of the organic by observing bacterial cell division through his microscope lens, and realizing that this division could be arrested by heat. That new knowledge, married with the industrial technologies of the early twentieth century, gave birth to the bottling and canning of food. Yet one more shift from the organic to the chemical marked yet another conquest over time and the natural process of decay. In the Parisian *salles des restaurateurs*, from their beginnings in the mid-eighteenth century, the ideas of scientific control over things organic were taking hold in relation to the body, the city, and the circulation of goods in the world. They were also taking hold in the arena of food production, and the farmer's engagement with the soil.[18]

A global village

Across the rural grasslands of the midlands of England, we can see two contrasting relics of past human engagements with the soil. The older relic is known as 'ridge and furrow', a corduroy effect of gentle undulating earthen ridges following the general topography of the land. The ridges are segmented into clusters, reflecting not individual ownership, but management of the landscape at the scale of the village community, collectively organizing cycles of harvest, grazing, and rest for the soil. The ridges are not straight, but are skewed in the shape of a reversed 'S', a signature of the toil of an ox team dragging and turning a heavy plough back and forth through the earth. The combined pattern is testimony to an ongoing organic negotiation between soil, landforms, oxen, and village communities.[19]

Superimposed over the ridge and furrow is a rectilinear systems of boundaries, ignoring the general topography and instead respecting the enclosure roads, many of them laid out during the eighteenth and nineteenth centuries to provide networks of communication through the new landscapes of soil as a commodity, rather than an organic force, owned and managed scientifically, rather than negotiated with. While the medieval system had concerned the resting and rejuvenation of the living soil, the modern system involved the appropriate management and circulation of mineral nutrients.

This new world of scientific control and efficient circulation had its great monuments, vast spaces, richly decorated and aisled with classical columns, but whereas aisled halls were erected in other times at the hearts of royal palaces and religious places, in the nineteenth century they were erected at nodes of the commercial world, at city markets, and at department stores. The age of technology gave birth to its own radically modern material culture of food and food containers. The alchemist's steam kettle had transformed one key component of the diet, meat, to a refined distillate; the Industrial Revolution would similarly transform that other key component, cereal grain.

For millennia, sweetened mixtures of cereal flour, moistened with water, had been fed to yeast colonies to create the billowing organic shapes of loaves and bread rolls, mirroring the pattern of growth of the yeast. After the Industrial Revolution, the same mixtures were now being fed, not to living yeast but to machines. From the early nineteenth century, sweetened dough was being fed into equipment with more than a passing resemblance to the printing press, and many of them did indeed print text into the dough. One early device developed in a factory alongside the London Road at the market town of Reading in England produced a sequence of rectangular tablets with the proprietor's name 'Huntley', filling their entire surface. Joseph Huntley later teamed up with George Palmer to mechanize the process yet further. Their steam-powered prints churned out inscribed biscuits that travelled across the world in brightly decorated tins. Just as the sinuous folds of ridge and furrow across the landscape had been superseded by the sharp rectangles of modern scientific agriculture, so, the bulbous loaves of leavened bread made way for the rectangular biscuit.[20]

Our imaginary nineteenth-century astronauts would surely have packed some of these inscribed tablets of dough along with bouillon cubes from a Parisian restaurateur. Space travel there was not, but travel over land and sea was expanding massively, and Huntley and Palmer's biscuits were following their journeyers. Kept dry and enclosed within tin boxes, science had separated these morsels of dough from the organic perils of breakdown and decay. The whole landscape of biscuit production and consumption mapped out the world of which Roze de Chantoiseau had dreamed, of efficient economic circulation across land and sea. Biscuit factories were strategically placed at nodes on the axes of commerce, along trading routes and ports.

Over the course of the next 100 years, this distinctly modernist strand of food production diversified further, with such notable products as margarine, ketchup, and the chocolate bar. They continued the stylistic tradition of the bouillon and biscuit in taking the form either of a uniform featureless fluid of paste, or a geometric tablet inscribed with text. For all the romantic potential for nostalgia they offered, South Sea whalers harvesting the source of margarine, Inca and Aztec gathering cocoa beans and tomatoes, that was not how these modern products were marketed. In the absence of nostalgia, there were no regional or

33. The first McDonald's Hamburger bar, opened in 1948 at San
Bernadino in California.

national allusions in this cuisine. Instead of nation states, it was captains
of industry that were celebrated, the proprietor's name branded across
either the product, or its factory-produced container. While margarine
was a true scientific invention, chocolate and ketchup each has a long
culinary heritage, but a heritage consciously ruptured in the reinvention
of the modern product. The same is true of the most emblematically
modern food of all.[21]

Mechanically tenderizing meat is an ancient concept, as is eating it
with bread. Only a slight shift was required to streamline its production
into unified and standardized tablet form. It was possibly not so much
the 'invention' of the hamburger in 1921 that marked out its modernity,
but a revolution in the culture of its production and consumption a
quarter of a century later.

In December 1948, a new establishment for dispensing food opened in
the Californian town of San Bernadino. In architectural terms, it was a
'drive-in' classic; a functional hexagonal building with counters opening
to an ample car park, bordered by large panels of hoarding covered in
gigantic text, proclaiming its business to drivers on the adjacent highway.

Those drivers could pull off the highway, park their Buick Roadmaster or Cadillac Fastback, and for 25 cents order a hamburger and fries. A logical extension of the landscape archaeology of biscuit production and consumption, it might seem the ultimate departure from the hearth and the conversational circle. While customers could perch at a counter bar, they could also return to their vehicle and switch on the radio. The first McDonald's hamburger bar had dispensed with tables, and unlike earlier hamburgers, theirs were distributed with neither plates, nor those key instruments of refined table manners, knives and forks.[22]

A solitary driver, listening to the car radio while eating with his hands may seem an odd point to conclude an exploration into the origins of sharing food. We might ask whether or not this thoroughly modern form of feeding, which by the end of the second millennium was netting over \$40 billion and an average of five customer visits for each person alive on the planet, was more akin to the itinerant munching of Passion the chimp in the Gombe forest. The exploration of meals in the course of this book does not lead me to that conclusion. Instead, the hamburger and fries and the Swanton TV dinner alike seem to continue some very ancient theme. To see how, let us return to the questions posed at the book's outset.

The first question asked what the drama of the human meal was all about. We can conclude that it was about two things. First, while many species adapted to the changeable Quaternary environment through their rapid response and fast turnover, early humans adapted by extending the scale of their feeding in space and time. Social cooperation in feeding steadily increased among early humans, in turn placing considerable demands on the brain. The unique abilities of the modern human brain brought us to a most unusual behavioural pattern, the gathering around a hearth in a conversational circle to share food. From this point onwards, the second element of the drama unfolded, and continues to unfold today. This is the endless interplay between community and network.

When and how did this happen? Pro-social feeding has its roots in the much deeper origins of birds and mammals, but has gathered considerable pace during the evolution of early humans. The most durable markers of this evolutionary pathway are the explosion in the size of hunted prey, and the enlargement of the brain cavity. The diminution of the teeth and the emergence of cooking are signs that the digestive system had to pay the price. By the time modern humans appeared in Europe, all the key elements of the modern human meal were in place.

The brain of those first modern humans was much like our own. From the time that the earliest adorned bodies gathered around the hearth, sharing food and drink and deep in conversation, the most significant developments in biological evolution had already happened. Various aspects of the ensuing interplay between community gathered around the hearth, the network reaching out into the far distance, have been explored in the context of Lévi-Strauss's *endocuisine* and *exocuisine*, and Goody's *basse cuisine* and *haute cuisine*. In the series of archaeologic-ally attested meals we can follow the network as it initially carried foraging parties across the landscape, to return with a rich and diverse wild harvest. It later carried precious objects, obsidian blades, and exotic shells. Subsequently, settlers and a mobile food web travelled along those networks establishing new communities and new nodes. The tempos of a compartmented culture become more multiple and deep, while the tempos of a compartmented nature became more uniform and shallow. With time, the network comes to define the community, which itself is now diffusing along the network, and becoming increasingly virtual.

Does this trend towards increasing mobilization have its radical thresh-olds, its revolutions, or points of inflection? The Neolithic revolution was clearly a highly consequential change along that trajectory, but just one of a series of profound changes, of conceptual and ecological transformations in the food quest and the meal. Among modern humans, one of the earliest of these transformations came with the new technologies of weaving and baskestry, technologies that not only revolutionized the gathering of food from the seas and the skies, but also enabled the gathering of small seeds. Some of those seeds now dominate our food web. Moreover, it completely transformed the gender relations of the food quest.

The mobilization of precious materials, and then of the farming food chains need not have upset intrinsic hierarchies and temporalities within the human ecosystem. The multi-track webs within which early farmers operated probably had similar dynamic relations within the ecosystem as the foraging webs that preceded them. When the relative scales, tempos, and hierarchies of human society did begin to equal, then supersede those in the natural world, the change was profound, and is visible in both the human record, in the architectural elaboration of the homes of the living, the ancestors, and the gods, and in the environment in the structured landscapes, the partition of the wild, and many signs of environmental 'stress'.

The reshuffling of scales and temporalities that has taken place at various stages over the last 5,000 years has confused and challenged the nested hierarchy of histories once proposed by the historian Fernand Braudel. No longer is it entirely clear that social engagements are the realm of a rapid, local *histoire d'événement*, or that environmental influences are primarily features of the *longue durée*. Environmental factors can be short term, especially if compartmented into the annual cycle of fixed individual fields, while social factors can reach across undreamt distances of space and time, beyond the elders and elite, to spirits, ancestors, and gods.[23]

Ecology and society become interwoven as shapers of the food quest, bringing us to the third question posed at the outset. What has been the impact of the social drama of the meal on the food quest itself? A large part of our food quest relates to a prevalent great ape pattern, of a considerable diversity of leaves, stems, and fruits complemented by a smaller range of mammals, extended across the planet as a consequence of our species evolutionary success. Ranked according to annual production, the biggest food species are, however, not those that are central to other great ape diets; they instead reflect features that are specifically human. As it so happens, the 25 cent hamburger and fries lead us to each of these.

The fries are made from the world's most popular underground tuber, but the potato is just one of several tubers that have been central to human diet, particularly in tropical latitudes. There are other species of ape which dig down to unpack tubers from the soil; timely dextrous unpacking is a facility we share with many other primates. The potential of tubers, however, was considerably enhanced by the cooking, raising them to a higher importance within the food web. The meat from the hamburger derives from the world's most popular 'big beast'. The culling and consumption of big beasts now, as ever, depended upon extensive social cooperation, and the massive human brain. The third component of the hamburger and fries, the bun, derives from the highest-producing food species of all, a grass seed called bread wheat. Indeed, grass seeds, wheat, rice, and maize in particular, occupy many of the upper rungs of the productivity ladder. Some primates do eat grass seeds but, more than anything else, their copious consumption depends heavily on the cognitive abilities of the modern human brain. While stone tools were used to gather their heads and pound them, the seed-harvester's equipment is greatly enhanced by basketry, weaving, sacking, and other technologies of the interconnected modern mentality. The route from fresh grass seeds to porridge, bread, boiled grain, or beer involves several steps and forward planning, features again associated with the modern human brain. Some, most famously Dr Robert Atkins, have argued that our guts have failed to keep evolutionary pace with the creative inventiveness of our brains, and carbohydrates, particularly from these most recent additions to our ancestral diet, are doing our bodies little good. While the return to palaeolithic nutrition advocated in the 'Atkins Diet' has apparently made a dent in sales of bread, there is little sign that the hamburger and fries will disappear from the modern scene.[24]

If ingredients of the solitary driver's hamburger and fries emblemize those key distinctive features of the human food quest, what about the final question: how has the food quest found itself at the heart of social life? In addressing this, we can reflect on how a series of archaeologically attested meals resonates with the arguments put forward by such anthropologists as Mary Douglas, Claude Lévi-Strauss, and Jack Goody. A recurrent theme of their arguments is a distinction between community and network, close kin and stranger, inside and outside. The community is the place of order and of fixed secure categories around the hearth. The network is the realm of transition and danger, of competition, exchange, and expansion of influence. In the archaeological record, we can place these patterns within a chronological framework. We can see, for example, that the hearth-centred community comes into being in the context of modern humans, whereas various of its separate elements are in a process of evolution among early humans. Just as one recurrent theme among modern humans is a complex interplay between social and ecological scales, we can also see a complex interplay between community and network. At Ohalo, it seemed that the meal was embedded in social relations, whereas at the later site of Roman Colchester, it could be argued that social relations and identity were embedded in the sharing and food and drink. At Moreaucourt Priory, network and community are indistinguishable; they are one and the same.

302

That brings me back to the solitary driver, who I very much doubt was eating his hamburger without either a newspaper in front of him or the car radio on. Rather than being solitary, he had connected with a network that spanned the State, the continent, and possibly the world. Today, hundreds of thousands of burger outlets across the world mirror each other in their common layout and precise branding, revealing that their clients are not liberated from a protocol of performance and gesture, involving queueing, financial transaction, rubbish disposal, and so on. It is simply that the protocol is global, and can now be transferred from California to Shanghai.

Community and network have merged. They now span the globe and draw diners around a vast campfire, which happens to be virtual rather than material. The most abundant component of global dining is a grass seed chosen not for its adaptability to the planet's varied ecosystems, but its association with a Christian god.

This is all a long way from the harsh material worlds of the ancestral humans with whom this book opened, struggling for sustenance and survival within the chilly wind-storms of Moravia, but perhaps not so far as it at first seems. They too had a virtual world, captured in the stories told around the hearth, stories of journeys to gather the mottled grey and blood-red stones from which their blades were fashioned, and journeys to ambush a migrating herd, or to gather roots for food and fibre for weaving. Some participants routinely travelled 100 kilometres or more on these journeys, to places unseen by several of their fellow diners around the hearth. Over thousands of kilometres stretching from Europe and Asia, comparable stories were being told around comparable hearths, around which diners sat, their bodies similarly adorned, and carrying the same style of stone blades in their hands. Those stories were sometimes told with the aid of small hand-held models, of faces, people, mammoths, deer, and wolves, all the principal players in the food quest, brought to life by the movement of the flames from the hearth. By the time the unique ritual of the human meal was recurrently depicted in images, to be viewed by an impressed audience, a long episode of evolutionary history was behind it, and the constantly changing interplay between the social person and biological organism, at the sharing of food and drink, had begun.

Notes

Chapter 1: A return to the hearth

1. Lévi-Strauss 1964.
2. The clearest examples of communities of the 'Gravettian' culture using mammoth bone as a constructional material come from sites further to the east, in Russia and the Ukraine, and the Moravian sites have been depicted as constructed of skin and branches. However, there are three known Moravian sites in which mammoth bone construction is envisaged as a possibility (Klima 1954; Oliva 1988; Svoboda 2001; Svoboda and Sedláčková 2004).
3. Eibes-Eibesfeldt 1970.
4. Schmandt-Besserat 2001.
5. Svoboda 1991; Svoboda et al. 2000; Svoboda and Sedláčková 2004.
6. The central figures have been Karel Absolon, Bohuslav Klima, and Jiří Svoboda.
7. The current project, co-directed by Jiří Svoboda and myself, explores some of the issues raised in Van Andel and Davies 2003.
8. In relation to early research in Mozambique, see Harris 1958; 1959; for developed accounts of his 'cultural materialism', see Harris 1974; 1977; 1979; and for texts focusing specifically on the food quest: Harris 1985; Harris and Ross 1987.
9. Goody 1982; 1988.
10. Douglas's biographer, Richard Farndon (1999), explores the way in which two of her most influential works (Douglas 1966, 1970) and her intellectual trajectory in general, were shaped by her convent years and lifelong Catholicism.
11. Lévi-Strauss 1955.
12. Lévi-Strauss 1962; 1964; 1968; Douglas 1966; 1970; 1972; 1984. This social anthropological tradition is most conspicuous in studies of the Neolithic by, for example, Hodder 1990; Tilley 1994; and Thomas 1999. Hodder's articulation of *domus* and *agrios* in particular mirrors the explorations of Lévi-Strauss and Douglas into manifestations of inside and outside, core and boundary.

13. Lévi-Strauss 1955; Goody 1962; Douglas 1963.
14. Soffer *et al.* 1993; 2000.
15. Douglas 1972; 1984.
16. Harris (1987), 'Foodways: Historical Overview and Theoretical Progomenon' in Harris and Ross 1987.
17. Godwin 1793; Malthus 1798.
18. Mason *et al.* 1994.
19. Jones 2001.
20. Evershed *et al.* 1999; Evershed and Dudd 2000; Tzedakis *et al.* 2006.
21. For the potential of faecal DNA see Poinar *et al.* 1998; for bog bodies, Brothwell 1987; Turner and Scaife 1995.
22. O'Connell and Hedges 1999; 2001.
23. French 2002.
24. Braudel 1958.
25. Goody 1982: chapter 3.

Chapter 2: Are we so different? How apes eat

1. Goodall 1986: 231.
2. Goodall 1971.
3. There are a number of publications on chimpanzee diet in the wild, for example: Nishida *et al.* 1983; Richard 1985; Milton 1993; Malenky *et al.* 1994; Conklin-Brittain *et al.* 1998; Wrangham *et al.* 1998. For this chapter I drew direct from Richard Wrangham's seminal Ph.D. thesis (Wrangham 1975).
4. Goodall 1986: 219–20.
5. Goodall 1986: 283–5 and 351–6.
6. Teleki 1973.
7. *Sunday Times* (London), September 1972, cited in Goodall 1986: 79.
8. Nishida *et al.* 1983; also Malenky *et al.* 1994.
9. Rosenblatt 2003; Eibes-Eibesfeldt 1970: chapter 7, 'Antidotes to aggression'.
10. Eibes-Eibesfeldt 1970: chapter 8, 'What keeps people together?'
11. Hohmann and Fruth 1996; Fruth and Hohmann 2002 for specific studies; Kano 1992; De Waal 1997 for a broader account of bonobo life.
12. For consideration of the evolution of ape and human sociality generally, see Foley 1989; Foley and Lee 1989; 1996; Maryanski 1996; and specifically for its relationship with brain size, see Milton 1988; Foley and Lee 1991; Dunbar 1993.
13. Foley 1989; Foley and Lee 1989; 1996; Maryanski 1996.
14. Wrangham *et al.* 1994.

Chapter 3: In search of big game

1. Roberts and Parfitt 1999: 372–8; Robert *et al.* (forthcoming).
2. For an analysis of the flint fragmentation patterns, in relation to specific activities, see Pope 2004; 2005. See also Bergman 1986; Bergman *et al.* 1990; and Rees 2000.
3. For Simon Parfitt's detailed work on the butchery, see Roberts and Parfitt 1999: chapter 6.5, pp. 395–405.
4. For the Schöningen spears, see Thieme 1997; and for the Boxgrove scapula wound, see Roberts and Parfitt 1999: 378 and fig. 279.
5. Roberts and Parfitt 1999: chapters 2, 3 and 5.
6. Morgan 1877; 1959. A valuable account of Morgan's western trips was compiled by Leslie White 1951.
7. Roberts *et al.* 1994; Stringer *et al.* 1998; Trinkaus *et al.* 1999; Streeter *et al.* 2001.
8. The seminal article for Neanderthal DNA was Krings *et al.* 1997; a general overview of the research is found in Jones 2001: chapter 3; and a recent review of research progress in Pääbo *et al.* 2004.
9. Mithen 1996; Mellars and Gibson 1996 for Palaeolithic mentalities; and Gamble 1999 for Palaeolithic sociality.
10. Hawkes 2003; 2004*a* and *b*; Foley and Lee 1989; McHenry 1996.
11. Blytt 1876; Sernander 1908.
12. Clements 1916.
13. For accessible overviews of methodologies and results see Birks and Birks 1980; Bell and Walker 1992.
14. There are many features of the stratigraphy that track the thermal trajectory, and thus the isotope sequence. A series of radiometric methods indicate an episode somewhere between isotope stages 6 and 11. The animal bones indicate a range of species whose best match would be with stage 13. However, the microbiological and biomolecular markers point to stage 11. On balance, stage 11 seemed the most probable (Roberts and Parfitt 1999: 303–11).
15. Roberts and Parfitt 1999: chapter 5.9, pp. 303–7.
16. For the evidence that insect and pollen records might be out of sync, see Coope and Brophy 1972; Coope 1977; for a general discussion of disequilibrium ecology, see Berryman and Millstein 1989.
17. The idea of Arctic Steppe or Mammoth Steppe goes back to the 1970s (Matthews 1976; Cwynar and Ritchie 1980; Ritchie and Cwynar 1982; Guthrie 1982). For a recent example of a fine detail analysis of the composition of this vanished plant community see Zazula *et al.* 2003.
18. The novel interpretation of pollen spectra, going beyond using present vegetation as a direct analogue, to exploring vegetation groupings that

may have disappeared, is marked in such publications as Overpeck *et al.* 1985; Webb 1986; Huntley 1990.

19. Hays *et al.* 1976; Imbrie and Imbrie 1979; COHMAP 1988.

Chapter 4: *Fire, cooking, and growing a brain*

1. Accounts of current and previous excavations at Abric Romaní can be found at Carbonell and Vaquero 1996; 1998; Vaquero and Carbonell 2000; Vaquero *et al.* 2001; Vallverdu *et al.* 2005.

2. For the 'pseudomorphs' (voids from decayed wooden items) see Carbonell and Castro-Curel 1992; Castro-Curel and Carbonell 1995; for small animal consumption see Walker *et al.* 1999; Stiner *et al.* 2000; for legume pods, Lev *et al.* 2005; and grass seed heads Madella *et al.* 2002.

3. There have been several papers on the early archaeological evidence for fire, of which Barbetti 1986, James 1989, Straus 1989, Bellomo 1993, and Clark and Harris 1985, are valuable contributions, broadly supporting the point that evidence for actual *lighting* of fires is not confidently attested beyond modern humans and Neanderthals. Arguing from human physiology and digestive potential, Wrangham *et al.* (1999) argue for the greater antiquity of cooking; however cooking, or external digestion more generally, could proceed through harvested fire (from volcanos, lightning strikes) or 'cool' methods such as fermentation and rotting.

4. Rigault, Simek, and Ge 1995; Pastó *et al.* 2000.

5. Lévi-Strauss 1968.

6. Nurston 2005.

7. For a discussion of the evolutionary issues around weaning, see Kennedy 2005.

8. The Shanidar skeletal evidence was recovered by Solecki 1971; and the old man at Chapelle-aux-Saints by Bouyssonie *et al.* 1908.

9. Aiello and Wheeler 1995.

10. For social implications of changes in brain size in our evolutionary history, see Dunbar 1993; Aiello and Dunbar 1993.

11. Personal observation by Ephraim Lev.

12. Dunbar 1993; 1996.

13. Kennedy 2005.

14. Mostofsky *et al.* 2001.

15. Information on the Doura Cave Boraginaceae from Hillman 2004; and on horse EFAs Levine 1998; Crawford *et al.* 1970.

16. Pettitt 1997.

17. James 1989.

18. Walker *et al.* 1999; Stiner *et al.* 2000; for the context of Neanderthal subsistence behaviours across Europe, see Pathou-Mathis 2000; and other papers in Stringer *et al.* 2000.
19. Barton 2000.
20. Dederiyeh Cave: Akazawa *et al.* 1999; Kebara cave: Lev *et al.* 2005; Amud Cave: Madella *et al.* 2002; Goreham's and Vanguard Caves: Gale and Carruthers 2000.
21. Burjachs and Julià 1994.
22. Mithen 1996; Mellars 1995; Mellars and Gibson 1996.
23. Cardini 1942; Bernabo Brea 1946.
24. Cardini 1942; Bernabo Brea 1946; Svoboda and Sedláčková 2004.

Chapter 5: Naming and eating

1. Heer 1866.
2. Nadel excavations: Nadel 1990; 1991; 2002. Some publications use the uncalibrated radiocarbon estimate of 19.5 thousand years ago, others the calibrated age of 23 thousand years. My text uses calibrates ages throughout.
3. Ohalo human remains: Hershkovitz *et al.* 1993; 1995; Nadel 1994a.
4. Alley 2000; Rahmsdorf 2003.
5. Brushwood huts: Nadel and Werker 1999; Liphschitz and Nadel 1997; Nadel *et al.* 2004.
6. Overview of site Nadel 2002; for plant foods: Weiss *et al.* 2004, 2005; Kislev *et al.* 1992; Piperno *et al.* 2004; for animals: Rabinovich and Nadel 2005; for birds: Simmons and Nadel 1998.
7. For the twisted fibres see Nadel 1994b; Nadel *et al.* 1994; for the net sinkers, see Nadel and Zaidner 2002.
8. Soffer *et al.* 2000.
9. Douglas 1966.
10. This passage draws upon both Claude Lévi-Strauss and Mary Douglas in exploring the use of space at Ohalo II. The *endocuisine* (core) and *exocuisine* (periphery) opposition, comes from Lévi-Strauss 1968, whereas the categorization/order/safety (core) and transitional/uncertain/dangerous (periphery) opposition follows Douglas 1966.
11. Nadel 1996, 2002.
12. Krupp 1992.
13. Rappaport 1968.
14. Rappaport 1979.
15. Nadel 2002.
16. Douglas 1966; 1970.

17. Drouin 1999.
18. For an overview of recent research in the field, see Ambrose and Katzenberg 2000.
19. The initial study is reported in Richards *et al.* 2001, and the continental data-set is currently being greatly extended through Richards's research at Leibnitz. The broad spectrum revolution was a concept originally coined by Flannery (1969), and it retains a great deal of utility in terms of exploring diversification of human diet. However, the timing of this diversification has been pushed back in time, from a period just antecedent to agriculture, by sites such as Ohalo to a much earlier date, and it may possibly be deep-rooted in the ecology of anatomically modern humans. See Stiner 2001 for a retrospective review of the broad spectrum revolution in scholarship and research.
20. Pimm 1982; Cohen and Briand 1984; Briand and Cohen 1987; Lawton and Warren 1988; Pimm *et al.* 1990; Cohen *et al.* 1990*a* and *b*.
21. Gardner and Ashby (1970) demonstrated that, as network size grows, there is an increasingly steep decline in the probability of stability when intercon-nections rise beyond around 15–20 per cent. Two years later, Robert May confirmed and elaborated this idea of a critical level of connectance, in a paper that was to form one of the seminal inspirations of chaos theory (May 1972).
22. The argument of Robert May (1972) drew from a widely accepted math-ematical model for a feeding relationship through time of predator and prey, a relationship which was assumed to be self-stabilizing, but which, as May showed mathematically, could move into disequilibrium patterns by minor adjustments of the equation parameters.
23. Schaffer 1984.
24. The citations in notes 18, 19, and 20 (above) mark a change in our under-standing of how ecosystem connections relate to stability. Intuitively, it had been previously assumed that interconnections confer stability, rather in the manner of cross-bracing a building. However, mathematical ecology has demonstrated the reverse to be the case; loosely connected food webs are more stable than over-connected webs (De Angelis 1975).
25. Scale and compartmentalization in ecosystems is explored, in particular in relation to bird ecology in Allen and Starr 1982: chapter 8.
26. I am using 'seed' in the lay sense here; in strict botanical terminology, they are not 'seeds' but grass 'caryopses'.
27. William Banting 1863 was an early advocate of low carbohydrate diets. For the most prominent recent advocate see Atkins 1972; and for a discussion of potential health problems of grain-rich diets, see Eaton *et al.* 1988; and

Cordain *et al.* 2005. For evidence of deterioration from the Palaeolithic onwards, see Cohen and Armelagos 1984.
28. Harvey *et al.* 1998; Hollox *et al.* 2001.

Chapter 6: Among strangers

1. Stordeur *et al.* 1997; Stordeur 1999.
2. Willcox 2002.
3. Cauvin 1977; 1997; Stordeur 1999.
4. Cauvin 1977; 1997.
5. Goody 1982.
6. Moore *et al.* 2000.
7. Molleson 1994; and in Moore *et al.* 2000.
8. Peterson 2002 for a general survey; and Schmitt *et al.* 2003, for a deep time consideration of physiological evidence for spear-throwing.
9. Recent publications on isotopic tracing of humans include Dupras and Schwarcz 2001; Price *et al.* 2001; Bentley *et al.* 2002; Schwarcz 2002.
10. Sherratt 2006.
11. Cauvin *et al.* 1998.
12. Cauvin 1977.
13. Mauss 1925.
14. Flannery 1972; Cauvin 1997.
15. Hillman 1996.
16. Younger Dryas: Iverson 1954 for the origin of the concept; Harris 2003 for a global survey of its relationship to agricultural origins, and a résumé (p. 383) of recognition in the Quaternary record for its occurrence. See also Alley 2000 for ice core evidence; and Moore and Hillman 1992 for its relationship with human activity at Abu Hureyra.
17. Willcox 1996; Moore *et al.* 2000; Van Zeist and Bakker-Heeres 1982.
18. See Bar-Yosef 1998 for a review of the archaeological context.
19. Cauvin *et al.* 1998.
20. Cauvin 1997.
21. Cauvin *et al.* 1998 for a discussion of the export of 'redundant' males and agricultural spread; van Andel and Runnels 1995 for the 'leapfrog' effect of the spread, jumping past unsuitable soils.
22. For the original difference of view on migration, compare Cavalli-Sforza *et al.* 1994 (based on expressed genes) with Richards *et al.* 1996 (based on maternally inherited mitochondrial DNA). For studies considering relative mobility of males (through the Y chromosome) and females (through mitochondrial DNA) see Seielstad *et al.* 1998; and Kayser *et al.* 2001.

23. Childe 1929; 1936.
24. A seminal paper on this topic is Hayden (1990). He argues that many of the very first species displaying signs of domestication (e.g. dogs, gourds, chilli peppers, avocados) are not core staples but instead species that could be understood in the context of prestige and display. His most detailed examples come from the New World. His chronology for the Old World will need to be adjusted in the light of results from such sites as Ohalo II (cf. Chapter 5), but the overall thesis is nevertheless of global interest.

Chapter 7: Seasons of the feast

1. Mercer 1980; Mercer and Healey (forthcoming). The primary focus of the narrative was an assembly of bones from the upper fill of segment 1 comprising most of the elements of the skeletons of two cattle, together with the bones of a few calves, pigs and sheep or goat. Two articulated cattle vertebrae were carbon dated to 2920–2700 cal BC (4255 ± 50 BP: OxA-8893). The archaeozoologist Tony Legge infers from the context of the deposit and the state of the bones that they derive from a single event of consumption.
2. Bell *et al.*, 'Mollusc and sedimentary evidence for the palaeoenvironmental history of Hambledon Hill and its surroundings' in Mercer and Healey (forthcoming): chapter 5.
3. Tony Legge, 'The Animal Remains' in Mercer and Healey (forthcoming): chapter 5.
4. Tilley 1994.
5. McKinley, 'The Human Remains' in Mercer and Healey (forthcoming): chapter 5.
6. Thomas and Ray 2003; Thomas 2001.
7. Jones and Legge 1987; and 'Evaluating the Role of Cereal Cultivation in the Neolithic: Charred Plant Remains from Hambledon Hill, Dorset' in Mercer and Healey (forthcoming): chapter 5.
8. Yasuda 2002.
9. Mercer and Healey (forthcoming): chapter 6.
10. See pp. 117–119.
11. Copley *et al.* 2003; and in Mercer and Healey (forthcoming): chapter 5.
12. Richards *et al.* 2003.
13. Korn *et al.* 2001 (p. 9 for the Umeda); for the Kuru, see Lindenbaum 1979.
14. See Richards *et al.* 2003 for the hypothesis on dietary change, and papers by Milner *et al.* (2004), Lidén *et al.* (2004), and Hedges (2004) in *Antiquity* 78 (2004) debating whether the isotopic and archaeozoological data are in conflict. It remains an area of much debate, which may well be resolved

by the substantial enlargement of the isotopic database currently being undertaken by Richards.

15. Schulting and Wysocki 2002; Mercer 1999.
16. Schulting 1996.
17. Papers by Michael Dietler in Wiessner and Schiefenhövel 1997; and Dietler and Hayden 2001. Also Dietler 1990.
18. The 'ard' is the term for an animal-drawn cultivation implement, that tears through the topsoil, but without turning it upside down. It is sometimes referred to as a 'scratch plow', but the term plow is normally reserved for a heavier implement with a mouldboard for turning over the furrow. The latter implement came into use during the first millennium AD, and cultivation in prehistory was conducted by some version of either a digging stick, hoe or ard.
19. Bell and Walker 1992.
20. Bell *et al.* in Mercer and Healey (forthcoming): chapter 5.
21. Jones and Legge 1987.
22. Smith, 'Stone Axes', in Mercer and Healey (forthcoming): chapter 5.
23. Richards, 'Hambledon Hill Stable Isotope Values' in Mercer and Healey (forthcoming): chapter 5.
24. Ibid.
25. Ashbee *et al.* 1979.
26. Cunliffe 2006.

Chapter 8: Hierarchy and the food chain

1. Butler 1900.
2. Blegen and Rawson 1966–73.
3. Evans 1921.
4. Chadwick 1958; 1976; 1977; Killen 1985.
5. Blegen and Rawson 1966–73.
6. Bendall 2004; kylikes illustrated and discussed in Blegen and Rawson 1966, vol. i, pp. 350–418 and plates 324 ff.
7. Isaakidou *et al.* 2002.
8. McGovern *et al.* 1999.
9. Tzedakis and Martlew 1999.
10. Tsedakis *et al.* 2006.
11. Bendall 2004; Wright 2004.
12. Killen 1985.
13. Unearthed during Sir Leonard Woolley's excavations at Ur, see Woolley and Moorey 1982; 98–102.

14. Genesis 41.

15. There are various elements to this argument. The data on small garden plots in an earlier episode comes primarily from preserved weed assemblages, which a number of authors have associated with 'hoe-plot' communities during the Neolithic; see e.g. Jones 1992. Archaeological evidence for field systems comes largely from the third and second millennia BC in northern Europe; see e.g. Bowen and Fowler 1978, but occasional fragments of Bronze Age terracing are now showing up in the Mediterranean, and this is also a period when reference to enclosed, monocropping, prairie-like landscapes are alluded to further east in the Sumerian texts, cf. Halstead 1990.

16. Bell and Walker 1992 for a general survey of environmental trends in later prehistory.

17. Halstead 1990; 1992; 1999; 2003.

18. Behre 1990.

19. Jones 1981; Jones *et al.* 1986.

20. The idea of a Janus-faced holon is central to the argument of Allen and Starr 1982. It is drawn from an illusion to classical mythology by Arthur Koestler (1967). The god Janus was endowed with two faces, and both looked back into the past and forward into the future, a doorway connecting two states of being. Allen and Starr (1982) extend the metaphor of a doorway in time to doorways between tempos more generally.

21. Weber, Depew, and Smith 1988 for a range of studies of tempos in ecology.

22. Allen and Starr (1982) argue that the differentiation of rhythms is what actually constitutes the boundary around a whole range of ecological entities. Following this logic organelles, cells, organs, individuals, trophic groups, food webs, and the biosphere are all bounded by changes in tempos and the portal of these changes are the 'holons', which are central to their argument. These holons form a hierarchy of information nodes, ranked according the tempos of their individual rhythms of information flow. Outside the body that hierarchical ranking of tempos can be extended through each of the rhythms comprising the dynamic of the 'physical world'.

23. This shift of emphasis from 'adaptation' to an environment that is reasonably static, to 'coupling' between two dynamic rhythms, and the tracking of the slower by the faster draws on the mathematical ecology of, for example, De Angelis *et al.* 1989. See also Chapter 5, nn. 18–22.

24. Pimm 1982; Cohen and Briand 1984; Briand and Cohen 1987; Lawton and Warren 1988; Pimm *et al.* 1990; Cohen *et al.* 1990*a* and *b*.

25. See Chapter 5, nn. 21 and 22.

26. Cohen and Armelagos 1984.

Chapter 9: Eating in order to be

1. Crummy 1992: chapter 3, p. 21.
2. Murphy in Crummy 1992: chapter 8.
3. Crummy 1992: chapter 7 for bones, chapter 8 for other food remains.
4. Crummy 1984; 1992.
5. Van der Veen 1998; 1999; 2001.
6. King 1999.
7. As papyrus was expensive, short notes, brief accounts and other such things were instead written on stone flakes and fragments of broken pottery. These are collectively referred to as 'ostraca'. The word comes from the Greek 'ostrakon' meaning 'shell'.
8. Walsh 1999.
9. Crummy 1992.
10. Garnsey 1999.
11. Bowman 2003.
12. Dietler 1990; and in Dietler and Haydon 2001. These authors use the term 'diacritical' (from the Greek for 'distinguishing') for such feasts.
13. The emperor in question is Septimus Severus, born in Lepcis Magna in modern-day Libya. His Syrian wife was Julia Domna. As for contemporary religious plurality, see Beard *et al.* 1998; and Beard 1998.
14. Gaius Cornelius Tacitus, *De Origine et Situ Germanorum (Germania)* composed around AD 98.
15. Foster 1986.
16. Dietler 1990.
17. Hill 1997; Jundi and Hill 1998; Carr 2000.
18. Cunliffe 1991; Jones 1989; 1996; Hawkes 2000.
19. Hingley 1989 for a discussion in the context of the archaeological evidence.
20. Athenaeus 1927–41.
21. Hill 1995.
22. Slater 1991; Garnsey 1999; Dunbabin 1996.
23. Goody 1982.
24. Strabo lived from 64 BC to AD 23, travelled widely in Europe and the Nile, and is a major source on contemporary geography and economics. He writes of Britain: 'Most of the island is low-lying and wooded, but many parts are hilly. Britain produces corn, cattle, gold, silver and iron. These are exported together with hides, slaves, and hunting dogs' (Strabo, *Geography* 4. 5. 2).
25. Jacomet *et al.* 2002; and Bakels and Jacomet 2003 for Central European luxury foods; Roman pomegranates, almonds, melons, peaches, peppercorns. Further up the coast from Berenike at Quseir al-Qadim, Van der Veen

(2004) has recovered, not just peppercorns, but also coconut and rice, also imported from India.

26. Tacitus 1970.
27. Cunliffe 1971; 1998.
28. Hingley 1989.
29. Jones 1989; 1991b; 1996.
30. Rees 1979.
31. Jones 1991a.
32. Cunliffe 1998.
33. Jones 1989; 1991a.

Chapter 10: Far from the hearth

1. Glob 1969.
2. Helbaek 1950, 1958a and b; Holden 1986; 1995; Turner and Scaife 1995; Van der Sanden 1996.
3. Brothwell *et al.* 1990a and b; Holden 1996/7.
4. Stead *et al.* 1986.
5. The archaeologists were Glyn Daniel and Mortimer Wheeler who shared the meal in 1954 for the British television series *Buried Treasure*. Apparently, they quickly washed down the 'awful taste' with Danish brandy drunk from a cow's horn.
6. Ruth 2–3.
7. For an archaeological study of minor Chenopodiums and other lesser known American domesticates, see Smith 1992; also Smith 1995 for a wider survey.
8. Lindow: Stead *et al.* 1986; Turner and Scaife 1995 for a useful resume of bog body 'last meals'.
9. For an idea of available plant foods in this kind of ecosystem I have drawn upon plant remains from the very much earlier sites of Halsskov and Tybrind Vig (Kubiak-Martens 1999; 2002). See also Robinson 1994.
10. Fischer 1980.
11. The symptoms can also arise from parasite infection or vitamin B deficiency (Molleson, personal communication).
12. McKinley in Mercer and Healey (forthcoming): chapter 5.
13. Cohen and Armelagos 1984.
14. For Hambledon, McKinley in Mercer and Healey (forthcoming): chapter 5; for Poundbury, Molleson 1989.
15. Roberts and Cox 2003.
16. Angel 1984.

17. Roberts and Cox 2003*b*.
18. Farwell and Molleson 1993.

Chapter 11: The stomach and the soul

1. Clavel 2001; Lancel n.d.; Cahon 1993; 2005; Lawrence 2000.
2. Clavel 2001 studied the bones from a range of urban, rural, and religious sites, and châteaux along the Oise, Seine, and Aisne valleys, occupied between the twelfth and seventeenth centuries.
3. Cahon, cited in Clavel 2001: 158.
4. Aston 2000.
5. The 'Bulle de Moreaucourt' is held to have been written by the future Pope Gregory VIII when he was Albert de Morra, chancellor of the Roman Church. Fifteenth- and seventeenth-century copies are known (cf. Giry 1894: 458).
6. Clavel 2001: 152 ff.
7. Yvinec 1999.
8. Bakels 1999; Jones 1989; 1991*a* and *b*.
9. An early and valuable source is Fitzherbert 1523 which lists the most problematic weeds of the day. Some decades later, William Shakespeare alludes to some of the same weeds, for example, in *Coriolanus* Act 3 scene 1: 'In soothing them we nourish 'gainst our senate the *cockle* of rebellion, insolence, sedition, which we ourselves have plough'd for, sow'd and scatter'd.'
10. Jones 1989; 1991*a* and *b*.
11. Reynolds 1979.
12. Alongside the well-known Christian symbolism of bread wheat, rye features in Slav mythology, for example in relation to Jaryla, god of the fields and harbinger of spring, who rides on horseback, carrying with his left arm a sheath of rye, and with his right a human skull.
13. These anecdotes all come from Athenaeus of Naucratis, and a long passage he devoted to the subject of bread within the *Deipnosophistae* (Banquet of the Learned). In the final anecdote, the double entendre within Plato's composition *A Long Night* reads: 'and then he bought and sent us some loaves; don't think they were the clean and tidy kind; they were large Cilicians'.
14. Samuel 1996.
15. Inferred from citations within Athenaeus' *Deipnosophistae*.
16. Dunbanin 1996 for range of Roman dining patterns; Vroom 2003 on late Roman/early medieval frescos representing dining and the Eucharist.
17. Hawthorne 1997; Vroom 2003; Garnsey 1999.
18. Aston 2000.

19. Harmless 2004.
20. Hirschfeld 1992.
21. Wilpert 1896.
22. Lawrence 2000.
23. Cited in Bartlett 1993.
24. The idea of 'cerealization' as a convergence of agricultural, ideological, and political expansion is developed by Bartlett 1993.
25. Bartlett 1993 for the perspective revealed in Christian texts. Earliest evidence of mould-board plowing from Feddersen Wierde in North Germany (Haarnagel 1979). Berglund (forthcoming) infers from a range of pollen diagrams that during the third millennium BC, agriculture expanded northwards along the Norwegian coast, as far north as the Lofoten islands. Over the following millennia, there were various fluctuations in Scandinavian agricultural activity, but the centuries prior to Christianization certainly witness agricultural activity. AD 800–1000 in particular he sees as characterized by strong expansion of settlements, including the establishment of villages and towns in Scandinavia, and agriculture. See also Berglund 1985.
26. The reference to wheat and grapes comes from the record of the journey in the *Eiríks saga rauða* (*Saga of Eric the Red*).
27. The seminal work is Crosby 1972, in which he coined the phrase 'the Columbian exchange'. See also Crosby 1986; and Fernández-Armesto 2001.
28. Fernández-Armesto 2001.
29. Bernabé Cobo was a Spanish priest who lived and evangelized in seventeenth-century South and Central America. His book, *The History of the New World*, remains a major ethnographic source.
30. Malagon-Barcelo 1963.
31. Walker Bynum 1987.
32. Kolde 1911, cited in Farndon 1999.
33. Hunter 1952; Briggs 1978.
34. Worster 1977; 1979.
35. Hamilton 2004 surveys the symbolic and ritual manifestations of rice in Asian symbolism. Miller and Taube 1993 is a useful reference source for Chicomecoatl and other American maize deities.

Chapter 12: A global food web

1. Rathje and Murphy 2001.
2. e.g. Strong 2002.
3. The first two quotations are direct from Rathje and Murphy 2001. The third is entirely plausible chronologically, but inserted by me.

4. Gitelson 1992; Adema 2000.
5. cf. Brain *et al.* 1999.
6. Strong 2002: chapter 6.
7. Osepchuk J. 1984.
8. Introduction to Spang 2000.
9. Spang 2000: chapters 4 and 6.
10. Spang 2000: chapters 7 and 8.
11. Fernández-Armesto 2001.
12. Shortly after Thomas's death in September 2005, Roy Rivenburg of the *Los Angeles Times* argued that the entire story was a fabrication, and that frozen meals had been supplied to the Navy ten years earlier, by the W. L. Maxwell Company (Rivenburg 2005).
13. Extract from record of Winslow's record, reproduced in Heath 1963: 82.
14. Spang 2000: chapter 7.
15. Goody 1982.
16. Goody 1982; Spang 2000; Fernández-Armesto 2001.
17. Spang 2000: chapters 2 and 3.
18. Lazaro Spallanzani (1729–99) was a major figure in biology, and a pioneer of microbiology and studies of the digestive system. He demonstrated that microbes could be destroyed by boiling. Nicolas Appert (1750–1841) was an innovative chef, who introduced many new ideas, including compressing bouillon into a storable tablet, and capturing Spallanzani's science, by sealing boiled food in glass jars and metal cans (Appert 1810).
19. The seminal study, which has inspired the whole field of landscape archaeology, is Hoskins 1955.
20. Goody 1982; Spang 2000; Fernández-Armesto 2001.
21. Fernández-Armesto 2001: chapter 8.
22. Kottak 1978; Fitzell 1978.
23. Braudel 1958.
24. See Chapter 5, note 27.

References

ADEMA, P. (2000), 'Consumption: Food, Television and the Ambiguity of Modernity', *Journal of American and Comparative Cultures* 23/3: 113.

AIELLO, L. C., and DUNBAR, R. I. M. (1993), 'Neocortex Size, Group Size and the Evolution of Language', *Current Anthropology* 36: 199–221.

—— and WHEELER, P. (1995), 'The Expensive Tissue Hypothesis', *Current Anthropology* 34: 184–93.

AKAZAWA, T., MUHESEN, S., ISHIDA, H., KONDO, O., and GRIGGO, C. (1999), 'New Discovery of a Neanderthal Child Burial from the Dederiyeh Cave in Syria', *Paleorient* 25/2: 127–40.

ALLEN, T. F. H., and STARR, T. B. (1982), *Hierarchy: Perspective for Ecological Complexity* (Chicago: Chicago University Press).

ALLEY, R. B. (2000), 'Ice-core Evidence of Abrupt Climate Changes', *Proceedings of the National Academy of Sciences* 97/4: 1331–4.

AMBROSE, S. H., and KATZENBERG, M. A. (eds.) (2000), *Biogeochemical Approaches to Paleodietary Analysis* (New York: Kluwer Academic/Plenum).

ANGEL, L. (1984), 'Health as a Crucial Factor in the Changes from Hunting to Developed Farming in the Eastern Mediterranean', in M. N. Cohen and G. J. Armelagos (eds.), *Palaeopathology at the Origins of Agriculture* (Orlando: Academic Press): 51–73.

APPERT, N. (1810), *L'Art de conserver, pendant plusieurs années, toutes les substances animales et végétales* (Paris: Patris et Cie).

ASHBEE, P., SMITH, I. F., and EVANS, J. G. (1979), 'Excavation of Three Long Barrows Near Avebury, Wiltshire', *Proceedings of the Prehistoric Society* 45: 207–300.

ASTON, M. (2000), *Monasteries in the Landscape* (Stroud: Tempus).

ATHENAEUS (1927–41), *The Deipnosophists*, trans. Charles Burton Gulick (London: William Heinemann; New York: E. P. Putnam's).

ATKINS, R. C. (1972), *Dr. Atkins' Diet Revolution. The High Calorie Way to Stay Thin Forever* (New York: David McKay).

BAKELS, C. (1999), 'Dury "le Moulin" (Somme) Étude des restes botaniques', *Revue archéologique de Picardie* 1: 237–45.

—— and JACOMET, S. (2003), 'Access to Luxury Foods in Central Europe during the Roman Period: The Archaeobotanical Evidence', *World Archaeology* 34: 542–57.

References

BANTING, W. (1863), *Letter on Corpulence Addressed to the Public* (London: Harrison).

BARBETTI, M. (1986), 'Traces of Fire in the Archaeological Record before One Million Years Ago?' *Journal of Human Evolution* 15: 771–81.

BARTLETT, R. (1993), *The Making of Europe: Conquest, Colonisation and Cultural Change 950–1350* (London: Penguin).

BARTON, R. N. E. (2000), 'Mousterian Hearths and Shellfish: Late Neanderthal Activities in Gibralter', in C. B. Stringer, R. N. E. Barton, and J. C. Finlayson (eds.), *Neanderthals on the Edge: Papers from a Conference Marking the 150th Anniversary of the Forbes' Quarry Discovery, Gibralter* (Oxford: Oxbow Books).

BAR-YOSEF, O. (1998), 'The Natufian Culture in the Levant, Threshold to the Origins of Agriculture', *Evolutionary Anthropology* 6: 159–77.

BEARD, M. (1998), *Religions of Rome*, ii, *A Source Book* (Cambridge: Cambridge University Press).

—— NORTH, J. A., and PRICE, S. R. F. (1998), *Religions of Rome*, i, *A History* (Cambridge: Cambridge University Press).

BEHRE, K. E. (1990), 'Some Reflections on Anthropogenic Indicators and the Record of Prehistoric Occupation Phases in Pollen Diagrams from the Near East', in S. Bottema, G. Entjes-Nieborg, and W. Van Zeist (eds.), *Man's Role in the Shaping of the Eastern Mediterranean Landscape* (Rotterdam: A. A. Balkema): 219–31.

BELL, M., and WALKER, M. J. C. (1992), *Late Quaternary Environmental Change: Physical and Human Perspectives* (London: Longman).

BELLOMO, R. (1993), 'A Methodological Approach for Identifying Archaeological Evidence of Fire Resulting from Human Activities', *Journal of Archaeological Science* 20: 525–53.

BENDALL, L. (2004), 'Fit for a King? Exclusion, Hierarchy, Aspiration and Desire in the Social Structure of Mycenaean Banqueting', in P. Halstead and J. Barrett (eds.), *Food, Cuisine and Society in Prehistoric Greece. Proceedings of the 10th Aegean Round Table, University of Sheffield* (Sheffield: Sheffield University Press).

BENTLEY, R. A., PRICE, T. D., LÜNING, J., GRONENBORN, D., WAHL, J., and FULLAGAR, P. D. (2002), 'Prehistoric Migration in Europe: Strontium Isotope Analysis of Early Neolithic Skeletons', *Current Anthropology* 43: 799–804.

BERGLUND, B. E. (1985), 'Early Agriculture in Scandinavia: Research Problems Related to Pollen-Analytical Studies', *Norwegian Archaeological Review* 18: 77–105.

—— (forthcoming), 'The Agrarian Landscape Development in Northwest Europe since the Neolithic. Cultural and Climatic Factors behind a Regional/Continental Pattern', *World System History and Global Environmental Change*, conference in Lund, September 2003.

BERGMAN, C. A. (1986), 'Refitting of the Flint Assemblages', in M. B. Roberts (ed.), 'Excavation of the Lower Palaeolithic Site at Amey's Eartham Pit, Boxgrove, West Sussex: A Preliminary Report', *Proceedings of the Prehistoric Society* 52: 235–6.

—— ROBERTS, M. B., COLLCUTT, S. N., and BARLOW, P. (1990), 'Refitting and Spatial Analysis of Artefacts from Quarry 2 at the Middle Pleistocene Acheulian Site of Boxgrove, West Sussex, England', in E. Cziesla, S. Eickhoff, N. Arts, and D. Winter (eds.), *The Big Puzzle* (Bonn: Holos): 265–82.

BERNABO BREA, L. (1946), *Gli scavi nella caverna delle Arene Candide* (Bordighera: Istituto di Studi Liguri).

BERRYMAN, A. A., and MILLSTEIN, J. A. (1989), 'Are Ecological Systems Chaotic—and If not, Why not?' *Trends in Ecology and Evolution* 4/1: 26–8.

BIRKS, H. J. B., and BIRKS, H. H. (1980), *Quaternary Palaeoecology* (Baltimore: University Park Press).

BLEGEN, C. W., and RAWSON, M. (1966–73), *The Palace of Nestor at Pylos in Western Messenia*, 3 vols. (Princeton: Princeton University Press).

BLYTT, A. (1876), *Essay on Immigration of the Norwegian Flora during Alternating Rainy and Dry Periods* (Cammermeye: Christiania).

BOUYSSONIE, A, BOUYSSONIE, L., and BARDON, L. (1908), 'Découverte d'un squelette humain Moustérien à la bouffia de la Chapelle-aux-Saints (Corrèze)', *Anthropologie (Paris)* 19: 513–18.

BOWEN, H. C., and FOWLER, P. J. (1978), *Early Land Allotment in the British Isles* (Oxford: British Archaeological Reports 48).

BOWMAN, A. K. (2003), *Life and Letters on the Roman Frontier: Vindolanda and its People* (London: British Museum Press).

BRAIN, M., ELASMAR, M., and HASEGAWA, K. (1999), 'The Portrayal of Women in U.S. Prime Time Television', *Journal of Broadcasting & Electronic Media* 43/20.

BRAUDEL, F. (1958), 'Histoire et Sciences sociales: la longue durée', *Annales* 13/4: 725–53.

BRIAND, F., and COHEN, J. E. (1987), 'Environmental Correlation of Food Chain Length', *Science* 238: 956–60.

BRIGGS, D. E. (1978), *Barley* (London: Chapman & Hall).

BROTHWELL, D. (1987), *The Bog Man and the Archaeology of People* (Cambridge, Mass.: Harvard University Press).

—— LIVERSAGE, D., and GOTTLIEB, B. (1990a), 'Radiographic and Forensic Aspects of the Female Huldremose Body', *Journal of Danish Archaeology* 9: 157–278.

—— HOLDEN, T., LIVERSIDGE, D., GOTTLIEB, B., BENNIKE, P., and BOESEN, J. (1990b), 'Establishing a Minimum Damage Procedure for the Gut Sampling of Intact Human Bodies: The Case of Huldremose Woman', *Antiquity* 64: 830–5.

References

Burjachs, F., and Julià, R. (1994), 'Abrupt Climatic Changes during the Last Glaciation, Based on Pollen Analysis of the Abric Romaní, Catalonia, Spain', *Quaternary Research* 42: 308–15.

Butler, S. (1990), *The Odyssey: Rendered into English Prose for the Use of those who cannot Read the Original* (London: Longmans, Green & Co.).

Cahon, G. (1993), 'Le Prieuré de Moreaucourt', *Bulletin de la Société des Antiquaires de Picardie. Amiens* 629: 296–326.

—— (ed.) (2005), *EUREKA; les Amis de Moreaucourt: 35 ans de recherches sur Moreaucourt* (Picardie).

Carbonell, E., and Castro-Curel, Z. (1992), 'Palaeolithic Wooden Artifacts from the Abric Romaní (Capellades, Barcelona, Spain)', *Journal of Archaeological Science* 19: 707–19.

—— and Vaquero, M. (eds.) (1996), *The Last Neanderthals, the First Anatomically Modern Humans* (Tarragona: URV).

—— and Vaquero, M. (1998), 'Behavioural Complexity and Biocultural Change in Europe around Forty Thousand Years Ago', *Journal of Anthropological Research* 54: 373–97.

Cardini, L. (1942), 'Nuovi documenti sull'antichità dell'uomo in Italia: reperto umano del Paleolitico superiore nella Grotta delle Arene Candide', *Razza e Civiltà* 3: 5–25.

Carr, G. (2000), ' "Romanisation" and the Body', *Proceedings of the 10th Theoretical Roman Archaeology Conference* (Oxford: Oxbow Books): 112–24.

Castro-Curel, Z., and Carbonell, E. (1995), 'Wood Pseudomorphs from Level I at Abric Romaní, Barcelona, Spain', *Journal of Field Archaeology* 22: 376–84.

Cauvin, J. (1977), 'Les Fouilles de Mureybet (1971–1984) et leur significance pour les origines de sédentarisation au Proche Orient', *Annals of the American School of Oriental Research* 44: 19–48.

—— (1997), *Naissances des divinités, naissance d'agriculture. Le révolution des symboles au Néolithique*, 2nd edn. (Paris: CNRS).

—— Cauvin, M. C., Helme, D., and Willcox, G. (1998), 'L'Homme et son environment au Levant Nord entre 30,000 et 7,500 BP', *Paléorient* 23: 51–69.

Cavalli-Sforza, L. L., Menozzi, P., and Piazza, A. (1994), *The History and Geography of Human Genes* (Princeton: Princeton University Press).

Chadwick, J. (1958), *The Decipherment of Linear B* (Cambridge: Cambridge University Press).

—— (1976), *The Mycenaean World* (Cambridge: Cambridge University Press).

—— (1977), 'The Interpretation of Mycenaean Documents and Pylian Geography', in J. Bintliff (ed.), *Mycenaean Geography* (Cambridge: Cambridge University Press): 36–9.

Childe, V. G. (1928), *The Most Ancient East: The Oriental Prelude to European Prehistory* (London: Kegan Paul).

—— (1936), *Man Makes Himself* (London: Watts & Co.).

CLARK, J. D., and HARRIS, J. W. K. (1985), 'Fire and its Roles in Early Hominid Lifeways', *African Archaeological Review*: 3–27.

CLAVEL, B. (2001), 'L'Animal dans l'alimentation medievale et moderne en France du Nord (XIIe–XVIIe siècles)', *Revue archéologique de Picardie* 19: 1–204.

CLEMENTS, F. E. (1916), *Plant Succession: An Analysis of the Development of Vegetation* (Washington: Carnegie).

COHEN, J. E., and BRIAND, F. (1984), 'Trophic Links of Community Food Webs', *Proceedings of the National Academy of Sciences* 81/13: 4105–9.

—— BRIAND, F., and NEWMAN, C. M. (1990), *Community Food Webs: Data and Theory* (*Biomathematics* 20) (New York: Springer Verlag).

—— LUCZAK, T., NEWMAN, C. M., and ZHOU, Z. M. (1990), 'Stochastic Structure and Nonlinear Dynamics of Food Webs: Qualitative Stability in a Lotka–Volterra Cascade Model', *Proceedings of the Royal Society (London) Series B* 240: 607–27.

COHEN, M. N., and ARMELAGOS, G. J. (1984), *Palaeopathology at the Origins of Agriculture* (Orlando: Academic Press).

COHMAP Members (1988), 'Climatic Changes of the Last 18,000 Years: Observations and Model Simulations', *Science* 241: 1043–52.

CONKLIN-BRITTAIN, N. L., WRANGHAM, R. W., and HUNT, K. D. (1998), 'Dietary Response of Chimpanzees and Cercopithecines to Seasonal Variation in Fruit Abundance II: Nutrients', *International Journal of Primatology* 19: 949–70.

COOPE, G. R. (1977), 'Fossil Coleopteran Assemblages as Sensitive Indicators of Climatic Changes during the Devensian (Last) Cold Stage', *Philosophical Transactions of the Royal Society (London) Series B* 280: 313–48.

—— and BROPHY, J. A. (1972), 'Late Glacial Environmental Changes Indicated by a Coleopteran Succession from North Wales', *Boreas* 1: 97–142.

COPLEY, M. S., BERSTAN, R., DUDD, S. N., DOCHERTY, G. D., MUKHERJEE, A. J., PAYNE, S., EVERSHED, R. P., and STRAKER, V. (2003), 'Direct Chemical Evidence for Widespread Dairying in Prehistoric Britain', *Proceedings of the National Academy of Sciences* 100/4: 1524–9.

CORDAIN, L., EATON, S. B., SEBASTIAN, A., MANN, N., LINDEBERG, S., WATKINS, B. A., O'KEEFE, J. H., and BRAND-MILLER, J. (2005), 'Origins and Evolution of the Western Diet: Health Implications for the 21st Century', *American Journal of Clinical Nutrition* 81: 341–54.

CRAWFORD, M. A., GALE, M. M., WOODFORD, M. H., and CAWED, N. M. (1970), 'Comparative Studies on Fatty Acid Composition of Wild and Domestic Meats', *International Journal of Biochemistry* 1: 295–305.

CROSBY, A. W. (1972), *The Columbian Exchange, Biological and Cultural Consequences of 1492* (Westport, Conn.: Greenwood Press).

References

CROSBY, A. W. (1986), *Ecological Imperialism: The Biological Expansion of Europe, 900–1900* (Cambridge: Cambridge University Press).

CRUMMY, P. (1984), *Excavations at Lion Walk, Balkerne Lane, and Middleborough, Colchester, Essex* (Colchester: Colchester Archaeological Trust).

—— (1992), *Excavations at Culver Street, the Gilberd School, and Other Sites in Colchester (1971–85)* (Colchester: Colchester Archaeological Trust).

CUNLIFFE, B. W. (1971), *Excavations at Fishbourne, 1961–1969* (London: Society of Antiquaries).

—— (1991), *Iron Age Communities in Britain: An Account of England, Scotland and Wales from the Seventh Century BC until the Roman Conquest* (London: Routledge).

—— (1998), *Fishbourne Roman Palace* (Stroud: Tempus).

—— (2006), 'The Roots of Warfare', in M. Jones and A. Fabian (eds.), *Conflict* (Cambridge: Cambridge University Press).

CWYNAR, L. C., and RITCHIE, J. C. (1980), 'Arctic Steppe-Tundra: A Yukon Perspective', *Science* 20/8: 1375–7.

DE ANGELIS, D. L. (1975), 'Stability and Connectance in Food Web Models', *Ecology* 56: 238–43.

—— MULHOLLAND, P. J., PALUMBO, A. V., STEINMAN, A. D., HUSTON, M. A., and ELWOOD, J. W. (1989), 'Nutrient Dynamics and Food Web Stability', *Annual Review of Ecology and Systematics* 20: 71–95.

DE WAAL, F. B. M. (1997), *Bonobo: The Forgotten Ape* (Berkeley: University of California Press).

DIETLER, M. (1990), 'Driven by Drink: The Role of Drinking in the Political Economy and the Case Study of Iron Age France', *Journal of Anthropological Archaeology* 9: 352–406.

—— and HAYDEN, B. (eds.) (2001), *Feasts: Archaeological and Ethnographic Perspectives on Food, Politics, and Power* (Washington: Smithsonian).

DOUGLAS, M. (1963), *The Lele of the Kasai* (Oxford: Oxford University Press).

—— (1984), *Food in the Social Order: Studies of Food and Festivities* (New York: Russell Sage Foundation).

—— (1966), *Purity and Danger: An Analysis of Concepts of Pollution and Taboo* (London: Routledge & Kegan Paul).

—— (1970) *Natural Symbols, Explorations in Cosmology* (New York: Pantheon Books).

—— (1972) 'Deciphering a Meal', *Daedalus* 101: 61–82.

DROUIN, J.-M. (1999), *L' Écologie et son histoire: Réinventer la nature* (Paris: Flammarion).

DUNBABIN, K. M. D. (1991), 'Triclinium and Stibadium', in W. J. Slater (ed.), *Dining in a Classical Context* (Ann Arbor: Michigan University Press): 121–48.

—— (1996), 'Convivial Spaces: Dining and Entertainment in the Roman Villa', *Journal of Roman Archaeology* 9: 66–80.

References

DUNBAR, R. I. M. (1993), 'Co-evolution of Neocortical Size, Group Size and Language in Humans', *Behavioural and Brain Sciences* 16: 681–735.

—— (1996), *Grooming, Gossip, and the Evolution of Language* (London: Faber & Faber).

DUPRAS, T. L., and SCHWARCZ, H. P. (2001), 'Strangers in a Strange Land: Stable Isotope Evidence for Human Migration in the Dakhleh Oasis, Egypt', *Journal of Archaeological Science* 28: 1199–208.

EATON, S. B., KONNER, M., and SHOSTAK, M. (1988), 'Stone-Agers in the Fast Lane: Chronic Degenerative Diseases in Evolutionary Perspective', *American Journal of Medicine* 84: 739–49.

EIBES-EIBESFELDT, I. (1970), *Ethology: The Biology of Behavior* (New York: Holt, Rinehart & Winston).

EVANS, A. (1921), *The Palace of Minos: A Comparative Account of the Successive Stages of the Early Cretan Civilization as Illustrated by the Discoveries at Knossos* (London: Macmillan).

EVERSHED, R. P., and DUDD, S. N. (2000), 'Lipid Biomarkers Preserved in Archaeological Pottery: Current Status and Future Prospects', in S. Pike and S. Gitin (eds.), *The Practical Impact of Science on Near Eastern and Aegean Archaeology* (London: Archetype): 155–69.

—— DUDD, S. N., CHARTERS, S., MOTTRAM, H. R., STOTT, A. W., RAVEN, A. M., VAN BERGEN, P. F., and BLAND, H. A. (1999), 'Lipids as Carriers of Anthropogenic Signals from Prehistory', *Philosophical Transactions of the Royal Society (London) Series B*, 354: 19–31.

FARNDON, R. (1999), *Mary Douglas: An Intellectual Biography* (London: Routledge).

FARWELL, D. E., and MOLLESON, T. L. (1993), *Excavations at Poundbury*, ii, *The Cemeteries* (Dorchester: Dorsert Natural History and Archaeology Society).

FERNÁNDEZ-ARMESTO, F. (2001), *Food: A History* (London: Macmillan).

FISCHER, C. (1980), 'Bog Bodies of Denmark', in A. Cockburn and E. Cockburn (eds.), *Mummies, Disease and Ancient Cultures* (Cambridge: Cambridge University Press).

FITZELL, P. (1978), 'The Man Who Sold the First McDonald's', *Journal of American Culture* 1/2: 392.

FITZHERBERT, J. (1523), *Boke of Husbandrie* (London: Thomas Berthelet).

FLANNERY, K. V. (1969), 'Origins and Ecological Effects of Early Domestication in Iran and the Near East', in P. J. Ucko and G. W. Dimbleby (eds.), *The Domestication and Exploitation of Plants and Animals* (Chicago: Aldine): 73–100.

—— (1972), 'The Origins of the Village as a Settlement Type in Mesoamerica and the Near East', in P. Ucko, R. Tringham, and G. W. Dimbleby (eds.), *Man, Settlement and Urbanism* (London: Duckworth): 23–53.

FOLEY, R. A. (1989), 'The Evolution of Hominid Social Behaviour', in V. Standen and R. A. Foley (eds.), *Comparative Socioecology* (Oxford: Blackwell Scientific): 473–94.

References

FOLEY, R. A. and LEE, P. C. (1989), 'Finite Social Space, Evolutionary Pathways and Reconstructing Hominid Behaviour', *Science* 243: 901–6.

—— (1991), Ecology and Energetics of Encephalization in Hominid Evolution', *Philosophical Transactions of the Royal Society (London) Series B* 334: 223–32.

—— (1996), 'Finite Social Space and the Evolution of Human Behaviour', in J. Steele and S. Shennan (eds.), *The Archaeology of Human Ancestry: Power, Sex and Tradition* (London: Routledge): 47–66.

FOSTER, J. (1986), *The Lexden Tumulus: A Re-appraisal of an Iron Age Burial from Colchester, Essex* (Oxford: British Archaeological Reports 156).

FRENCH, C. A. I. (2002), *Geoarchaeology in Action: Studies in Soil Micromorphology and Landscape Evolution* (London: Routledge).

FRUTH, B., and HOHMANN, G. (2002), 'How Bonobos Handle Hunts and Harvests: Why Share Food?', in C. Boesch, G. Hohmann, and L. Marchant (eds.), *Behavioural Diversity in Chimpanzees and Bonobos* (Cambridge: Cambridge University Press).

GALE, R., and CARRUTHERS, W. (2000), 'Charcoal and Charred Seed Remains from Middle Palaeolithic Levels at Goreham's and Vanguard Caves', in C. B. Stringer, R. N. E. Barton, and J. C. Finlayson (eds.), *Neanderthals on the Edge: Papers from a Conference Marking the 150th Anniversary of the Forbes' Quarry Discovery, Gibralter* (Oxford: Oxbow Books).

GAMBLE, C. (1999), *The Palaeolithic Societies of Europe* (Cambridge: Cambridge University Press).

GARDNER, M. R., and ASHBY, W. R. (1970), 'Connectance of Large Dynamic (Cybernetic) Systems-Critical Values for Stability', *Nature* 228: 784.

GARNSEY, P. (1999), *Food and Society in Classical Antiquity* (Cambridge: Cambridge University Press).

GIRY, A. (1894), *Manuel de diplomatique: Diplômes et chartes* (Paris).

GITELSON, J. (1992), 'Populox: The Suburban Cuisine of the 1950s', *Journal of American Culture* 15: 73–8.

GLOB, P. V. (1969), *The Bog People: Iron-Age Man Preserved* (Ithaca, NY: Cornell University Press).

GODWIN, W. (1793), *An Enquiry Concerning Political Justice, and its Influence on General Virtue and Happiness* (London: G.G.J. & J. Robinson).

GOODALL, J. (1971), *In the Shadow of Man* (Boston: Houghton Mifflin).

—— (1986), *The Chimpanzees of Gombe: Patterns of Behaviour* (Cambridge, Mass.: Harvard University Press).

GOODY, J. (1962), *Death, Property and the Ancestors: A Study of the Mortuary Customs of the LoDagaa of West Africa* (Standford, Calif.: Stanford University Press).

—— (1982), *Cooking, Cuisine and Class: A Study in Comparative Sociology* (Cambridge: Cambridge University Press).

—— (1998), *Food and Love: A Cultural History of East and West* (London: Verso).

Guthrie, R. D. (1982), 'Mammals of the Mammoth Steppe as Paleoenvironmental Indicators', in D. M. Hopkins, J. V. Matthews, C. E. Schweger, Jr., and S. B. Young (eds.), *Paleoecology of Beringia* (New York: Academic Press): 307–26.

Haarnagel, W. (1979), *Die Grabung Feddersen Wierde*, ii, *Methode, Hausbau, Siedlungs- und Wirtschaftsformen sowie Sozialstruktu* (Stuttgart: Franz Steiner Verlag).

Halstead, P. (1990), 'Quantifying Sumerian Agriculture—Some Seeds of Doubt and Hope', *Bulletin of Sumerian Agriculture* 5: 187–95.

—— (1992), 'The Mycenaean Palatial Economy: Making the Most of the Gaps in the Evidence', *Proceedings of the Cambridge Philological Society* 38: 57–86.

—— (1999), 'Surplus and Share-croppers: The Grain Production Strategies of Mycenaean Palaces', in P. Betancourt, V. Karageorghis, R. Laffineur and W.-D. Niemeier (eds.), *MELETHMATA. Studies Presented to Malcolm H. Weiner as he Enters his 65th Year*: ii. 319–26.

—— (2003), 'Texts and Bones: Contrasting Linear B and Archaeozoological Evidence for Animal Exploitation in Mycenaean Southern Greece', in E. Kotjabopoulou, Y. Hamilakis, P. Halstead, C. Gamble, and P. Elefanti (eds.), *Zooarchaeology in Greece: Recent Advances* (London: British School at Athens): 257–61.

Hamilton, R. W. (2004), *The Art of Rice: Spirit and Sustenance in Asia* (Los Angeles: UCLA, Fowler Museum of Cultural History).

Harmless, W. (2004), *Desert Christians: An Introduction to the Literature of Early Monasticism* (Oxford: Oxford University Press).

Harris, D. R. (2003), 'Climatic Change and the Beginnings of Agriculture: The Case of the Younger Dryas', in L. J. Rothschild and A. M. Lister (eds.), *Evolution on Planet Earth: The Impact of the Physical Environment* (London: Academic Press): chapter 20.

Harris, M. (1958), *Portugal's African 'Wards': A First-Hand Report on Labor and Education in Mocambique* (New York: American Committee on Africa).

—— (1959), 'Labor Migration among the Mocambique Thonga: Cultural and Political Factors', *Africa* 29: 50–64.

—— (1974), *Cows, Pigs, Wars and Witches: The Riddles of Culture* (New York: Random House).

—— (1977), *Cannibals and Kings: The Origins of Culture* (New York: Random House).

—— (1979), *Cultural Materialism: The Struggle for a Science of Culture* (New York: Random House).

—— (1985), *Good to Eat: Riddles of Food and Culture* (New York: Simon & Schuster).

—— and Ross, E. B. (eds.) (1987), *Food and Evolution: Towards a Theory of Human Food Habits* (Philadelphia: Temple University Press).

References

HARVEY, C. B., HOLLOX, E. J., POULTER, M., WANG, Y., ROSSI, M., AURICCHIO, S., IQBAL, T. H., COOPER, B. T., BARTON, R., SARNER, M., KORPELA, R., and SWALLOW, D. M. (1998), 'Lactase Haplotype Frequencies in Caucasians: Association with the Lactase Persistence/Non-persistance Polymorphism', *Annals of Human Genetics* 62: 215–23.

HAWKES, G. (2000), 'An Archaeology of Food: A Case Study from Roman Britain', *Proceedings of the 10th Theoretical Roman Archaeology Conference* (Oxford: Oxbow Books): 94–103.

HAWKES, K. (2003), 'Grandmothers and the Evolution of Human Longevity', *American Journal of Human Biology* 15: 380–400.

—— (2004a), 'Mating, Parenting and the Evolution of Human Pair Bonds', in B. Chapais and C. Berman (eds.), *Kinship and Behavior in Primates* (Oxford: Oxford University Press): 443–73.

—— (2004b), 'The Grandmother Effect', *Nature* 428: 128–9.

HAWTHORNE, J. W. J. (1997), 'Pottery and Paradigms in the Early Western Empire', *Proceedings of the 10th Theoretical Roman Archaeology Conference* (Oxford: Oxbow Books): 160–72.

HAYDEN, B. (1990), 'Nimrods, Piscators, Pluckers, and Planters: The Emergence of Food Production', *Journal of Anthropological Archaeology* 9: 31–69.

HAYS, J. D., IMBRIE, J., and SHACKLETON, N. J. (1976), 'Variations in the Earth's Orbit: Pacemaker of the Ice Ages', *Science* 194/4270: 1121–32.

HEATH, D. (ed.) (1963), *A Journal of the Pilgrims at Plymouth (Mourt's Relation: A Relation or Journal of the English Plantation settled at Plymouth in New England, by certain English adventurers both merchants and others* (New York: Corinth Books).

HEDGES, R. E. M. (2004), 'Isotopes and Herrings: Comments on Milner *et al.* and Lidén *et al.*', *Antiquity* 78: 34–7.

HEER, O. (1866), *Die Pflanzen der Pfahlbauten* (Zurich: Druck von Zürcher und Furrer).

HELBAEK, H. (1950), 'Tollundmandens sidsde maltid (the Tollund man's last meal)', *Arboger for Nordisk Oldkyndighed og Historie* 1950: 328–41.

—— (1958a), 'Grauballemandens sidste måltid', *Kuml* (Århus) 1958: 83–116.

—— (1958b), 'Studying the Diet of Ancient Man', *Archaeology* 14: 95–101.

HERSHKOVITZ, I., EDELSON, G., SPIERS, M., ARENSBURG, B., NADEL, D., and LÉVI, B. (1993), 'Ohalo II Man—Unusual Findings in the Anterior Rib Cage and Shoulder Girdle of a 19,000 Years-Old Specimen', *International Journal of Osteoarchaeology* 3: 177–88.

—— SPIERS, M., FRAYER, D., NADEL, D., WISH-BARATZ, S., and ARENSBURG, B. (1995), 'Ohalo II—A 19,000 Years Old Skeleton from a Water-Logged Site at the Sea of Galilee', *American Journal of Physical Anthropology* 96: 215–34.

HILL, J. D. (1995), 'The Pre-Roman Iron Age in Britain and Ireland: An Overview', *Journal of World Prehistory* 9/1: 47–98.

References

—— (1997), 'The End of One Kind of Body and the Beginning of Another Kind of Body? Toilet Instruments and "Romanization" in Southern England during the First Century AD', in A. Gwilt and C. Haselgrove (eds.), *Reconstructing Iron Age Societies* (Oxford: Oxbow monograph 71): 96–107.

HILLMAN, G. C. (1996), 'Late Pleistocene Changes in Wild Plant Foods Available to the Hunter-Gatherers of the Northern Fertile Crescent: Possible Preludes to Cereal Cultivation', in D. Harris (ed.), *The Origins and Spread of Agriculture and Pastoralism in Eurasia* (London: University College Press): 159–203.

—— (2004), 'The Rise and Fall of Human Dietary Diversity: An Overview of Archaeobotanical Evidence from Western Eurasia, and of Experiments with Some of the Key Food Plants', *The International Society of Ethnobiology—Ninth International Congress*—abstract.

HINGLEY, R. (1989), *Rural Settlement in Roman Britain* (London: Seaby).

HIRSCHFELD, Y. (1992), *The Judean Desert Monasteries in the Byzantine Period* (New Haven: Yale University Press).

HODDER, I. R. (1990), *The Domestication of Europe: Structure and Contingency in Neolithic Societies* (Oxford: Blackwell).

HOHMANN, G., and FRUTH, B. (1996), 'Food Sharing and Status in Unprovision Bonobos', in P. Wiessner and W. Schiefenhovel (eds.), *Food and the Status Quest: An Interdisciplinary Perspective* (New York: Berghahn Books): 47–67.

HOLDEN, T. G. (1986), 'Preliminary Report on the Detailed Analysis of the Macroscopic Remains from the Gut of Lindow Man', in I. M. Stead, J. B. Bourke, and D. Brothwell (eds.), *Lindow Man: The Body in the Bog* (London: British Museum).

—— (1995), 'The Last Meals of the Lindow Bog Men', in R. C. Turner and R. G. Scaife (eds.), *Bog Bodies: New Discoveries and New Perspectives* (London: British Museum Press): 76–82.

—— (1996/7), 'Food Remains from the Gut of the Huldremose Bog Body', *Journal of Danish Archaeology* 13: 49–55.

HOLLOX, E. J., POULTER, M., ZVARIK, M., FERAK, V., KRAUSE, A., JENKINS, T., SAHA, N., KOZLOV, A., and SWALLOW, D. M. (2001), 'Lactase Haplotype Diversity in the Old World', *American Journal of Human Genetics* 68: 160–72.

HOSKINS, W. G. (1955), *The Making of the English Landscape* (London: Hodder & Stoughton).

HUNTER, H. H. (1952), *The Barley Crop* (London: Crosby Lockwood).

HUNTLEY, B. (1990), 'Dissimilarly Mapping between Fossils and Contemporary Pollen Spectra in Europe for the Past 13,000 Years', *Quaternary Research* 33: 360–76.

IMBRIE, J., and IMBRIE, K. P. (1979), *Ice Ages: Solving the Mystery* (Cambridge, Mass.: Harvard University Press).

References

ISAAKIDOU, V., HALSTEAD, P., DAVIS, J., and STOCKER, S. (2002), 'Burnt Animal Sacrifice at the Mycenaean "Palace of Nestor", Pylos', *Antiquity* 76: 86–92.

IVERSON, J. (1954), 'The Late Glacial Flora of Denmark and its Relation to Climate and Soil', *Danmarks Geologiske Undersøgelse* II 80: 87–119.

JACOMET, S., Kučan, D., RITTER, A., SUTER, G., and HAGENDORN, A. (2002), '*Punica granatum* L. (pomegranates) from Early Roman Contexts in Vindonissa (Switzerland)', *Vegetation History and Archaeobotany* 11: 79–92.

JAMES, S. (1989), 'Hominid Use of Fire in the Lower and Middle Pleistocene: A Review of the Evidence', *Current Anthropology* 30: 1–26.

JONES, G. E. M. (1981), 'Crop Processing at Assiros Toumba: A Taphonomic Study', *Zeitschrift für Archäologie* 15: 105–11.

—— (1992), 'Weed Phytosociology and Crop Husbandry: Identifying a Contrast between Ancient and Modern Practice', *Review of Palaeobotany and Palynology* 73: 133–43.

—— and LEGGE, A. J. (1987), 'The Grape (*Vitis vinifera* L.) in the Neolithic of Britain', *Antiquity* 61/233: 452–5.

—— WARDLE, K., HALSTEAD, P., and WARDLE, D. (1986), 'Crop Storage at Assiros', *Scientific American* (March) 254: 96–103.

JONES, M. K. (1989), 'Agriculture in Roman Britain: The Dynamics of Change', in M. Todd (ed.), *Research on Roman Britain (1960–1989)* (London: Britannia Monograph 11).

—— (1991*a*), 'Agricultural Change in the Pre-documentary Past', in B. Campbell and M. Overton (eds.), *Productivity Change and Agricultural Development* (Manchester: Manchester University Press): 78–93.

—— (1991*b*), 'Food Production and Consumption', in R. F. J. Jones (ed.), *Roman Britain: Recent Trends* (Sheffield: Sheffield University Press): 21–8.

—— (1996), 'Plant Exploitation', in T. Champion and J. Collis (eds.), *The Iron Age in Britain and Ireland* (Sheffield: Sheffield Academic Press): 29–40.

—— (2001), *The Molecule Hunt* (London: Allen Lane).

JUNDI, S., and HILL, J. D. (1998), 'Brooches and Identities in First Century AD Britain: More than Meets the Eye?' in *Proceedings of the Seventh Annual Theoretical Roman Archaeology Conference: Nottingham* (Oxford: Oxford Books): 125–37.

KANO, T. (1992), *The Last Ape: Pygmy Chimpanzee Behaviour and Ecology* (Stanford, Calif.: Stanford University Press).

KAYSER, M., BRAUER, S., WEISS, G., SCHIEFENHOVEL W., and STONEKING, M. (2001), 'Independant Histories of Human Y Chromosomes from Melanesia and Australia', *American Journal of Human Genetics* 68: 173–90.

KENNEDY, G. E. (2005), 'From the Ape's Dilemma to the Weanling's Dilemma: Early Weaning and its Evolutionary Context', *Journal of Human Evolution* 48: 123–45.

KILLEN, J. T. (1985), 'The Linear B Tablets and the Mycenaean Economy', in A. Morpurgo Davies and Y. Duhoux (eds.), *Linear B: A 1984 Survey* (Bibliothèque des Cahiers de l'Institut de Linguistique de Louvain): 241–305.

KING, A. J. (1999), 'Diet in the Roman World: A Regional Inter-site Comparison of the Mammal Bones', *Journal of Roman Archaeology* 12: 168–202.

KISLEV, M. E., NADEL, D., and CARMI, I. (1992), 'Epipalaeolithic (19,000) Cereal and Fruit Diet at Ohalo II, Sea of Galilee, Israel', *Review of Palaeobotany and Palynology* 73: 161–6.

KLIMA, B. (1954), 'Palaeolithic Huts at Dolní Vestonice, Czechoslovakia', *Antiquity* 28/109: 4–14.

KOESTLER, A. (1967), *The Ghost in the Machine* (London: Arkana).

KOLDE, T. (1911), 'Sacred Heart of Jesus, Devotion to', in S. M. Jackson (ed.), *The New Schaff–Herzog Religious Encyclopedia* (New York: Funk & Wagnells).

KORN, D., RADICE, M., and HAWES, C. (2001), *Cannibal: The History of the People Eaters* (London: Macmillan).

KOTTAK, C. (1978), 'Rituals at Mcdonalds', *Natural History* 87: 74–83.

KRINGS, M., STONE, A., SCHMITZ, R. W., KRAINITZKI, H., STONEKING, M., and PÄÄBO, S. (1997), 'Neanderthal DNA Sequences and the Origin of Modern Humans', *Cell* 90: 19–30.

KRUPP, E. C. (1992), *Beyond the Blue Horizon: Myths and Legends of the Sun, Moon, Stars, and Planets* (Oxford: Oxford University Press).

KUBIAK-MARTENS, L. (1999), 'The Plant Food Component of the Diet at the Late Mesolithic (Ertebølle) Settlement at Tybrind Vig, Denmark', *Vegetation History and Archaeobotany* 8: 117–27.

—— (2002), 'New Evidence for the Use of Root Foods in Pre-agrarian Subsistence Recovered from the Late Mesolithic Site at Halsskov, Denmark', *Vegetation History and Archaeobotany* 11: 23–31.

LANCEL, G. (n.d.), 'L'Étoile et son histoire', http://g.lancel.free.fr/

LAWRENCE, C. H. (2000), *Medieval Monasticism: Forms of Religious Life in Western Europe in the Middle Ages (The Medieval World)* (London: Longman).

LAWTON, J. H., and WARREN, P. H. (1988), 'Static and Dynamic Explanations for Patterns in Food Webs', *Trends in Ecology and Evolution* 3/9: 242–4.

LEV, E., KISLEV, M. E., and BAR-YOSEF, O. (2005), 'Mousterian Vegetal Food in Kebara Cave, Mt Carmel', *Journal of Archaeological Science* 32: 475–84.

LÉVI-STRAUSS, C. (1955), *Tristes tropiques* (Paris: Plon).

—— (1962), *La Pensée sauvage* (Paris: Plon).

—— (1964), *Les Mythologiques: Le Cru et le cuit* (Paris: Plon).

—— (1968), *Les Mythologiques: L'Origine des manières de table* (Paris: Plon).

LEVINE, M. A. (1998), 'Eating Horses: The Evolutionary Significance of Hippophagy', *Antiquity* 72: 90–100.

References

LIDÉN, K., ERIKSSON, G., NORDQVIST, B., GÖTHERSTRÖM, A., and BENDIXEN, E. (2004), 'The Wet and the Wild Followed by the Dry and the Tame—or did they Occur at the Same Time? Diet in Mesolithic-Neolithic Southern Sweden', *Antiquity* 78: 23–33.

LINDENBAUM, S. (1979), *Kuru Sorcery* (Mountain View, Calif.: Mayfield Publishing Company).

LIPSCHITZ, N., and NADEL, D. (1997), 'Epipalaeolithic (19,000 B.P.) Charred Wood Remains from Ohalo II, Sea of Galilee, Israel', *Mitekufat Haeven, Journal of the Israel Prehistoric Society* 27: 5–18.

McGOVERN, P. E., GLUSKER, D. L., MOREAU, R. A., NUÑEZ, A., BECK, C. W., SIMPSON, E., BUTRYM, E. D., EXNER, L. J., and STOUT, E. C. (1999), 'A Funerary Feast Fit for King Midas', *Nature* 402: 863–4.

McHENRY, H. (1996), 'Sexual Dimorphism in Fossil Hominids and its Socioecological Implications', in J. Steele and S. Shennan (eds.), *The Archaeology of Human Ancestry: Power, Sex and Tradition* (London: Routledge): 91–109.

MADELLA, M., JONES, M. K., GOLDBERG, P., GOREN, Y., and HOVERS, E. (2002), 'The Exploitation of Plant Resources by Neandertals in Amud Cave (Israel): The Evidence from Phytolith Studies', *Journal of Archaeological Science* 29: 703–19.

MALAGON-BARCELO, J. (1963), 'Toledo and the New World in the Sixteenth Century', *Americas* 20/2: 97–126.

MALENKY, R. K., KURODA, S., VINEBERG, E. O., and WRANGHAM, R. W. (1994), 'The Significance of Terrestrial Herbaceous Foods for Bonobos, Chimpanzees and Gorillas', in R. W. Wrangham, W. C. McGrew, F. B. de Waal, and P. G. Heltne (eds.), *Chimpanzee Cultures* (Cambridge, Mass.: Harvard University Press): 59–75.

MALTHUS, T. (1798), *An Essay on the Principle of Population, as it Affects the Future Improvement of Society with Remarks on the Speculations of Mr. Godwin, M. Condorcet, and Other Writers* (London: Johnson, St Paul's Church-yard).

MARYANSKI, A. (1996), 'African Ape Social Networks: A Blueprint for Reconstructing Early Hominid Social Structures', in J. Steele and S. Shennan (eds.), *The Archaeology of Human Ancestry: Power, Sex and Tradition* (London: Routledge): 67–90.

MASON, S. L. R., HATHER, J. G., and HILLMAN, G. C. (1994), 'Preliminary Investigation of the Plant Macro-remains from Dolní Vestonice II, and its Implications for the Role of Plant Foods in Palaeolithic and Mesolithic Europe', *Antiquity* 68: 48–57.

MATTHEWS, J. V. (1976), 'Arctic-Steppe—an Extinct Biome', *Abstracts of the Fourth Biennial Meeting of the American Quaternary Association*: 73–7.

MAUSS, M. (1925), *The Gift: Forms and Functions of Exchange in Archaic Societies* (New York: Norton).

References

MAY, R. M. (1972), 'Will a Large Complex System be Stable?' *Nature* 238: 413–14.

MELLARS, P. A. (1995), *The Neanderthal Legacy: An Archaeological Perspective from Western Europe* (Princeton: Princeton University Press).

—— and GIBSON, K. (1996), *Modelling the Early Human Mind* (Cambridge: McDonald Institute Monographs).

MERCER, R. J. (1980), *Hambledon Hill: A Neolithic Landscape* (Edinburgh: Edinburgh University Press).

—— (1999), *The Origins of Warfare in the British Isles*, in J. Carman and A. Harding (eds.), *Ancient Warfare* (Stroud: Sutton): 143–56.

—— and HEALEY, F. (forthcoming), *Hambledon Hill, Dorset, England. Excavation and Survey of a Neolithic Monument Complex and its Surrounding Landscape* (London: English Heritage Monograph Series).

MILLER, M., and TAUBE, K. (1993), *The Gods and Symbols of Ancient Mexico and the Maya* (London: Thames & Hudson).

MILNER, N., CRAIG, O. E., BAILEY, G. N., PEDERSEN, K., and ANDERSEN, S. H. (2004), 'Something Fishy in the Neolithic? A Re-evaluation of Stable Isotope Analysis of Mesolithic and Neolithic Coastal Populations', *Antiquity* 78: 9–22.

MILTON, K. (1988), 'Foraging Behavior and the Evolution of Primate Cognition', in A. Whiten and R. Byrne (eds.), *Machiavellian Intelligence: Social Expertise and the Evolution of Intellect in Monkeys, Apes, and Humans* (Oxford: Oxford University Press): 285–305.

—— (1993), 'Diet and Primate Evolution', *Scientific American* 269: 86–93.

MITHEN, S. (1996), *The Prehistory of the Mind: The Cognitive Origins of Art and Science* (London: Thames & Hudson).

MOLLESON, T. (1989), 'Social Implications of the Mortality Patterns of Juveniles from Poundbury Camp, Romano-British Cemetery', *Anthropologischer Anzeiger* 47: 27–38.

—— (1994), 'The Eloquent Bones of Abu Hureyra', *Scientific American* 271/2: 70–5.

MOORE, A. M. T., and HILLMAN, G. C. (1992), 'The Pleistocene to Holocene Transition and Human Economy in Southwest Asia: The Impact of the Younger Dryas', *American Antiquity* 57/3: 482–94.

—— and LEGGE, A. J. (2000), *Village on the Euphrates* (Oxford: Oxford University Press).

MORGAN, L. H. (1877), *Ancient Society or Researches in the Lines of Human Progress from Savagery Through Barbarism to Civilization* (London: Macmillan).

—— (1959), *The Indian Journals, 1859–62* (Ann Arbor: University of Michigan Press).

MOSTOFSKY, D. I., YEHUDA, S., and SALEM, N. (2001), *Fatty Acids: Physiological and Behavioral Functions* (New Jersey: Humana Press).

NADEL, D. (1990), 'Ohalo II—a Preliminary Report', *Mitekufas Haevan, Journal of the Israel Prehistoric Society* 23: 48–59.

References

NADEL, D. (1991), 'Ohalo II—the Third Season (1991)', *Mitekufas Haevan, Journal of the Israel Prehistoric Society* 24: 158–63.

—— (1994a), 'Levantine Upper Palaeolithic—Early Epipalaeolithic Burial Customs: Ohalo II as a Case Study', *Paleoriént* 20/1: 113–21.

—— (1994b), '19,000-year-old Twisted Fibers from Ohalo II', *Current Anthropology* 35/4: 451–8.

—— (1996), 'The Organization of Space in a Fisher–Hunter-Gatherers' Camp at Ohalo II, Israel', in M. Otte (ed.), *Nature et Culture*, Colloque de Liège, E.R.A.U.L. 68 (Liege): 373–88.

—— (ed.) (2002), *Ohalo II, A 23,000-Year-Old Fisher–Hunter-Gatherers' Camp on the Shore of the Sea of Galilee* (Haifa University: Hecht Museum).

—— and WERKER, E. (1999), 'The Oldest Ever Brushwood Hut Plant Remains from Ohalo II, Jordan Valley, Israel' (19,000 BP).

—— and ZAIDNER, Y. (2002), 'Upper Pleistocene and mid-Holocene Net Sinkers from the Sea of Galilee, Israel', *Mitekufat Haeven, Journal of the Israel Prehistoric Society* 32: 37–59.

—— DANIN, A., WERKER, E., SCHICK, T., KISLEV, M. E., and STEWART, K. (1994), '19,000 years-old Twisted Fibers from Ohalo II', *Current Anthropology* 35/4: 451–8.

—— WEISS, E., SIMCHONI, O., TSATSKIN, A., DANIN, A., and KISLEV, M. E. (2004), 'Stone Age Hut in Israel Yields World's Oldest Evidence of Bedding', *Proceedings of the National Academy of Sciences* 101: 6821–6.

NISHIDA, T., WRANGHAM, R. W., GOODALL, J., and UCHARA, S. (1983), 'Local Differences in Plant Feeding Habits of Chimpanzees between Mahale Mountains and Gombe National Park, Tanzania', *Journal of Human Evolution* 12: 467–89.

NURSTEN, H. E. (2005), *The Maillard Reaction: Chemistry, Biochemistry and Implications* (London: Royal Society of Chemistry).

O'CONNELL, T. C., and HEDGES, R. E. M. (1999), 'Isotopic Comparison of Hair and Bone: Archaeological Analyses', *Journal of Archaeological Science* 26/6: 661–5.

—— (2001), 'Isolation and Isotopic Analysis of Individual Amino Acids from Archaeological Bone Collagen: A New Method Using RP-HPLC', *Archaeometry,* 43/3: 421–38.

OLIVA, M. (1988), 'A Gravettian Site with Mammoth-Bone Dwelling in Milovice (Southern Moravia)', *Anthropologie* 26: 105–12.

OSEPCHUK, J. M. (1984), 'A History of Microwave Heating Applications', *Microwave Theory and Techniques, IEEE Transactions* 32/9: 1200–24.

OVERPECK, J. T., WEBB, T. IV, and PRENTICE, I. C. (1985), 'Quantitative Interpretation of Fossils Pollen Spectra: Dissimilarity Coefficients and the Method of Modern Analogs', *Quaternary Research* 23: 87–108.

PÄÄBO, S., POINAR, H., SERRE, D., JAENICKE-DESPRÉS, V., HEBLER, J., ROH-
LAND, N., KUCH, M., KRAUSE, J., VIGILANT, L., and HOFREITER, M. (2004),
'Genetic Analyses from Ancient DNA', *Annual Review of Genetics* 38: 645–79.

PASTÓ, I., ALLUÉ, E., and VALLVERDÚ, J. (2000), 'Mousterian Hearths at Abric
Romaní, Catalonia (Spain)', in C. B. Stringer, R. N. E. Barton, and J. C.
Finlayson (eds.), *Neanderthals on the Edge: Papers from a Conference Marking
the 150th Anniversary of the Forbes' Quarry Discovery, Gibralter* (Oxford: Oxbow
Books): 59–67.

PATHOU-MATHIS, M. (2000), 'Neanderthal Subsistence Behaviours in Europe',
International Journal of Osteoarchaeology 10: 379–95.

PETERSON, J. (2002), *Sexual Revolutions: Gender and Labor at the Dawn of Agriculture* (Walnut Creek, Calif.: AltaMira Press).

PETTITT, P. (1997), 'High Resolution Neanderthals? Interpreting Middle Palaeolithic Intrasite Spatial Data', *World Archaeology* 29: 208–24.

PIMM, S. L. (1982), *Food Webs* (London: Chapman & Hall).

—— LAWTON, J. H., and COHEN, J. E. (1990), 'Food Web Patterns and their
Consequences', *Nature* 350: 669–74.

PIPERNO, D. R., WEISS, E., HOLST, I., and NADEL, D. (2004), 'Processing of
Wild Cereal Grains in the Upper Palaeolithic Revealed by Starch Grain
Analysis', *Nature* 430: 670–3.

POINAR, H. N., HOFREITER, M., SPAULDING, W. G., MARTIN, P. S., STANKIE-
WICZ, B. A., BLAND, H. A., EVERSHED, R. P., POSSNERT, G., and PÄÄBO, S.
(1998), 'Molecular Coproscopy: Dung and Diet of the Extinct Ground Sloth,
Northrotheriops shastensis', *Science* 281: 402–6.

POPE, M. I. (2004), 'Behavioural Implications of Biface Discard: Assemblage
Variability and Land-Use at the Middle Pleistocene Site of Boxgrove', in
Lithics in Action. Lithic Studies Society Occasional Paper 24 (Oxford: Oxbow
Books).

—— (2005), 'Observations on the Relationship between Palaeolithic Individuals
and Artefact Scatters at the Middle Pleistocene Site of Boxgrove, UK', in
C. S. Gamble and M. Porr, *The Individual in the Palaeolithic* (London: Routledge).

PRICE, T. D., BENTLEY, R. A., LÜNING, J., GRONENBORN, D., and WAH, J. (2001),
'Prehistoric Human Migration in the Linearbandkeramik of Central Europe',
Antiquity 75/289: 593–603.

RABINOVICH, R., and NADEL, D. (2005), 'Broken Mammal Bones: Taphonomy
and Food Sharing at the Ohalo II Submerged Prehistoric Camp', in
H. Buitenhuis, A. M. Choyke, L. Martin, L. Bartosiewicz, and M. Mashkour
(eds.), *Archaeozoology of the Near East VI, Proceedings of the Sixth International
Symposium on the Archaeozoology of Southwestern Asia and Adjacent Areas*
(Groningen: ARC-Publicaties) 123: 34–50.

RAHMSTORF, S. (2003), 'Timing of Abrupt Climate Change: A Precise Clock', *Geophysical Research Letters* 30/10: 1510.

RAPPAPORT, R. (1968), *Pigs for the Ancestors* (New Haven: Yale University Press).

—— (1979), *Ecology, Meaning and Religion* (Richmond, Calif.: North Atlantic Books).

RATHJE, W., and MURPHY, C. (2001), *Rubbish: The Archaeology of Garbage* (Tucson: University of Arizona Press).

REES, D. A. (2000), 'The Refitting of Lithics from unit 4c Area Q2/D Excavations at Boxgrove, West Sussex, England', *Lithic Technology* 25/2: 120–34.

REES, S. E. (1979), *Agricultural Implements in Prehistoric and Roman Britain* (Oxford: British Archaeological Reports 69).

REYNOLDS, P. J. (1979), *Iron-Age Farm: The Butser Experiment* (London: British Museum Publications).

RICHARD, A. (1985), 'Primate Diets: Patterns and Principles', in A. Richard (ed.), *Primates in Nature* (New York: W. H. Freeman).

RICHARDS, M. B., CÔRTE-REAL, H., FORSTER, P., MACAULAY, V., WILKINSON-HERBOTS, H., DEMAINE, A., PAPIHA, S., HEDGES, R., BANDELT, H.-J., and SYKES, B. C. (1996), 'Palaeolithic and Neolithic Lineages in the Human Mitochondrial Gene Pool', *American Journal of Human Genetics* 59: 185–203.

RICHARDS, M. P., PETTITT, P. B., STINER, M. C., and TRINKAUS, E. (2001), 'Stable Isotope Evidence for Increasing Dietary Breadth in the European Mid-Upper Palaeolithic', *Proceedings of the National Academy of Sciences* 98: 6529–32.

—— SCHULTING, R. J., and HEDGES, R. E. M. (2003), 'Sharp Shift in Diet at the Onset of the Neolithic', *Nature* 425: 366.

RIGAUD, J., SIMEK, J., and GE, T. (1995), 'Mousterian Fires from Grotte XVI (Dordogne, France)', *Antiquity* 69: 902–12.

RITCHIE, J. C., and CWYNAR, L. C. (1982), 'Late Quaternary Vegetation of the North Yukon', in D. M. Hopkins, J. V. Matthews, Jr., C. E. Schweger, and S. B. Young (eds.), *Paleoecology of Beringia* (New York: Academic Press): 113–26.

RIVENBURG, R. (2005), 'False Tales of Turkey on a Tray', *Los Angeles Times* (31 July).

ROBERTS, C. A., and COX, M. (2003a), 'The Human Population: Health and Disease', in M. A. Todd (ed.), *Companion to Roman Britain* (Oxford: Blackwell): 242–72.

—— (2003b), *Health and Disease in Britain: Prehistory to the Present Day* (Stroud: Sutton Publishing).

ROBERTS, M. B., and PARFITT, S. A. (eds.) (1999), *Boxgrove: A Middle Pleistocene Hominid Site at Eartham Quarry, Boxgrove, West Sussex* (London: English Heritage Monograph 17).

—— and POPE, M. I. (forthcoming), *The Archaeology of the Middle Pleistocene Hominid Site at Boxgrove, West Sussex, UK. Excavations 1991–1996* (London: English Heritage Monograph Series).

—— STRINGER, C. B., and PARFITT, S. A. (1994), 'A Hominid Tibia from Middle Pleistocene Sediments at Boxgrove, UK', *Nature* 369: 311–13.

ROBINSON, D. E. (1994), 'Dyrkede planter fra Danmarks forhistorie', *Arkæologiske Udgravninger i Danmark* 1993 (Copenhagen: Det Arkæologiske Nævn): 1–7.

ROSENBLATT, J. S. (2003), 'Outline of the Evolution of Behavioural and Non-behavioural Patterns of Parental Care among the Vertebrates: Critical Characteristics of Mammalian and Avian Parental Behaviour', *Scandinavian Journal of Psychology* 44: 265–71.

SAMUEL, D. (1996), 'Investigation of Ancient Egyptian Baking and Brewing Methods by Correlative Microscopy', *Science* 273/274: 488–90.

SCHAFFER, W. (1984), 'Stretching and Folding in Lynx Fur Returns: Evidence for a Strange Attraction in Nature?' *American Naturalist* 124/6: 798–820.

SCHMANDT-BESSERAT, D. (2001), Feasting in the Ancient Near East', in M. Dietler and B. Hayden (eds.), *Feasts: Archaeological and Ethnographic Perspectives on Food, Politics, and Power* (Washington: Smithsonian): 391–403.

SCHMITT, D., CHURCHILL, S. E., and HYLANDER, W. L. (2003), 'Experimental Evidence Concerning Spear Use in Neandertals and Early Modern Humans', *Journal of Archeological Science* 30: 103–14.

SCHULTING, R. J. (1996), 'Antlers, Bone Pins and Flint Blades: The Mesolithic Cemeteries of Téviec and Hoëdic, Brittany', *Antiquity* 70: 335–50.

—— and WYSOCKI, M. (2002), 'Cranial Trauma in the British Earlier Neolithic', *Past* 41: 4–6.

SCHWARCZ, H. P. (2002), 'Tracing Human Migration with Stable Isotopes', in K. Aoki and T. Akazawa (eds.), *Human Mate Choice and Prehistoric Marital Networks* (Kyoto: International Research Center for Japanese Studies).

SEIELSTAD, M. T., MINCH, E., and CAVALLI-SFORZA, L. L. (1998), 'Genetic Evidence for a Higher Female Migration Rate in Humans', *Nature Genetics* 20: 278–80.

SERNANDER, R. (1908), 'On the Evidence of Postglacial Changes of Climate Furnished by the Peat-Mosses of Northern Europe', *Geologiska föreningens i Stockholm Förhandlingar* 30: 456–78.

SHERRATT, A. (2006), 'Diverse Origins: Regional Contributions to the Genesis of Farming', in S. Colledge, J. Conolly, and S. J. Shennan (eds.), *Origins and Spread of Agriculture in SW Asia and Europe: Archaeobotanical Investigations of Neolithic Plant Economies* (London: University College).

SIMMONS, T., and NADEL, D. (1998), 'The Avifauna of the Early Epipalaeolithic Site of Ohalo II (19,400 B.P.), Israel: Species Diversity, Habitat and Seasonality', *International Journal of Osteoarchaeology* 8/2: 79–96.

SLATER, W. J. (ed.) (1991), *Dining in a Classical Context* (Ann Arbor: University of Michigan Press).

SMITH, B. D. (1992), *Rivers of Change: Essays in Early Agriculture in Eastern North America* (Washington: Smithsonian).

—— (1995), *The Emergence of Agriculture* (New York: W. H. Freeman & Co.).

SOFFER, O., VANDIVER, P., KLÍMA, B., and SVOBODA, J. (1993), 'The Pyrotechnology of Performance Art: Moravian Venuses and Wolverines', in H. Knecht, A. Pike-Tay, and R. White (eds.), *Before Lascaux: The Complex Record of the Early Upper Paleolithic* (New York: CRC Press): 259–75.

—— ADOVASIO, J. M., and HYLAND, D. C. (2000), 'The "Venus" Figurines: Textiles, Basketry, Gender and Status in the Upper Paleolithic', *Current Anthropology* 41: 511–37.

SOLECKI, R. S. (1971), *Shanidar: The First Flower People* (New York: Alfred A. Knopf).

SPANG, R. (2000), *The Invention of the Restaurant* (Cambridge, Mass.: Harvard University Press).

STEAD, I. M., BOURKE, J. B., and BROTHWELL, D. (1986), *Lindow Man: The Body in the Bog* (London: British Museum).

STINER, M. C. (2001), 'Thirty Years on the "Broad Spectrum Revolution" and Paleolithic Demography', *Proceedings of the National Academy of Sciences* 98/13: 6993–6.

—— MUNRO, N. D., and SUROVELL, T. A. (2000), 'The Tortoise and the Hare: Small-Game Use, the Broad Spectrum Revolution, and Palaeolithic Demography', *Current Anthropology* 41: 39–79.

STORDEUR, D (1999), 'Jerf el Ahmar et l'émergence du Néolithique au Proche Orient', in J. Guilaine (ed.), *Premiers paysans du Monde: naissance des agricultures* (Paris: Édition Errance): 31–60.

—— HELMER, D., and WILLCOX, G. (1997), 'Jerf el Ahmar: un nouveau site de l'horizon PPNA sur le moyen Euphrate Syrien', *Bullétin de la Société Préhistorique Française* 94/2: 282–5.

STRAUS, L. G. (1989), 'On Early Hominid Use of Fire', *Current Anthropology* 30: 488–91.

STREETER, M., STOUT, S. D., TRINKAUS, E., STRINGER, C. B., and ROBERTS, M. B. (2001), 'Histomorphometric Age Assessment of the Boxgrove 1 Tibial Diaphysis', *Journal of Human Evolution* 40/4: 331–8.

STRINGER, C. B., TRINKAUS, E., ROBERTS, M. B., PARFITT, S. A., and MACPHAIL, R. I. (1998), 'The Middle Pleistocene Human Tibia from Boxgrove', *Journal of Human Evolution*, 34/5: 509–47.

—— BARTON, R. N. E., and FINLAYSON, J. C. (eds.) (2000), *Neanderthals on the Edge: Papers from a Conference Marking the 150th Anniversary of the Forbes' Quarry Discovery, Gibralter* (Oxford: Oxbow Books).

STRONG, R. (2002), *Feast: A History of Grand Eating* (London: Jonathan Cape).

SVOBODA, J. (ed.) (1991), *Dolní Věstonice II—Western Slope* (Liege: ERAUL 54).

—— (2001), 'Gravettian Mammoth Bone Deposits in Moravia', in *La terra degli elephanti—The world of elephants, Atti del 1 congresso internationale* (Rome): 359–62.

—— and SEDLÁČKOVÁ, L. (eds.) (2004), *The Gravettian along the Danube* (Brno: Dolnověstonické studie 11).

—— KLÍMA, B., JAROŠOVÁ, L., and ŠKRDLA, P. (2000), 'The Gravettian in Moravia: Climate, Behaviour and Technological Complexity', in W. Roebroeks, M. Mussi, J. Svoboda, and K. Fennema (eds.), *Hunters of the Golden Age. The Mid Upper Palaeolithic of Eurasia, 30,000–20,000 B.P.* (Leiden): 197–217.

TACITUS (1970), *Agricola*, trans. M. Hutton (Cambridge, Mass.: Harvard University Press (Loeb)).

TELEKI, G. (1973), 'The Omnivorous Chimpanzee', *Scientific American* 228: 32–42.

THIEME, H. (1997), 'Lower Palaeolithic Hunting Spears from Germany', *Nature* 385: 807–10.

THOMAS, J. (1999), *Understanding the Neolithic* (London: Routledge).

—— (2001), 'Neolithic Enclosures: Some Reflections on Excavations in Wales and Scotland', in T. Darvill and J. Thomas (eds.), *Neolithic Enclosures of North-West Europe* (Oxford: Oxbow Monographs), 132–43.

—— and Ray, K. (2003), 'In the Kinship of Cows: the Social Centrality of Cattle in the Earlier Neolithic of Southern Britain', in M. Parker Pearson (ed.), *Food and Culture in the Neolithic* (Oxford: British Archaeological Reports).

TILLEY, C. (1994), *A Phenomenology of Landscape Places, Paths and Monuments* (Oxford: Berg).

TRINKAUS, E., STRINGER, C. B., RUFF, C. B., HENNESSEY, R. J., ROBERTS, M. B., and PARFITT, S. A. (1999), 'Diaphyseal Cross-Sectional Geometry of the Boxgrove 1 Middle Pleistocene Human Tibia', *Journal of Human Evolution* 37: 1–25.

TURNER, R., and SCAIFE, R. (eds.) (1995), *Bog Bodies: New Discoveries and New Perspectives* (London: British Museum Press).

TZEDAKIS, Y., and MARTLEW, H. (1999), *Minoans and Mycenaeans: Flavours of their Time* (Athens: Greek Ministry of Culture and National Archaeological Museum).

—— and JONES, M. K. (eds.) (2006), *Archaeology Meets Science: Biomolecular Investigations in Bronze Age Greece* (Oxford: Oxbow Books).

VALLVERDU, J., ALLUE, E., BISCHOFF, J. L., CACERES, I., CARBONELL, E., CEBRIA, A., GARCIA-ANTON, D., HUGUET, R., IBANEZ, N., MARTINEZ, K., PASTO, I., ROSELL, J., SALADIE, P., and VAQUERO, M. (2005), 'Short Human Occupations in the Middle Palaeolithic Level I of Abric Romani Rock-Shelter', *Journal of Human Evolution* 48: 157–74.

VAN ANDEL, T., and DAVIES, W. (eds.) (2003), *Neanderthals and Modern Humans in the European Landscape during the Last Glaciation* (Cambridge: McDonald Institute Monographs).

VAN ANDEL, T., and RUNNELS, C. N. (1995), 'The Earliest Farmers in Europe: Soil Preferences and Demic Diffusion Pathways', *Antiquity* 69: 481–500.

VAN DER SANDEN, W. (1996), *Through Nature to Eternity. The Bog Bodies of Northwest Europe* (Amsterdam: Batavian Lion International).

VAN DER VEEN, M. (1998), 'A Life of Luxury in the Desert? The Food and Fodder Supply to Mons Claudianus', *Journal of Roman Archaeology* 11: 101–16.

—— (1999), 'The Food and Fodder Supply to Roman Quarry Settlements in the Eastern Desert of Egypt', in M. van der Veen (ed.), *The Exploitation of Plant Resources in Ancient Africa* (New York: Kluwer Academic/Plenum Press): 171–83.

—— (2001), 'The Botanical Evidence' (chapter 8), in V. A. Maxfield and D. P. S. Peacock (eds.), *Survey and Excavations at Mons Claudianus 1987–1993*, ii, *The Excavations: Part 1* (Cairo, Institut Français d'Archéologie Orientale du Caire: Documents de Fouilles 43): 174–247.

—— (2004), 'The Merchants' Diet: Food Remains from Roman and Medieval Quseir al-Qadim', in P. Lunde and A. Porter (eds.), *Trade and Travel in the Red Sea Region* (British Archaeological Reports: International Series 1269): 123–9.

VAN ZEIST, W., and BAKKER-HEERES, J. A. H. (1982), 'Archaeobotanical Studies in the Levant. I. Neolithic Sites in the Damascus Basin: Aswad, Ghoraifé, Ramad', *Palaeohistoria. Acta et Communicationes Instituti Bio-Archaeologici Universitatis Groninganae* 24: 165–257.

VAQUERO, M., and CARBONELL, E. (2000), 'The Late Middle Palaeolithic in the Northeast of the Iberian Peninsula', in C. B. Stringer, R. N. E. Barton, and J. C. Finlayson (eds.), *Neanderthals on the Edge: Papers from a Conference Marking the 150th Anniversary of the Forbes' Quarry Discovery, Gibralter* (Oxford: Oxbow Books): 69–83.

—— VALLVERDU, J., ROSELL, J., PASTO, I., and ALLUE, E. (2001), 'Neandertal Behaviour at the Middle Palaeolithic Site of Abric Romani, Capellades Spain', *Journal of Field Archaeology* 28: 93–115.

VROOM, J. (2003), *After Antiquity: Ceramics and Society in the Aegean from the 7th to the 20th Century AC. A Case Study from Boeotia, Central Greece* (Leiden University: Archaeological Studies).

WALKER, M. J., GIBERT, J., SANCHEZ, F., LOMBARDI, A. V., SERRANO, I., GOMEZ, A., EASTHAM, A., RIBOT, F., ARRIBAS, A., CUENCA, A., GIBERT, L., ALBALADEJO, S., and ANDREU, J. A. (1999), 'Excavations at New Sites of Early Man in Murcia: Sima de las Palomas del Cabezo Gordo and Cueva Negra del Estrecho del Rio Quipar de la Encamacion', *Human Evolution* 14: 99–123.

WALKER BYNUM, C. (1987), *Holy Feast and Holy Fast: The Religious Significance of Food to Medieval Women* (Berkeley: University of California Press).

WALSH, P. G. (1999), The *Satyricon* / Petronius, trans. with an introduction and notes (Oxford: Oxford University Press).

WEBB, T. (1986), 'Is Vegetation in Equalibrium with Climate? How to Interpret Late Quaternary Pollen Data', *Vegetatio* 67: 75–91.

WEBER, B. H., DEPEW, D. J., and SMITH, J. D. (eds.) (1988), *Entropy, Information and Evolution* (Cambridge, Mass.: MIT Press).

WEISS E., KISLEV, M. E., SIMCHONI, O., and NADEL, D. (2005), 'Small-Grained Wild Grasses as Staple Food at the 23,000 Year-Old Site of Ohalo II, Israel', *Economic Botany* 588: 125–34.

—— Wetterstrom, W., Nadel, D., and Bar-Yosef, O (2004), 'The Broad Spectrum Revisited: Evidence from Plant Remains', *Proceedings of the National Academy of Science* 101/26: 9551–5.

WHITE, L. A. (1951), 'Lewis S. Morgan's Western Field Trips', *American Anthropologist* 53: 11–18.

WIESSNER, P., and SCHIEFENHÖVEL, W. (eds.) (1997), *Food and the Status Quest: An Interdisciplnary Perspective* (Oxford: Berghahn).

WILLCOX, G. (1996), 'Evidence for Plant Exploitation and Vegetation History from Three Early Neolithic Pre-pottery Sites on the Euphrates (Syria)', *Vegetation History and Archaeobotany* 5: 143–52.

—— (2002), 'Charred Plant Remains from a 10th Millennium B.P. Kitchen at Jerf el Ahmar', *Vegetation History and Archaeobotany* 11: 55–60.

WILPERT, J. (1896), *Fractio Panis. La plus ancienne représentation du sacrifice eucharistique à la ≪cappella Greca≫ découverte et expliquée par Mgr Joseph Wilpert* (Paris: Firmin-Didot et Cie).

WOOLLEY, C. L., and MOOREY, P. R. S. (1982), *Ur 'of the Chaldees'*, rev. edn. (Ithaca, NY: Cornell University Press).

WORSTER, D. (1977), *Nature's Economy: A History of Ecological Ideas* (Cambridge: Cambridge University Press).

—— (1979), *Dust Bowl: The Southern Plains in the 1930s* (Oxford: Oxford University Press).

WRANGHAM, R. W. (1975), 'The Behavioural Ecology of Chimpanzees in Gombe National Park, Tanzania' (Ph.D. Dissertation, University of Cambridge).

—— CONKLIN-BRITTAIN, N. L., and HUNT, K. D. (1998), 'Dietary Response of Chimpanzees and Cercopithecines to Seasonal Variation in Fruit Abundance I. Antifeedants', *International Journal of Primatology* 19: 949–70.

—— MCGREW, W. C., DE WAAL, F. B. M., and HELTNE, P. G. (1994), *Chimpanzee Cultures* (Cambridge, Mass.: Harvard University Press).

—— JONES, J. H., LADEN, G., PILBEAM, D., and CONKLIN-BRITTAIN, N. L. (1999), 'The Raw and the Stolen: Cooking and the Ecology of Human Origins', *Current Anthropology* 40: 567–94.

References

WRIGHT, J. (ed.) (2004), 'The Mycenaean Feast', *Hesperia* 73/2: 1–217.

YASUDA, Y. (ed.) (2002), *The Origins of Pottery and Agriculture* (New Delhi: Roli Books).

YVINEC, J.-H. (1999), Étude archéozoologique du site de Dury "le Moulin" (Somme)', *Revue archéologique de Picardie* 1: 247–55.

ZAZULA, G. D., FROESE, D. G., SCHWEGER, C. E., MATHEWES, R. W., BEAUDOIN, A. B., TELKA, A. M., HARINGTON, C. R., and WESTGATE, J. A. (2003), 'Ice-Age Steppe Vegetation in East Beringia', *Nature* 423: 603.

Index

Note: Page numbers in italics refer to illustrations, e.g. Acheulian hand axes 56, *57*, 71 Page numbers followed by 'n.' and a number refer to Notes, e.g. ards 169, 174, 259, 312n.18